PSYCHOANALYSIS AND GENDER

Since its creation by Sigmund Freud, psychoanalytic theory has informed, influenced and sometimes enraged writers who are concerned with issues of gender and feminism. Rosalind Minsky's volume provides a clear, accessible and unpretentious introduction to the concepts of and key thinkers in psychoanalytic theory.

The first part of the volume offers the fundamentals of psychoanalytic theory and the major writers who worked in the field, exploring how the theory is relevant in both the academic and political realms. The second part demonstrates this theory in practice with an anthology of seminal essays by Freud, Klein, Winnicott, Lacan, Kristeva and Irigaray. Together these parts combine to provide readers with the necessary vocabulary and knowledge to apply psychoanalytic theory to their studies.

Writing specifically for students, Minsky discusses the key issues in straight-forward, jargon-free prose. *Psychoanalysis and Gender: An introductory reader* is an essential guide to this major field. Any student interested in issues of gender will find it an invaluable introduction.

Rosalind Minsky is a lecturer in the Department of Arts and Letters at Anglia Polytechnic University.

301   D0417824

Critical Readers in Theory and Practice

GENERAL EDITOR: Rick Rylance, *Anglia Polytechnic University*

The gap between theory and practice can often seem far too wide for the student of literary theory. *Critical Readers in Theory and Practice* is a new series which bridges that gap: it not only offers an introduction to a range of literary and theoretical topics, but also *applies* the theories to relevant texts.

Each volume is split into two parts: the first consists of an in-depth and clear introduction, setting out the theoretical bases, historical developments and contemporary critical situation of the topic. The theory is then applied to practice in the second part in an anthology of classic texts and essays.

Designed specifically with the student in mind, *Critical Readers in Theory and Practice* provides an essential introduction to contemporary theories and how they relate to textual material.

Bakhtinian Thought: An introductory reader Simon Dentith

War Poetry: An introductory reader Simon Featherstone

The Postmodern Arts: An introductory reader Nigel Wheale

Psychoanalysis and Gender: An introductory reader Rosalind Minsky

PSYCHOANALYSIS AND GENDER

An introductory reader

ROSALIND MINSKY

LONDON AND NEW YORK

BARCODE No.
X   3604854

CLASS No.
150.195 082 MIN

BIB CHECK   20 NOV 1996   PROC CHECK

92 1/96   FINAL CHECK
92 1/96

OS   SYSTEM No.
242975

LOAN CATEGORY
SL

First published 1996
by Routledge
11 New Fetter Lane, London EC4P 4EE

Simultaneously published in the USA and Canada
by Routledge
29 West 35th Street, New York, NY 10001

© 1996 Rosalind Minsky

Typeset in Janson by
Ponting–Green Publishing Services, Chesham, Bucks

Printed and bound in Great Britain by
Clays Ltd, St Ives PLC

All rights reserved. No part of this book may be reprinted or
reproduced or utilized in any form or by any electronic,
mechanical, or other means, now known or hereafter
invented, including photocopying and recording, or in any
information storage or retrieval system, without permission
in writing from the publishers.

British Library Cataloguing in Publication Data
A catalogue record for this book is available from
the British Library

Library of Congress Cataloguing in Publication Data
Minsky, Rosalind.
Psychoanalysis and Gender : An introductory reader / Rosalind Minsky.
p.   cm. – (Critical Readers in Theory and Practice)
Includes bibliographical references and index.
1. Psychoanalysis and feminism.   2. Femininity (Psychology)
I. Title.   II. Series.
BF175.4.F45M56   1996
150.19'5'082–dc20   95–16457

ISBN 0–415–09220–5 (hbk)
ISBN 0–415–09221–3 (pbk)

For David, Rod, Simon and Genia

We know more than we know we know.

(Michael Polanyi)

Concepts can never be presented to me merely, they must be knitted into the structure of my being, and this can only be done through my own activity.

(M.P. Follett, 'Creative Experience')

Creativity, as has been said, consists largely of re-arranging what we know in order to find out what we do not know.... Hence, to think creatively we must be able to look *afresh* at what we normally take for granted.

(George Kneller, 'The Art and Science of Creativity')

Contents

General editor's preface   xi

Preface   xii

Acknowledgements   xiv

List of abbreviations   xv

Part I

Introduction: psychoanalysis and the unconscious   3

1 Freud: the rejection of femininity   25
   Commentary on 'Femininity'   47
   Discussion   62
   Presences and absences   72
   Suggested reading   75

2 Klein: phantasy and the mother   78
   Commentary on 'A Study of Envy and Gratitude'   91
   Discussion   97
   Presences and absences   106
   Suggested reading   107

3 Winnicott: the 'good enough' mother   110
   *Commentary on 'Transitional Objects and
      Transitional Phenomena'*   124
   Discussion   128
   Presences and absences   133
   Suggested reading   135

4 Lacan: the meaning of the phallus   137
   Commentary on 'The Meaning of the Phallus'   163
   Discussion   168
   Presences and absences   175
   Suggested reading   176

[ix]

5 Feminist interpretations   178
   Julia Kristeva: *ending the 'fight to the death'*   180
   Commentary on an extract from 'Women's Time'   184
   Discussion   188
   Luce Irigaray: *'two lips touching and re-touching'*   192
   Commentary on an extract from Speculum of the Other Woman 200
   Discussion   201
   Suggested reading   203

6 Conclusions   206

Part II

7   Sigmund Freud: 'Femininity' (1933)   215

8   Melanie Klein: 'A Study of Envy and Gratitude' (1956)   236

9   Donald Winnicott: from 'Transitional Objects and
   Transitional Phenomena' (1971)   254

10 Jacques Lacan: 'The Meaning of the Phallus' (1958)   269

11 Julia Kristeva: from 'Women's Time' (1981)   281

12 Luce Irigaray: from *Speculum of the Other Woman* (1985)   289

   Bibliography   294

   Index   306

General editor's preface

The interpretation of culture never stands still. Modern approaches to familiar problems adjust our sense of their importance, and new ideas focus on fresh details or remake accepted concepts. This has been especially true over recent years when developments across the humanities have altered so many ideas.

For many this revolution in understanding has been exciting but difficult, involving the need to integrate advanced theoretical work with attention to specific texts and issues. This series attempts to approach this difficulty in a new way by putting together a new balance of basic texts and detailed, introductory exposition.

Each volume in the series will be organized in two parts. Part I provides a thorough account of the topic under discussion. It details important concepts, historical developments and the contemporary context of interpretation and debate. Part II provides an anthology of classic texts or – in the case of very recent work – essays by leading writers which offer focused discussions of particular issues. Commentary and editorial material provided by the author connect the explanations in Part I to the materials in Part II, and in this way the reader moves comfortably between original work and enabling introduction.

The series will include volumes on topics which have been of particular importance recently. Some books will introduce specific theoretical ideas; others will re-examine bodies of literary or other material in the light of current thinking. But as a whole the series aims to reflect, in a clear-minded and approachable way, the changing ways in which we understand the expanding field of modern literary and cultural studies.

Rick Rylance

Preface

Although Freud died over half a century ago, psychoanalytic theory continues to represent a largely unknown quantity for many students and academics despite the impact of post-modern theory and the interest in it within some areas of feminism. Although post-modernism challenges both the meanings of our identities and the knowledge we produce, many students and academics are still not sure quite how psychoanalytic theory is involved in this challenge. In stressing the central role of the unconscious in all identity (that is in everything with which we make an identification, including language and knowledge), psychoanalysis inevitably suggests that all meanings can be potentially subverted, including those of gender divisions.

Despite increased interest in psychoanalytic theory during the 1980s, substantial areas of theoretical insight still seem to constitute a little known area of knowledge which is the exclusive possession of a tiny minority consisting of psychoanalysts, analytical psychotherapists and their patients and ex-patients. In my view this intellectually rich and fascinating area of theory and insight is of enormous significance for us all and yet many students and academics are still largely unaware of its existence or treat it as a kind of taboo area best left alone. For me, psychoanalysis provides the essential 'missing link' between biology and history and culture. In both its modern and post-modern forms, it offers a powerful tool of analysis to students and academics and all those seeking new ways of understanding the complexities of history and the contemporary social world which demand our attention.

The aim of this book is to try to provide both a way into psychoanalytic theory generally and specifically into the study of the unconscious construction of men and women, or gendered identities, and the knowledge they produce. I hope it will become clear that psychoanalytic theory is a form of knowledge and practice which works best through the integration of both the intellectual and the emotional levels of our existence, much more like an art than a science. Although our identity may nowadays be theorised as an event in language, I hope the theories described in this book will convince the reader that human identity is something even more complicated than this and perhaps is ultimately untheorisable in any single approach.

I hope that the papers included in Part II will, with the aid of the introductory chapters, the commentaries and footnotes, be accessible to those who are unfamiliar with this area of theory. I also hope that the material in this book will be a stimulating source of discussion and insight and perhaps suggest the basis for a form of knowledge and practice which successfully combines emotional insight, intuition, empathy and an attention to the ordinary human dramas of life with the intellectual and structural levels of our existence without doing violence to either.

Acknowledgements

I would like to thank my partner David Pickles for his support and encouragement throughout the preparation and writing of this book and for his invaluable and insightful comments on my manuscripts. I would especially like to thank Marina Voikhanskaya for her wisdom and generosity in my discussions with her and Christina Marshall for her interest and encouragement. I would also like to express my appreciation to all those students, colleagues and friends whose questions, comments and, sometimes, prejudices have contributed to my thinking and the preparation of this book. I would like to thank Alison Ainley for her comments on my section on Irigaray. Finally, I would like to thank my colleague and series editor Rick Rylance for giving me the opportunity to write this book and for his comments and help in the final production of my typescript and also Talia Rodgers, my editor and her assistant Tricia Dever, at Routledge.

I would like to express my gratitude to the following for permission to include their copyright material in the anthology:

Chatto and Windus, London, for Sigmund Freud's Lecture 33 'Femininity' (1933) from the Standard Edition of *The Complete Psychological Works*, vol. 22: 112; the Melanie Klein Trust and Penguin Books, London, for Melanie Klein's 'A Study of Envy and Gratitude' from *The Selected Melanie Klein*, ed. Juliet Mitchell (1986); Routledge, London, for Winnicott's 'Transitional Objects and Transitional Phenomena': 1–14, from *Playing and Reality* (1970); Macmillan Press, London, for the English translation by Jacqueline Rose of Jacques Lacan's 'The Meaning of the Phallus' from *Lacan and the Ecole Freudienne: Feminine Sexuality*, ed. Juliet Mitchell and Jacqueline Rose (1982); Blackwell, Oxford, for Julia Kristeva's 'Women's Time': 205–13, from *The Kristeva Reader*, ed. Toril Moi (1986); Cornell University Press, Ithaca, for Luce Irigaray's *Speculum of the Other Woman*: 25–8, (1985).

[xiv]

Abbreviations

The following abbreviations have been used throughout:

SE   Standard Edition of the *Complete Psychological Works of Sigmund Freud*, vols 1–24 (1953–74) London, Hogarth Press and The Institute of Psychoanalysis.

PFL   Pelican Freud Library (1973–) Harmondsworth, Penguin.

PART I

Introduction: psychoanalysis and the unconscious

The idea that we could think out a theory of the structure and functioning of the personality without it having any relation to the structure and functioning of our own personality, should be a self evident impossibility.

(Harry Guntrip, 1975)

Overview

Psychoanalytic theory is radically different from other theories because it makes the unconscious its central organising concept. The unconscious, however, is something which, by definition is largely inaccessible to us. In the modern age it was Freud who first called this hidden, wordless dimension of identity the unconscious or psychical reality. What is most distinctive about the unconscious, as Freud defined it, is that, although it is constructed in early childhood out of our earliest desires and losses, its system of frozen meanings influences everything we do, whether we are five or eighty-five, without our being aware of it. Freud thought that we can only catch glimpses of its meanings in dreams, or random slips of the tongue or pen, in jokes, in what he described as neurotic symptoms in the form of anxiety, guilt, depression, obsessions, phobias, psychosomatic illness or in sudden eruptions of emotion which we find impossible to explain. We sometimes say in bewilderment 'I don't know what came over me'. We seem to have slipped out of what we normally think of as our identity. We may say 'It's not like me. I'm not myself'. Although psychoanalytic theory provides the basis for the therapeutic practice of psychoanalysis out of which it emerged, it also provides a structural theory of the construction of identity and has increasingly been used, especially by feminists, to expose and explore the unconscious dimensions of both history and contemporary culture. It makes possible the exploration of a territory of meaning beyond the boundaries of other theories such as conventional psychology and

[3]

sociology which have been primarily concerned with the analysis of consciousness and the processes of socialisation. By focusing on unconscious processes and states of mind conceived as a psychical domain which may not be entirely determined by culture, psychoanalytic theory has made it possible to analyse the unconscious, as well as conscious, meanings which contribute to the complexity of ourselves and the world in which we live and, ultimately, in the work of Lacan, to question the very meaning and status of consciousness and language. It is in Lacan's post-structuralist development of Freud, that the unconscious, now conceptualised as the driving force of language, begins to have an integral role in the construction of consciousness and culture. An unconscious sense of lack of being is transformed into desire, a want to be.

In particular, in this book, we shall use psychoanalytic theory to examine one of the most important issues in contemporary life: the construction of 'masculine' and 'feminine' identity. Freud's psychoanalytic theory, hovering between natural and human science, sees identity in terms of the unconscious negotiation of painful feelings of loss and desire in relation to a complicated web of social or cultural constraints but never solely determined by them. In his theory the silent world of hidden meanings never displaces the ordinary human suffering which gives rise to them. However, in Lacan's development of Freud's work, the stuff of psychoanalysis – difference, desire and identity – is transformed into language. Difference orders the meanings within language and desire energises the movement from one meaning to the next. In describing the unconscious construction of patriarchal ideology, he makes a dramatic link between sexuality on the one hand, and culture on the other. Gendered desiring identity becomes gendered eroticised language and knowledge out of which our gendered subjectivity is constructed. Language can no longer be seen as neutral and objective.

But at the same time Lacan's work raises yet more questions about the nature of the baby's earliest experiences of sexuality and meaning in relation to the mother which have been pursued in the work of the French feminists, in particular, in the writings of Hélène Cixous, Luce Irigaray and Julia Kristeva. In focusing on an unconscious domain which exists, it is argued, at some level beyond the reach of theories of socialisation or symbolic practices, psychoanalytic theory poses questions about the origins of the unconscious meanings of the body, desire, pleasure, phantasy and identification. These unconscious meanings al-

[4]

ways potentially challenge the status of cultural meanings and identities based on the apparently safe, rational categories of language. In particular, Freud's concept of mastery as control of painful loss and desire through language pre-figures Lacan's view of language as a system of control as well as subjectivity.

Evidence of the unconscious

Before we look further into the different psychoanalytic theories let us begin by considering the question of what constitutes 'evidence' of the unconscious at the level of our everyday experience. We can take as examples the powerful experiences of feeling an irrational dislike or hostility towards an individual or a group of people and the experience of falling in love.

The following kind of behaviour is probably recognisable to many of us. We feel rather anxious, guilty or vulnerable, so we hit out at other people, often the people closest to us, and act as if they were attacking us. This mechanism is known in psychoanalytic theory as 'projection'. We find a part of ourselves unacceptable and painful (the thing we feel guilty about – our anxiety, insecurity or vulnerability) and instead of allowing ourself consciously to feel and own the emotions we don't like, we project them onto other people and then feel attacked by them. These same people then represent to us the alienated part of ourselves that we've thrown out into the external world. Feeling under attack, we attack them – usually much to their surprise! The concept of projection is important because it describes one of the many unconscious defensive behaviours by means of which which we protect ourselves from knowing about the contents of our inner world. Unacceptable feelings which, if we allow ourselves to feel them consciously, are potentially very painful may be projected into the world and onto other people where we mistakenly imagine ourselves rid of them. Unfortunately we are not, and we subsequently experience paranoia to a greater or lesser extent. We feel under attack from these alienated parts of ourself over which we no longer have any control. Racism, forms of ethnocentric or nationalist hatred, class antagonism, sexism and homophobia may be generalised examples of this kind of unconscious behaviour. Feelings of anxiety or inferiority are projected or externalised onto others so that these hated parts of the self are experienced as hostile elements contained in the external rather than internal world, which therefore have to be controlled.

Within the conceptual framework of psychoanalytic theory, some-times whole relationships are perceived to be based on what is known as 'projective identification'. Individuals often marry or live together in a symbiotic relationship of mutual dependency where one person seems to express all the anger for both partners and the other all the vulner-ability. Together they seem to inhabit one identity with complementary roles which are wholly unconscious. The amazing sensation of being in love – the feeling of oneness and completion accompanied by a feeling of exhilaration or euphoria – can be seen from a psychoanalytic perspective to be about meeting someone through whom we can express, using the mechanism of projection, that part of ourself that we do not want consciously to acknowledge. Both parties unconsciously recognise that they can complete each other and increase each other's sense of identity and self-worth. Often, this seems to become clear only when one partner suddenly starts expressing emotions which were not part of the original unconscious 'deal' – which belonged to the terrain of the other. The fragile equilibrium may be disturbed, for example, when a woman stops being the person in the relationship 'in charge' of the vulnerability and starts to break out of this role by becoming strong and active. Very often the husband/lover may feel a sense of betrayal and doesn't understand why. (Of course this may happen just as easily the other way round.) When a relationship of very powerful mutual dependency, based on projective identification, breaks up, it often feels as if the leaver has literally gone off with a part of the self of the person who has been left. This is because the leaver has actually made him/herself absent, still carrying a substantial part of the projected self of the other partner, who is left feeling, not surprisingly, fragile, empty and incomplete.

Unconscious defences: projection and projective identification

Although Freud first used the concept of projection, the joint concepts of projection and projective identification are particularly associated with the work of Melanie Klein who, on the basis of her analysis of very young children, took the view radically different from that of Freud, that the unconscious is structured not between the age of three and five during the Oedipal crisis (a fuller explanation of this idea will be given below), but in the pre-Oedipal baby's developing relationship with its mother. In a relationship of projective identification in which the baby projects itself onto the mother and then re-identifies with her, the baby's self is characterised by Klein as being initially undifferentiated from that of the mother. Because of this total dependence, the baby, according to Klein, experiences alternating states of love and hate. When it is full and satisfied by the mother, it experiences itself as 'good'; psychically 'full' it loves and idealises the mother. When it feels frustrated and empty it experiences itself as 'bad' and in danger of psychical disintegration. To overcome this danger to its fragile sense of self the baby splits off its bad feelings and projects them onto the mother who is then experienced as attacking rather than loving. The baby, like the adult who projects in later life, is actually suffering from a paranoid fantasy: it feels itself under attack from its own externalised, split-off, feelings of hatred and envy now embodied by the mother, its psychical 'other half'. Being in love in the way I have described seems to hark back unconsciously to the young baby's feelings of fullness and love when it experienced the mother as totally satisfying and fulfilling.

The psychoanalytic concepts of projection and projective identi-fication allow us to begin to see the evidence for feelings or phantasies which are unconscious. (Phantasy is the usual way of indicating a powerful form of primitive thinking which pre-dates reason or emo-tional insight, and which originates in the unconscious, as distinct from a fantasy or piece of conscious day-dreaming.) They represent what Klein sees as defence mechanisms against the emergence of these feelings into consciousness which enable us to ignore and disown them. Psychoanalysis suggests that these may be seen at work, not just during crises, but in the smallest details of our day-to-day existence. Some of us will be able to remember the times when we have compulsively cleared out our cupboards, turned our houses or rooms upside down, wiped the last fragment of a tea leaf from the work surface, got up from our seat to straighten the edge of a curtain or felt a sudden need to go on a diet or take violent exercise. These are all ways in which we attempt to control our inner reality by trying to control the external world. Usually this is only of limited value. If this behaviour goes on for too long we may feel a sense of inner emptiness and impoverishment because so much of who we are has been disowned and split off somewhere outside ourselves; in short we feel lacking in substance and self-esteem and we feel depressed.

[7]

The origins of the unconscious

If we can accept that there is evidence for a dimension of identity which is outside our conscious knowledge, we have to ask how it came into being. Psychoanalytic theory is the discourse which attempts to provide the answer to this question because, alone among discourses, it deals with the human subject's unconscious coming into being and the kind of events which constitute an individual's hidden, unrecorded history. It charts not what we normally call history – the history of consciousness, of social power and domination, the social construction of reality – but another kind of story. This is the important history of the individual's unconscious construction, which takes place inside the wider social or cultural context, but maps how an individual has reacted to the powerful currents of emotion in his or her own family and the presences and absences, both physical and emotional, within this family. In Freud's version of this historical psychoanalytic reality, the crucial experiences seem to be the powerful desire of the male or female child for total possession of the mother, the loss of whom provides the origin for the formation of the unconscious and the split subject. ('Mummy, I'm going to marry you when I grow up.' 'But I'm already married to Daddy.') The fear of retribution from the spouse of the desired parent, feelings of loss and rejection by the parents we can't 'marry' and have to give up, feelings of rivalry and intense jealousy at the birth of new babies – in fact, all the feelings we would expect in a passionate love affair brought to an end by the existence of a rival, seem to be felt by many children, however sensitive individual parents might be, and even when stereotyped gender roles have been changed. Psychoanalytic case histories suggest that these Oedipal feelings (named after the Greek myth in which Oedipus unknowingly – unconsciously – killed his father and married his mother) which were first identified and described by Freud, seem to be experienced by most people, including those brought up in single-parent families. However, in order to cope in the outside world, such feelings have to be repressed for the individual to become a viable, coping human subject. Unfortunately, this viability seems to be at the cost of our sense of personal coherence; in order to function we have alienated or split-off some important part of ourselves.

Universal or social construction

One of the most common criticisms of the concept of the unconscious is that Freud considered that it was a universal phenomenon fixed in early

[8]

childhood and therefore ahistorical, or outside the influence of society or culture. This issue is a very important one, particularly in relation to the unconscious construction of the socially unequal categories of 'masculinity' and 'femininity' and the possibility of change. But although the existence of phenomena which are universal and ahistorical is widely contested, it does look as if the phenomenon of the unconscious is not historical in the usual sense of the word. It is difficult to see how a child's passionate feelings of desire and loss in relation to its mother around the age of three or four, or intense jealousy at the birth of a new sibling and its subsequent repression, can be totally dependent on historical contingencies and consciousness. Historical contingencies will obviously affect who is present or absent, how and what emotions can be expressed or repressed, what kind of defences are more socially acceptable at any one time. But they do not alter the possibility that the unconscious comes into being some time in early childhood, that desires seem to have to be repressed in favour of consciousness, in order for the subject to come into being and cope with the demands of life. Powerful emotions such as the ones that lie behind the statement 'Mummy, I'm going to marry you', that lie behind the recognition that someone, a rival, was there before us, or behind the statement 'But you can't have a baby like me, you're a boy', or behind the jealousy about a new sibling, look like experiences which might run through the heart of historical contingencies and consciousness which seem to determine the conceptual grid through which we interpret the world.

Even if we want to argue that the only universal experiences are birth and death, it could be argued, taking a more Lacanian view, that desire or the unconscious comes into being at birth, the moment of the baby's first experience of loss. This is the time when the baby is cut off from its first total unity with the mother for ever although it may hanker to regain this original state of bliss for the rest of its life. Subsequent losses are loss of the mother's breast after weaning, loss of acceptance of its own internal contents after toilet training and finally loss of the phantasy of the mother's desire. If these are not universal experiences, then we have at least to recognise that they may be so widespread that we cannot ignore their symbolic significance for our psychical development.

However, this view of the unconscious construction of identity does not disclaim the vital significance of social or cultural factors. Both Freud and Lacan recognised that there must always be a complex and subtle interaction between the historical, social and psychical dimensions of existence. As culturalists argue, and psychoanalysis also suggests, it seems that in a variety of complex symbolic ways, the social world or culture both 'picks up' and is 'picked up' and structured by the unconscious which, to the extent that it is implicated in creating history, is, at the same time, also historicised and subsequently disposed of in relation to the wider forces within culture and history. In yet more complex ways, as we shall see in the work of Freud and Lacan, the body acts as a kind of mediator in this interplay between the unconscious and the cultural.

Theoretically, Freud's unconscious seems to lie somewhere between biology and history while for Lacan, it lies exclusively within language in the spaces between the ordered categories of culture where many assume only reason and logic prevail. As we shall see, language is seen by Lacan as a cultural version of the child's pleasing mirror-image of its still uncoordinated body. (Intriguingly, long before Lacan, we referred to the idea of a 'body' of knowledge.) To the extent that the unconscious is something which, although intrinsically linked to the body, always lies outside our idea of ourselves and the cultural categories of language and knowledge which sustain our sense of these selves, it does seem to exist in some sense beyond culture and history although, as we shall see, Lacan argues that the unconscious *is* language and culture. However, if we accept that the unconscious consists of bodily processes and the phantasies associated with them mediated by language, and if we are also concerned to bring about social and cultural change, we will need to give the concept of the unconscious some careful attention, and particularly in the area of gender and difference, where unconscious processes seem to play such a powerful role. This attention needs to include our insight that difference is crucial to the meaning of our sexual identities but also to the meanings of the selves we create in language, which is also based on difference. But it must also include at the ordinary everyday level, how we respond to all those whom we perceive as different from ourselves. The issue of gender difference and the domination of women, including all those who have been 'feminised' within patriarchal societies, has been and continues to be, one of the most pressing problems we have to confront, since it manifests itself as an effect of language but also in other experiences which result in exclusion and suffering.

The therapeutic practice of psychoanalysis

Psychoanalytic theory has given rise to two distinct kinds of discourse. One arises directly out of therapeutic or 'clinical' practice and is centred on the fundamentals of family life and ordinary human events. This provides the basis for the understanding of neurotic disturbance and our 'normal' unconscious projections onto cultural objects, and was invented by Freud. The other is a structural theory which attempts to unveil the causal structures which determine the construction of human identity and, ultimately, strives after an understanding of the whole of human culture and knowledge. But for the sake of clarity, I want first to give a brief description of the therapeutic practice of psychoanalysis, since this forms the underlying basis for all the theoretical positions contained in this book.

At the moment, the practices of psychoanalysis or psychoanalytical psychotherapy seem to be the only activities whose specific purpose, within the security of a protected environment, is to allow individuals gradually to become more aware of unconscious or disassociated aspects of their identity. But the special nature of the practice of psychoanalytic theory – the exclusive relationship between two people crucially mediated by language, and the requirement for confidentiality – makes it impossible for anyone to eavesdrop on anyone else's therapy. However, we do have access to the numerous anonymous case-studies written by analysts and, more recently, accounts of psychoanalytic therapy by those who have experienced it. These help us to understand the complex dynamics of the psychoanalytic process and how the unconscious, however it is theorised, expresses itself in this setting.

Classical psychoanalytic practice which broadly follows the pattern laid down by Freud, focuses on the patient's unconscious phantasies and attempts to integrate the two worlds which constitute our identity, an inner world of phantasies, impulses and conflicts and an outer world we conventionally call external reality. It does this through the use of a special kind of language called 'free association' which is based on whatever 'comes to mind' during a session. Speech, the play of imagina-tion, dreams, phantasies and other forms of symbolic representation in the form of symptoms, reveal hidden meanings, previously unspoken and allows them to be articulated into words for the first time. Interpretation takes place through the therapist's access to a symbolic system based on unconscious processes. Some therapists emphasise the provision, in therapy, of a nurturing environment in which real, but repressed ex-periences can emerge with little interpretation. But in all psychoanalytic practice there are moments when the patient's recognition of un-conscious material plays a crucial role. It is this recognition which signals that something in the shared discourse, characteristic of that situation, is now 'hooking up' with something in the unconscious. The conscious and unconscious meet in that moment of rapport. The insight and acknowledgement of previously hidden feelings is based on this coincidence between what has been said at the level of consciousness and the hidden unknown and 'unfelt' unconscious material identified by both parties. If there is no resonance, then the observation, if it is made by the therapist, may be wrong or the patient may feel unable to 'let it in'. Sometimes there is no sense of recognition because we defend ourselves against it and refuse the awareness of a painful reality in favour of the familiar phantasies or stories we prefer to tell about ourselves. Even in the containing environment of therapy moments of recognition can cause anxiety, so we may reject them, often with boredom or anger. But once the suggestion has been made, if it is an insight, it is difficult for the individual to put it out of their mind. Often, other supporting evidence comes rushing in from the rest of their life and, if it tallies with what remains unconscious, their defences evaporate and the recognition takes over. It becomes impossible to sustain the defence and reject the insight and the feelings which accompany it. The unconscious is converted into consciousness, that is, silent, unconscious feeling is squeezed into speech.

Another crucial aspect of the practice of psychoanalysis generally is the phenomenon of 'transference'. This idea refers to the way patients seem to unconsciously transfer the kind of relationship they had with their parents, as very young children, onto the therapist. (This is something which also characterises close relationships outside the consulting room in certain circumstances which is why it is an important concept in the academic practice of psychoanalytic theory as a means of understanding cultural issues.) The process of transference and the therapist's own counter-transference give therapists the opportunity of seeing for themselves what is going on by experiencing, in a displaced and condensed form, the emotional texture of this unconscious re-run of the patient's earliest relationships. The therapist then uses this repetition in the here and now, to make the patient aware of feelings and phantasies which the child-like part of them has carried into adult life. The recognitions patients are then able to make during this 'repeat performance' allow them gradually to gain access to the parts of their identity which have been disowned and, within a context of trust, the transference eventually dissolves. The sense of increased confidence and creativity people frequently experience as a consequence of therapy seems to result from losing feelings of emptiness, impoverishment and futility because so much of who they were, and how they felt remained unspoken and outside their conscious identity. A sense of having both bodily and psychological substance often replaces feelings of fragility, vulnerability and inhibition and this is reinforced by, perhaps, the first experience of real understanding and unconditional love the patient has ever had.

Criticisms of the practice of psychoanalysis

Some critics have had serious misgivings about the practice of psycho-analysis, seeing it as essentially conservative, male-dominated authorit-arian and primarily concerned with adapting the patient to an acceptance of the status quo, including culturally acceptable gender roles. (This kind of criticism clearly affects the attitude of these critics to psychoanalytic theory.) Although this view may be justified in some cases, particularly in relation to ego-psychology, a mainly American variant of psycho-analysis based on a distorted version of Freud's work, it is not the norm in relation to most modern, humane psychoanalytic practice, though there are always individual instances of bad practitioners just as there are individual bad teachers, social workers or medical doctors. Although psychoanalytic knowledge may be used by some therapists to confine identities to rigid gender roles it is used by many as a means of liberating gender because 'masculinity' and 'femininity' are perceived to cross the boundaries of male and female bodies. We all, as small children, identify to different extents, with both mothers and fathers or their substitutes. Recent complaints about psychotherapy have focused on the failure of professional organisations to impose sanctions in instances of bad prac-tice which is an important but different issue. Rather than taking an authoritarian, or manipulative stance, on the contrary, most modern psychoanalysis or psychoanalytic therapy, is fundamentally concerned with the idea of persuading the client to recognise their own power when they may never before have had this kind of experience. Many people are unconsciously trapped in an attitude of submission or domination in relation to others. The special characteristic of psychoanalytic thera-peutic practice at its most eclectic and humane, is that it enables patients to grasp the reality that there is the possibility that human beings can creatively make their own lives in both their personal relationships and their social and political alliances. In Freudian terms, it puts them in touch with their unconscious desire which can then effectively empower their language and their subjectivity. This concern with empowerment places psychoanalysis firmly within wider modern debates about power and how we can achieve political as well personal change. At its core is the idea that individuals need no longer be in thrall to an unconscious drama which insists that they follow its agenda rather than one of their own choosing. This does not, of course, imply that we should under-estimate the imprisoning power of cultural and social circumstances which require collective action to bring about change.

The academic practice of psychoanalytic theory

Psychoanalytic theory attempts to create rational knowledge (though at one level the post-modernist dimension of Freudian psychoanalysis challenges the status of all knowledge) about the construction of identity which allows us to use it to analyse historical and cultural questions in distinctive ways. It focuses on the effects of unconscious desire and loss originating in early childhood. In prioritising rational interpretation of what are seen as irrational processes, the use of psychoanalytic theory as an academic discourse is very different from the experience of the therapeutic practice of psychoanalysis where, from the point of view of the patient, intellectual as opposed to emotional understanding, is discouraged. The strangeness and ultimate inpenetrability of the un-conscious is, of course, because it is not rational and many analytical therapists and analysts argue that what they do is more like an art than any variety of science.

However, in using psychoanalytic theory as an analytical tool with which we can explore the unconscious dimensions of cultural phenom-ena such as gender, there is always the possibility that we will make contact with our own inner world. Because of this, reading and thinking about psychoanalytic material presents a particular kind of challenge to the reader. We may feel pleasure at the recognition of ourselves in some of the material, but other parts of it may set up unconscious resonances in our experience which are disturbing and provoke anxiety. This is particularly true in relation to Freudian theory, where our sense of the 'oddness' of some of Freud's material may stem from the fact that he is describing normal thinking (the way we consciously live out our 'mascu-linity' or 'femininity' for example) but it is utterly transformed in his description by the nature and language of the unconscious. The strangeness of his very distinctive understanding of sexuality derived from the body-preoccupied world of the young child may provoke feelings of distaste in some readers, but these feelings may also arise from the anxiety this may activate in them because we have all been small children. On the other hand, Winnicott's strand of Object-Relations theory, described in chapter three of this book, takes a more socialised view of the unconscious as a container of real deprivations and offers us descriptions of ourselves which are much more recognisable and accessible.

So, although all psychoanalytic theory provides a powerful tool for the analysis of identity, culture and language, it is almost impossible to use it creatively and productively without at the same time developing a considerable degree of emotional insight. Resonances and reverberations within us eventually provide the basis for this insight. This is why so many academic psychoanalytic theorists such as Juliet Mitchell, Nancy Chodorow, Luce Irigaray and Julia Kristeva started out as or have become psychoanalysts or psychoanalytic therapists. In using psycho-analytic theory for academic analysis, recognitions of the unconscious dimensions of cultural questions which, at some level, flesh out the meanings of the concepts, are dependent on a degree of emotional insight into what constitutes those dimensions. For example, the idea of projection which, in one form or another, is central to all the theories discussed in this book and to the psychoanalytic study of women's subordination, is difficult to understand and use in academic analysis with any confidence, unless we have some conscious awareness of the ex-perience of it. As I have suggested earlier, this is what sometimes makes the use and development of psychoanalytic theory 'hard work' in the emotional as well as intellectual sense. This is as true of the structural theory of Freud, Lacan and the French feminists as it is of other theory because its structural coherence always rests on the family as an essential field of determining forces and the reverberations of the family within our individual identities.

Psychoanalytic theory and 'truth'

Although psychoanalytic theory at one level represents a very integrated form of knowledge because it pays attention to unconscious as well as conscious processes, like all other theories, it can only represent one among many ways of thinking the world and there is considerable theoretical variation within psychoanalytic theory itself. Many students and academics now accept the idea that no theory, however elegant, erudite or compelling offers any kind of over-arching certainty. All theories are seen as socially constructed discourses which contain different versions of what used to be called 'truth'; this has the effect of subtly keeping us in our place. This particular theoretical insight (labelled 'post-modernism') emerged partly as a result of Lacan's work on the relationship between the unconscious and language or knowledge. Lacan and others have argued that the words and categories through which we structure and interpret the world consciously, have meanings we can never totally pin down because of the ever-present potential of the unconscious to disrupt meaning. This means that discourses are constructed out of unconscious as well as social or conscious interests. In their gaps and incoherences, they reveal what their creators may have unconsciously disowned or repressed. All writers are 'writers in transference' as psychoanalytic language describes it. Their writing is invested with what Lacan calls unconscious desire, before, and in the process, of writing. So the different theories contained in the body of psychoanalytic theory – modern and post-modern – can provide us with powerful insights, but none of them, on their own, can give us a definitive answer to the question of how gendered identity is constructed. Since we cannot have identities which are free of unconscious determinations and be entirely consistent ourselves we cannot hope for a perfectly coherent form of knowledge. No one, single psychoanalytic theory can offer a definitive account of the unconscious construction of gender. However, each of them contains valuable ideas and insights which can be used to analyse different aspects of what we call reality alongside other theories (such as those of history, sociology, anthropology and semiotics).

Readers, as well as writers, also construct meanings out of their own conscious and unconscious interests. As readers of texts, including psychoanalytic ones, we bring to them not only our own understanding but also our unconscious experience which inevitably shapes and determines what we make of them. We are all, writers and readers, subject to our own unconscious agendas. We may therefore find that we need to read some psychoanalytic texts many times before our unconscious will allow us to take in the meanings of certain passages without a mental sensation of 'jogging over'. They may make us feel bored, angry or tired. In sociology and cultural studies, students and teachers refer to the 'negotiation' of the meanings made available to us by our social position within culture. But this is not always possible when our unconscious, as conceived by Freud, refuses to permit this negotiation in the interests of protecting us, as individuals, from psychical pain.

Psychoanalysis and feminism

Many feminists have taken up psychoanalytic theory, although others have been hostile to it. In particular, they have criticised Freud's theory for being father-centred and phallocentric (penis-centred). However, although some of Freud's remarks about women have laid him open to the charge of blatant sexism, his more considered ideas about 'femininity' have sometimes been taken out of the context of his overall theory. Juliet Mitchell has commented that 'Concepts such as penis-envy without such notions [of context] become either laughable or ideologically dangerous' (Mitchell 1975: xvi). Other feminists have rejected Freud on the basis that, since Freud was white, middle-class and male, his work embodies oppressive social relations which reflect this background. But many theories, including those of Freud, are of great intellectual interest in spite of the fact that they have been produced by people who occupy unjustified positions of social power. Many of these contain, embedded within them, insights about human experience which in my view, although it is controversial, may fruitfully be used in the interests of those who have the least power to represent their interests. In this book I shall suggest that the development of the distinctly mother-centred ap-proaches of Klein and Winnicott arise directly out of Freud's ostensibly father-centred work.

Since the mid-1970s interest in psychoanalytic theory has grown among feminists. Many have recognised that they share with psycho-analysis a common concern with gender identity, sexuality, the body, the family, power and the possibility of change. All of these are perceived to have a direct bearing on the position of women. At the time of writing, when the distinction between our biological sex and our gender is widely acknowledged, most people recognise the role played by socialisation and culture in the construction of the unequal categories of 'masculinity' and 'femininity'. However, many feminists have become attracted to psychoanalytic theory because it has become clear that socialisation theory, which deals only with conscious processes, cannot alone provide an adequate explanation of how these destructive categories come into being. Psychoanalytic theory offers another approach. By exploring how culturally approved definitions of 'masculinity' and 'femininity', and those which lie outside them, are unconsciously lived as identities by men and women, it dramatically extends the scope of the analysis of women's subordination in culture. In most societies, women, and those equated with the 'feminine', have been and continue to be largely dominated by male power. Psychoanalytic theory and practice suggest that political and personal violence frequently springs from unconscious anxieties and desires which may nevertheless masquerade as the language of consciousness and reason. It suggests that if we want to understand the subordination of women (and other groups on the basis of class, sexual orientation, race and ethnicity), we need to attend to the unconscious formations (such as projection) behind these responses to difference. The French feminists in particular (as we shall see in chapter five) have taken up the Freudian and Lacanian analysis of the ideology of patriarchal culture and the role and meaning of the unconscious and gender difference within it.

In this book I have chosen to retain the term 'patriarchal' to describe culture and society although the concept of 'patriarchy', has now been widely criticised. Post-modern theory, in particular, has theorised the collapse of all identities and totalising concepts including that of patriarchy. However, I think the idea of a patriarchal culture or society continues to be a useful way of describing a range of unconscious as well as conscious constraints, contained in a set of complex and interconnecting signifying practices or ways of 'thinking' the world which are historically contingent with the subordination of women. These practices are mediated by many, but not all cultural institutions and by many, but not all, men (and some women), at both public and private levels of experience, but not necessarily consistently or all the time.

Difference: across the boundaries of the body

At the more personal level, one of the strengths of Freud's theory, as we shall see in more detail later, is that it allows us to explain differences among women and men as well as the difference between them. In describing the unconscious reasons why people do not conform to the cultural norms of 'masculinity' and 'femininity', it allows us to explore why many people seem to circumvent their socialisation into cultural norms so that, for example, some women are more culturally 'masculine' in their drives (sexual and others) while some men remain more culturally 'feminine'. The problem in Western societies and perhaps all others is that, as Lacan argues, maleness signifies value and power, whether an individual's personal behaviour justifies it or not. Men, therefore, have a privileged status within culture which even the most culturally 'feminine' of them find difficult to give up. The problem for men is that to be more like women in any way – public or personal – is to accept a downgrading of status in social and sexual terms and risk being seen as less of a man on both fronts. The situation is different for women. For a woman to be more culturally 'masculine', as many women are and want to be, implies some upgrading of social status. But the problem for such women is that they may at the same time be downgraded in sexual terms, which is a problem experienced particularly by young girls. The fear of many adolescent girls is that to be clever and active is to be perceived as 'unsexy'. A woman may become well qualified, with a fulfilling, high-status, well-paid job, feel fulfilled but at the same time fear that she may be judged by men as less sexually attractive, less of a 'real woman' and more threatening than other women – and these kinds of feelings are painful to many women.

Freudian theory, assuming the existence of the unconscious, allows us to explain why some men and women repress sexual feelings dissonant with their gender roles in response to cultural prohibitions. The 'ultra macho' man is often compensating by unconsciously concealing his 'femininity' (perhaps because of an over-identification with his mother frequently brought about by a physically or emotionally absent father). The 'ultra feminine' woman is often compensating for an over-identification with a father, which has left her with unconscious anxiety about her status as a 'real woman'.

Freudian and Object-Relations theory

In this book we shall be dealing with the two main strands of psychoanalytic theory. Although the term 'psychoanalysis' has been associated particularly with the work of Freud who invented it, a second major tradition of psychoanalytic theory called Object-Relations theory developed from his work in the 1930s. This book introduces four major psychoanalytic writers who represent some of the most influential ideas within these two perspectives: Freud, Lacan and the early work of Klein (Freudian theory) and Klein's later work and Winnicott (Object-Relations theory). In addition, two more writers, introduced in chapter five, represent important feminist interpretations of Lacan's theory: Julia

Kristeva and Luce Irigaray. The first section of each chapter gives details of the theory; the second section provides a commentary on a selected text (contained in Part II) in the overall context of the theory in the first section, and the third section gives a discussion of the theory, particularly in the context of gender. The organisation of the book anticipates that the reader might first read the initial outline of the theory, then read the original text alongside the commentary, and then the discussion. At the end of each chapter there is a list of suggested reading as a guide to the reader. These are not scholarly bibliographies but intended as accessible guides to further reading.

Freudian and Object-Relations theory differ in how they conceptualise the unconscious and the degree to which the role of the unconscious is emphasised. But what both have in common is the idea that we cannot 'be' by thinking alone. Both approaches emphasise that something which forms part of our experience which is 'repressed' (Freud), 'split off' (Klein) or 'dissociated' (Winnicott) from consciousness. Both assume that appearance often masks a different underlying reality whether it is conceptualised as another 'scene' with a specific language of its own (Freud), as a melée of primitive phantasies (Klein), as an unreachable well of early deprivations (Winnicott), or as permanently unsatisfied desire which nevertheless generates subjectivity in language (Lacan). However the differences between them crucially affect their views of identity. Freudian theory sees identity as always divided, unstable and made precarious by a potentially subversive unconscious. This hidden agenda has a dynamic effect on what we do, how we think and the knowledge we are able to produce. Object-Relations theory, on the other hand, sees identity as capable of becoming unified, stable and authentic. The two schools also differ on the degree of emphasis they give to biology. Freudian theory, in spite of Freud's early pre-occupation with biological determinations, emphasises the unconscious construction of gendered subjectivity, whereas Object-Relations theory takes gender to be partly biologically determined at birth (though reinforced in early childhood).

The two streams of psychoanalytic theory are also disinguished by which parent is given prominence in the theory. Freud's early work, in particular, focuses on the father, whereas in Object-Relations theory the emphasis is on the mother. As I have already suggested, however, one argument of this book is that this distinction is not as clear as it is sometimes taken to be. Although Freud may not have recognised it fully himself, his theory (particularly in his later work) is concerned as much with the importance of the mother as the father, especially for the girl. It is this which provides the springboard for much of the Object-Relations theory which emerged after it. I shall argue that, in each of the four major theories we shall consider, the mother, explicitly or implicitly, stands at the centre of all identity and sexuality in the unconscious life of the child and adult. This may be a major factor in the subordination of women and the 'feminine' within culture.

We also need to compare each of the different perspectives in terms of the kind of theory they represent. They include theories which are centred around clinical experience and theories which attempt to build structural models which do not depend directly on experience. Freud's theory, while always concerned with early fundamental experiences within the family and the inter-subjective dramas of everyday life reflects his interest in the structural dimensions of identity and the language through which the complex fabric of the unconscious can be made accessible. For Freud, the central structural concept of the unconscious is both an explanatory device for making ordinary human speech and action intelligible, as well as the springboard for the other structural concepts he needed for a larger theory of human thought and culture. In this sense his work is simultaneously modern and post-modern. Klein's theory, although heavily dependent on Freud, is based on a developmental, stage-by-stage approach which is mainly concerned with therapeutic issues of interpretation rather than an overall structural theory of culture. Winnicott's theory is also primarily developmental rather than structural though he was always sceptical about the status of any theory, seeing it as potentially imprisoning. For this reason he frequently breaks into an idiosyncratic, often poetic use of language which inhabits a realm outside the domain of theoretical precision and coherence. In dramatic contrast, Lacan's development of Freud's theory is unrepentently post-structuralist, relying almost entirely on structural linguistics to generate a theory of psychoanalysis and the unconscious as language. His own notoriously difficult writing reflects his wish to demonstrate the action of the unconscious on all writing, including theoretical writing. The theory of the French feminists (now increasingly referred to as post-modern feminists) Cixous, Kristeva and Irigaray, though post-structuralist in their pre-occupation with language as identity, are also concerned with such fundamental issues as mothering and women's bodies which continually intermix with the structural elements.

Although these writers are often grouped together, by others, they do not form a group and the work of each is distinctively different from that of the others, as I hope will become clear in chapter five when we look at the work of Kristeva and Irigaray.

An eclectic perspective

This book adopts an eclectic approach. This does not reflect a lack of confidence in theory as such but a recognition that in our analysis of identities and culture this is the only way we can use what we value within each of the different modern and post-modern conceptual frameworks. This follows the actual therapeutic practice of much modern psychoanalysis. Many psychoanalysts who are now often called psycho-analytical psychotherapists succeed by using concepts drawn from different perspectives because rigid, orthodox, dogmatic approaches often close off possibilities and new thought. Within an eclectic approach rigour takes on a more human meaning. It consists of acknowledging the provisionality of everything that we think we know (without throwing out passion and commitment), understanding the points at which theories become incompatible, but nonetheless using each of them in our academic practice where they can help us illuminate different aspects of the construction of gendered identities and culture. Even within the natural sciences, the 'truth' of science is nowadays defined in terms of its usefulness. It is no longer seen as useful or powerful because it is 'true' but 'true' only in the sense that it is useful. In analysing gender, of course, this idea might be intended to undermine patriarchal ways of understanding the world, but, as Kristeva emphasises, it also threatens feminist forms of knowledge as well.

The theories of Freud, Klein, Winnicott and Lacan described in this book each illuminate different aspects of identity and power in their own distinctive way. Each is based on long therapeutic experience. What distinguishes them is what their writers have created out of similar 'clinical' material. As I have already suggested, each of their theories inevitably has built-in presences and absences which reflect their creators' unconscious interests in their theoretical constructions and I have included a brief discussion of this idea in each chapter. But this is not intended to underestimate the central role of cultural and historical factors in the construction of this theory.

Psychoanalytic jargon

One thing which has been most offputting about some (but not all) psychoanalytic theory is the rather heavy, abstract, language in which it is sometimes written. Another is its use as rigid, imprisoning, defensive dogma. In the chapters that follow, I shall try to avoid unnecessary jargon and each new concept we encounter will be clearly explained and put into context. If ideas are valuable they should be valuable in a language which allows us to maintain contact with our experience.

The theoretical break between modern and post-modern psycho-analytic approaches and the resulting change in the language used is most visible in this book in the transition from Winnicott's paper 'Transitional Objects and Transitional Phenomena' to Lacan's 'The Meaning of the Phallus'. Here, the contrast between Winnicott's more conventional language (in this paper though not in others) in which unconscious desire could be said to be firmly controlled and the galloping abundance of desire in Lacan's text is very striking. Lacan's efforts to make his writing reflect the complexity of his theory, and use language to imitate the texture and richness of the unconscious lead him to a difficult, sometimes tortured exploration of the ideas which lie behind it. One function of this book is to illuminate the theoretical intentions behind this self-conscious, sometimes exasperating style which has been hugely influential on contemporary psychoanalytic thinking.

Suggested reading

BARUCH, E. (1991) *Women Analyse Women*, New York, New York University Press.
BREEN, D. (1993) *The Gender Conundrum*, London, Routledge.
DINNAGE, R. (1988) *One to One*, Harmondsworth, Penguin [a personal account of the experience of analysis].
FORDHAM, M. (1993) *The Making of an Analyst*, London, Free Association Books.
GUNTRIP, H. (1975) 'My Experience of Analysis with Fairburn and Winnicott (How Complete a Result Does Psychoanalytic Therapy Achieve)', *International Review of Psychoanalysis*, 2: 145–56.
HERMAN, N. (1988) *My Kleinian Home*, London, Free Association Books [a personal account of the experience of Kleinian analysis].
HERMAN, N. (1987) *Why Psychotherapy?*, London, Free Association Books.
KENNEDY, R. (1993) *Freedom to Relate*, London, Free Association Books.
LAPLANCHE, J. and PONTALIS, J.B. (1985) *The Language of Psychoanalysis*, London, Hogarth Press [useful explanations of psychoanalytic terms and where they come from].

LINDNER, R. (1986) *The Fifty Minute Hour: A Collection of True Psychoanalytic Tales*, London, Free Association Books.

LOMAS, P. (1987) *The Limits of Interpretation: What's Wrong With Psychoanalysis?*, London, Penguin [a discussion of psychoanalysis by an analyst who uses an eclectic approach].

LOMAS, P. (1992) *The Psychotherapy of Everyday Life*, London, Penguin.

MINSKY, R. (1990) 'The Trouble is it's ahistorical – The Problem of the Unconscious', *Feminist Review*, 36: 4–14 [a discussion of the concept of the unconscious].

RYCROFT, C. (1995) *A Critical Dictionary of Psychoanalysis*, London, Penguin.

SEGAL, J. (1985) *Phantasy in Everyday Life*, London, Pelican.

STORR, A. (1979) *The Art of Psychotherapy*, London, Butterworth-Heinemann.

TONG, R. (1989) *Feminist Thought*, London, Routledge [chapters five, 'Psycho-analytic Feminism' and eight 'Post-Modern Feminism'].

WRIGHT, E. ed. (1992) *Feminism and Psychoanalysis: A Critical Dictionary*, Oxford, Blackwell.

The distinction between psychoanalysis, psychotherapy and psychiatry is sometimes unclear. Psychoanalysis is the process initiated by Freud and is practised by people who trained in particular training institutions such as the British Psychoanalytical Society and who refer to themselves as psychoanalysts or, increasingly, psychoanalytical psychotherapists although they may not be Freudian. Some forms of psychoanalytic psychotherapy use a psychoanalytic approach but are much less time-consuming than classical psychoanalysis and are thought by many to be equally effective. Confusingly, other forms of therapy which do not use a psychoanalytic approach are also often called 'psycho-therapy'. In Britain psychiatry normally has very little to do with psychoanalysis, being primarily concerned with the treatment of mental illness by drug therapy. Rather confusingly, in the United States psychoanalysts are sometimes called psychiatrists. However, the most common form of psychoanalysis in the United States is ego-psychology which is very different from the psychoanalysis invented by Freud.

I
Freud: the rejection of femininity

Born under one law, to another bound.
(Fulke Greville, poet (1554–1628), *Mustapha*)

Biographical background (1856–1939)

Sigmund Freud was born in Moravian Freiberg, now in the Czech Republic, the oldest of eight children and reputedly his mother's favourite. Before his discovery of the unconscious and psychoanalysis, Freud worked as a neurologist in Vienna, specialising in the study of organic nervous disease. However in 1885, just before his long-awaited marriage to Martha Bernays, he went on a six-month visit to Paris, where he became fascinated by Jean Martin Charcot's use of hypnosis with women who suffered from what was called hysteria, a physical illness for which there seemed to be no medical explanation. This visit was a source of inspiration for Freud and marked a dramatic change of direction in his career. In 1895, at the age of thirty-nine, he published his first book on psychoanalysis, *Studies on Hysteria* with his colleague Josef Breuer. This book grew directly out of their innovatory work with women suffering from hysterical symptoms. In 1900 he published his founding book on the unconscious, *The Interpretation of Dreams*. Although this book at first provoked disappointingly little interest, by 1909, when he was invited to lecture in America, psychoanalysis was beginning to establish a growing international reputation.

Freud spent his long life mainly in Vienna continually developing his ideas despite suffering from throat cancer diagnosed in 1923. These ideas were published in a series of major papers including *Beyond the Pleasure Principle* (1920) and *The Ego and the Id* (1923). He also worked in clinical practice with his patients, who provided him with the source of his theoretical ideas. Some of these patients he subsequently trained as psychoanalysts. As a Jew, he fled in 1938 with his family from Hitler's Germany to England where he died of cancer a year later, at the outbreak of the Second World War.

[25]

An overview of Freud's ideas

Freud's greatest achievement was to transform the way we think about ourselves. From the end of the nineteenth century for the next forty years, he put forward ideas which revolutionised our view of ourselves as rational, knowing subjects. This view had predominated since Descartes had written over two hundred years earlier that 'I think, therefore I am'. Freud pronounced that consciousness, knowledge about ourselves and everything else, is always threatened by the potential subversion of our unconscious. Before we look specifically at Freud's ideas about the construction of 'masculinity' and 'femininity' and how we live these identities in our minds, we need first to explore the wider context of Freud's ideas and to trace the vital links between Freud's interacting concepts of the unconscious, sexuality, identity, gender and subjectivity.

Freud's theory takes all identity to be fundamentally split into two entirely separate dimensions. One is consciousness, what we think we know about ourselves and what we call reality and the other is the unconscious, a part of us which determines much of what we do and how we feel but of which we are unaware – what Freud also called 'psychical reality'. Freud believed that this 'other scene' was completely concealed from conscious view by means of psychological blocking mechanisms which he called our defences. He thought the most important of these was *repression*, a means of shutting out potentially painful aspects of ourselves which nevertheless still form a substantial, but hidden part of who we are. Freud believed that identity is also inseparably interwoven with our sexuality. By sexuality Freud means a variety of drives which go beyond what we normally describe as sexual. These drives represent the major sources of pleasure in early childhood. But what interests Freud is how these are transformed into their psychical representations, that is, what they come to mean within our unconscious about who we are or our identity. These are meanings which are normally not accessible to consciousness, although they persistently influence what we do. The gendered human subject, Freud insisted, is inherently at odds with itself. Consciousness – what we call our identity – is always unstable, always at risk of sabotage from the unacceptable feelings of loss and desire which we have to repress into our unconscious in order to conform to the demands of culture. Our inner psychical or unconscious reality and the external world are always fundamentally in conflict.

There are sometimes said to be two distinct Freuds. One Freud is the enthusiastic, modernist product of the Enlightenment dedicated to scientific analysis of a new science of neurotic disorder based on his clinical experience. Within this new knowledge, which wavers between a natural and a human science, identity, or what Freud referred to as the 'psychical apparatus', is seen as the wordless interplay of biological drives. For this rationalist, modernist Freud there was always the underlying hope that identity or the ego could fight off the onslaughts of the unconscious. The second Freud is the post-modern theorist fascinated by the prospect of founding a new structural theory of the unconscious which would reveal the myth of identity. For this post-modern Freud, pre-occupied with conscious and unconscious symbolisation, gendered identity is inherently fragile, precarious and unstable because it is always vulnerable to disruption from the unconscious. In this situation in which the human subject cannot know itself, Freud suggests that language, knowledge and theory must also be precarious and incomplete, constantly encumbered with riddles and paradoxes. It is this post-modern Freud which interests Lacan and others in the contemporary development of his work.

The unconscious

Freud's life-long pre-occupation with the hidden but ultimately knowable meanings embedded in language and other forms of symbolisation dramatically influenced the development of his central concept of the unconscious. By the end of the late nineteenth century the idea of the unconscious was not new – as Freud himself recognised, poets, philosophers and many nineteenth-century psychologists had been aware of its existence. But Freud's concept of the unconscious grew directly from his early clinical work with women patients suffering from what were called hysterical conversion symptoms and he often referred to these women as his teachers. He recognised that his patients made significant progress through what he called *free association* (saying whatever comes to mind) and Bertha Pappenheim, a patient of Freud's colleague, Breuer, christened the technique 'the talking cure' (PFL 3: 83). Juliet Mitchell vividly describes this technique as 'the action or the language of the body squeezed into words' (Mitchell 1986: 11). The symptoms of hysteria suffered by these women took the form of physical illnesses or paralyses which seemed to have no underlying medical explanation and Freud became convinced that these symptoms carried a special kind of meaning deriving from painful experiences in the past. A hysterical woman, he insisted, 'suffers from reminiscences' (PFL 7: 58). He came to the conclusion that in childhood we repress forbidden and painful feelings into the unconscious where they remain in a dynamic state which always threatens to erupt back into consciousness. Eventually they express themselves in physical symptoms or psychological ways such as dreams or slips of the tongue which represent a kind of compromise between the power of our repressed feelings and the energy of our defences against them contained in our consciousness. This defensive part of ourselves is always intent on papering over the cracks and maintaining its own version of events at all costs. For Freud, repression produces a contradiction at the heart of all human identity and culture. In *Civilisation and its Discontents* (PFL 12) he emphasises the similarity 'between the process of civilisation and the libidinal development of the individual' in that 'Civilisation is built on the renunciation of instinct'. The loss involved in repression lies at the core of our identities.

Freud decided that everyone experiences symbolic expressions of the unconscious in the form of projections, compulsions, obsessions, anxieties, phobias or psychosomatic illness. One area of interest in which Freud has been especially influential is in his fascination with language and representation. This interest first became clear in his book, *The Interpretation of Dreams* (1900) in which he published his founding ideas on the symbolic structure of the language of the unconscious. He analysed the phenomenon of dreams (which he described as the 'royal road' to the unconscious) to demonstrate what he saw as the universal nature of the language of the unconscious (SE 4–5, PFL4). He argued that dreams, jokes, slips of the tongue, bungled speech and actions all shared the same kind of structure as neurotic symptoms. These frozen unconscious meanings produced from fundamental human experiences emerged symbolically in two modes – *condensation* and *displacement*.

Condensation occurs when one idea with several associations is symbolised by a single symbol or metaphor. Displacement takes place when an idea is displaced onto other ideas which originally had less intensity but which are related to the first idea through a chain of associations. These two complementary concepts allowed Freud to perceive the otherwise invisible structural laws or patterns of unconscious meaning. An example of condensation would be the common dream of finding oneself naked in the middle of a city. This could represent the condensation of several anxieties: a generalised fear of being exposed as less confident than one might appear, anxiety about an important job interview the next day and an experience on the day before the dream of having been lost on the way to the theatre with a group of children who were consequently late for a matinée. As examples of common forms of displacement found in dreams Freud included the following: steps, ladders and staircases symbolically represent sexual activity; rooms, tables, and tables laid for meals represent women; walls and houses represent bodies, bridges and woooded hills; landscapes in general symbolise genitals; hair-cutting, teeth falling out represent anxieties about sexuality and weapons, tools, complicated machinery, snakes and neck-ties symbolise the penis. The following dream is an example of condensation and displacement combined in a composite structure. A man dreams he is riding out into the countryside on a motorbike with his girl-friend. He stops and they go for a walk in the forested hills. When they return he finds a gang of jeering youths who have taken his motorbike apart. As he rushes after them he notices that they are running away with the crucial part whose loss would prevent him from ever being able to re-assemble his bike. The unconscious ideas which have been condensed into this incident might be the desire for a powerful 'masculine' identity (the motorbike), the wish to establish or continue a sexual relationship with the girl who accompanies him (going to the countryside and the walk), anxieties about sexual potency (the wrecking of the bike and the theft of the crucial component), his own self-contempt about the fragility of his 'masculinity' (the jeering boys represent displaced contemptuous aspects of the man's self intent on sabotaging the part trying to be powerful and potent).

In his much later paper 'The Unconscious' (1915), Freud emphasised and developed his description of the unconscious. He distinguished between two kinds of memories, what he called 'thing-presentations' in the unconscious and 'word-presentations' which occur only in language. Repression prevents the thing-presentation (in the unconscious) being translated into words, so that it remains attached to the idea in the unconscious. For Freud, these presentations represent memories which are mobilised initially by some wish or desire. Only when the silent thing-presentations are expressed in language can they lose their potential for sabotage and disruption.

So, for Freud, the fundamental assumption from which all his other concepts and ideas flow is the unconscious and the idea of a psychical (unconscious) reality or sub-text consisting of phantasies and forbidden desires. Paradoxically, as Juliet Mitchell comments, although it is not part of the external world 'it is a hard core, a nugget, felt to be as real as the grass and the trees, as real as (and not unconnected with) the fact that one is born to two parents and is either a boy or a girl' (Mitchell 1986: 13).

Freud refers to the unconscious as 'primary process' and to consciousness as 'secondary process'. Unfortunately, however, critics often apply the standards of consciousness to unconscious structures which is to miss the essential point because the unconscious is the level which is, by definition, normally unavailable to consciousness. One of the problems of speaking and writing about the unconscious, therefore, is that we do so in the language of consciousness and culture. As we shall see at an important level, language is a defence against the unconscious whose silent, desiring meanings are hidden beneath its surface.

Freud's conceptualisation of the precise relationship between conscious and unconscious processes changed in the course of his life. Over half a century during which he was trying to conceptualise an entirely new way of thinking human experience Freud constantly revised, reworked and developed his ideas within evolving conceptual frameworks. His later theory is, however, generally regarded as offering the most sophisticated basis for practice. Here the emphasis on the biological drives of his earlier work has been transformed into a concentration on their psychical representations, what they come to mean within a person's unconscious. This new three-dimensional theory of the id, ego and the superego was introduced in 1923, in *The Ego and the Id* (PFL II: 339). This replaced the dualism of his earlier work which divided the mind into two opposing systems – pre-conscious and conscious on the one hand, and the unconscious on the other. This new, tripartite model gave much more scope for complexity and overlap while continuing to separate the world of culture from that of the unconscious. Freud now argued that the baby gradually develops three distinguishable realms of identity – *id, ego* and *superego*. The id is the unconscious place into which drives and desires are repressed (including, controversially, a death drive). The ego is the organised sense of identity or 'self', and the superego is the critic and protector of the ego. Both the ego and later the super-ego are carved out of the id, but not completely and not for all time for the boundaries between these entities are frequently blurred and differences are often difficult to perceive.

For Freud the ego forms the basic building block for identity. It

LANCASHIRE LIBRARY

represents the means by which an individual becomes a human subject, and is constructed out of the child's earliest identifications or emotional ties and the symbolic remains of abandoned attachments to other people and things; what Freud calls 'objects'. Identification with another person as someone one would like to be becomes the means by which identity comes into being through the successive internalisations of other people's qualities and attributes. The ego is simultaneously part of both the past and the present. Freud summed up this view in his paper 'Group, Psychology and the Analysis of the Ego' (1921) and added that the ego must also be grounded in word-presentations in language, which provide it with a degree of mastery against unconscious desire. However, he thought that this makes the ego permanently precarious because the unconscious always contrives to be heard in the stumblings and hesitations of language. This emphasis on the construction of the ego through identification with other people and the part language plays in it, is crucial to Lacan's re-working of Freud, as we shall see in chapter four.

Freud's life-long preoccupation with the description of the nature of unconscious processes was paralleled by an equally intense conviction that it was indissolubly linked with the construction of sexuality. In fact, it is the twin concepts of the meaning of sexuality and the meaning of the unconscious, each determining the structure of the other, which form the central core of his work. So let us look now at what he means by his concept of sexuality.

Sexuality

By *sexuality*, Freud meant something very different from our conventional understanding of this idea. Freud's perception of sexuality transcends the simple idea of genital sexuality. He sees it not simply as animal instinct but as specific to both human culture and the form of conscious and unconscious life we live within it. For Freud sexuality is infinitely complicated and far reaching in its effects and its 'normal' development is a long and tortuous process which may be established in most of us only very precariously.

Freud perceives sexuality not as one drive but a compound of many '*component instincts*', each deriving from pleasurable experiences of the body in infancy. The use of the term 'instincts' is important here because it stems directly from the translation of the standard edition of his work. Freud used the word 'Trieb' in his original German text but the translators of the standard edition translated it as 'instinct', consequently losing the distinction Freud had made between 'Trieb' which belongs to the dimension of the mind and 'Instinkt' which is more appropriate to biology. In doing this, the translation suggests the idea of a programmed instinct derived directly from the body rather than an impulse related more to the mind. This confusion has had the effect of detracting from the radical quality of Freud's theory. Early in his career, in 1905, in his book titled *Three Essays on Sexuality* (PFL 7: 31), when he was still thinking very much in terms of drives rather than his later structural categories. Freud proposed the revolutionary idea of *infantile sexuality*, which was greeted at the time with moral outrage. In many ways this laid the groundwork for his later theory of sexuality which was absorbed into a larger theory of identity or subjectivity involving the structural concepts of the id, ego and superego. In the *Three Essays* he argues that children are sexual almost from the moment of birth. By 'sexual' Freud means only that the baby, small child and later adult gains pleasure from its own body, or, as we shall see, cultural substitutes for this body. He referred to these pleasure-seeking sexual drives as the libido or id. Freud describes the development of sexuality in terms of four broad, possibly successive, often co-existing but always overlapping stages. At each stage, the sexual instinct has a *source*, an *aim* and an *object*. The *source* is the part of the body, the erotogenic zone which experiences the need or later desire. The *aim*, which may be passive or active, is the discharge of sexual tension and the *object* is the part of the body, or later, person (the object of the child's or adult's love) 'appropriate' for providing satisfaction or pleasure. The idea of appropriateness is crucial to our understanding of the whole process. For example, natural activities like eating or defecating or being washed give rise to pleasure spontaneously and passively in the baby but then later these activities are also actively sought for their own sake in babies of both sexes (for example, sucking the thumb or fingers as well as the mother's breast). So before we are able to fall in love with another person, we fall in love with our mother's breast, our faeces, our clitoris or penis because they give us pleasure, and importantly, our first primitive sense of identity.

The first vital need is for feeding and Freud describes this as the *oral phase* (PFL 7: 116–17). At this time the baby seeks and obtains pleasure through its lips – through sucking. The erotogenic zone is the lips, the aim is the pleasure of incorporation and the object with which the baby could be said to be 'in love', is the mother's breast or its own thumb or fingers. This first phase then gives way to the *anal phase* and the beginning of muscular co-ordination and control. The 'holding on' and 'letting go' of the faeces is found to be a source of pleasure over which the child has more control than the breast, which comes and goes depending on the mother's presence or absence. The erotogenic zone is then the anus, the aim is the pleasure of control and the object is the faeces, the precious internal contents which are expelled as a gift. It is important to remember here that we are concerned with the body-preoccupied reality of the very small child who, Freud believed at this stage in his life, experiences its self largely in terms of pleasurable sensations.

The third phase Freud described as the *phallic phase*. Here we approach more familiar ground. The penis is the seat of tension and satisfaction for the small boy as is the clitoris for the little girl. The clitoris is physiologically structured in the same way as the penis. It is during this phase that, Freud argues, both children discover sexual difference and gender. This is the phase when both sexes, already primarily identified (sharing an identity) with the mother, fall in love with her and want to 'marry' her and be desired by her exclusively. At this stage, Freud argues, both children are active in the form their sexuality or pleasure-seeking takes. They want to possess the mother and the pleasure associated with her for ever. Initially masturbation is the small child's way of exploring its body, its own potential for pleasure. Pleasure associated with the mother's care and pleasure from its own body are merged into a phantasy of paradise and a perfect identity, which Freud thought most of us never ultimately give up. The penis or clitoris provide the connection between these two. Initially, Freud describes as 'masculine' the fact that both children are active rather than passive in their aim in relation to the mother. However, throughout his long career he was dissatisfied with this equation. He repeatedly comments on the difficulties of equating active sexual aims with masculinity and passive ones with femininity since both men and women can take up both positions – active or passive – towards any object of desire. There is further discussion of this issue in the commentary on his paper 'Femininity' later in this chapter. During this phase, Freud tells us, on the basis of what his patients said to him in his clinical practice, both male and female children assume that their mother has a penis. Only later in the Oedipal crisis do both children discover that she has not. As he pointed out to his critics, the adult sexual practice of fetishism pursued by men who have, in phantasy, partly disavowed the discovery that their mother lacks a penis seems to bear this out.

[33]

Something – a shoe, a suspender belt, an item of clothing – comes to 'stand in' for the penis which is experienced as frighteningly absent from the bodies of female lovers even though, contradictorily, to some degree, the woman's lack of a penis is consciously known. It is as if the unconscious negotiation of this reality which as we shall see has such a shattering consequence, when it is first discovered, is still going on. Male trans-sexuals who dress as women may be trying to represent themselves as the pre-Oedipal mother, the all-powerful 'woman with a penis' with whom, as babies, they originally shared an identity and continue, unconsciously, to share an identity. (However, a state of knowing and not knowing at the same time could describe the confusing contradictions within many forms of knowledge, including Freud's own work, pointing to the ultimate impossibility of knowledge as 'truth' and the idea that knowledge itself may be a form of fetish which stands in for phantasy of the powerful phallic mother.)

The stimulus for the child's phantasised love affair with its mother, which expresses itself in phallic activity (masturbation in relation to the penis or clitoris) is the mother's nurturing and touching behaviour towards the child which is experienced as seduction because it is so pleasurable. The baby, as well as receiving hugs and kisses from birth, has had its genitals sponged, patted dry and powdered repeatedly by its mother. Another important feature of this phallic stage, according to Freud, is that the mother is perceived by the child to desire the phallus in the form of the father who is increasingly seen as the child's rival. As Freud was again the first to admit, this area of who thinks whom has what and why is a very confusing one; we shall return to this later.

The fourth and final stage in infantile sexuality to which Freud thought everyone could progress if things went smoothly (though he admitted they often did not) was the stage of *genital sexuality.* He argued that this was not usually achieved until after a period of latency, at puberty (when he thought most girls, after the onset of menstruation, first discover that they have a vagina as well as a clitoris). During this period of latency the child's sexual drives are repressed after the disappointments of the phallic phase and the Oedipal crisis. We shall return to this crucial stage later. Genital sexuality is defined by Freud as heterosexuality, the only form of sexuality condoned by culture.

The important thing to remember about these phases is that Freud saw them as overlapping and co-existing so that the child could in practice gain pleasure from the whole range of pleasure-giving 'objects' at once. Freud sees sexuality as almost infinitely plastic. It can move from aim to aim and object to object, both passively and actively. One organ may be substituted for another and vice versa. Freud describes early childhood sexuality as fundamentally and normally '*polymorphously perverse*', that is, entirely promiscuous in the choice of object in order to achieve its aim of pleasure or satisfaction (PFL 7: 109). It may also continue in adult sexuality in the form of what Freud calls perversions, which he views simply as residues in the adult of infantile sexual behaviour. Freud went on to point out that much so-called 'perverse' infantile sexual behaviour frequently forms the basis of fore-play in what are regarded as 'normal' heterosexual relationships. Kissing and oral sexual behaviour probably represent a desire for a return to the satisfaction of the mother's breast. Undeterred by the scandalous response he must have expected, he declared that no clear line could be drawn between 'perverse' and 'normal' sexuality. However, although Freud's account of his clinical practice in his case studies suggests that he had an open-minded view of homosexuality, there are other moments in his theoretical writing when he retreats to a view of it as both perverse and pathological. As I shall suggest later in this chapter, Freud's ambivalence about the status of specifically homosexual identity may at least in part have stemmed, like that of many men, from his unconscious anxiety about the durability of his own 'masculinity'.

Freud stresses that sexuality develops along a course beset with obstacles in the form of painful experiences within the family. We repress our infantile oral, anal and phallic instincts as we become involved in genital pleasure but they never disappear completely. They remain in the unconscious where they are hidden from the disapproval of culture. But there they undergo various transformations which result in symptoms, sublimations or character traits. Freud makes a crucial connection between the overlapping stages of infantile sexuality and the development of neurosis. He argues that frustrating or traumatic experiences during any one of these stages can lead to a 'fixation'. Here, part of the libido or sexual drive gets stuck at one of the pre-genital phases and attached to the particular form of sexual pleasure associated with that phase. This means that the genital phase is not achieved satisfactorily, so that its hold on the child is insecure.

Let us now look at how Freud's 'sexual instincts' are transformed into character traits or their unconscious or psychical representations within the people we become. This issue is of crucial importance to our understanding of the enormous significance Freud attributed to sexuality as his work developed. One of Freud's achievements was that he brought the physical body into the public sphere where it could be discussed properly. However, for Freud, the body is the material basis for the constitution of human identity but it is in no way reducible or identical to it. For Freud, the sexual phases came to represent not simply sources of pleasure but the earliest ways in which the child tries to discover who and what it is through its sensations of pleasure-giving objects. He became convinced that we gain our first sense of identity by taking these objects into our imagination which then, one by one, we have to give up in response to the demands of culture in the processes of weaning, toilet training and the inhibition of masturbation. However, as we shall see, this early identity is still fused with the mother until the Oedipal crisis is resolved. These 'lost', previously loved objects which the baby makes into its 'self' through its imagination, represent the baby's earliest sensations of having an identity. Since these objects were loved, their unconscious absorption into the self makes the baby feel it too is lovable.

At the oral stage, Freud's baby derives pleasure from the satisfaction of its hunger (one of what Freud originally called its self-preservation instincts). It does this through its taking in of milk. This experience is then displaced onto the sexual/psychical plane where it is experienced as the pleasure of incorporation (in this case this is the incorporation of the idea of the 'goodness' of the mother's breast into the baby's internal world). This then comes to form a priceless psychical substance, the baby's earliest sense of identity and security which it swallows with its mother's milk. What Freud called the self-preservation instinct, hunger, 'props up' the sexual instinct, the need to incorporate objects. We are all familiar with the baby's need to explore the world through its mouth. But many of us in adult life still retain some of the need to incorporate associated with the oral phase. We still sometimes unconsciously seek to comfort ourselves or bolster our sense of having substance or identity with pleasurable cultural substitutes for our mother's breast. The most obvious example is the pleasure of eating for its own sake, but others include chocolates, alcohol, cigarettes, consumer goods, television, work (we call people workaholics), even knowledge (we speak of a 'thirst' or 'appetite' for knowledge) and lovers (we may describe someone as 'dishy'). In one sense everything from which we gain pleasure and comfort may symbolically 'stand in' for the 'good breast'. We sometimes describe those who feel a disabling, compulsive need for these substitutes as 'addicts', whether it be chocolate, love, shopping, drugs or something else. These are often people whose early experience of mothering left them feeling painfully short of the comfort and sense of substance or identity everyone needs.

Let us pursue Freud's idea of the displacement of the biological instinct onto the sexual/psychical plane in what he calls the anal phase. Here, we find that the small child's increased muscular control of its faeces, its new-found capacity to control its own pleasurable sensations, whether to hold on or let go, may, if we experienced this phase as a problem (our mother was over-concerned with keeping us clean and, from the baby's point of view, apparently rejected the gift of our inner contents), be displaced in our adult life onto substitutes, symbolic 'stand ins' for faeces, frequently represented by money (filthy lucre), orderliness or cleanliness. Freud suggested that the muscular control involved in toilet training in childhood, may, if this training is too severe, be transformed, in an adult, into a compulsive need for control of the self and other people. It may be expressed, for example, in the compulsion to 'hold on' to money (often referred to in slang as being 'tight arsed'). It may take the form of different kinds of obsessions with, for example, tidiness and cleanliness, exercise, diet, video games, collecting things or even compulsive work as a form of imposing order and control on the inner world. The wish for anal sexual penetration may be considered as part of the same search for pleasure associated with control. Finally, we can see a fixation in the phallic stage in its most extreme transformation in cultural representations of patriarchal, 'macho' men (Rambo, Bond, etc.) who need to constantly assert their power and virility by 'showing off' (to be cock-sure or 'cocky'). Fast cars with long bonnets and 'power bulges' may be seen as phallic substitutes. The characteristics of a woman who is stuck in the phallic phase are similar but not, of course, endorsed by culture. Mrs Thatcher however, for a time, proved an exception. Lacan, in his development of Freud's theory, argued that many women fetishise their entire body into a representation of the missing phallus through its adornment (what Freud called their vanity) – by making it attractive to men. This matter will be discussed further at the end of the commentary on 'The Meaning of the Phallus' in the chapter on Lacan.

If for any reason our sexual energy is inhibited, Freud thought that it may be transformed or 'sublimated' in the form of artistic and intellectual interests which also give rise to pleasure. In fact, Freud came to the conclusion that sublimation was the basis for all the artistic and

[37]

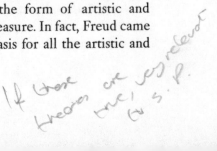

intellectual achievements of culture and civilisation (PFL 12: 267). He also saw the capacity for friendship and tenderness as sublimated forms of sexuality which could, in certain circumstances, suddenly re-emerge in an unsublimated form, as, for example, in some cases of child abuse (PFL 2: 129). Freud's theory of infantile sexuality is important for the understanding of the post-modernist work of the French feminists described in chapter five. Some of their work highlights the pre-Oedipal period of the baby's relationship with the mother before the imposition of gendered identity and heterosexuality required by culture.

Narcissism

In 1914, nine years after the publication of his *Three Essays on Sexuality*, Freud elaborated another theory related to infantile sexuality in his paper 'On Narcissism' (PFL 11: 59). Here the earlier instincts or drives are located firmly in the history of the formation of a person's subjectivity. Sexual drives, or what Freud now calls 'desire', are seen as directly involved in the construction of our identity. Freud thought *narcissism* represents a transitional stage between what he called the baby's auto-eroticism or self-love (a source of identity from pleasurable sensations from its own body – mouth, anus or genitals) and a relationship with an external object seen as a whole, separate person (the mother or, later, lover). In the narcissistic phase the child can, in phantasy, project its own body onto another, usually the mother, whom it then loves as its 'self'. In this way the baby forms an imaginary, but satisfying *image* of itself, reflected back by the mother's behaviour (earlier Freud had seen this self made up only of pleasurable *sensations*). The baby is given a self by the mother but one which is still fused with her. She is not yet seen as a separate person. This idea of the self as an 'other' was taken up by both Winnicott and Lacan but to very different effect, as we shall see.

Freud distinguished between two types of love: narcissistic love, characterised by the desire to be loved, and anaclitic love, characterised by the desire to love. Freud thought some narcissistic types of relationship conformed to the kind of love characteristic of normal heterosexual relationships, especially romantic love and the ideal of a perfect partner. (He also thought it was involved in some women's wish to be worshipped and adored.) In romantic love we often fall in love with our self projected onto the other. (We speak of finding our 'other half', our self in another.) He thought the love of parents for their children was another form of loving ourselves in the other. Here children are experienced by their parents as a psychological as well as a physical extension of themselves. He also thought love for a much younger partner was another form of narcissistic love which involves the idea of loving the 'self' we used to be or would like to have been. Freud argued that although we normally eventually transfer our narcissistic love from the narrow confines of a relationship in which our identity is fused with someone else to a love-object we experience as separate, we always retain some potential for love based on narcissism. The danger with relationships based on narcissism is that part of our unconscious identity is projected onto someone else in the external world which makes us very vulnerable if that person rejects us or dies. Clearly, narcissism or love of the same can express itself in both heterosexual and homosexual relationships since 'masculinity' and 'femininity' may exist in male or female bodies. In his paper 'Mourning and Melancholy' (1917), Freud's concept of narcissism illuminates the experience of mourning. Normal mourning entails an angry attack on the lost object (who has been internalised as part of the self) for dying. This amounts to a self-destructive attack on the self which is experienced by the mourner as painful feelings of loss or guilt. Gradually, as the new external reality is consciously acknowledged, the internal object can be given up, together with the loss and guilt, and even replaced with another. The film *Truly, Madly, Deeply* (director, Anthony Minghella, Great Britain, 1990) explores exactly this process. The bereaved young woman in the film is unable to get on with her life until she has been able to acknowledge and articulate all her feelings, including her anger, about the sudden death of her lover who remains internalised as part of her inner world. The process by which she does this is symbolised by the sudden return of her lover after his death, to her new flat, to comfort her. The new flat in which she confines herself for several days with the ghost of her lover, represents the woman's internal world. During these days of introspection, inside her flat, when she feels unable to go to work, she finds she is able to express her anger with her phantom lover as well as her love and loss. This represents the 'working through' of these painful, conflicting feelings. Once this has happened she begins to find the continuing, not to say demanding, unreal presence of her dead lover in the new flat (self) she is trying to assemble, stifling and disturbing. She tells him he must go and he leaves the flat to return finally to the 'other side'. In psychical terms this represents the woman's successful resolution of her bereavement.

She has managed to expel what had become a destructive rather than supportive phantasy object in her inner world, which allows her to get on with her life and begin a new relationship in the external world. If the process of bereavement is not adequately resolved in the way this film describes and, instead, serious depression develops, the same kind of situation exists except that the pain of inner reality prevails. The only way out of this predicament is to become able to withdraw the projection from the absent person by developing a form of identity which does not depend on someone else supporting us in our inner world.

In Freud's theory of narcissism the term 'drive' is replaced by 'desire' so that even consciousness and knowledge can be sexualised. Our desire for knowledge may involve us projecting ourselves onto it and then experiencing it as the mainstay of our identity like a substitute mother. For some people, a compulsive pre-occupation with intellectual knowledge is an attempt to mother the self exclusively with the mind. In this situation early experience of mothering has been unsatisfactory and separation has been difficult to achieve. This has the secondary comfort of appearing like independence to the outside world although intellectual activity is being substituted for feeling and emotional development. Although it is a culturally valued activity it is frequently emotionally impoverishing. Freud's theory of narcissism is particularly relevant to the understanding of Lacan's concept of the Imaginary in chapter four.

The Oedipal crisis and castration anxiety

For Freud, the crucial moment which simultaneously determines our future gender identity, forms our unconscious and, if all goes well, resolves the phallic phase, is the *Oedipal crisis*. This is the dramatic moment when the small girl or boy, locked in the phantasy of a passionate love affair with their mother, has to be prised apart from her permanently in order to become a gendered and autonomous human being, able to cope with a reality beyond the mother's potent body. This moment of separation is achieved by the entry of a third person, the potentially destructive rival in the form of the father and all he represents – the external world of culture, the law and, at this stage specifically, the law against incest which legislates that certain people in the family 'belong' to certain other people and not to others. Freud describes the means through which this is achieved as the castration complex. He came to see this as of central and crucial significance for the future sexual identity or gender of both male and female children and for their emotional well-being (that is, their freedom from neurotic symptoms).

The Oedipal crisis for Freud is the defining moment when each child takes on its future gender identity within culture and becomes a fully fledged human subject. In doing so, at the same time, it becomes a divided one because of the simultaneous construction of its unconscious. Initially Freud's theory of the Oedipal crisis was based on his *seduction theory*. This explained children's sexual feelings towards their parents in early childhood as the result of seduction by their nursemaids, servants, siblings, uncles and even fathers (SE 3: 195–9). He later abandoned this idea in favour of the theory that most children only phantasised seduction by their parents. This change of heart was largely, it seems, because Freud simply could not equate what he perceived as the widespread prevalence of neurosis with the same incidence of sexual abuse by middle-class fathers in late nineteenth-century society. He believed that actual child abuse by fathers was a cause of neurosis but that most neuroses were the result of children's early phantasies about erotic events with their fathers. As Peter Gay argues, 'What Freud repudiated was the seduction theory as a general explanation of how all neuroses originate' (Gay 1988: 95). Freud continued to recognise the existence of child abuse and its severe psychological consequences. However, our own knowledge of the prevalence of child abuse in late twentieth-century society must make us question Freud's eventual attribution of almost everything his patients told him to phantasy. Recently the work of Alice Miller has highlighted the serious psychological effects of children's actual experience of child abuse rather than the phantasised experiences made central in Freud's work (Miller 1991).

Let us look now in more detail at what happens in Freud's later, more developed theory, when the child anywhere between the age of three and five enters the Oedipal phase in his/her family. Let us start with the small boy, as Freud does, for the sake of clarity. The small boy, passionately in love with his mother, is suddenly overtaken by the '*castration complex*', that is, a consuming anxiety that he will lose his penis. This phantasy of castration is triggered by two factors: his recognition of sexual difference – his mother now appears to be castrated – and his guilt and murderous feelings towards his father whom he now sees as a rival. The small boy, becoming aware of what his mother lacks, is suddenly beset by the terror of losing his own penis, significantly his primary source of sexual phantasy and pleasure at this time and, importantly, also his source of narcissistic identity. This fear is often reinforced, even today, by parental threats in relation to the child's masturbation. In Freud's case-study 'Little Hans' (1909) Hans's mother says 'If you do that I shall send for doctor A. to cut off your widdler' (PFL 8: 165). Fear, perhaps reinforced by threats, resolves the crisis. In order to protect himself and his narcissism, the small boy has to give up his sexual ambitions towards his mother and, most importantly of all, to acknowledge the idea of *symbolic castration* by his father. This takes the form of submitting to the painful and humiliating reality that he must lose the mother to his more powerful father whom she apparently desires more than him anyway. Importantly, he must also give up his primary identification with her. Henceforth he must content himself with an alliance, an identification with his father whom he both loves and has hated as a rival. This identification forms the basis for another fundamental component of Freud's structural theory, the '*superego*' which is forged out of the child's guilt and fear, and exists in a separate 'compartment' of the self or ego. In future the father, internalised as the superego (an authoritarian version of the idealised ego characteristic of the narcissistic phase) will be the agency which represents the world beyond the mother's body, the culture in which he must take his place. He will also compensate for the loss of the mother by forming a crucial part of the identity of the small boy in future. To make this possible the boy has to *repress* his desire for his mother, and out of the *repression* of the pain and loss associated with this, the *unconscious* is formed.

For Freud, the child's acceptance of symbolic castration, the psychical 'cut', is the pivotal unconscious event in psychoanalytic theory which also provides the central moment in its practice. The concept of castration implies a threat to the child's fragile sense of identity derived from the narcissistic phase, as well as being a physical threat. It also threatens the child's ability to connect and make relationships with others. If symbolic castration by the father is not accepted, fetishism or homosexuality may be the resulting forms of identity for the male adult. Symbolic castration involves the acceptance of both these forms of identity only in the sense of the prohibition of heterosexual desires for the mother. Later, this formed the basis of Lacan's concept of phallic power as we shall see in chapter four. Symbolic castration represents the moment of 'truth', the acceptance of reality rather than phantasy, the closing of the door on most of the child's early personal history. The first repression, the giving up of both his desire for his mother and his identification with her, and his new kind of identification with the father as an authority figure, not a 'lost object' as in previous identifications, leads the boy out of the Oedipal crisis in the unconscious knowledge that if he allies himself with his father and becomes, like him, a 'man', he will eventually be able to have a substitute for his mother – a woman of his own. So the boy's entry into his 'masculinity' can only be achieved through his castration complex which sets in motion his separation from the mother and identification with the father. The cultural requirement of 'masculinity' crucially depends on acceptance of symbolic castration by the father and the repression of the boy's mother, and all she represents, into the unconscious. This severing from his 'femininity', half of what constituted his potential self, is the enormous emotional price which must be paid for a 'masculine' identity within patriarchal cultures.

Before we look specifically at the girl's experience of the Oedipal crisis, let us examine for a moment Freud's concept of the superego in a little more detail. Symbolic castration and the internalisation of the father in the form of the superego allows the child to achieve separation from the mother so that, with an identity no longer fused with her, it is able to develop a separate, viable sense of identity of its own. For Freud, the child's internalisation of the father as the superego is the means by which we are inserted into the historical and cultural meanings through which we are all partly constituted. (Girls, according to Freud, having nothing to lose and therefore fearing the father less, do not internalise such a powerful superego, that is such a rigid set of moral values.) The superego presides over us, to varying degrees, as an ever-present moral authority which produces a sense of guilt or conscience from which we cannot escape. In *Civilisation and its Discontents* (1930) Freud suggested that the capacity for guilt originates from two sources within the superego (PFL 12: 322). The first is in response to the authority of the father who forbids the child's incestuous desires for the mother. However, the child, although he cannot act on them, continues to harbour these desires, only now terrifyingly, under the surveillance of his father in the father's new unconscious, psychical incarnation as the superego. The second source of guilt stems from what the child does with his earlier aggressive impulses towards the father. The sense of being attacked by an internal saboteur in the form of guilt even when we have nothing to feel guilty about, arises, Freud suggests, because the child as well as internalising the loved father, at the same time internalises his aggression towards the father as the previously hated rival. This aggression then, as part of his superego, attacks the child from within, in effect doing to him what he would like to have done to his father. Freud is at pains to point out that the severity of the child's superego or conscience does not necessarily represent the actual severity of the father, although this may be a major factor. Rather it represents the child's own severity towards himself, derived from his anger towards the father. Through internalising the father, the child becomes both victim and executioner. Freud saw the direction of aggression inwards, into the individual's internal world where it could only harm its owner in the form of guilt, as the price of civilisation. For him, guilt provided the means for some containment, at least, of the destructive instincts he came to see as an inevitable component of human nature.

So, with the creation of the superego, castration anxiety is transformed into more generalised moral and social anxiety and 'normal' anxiety about such things as loss of love, punishment and death. Freud recognised that the Oedipal crisis represents the touchstone of his theory. It initiates the single most momentous sign of the child's entry into human culture, the formation of the superego. This seems to be the moment when culture drives a wedge between the child and the world of the body associated with the mother. Culture for Freud sometimes seems to be conceived as everything which for the child is not associated with the mother's body. From this time the public and the private spheres seem to become synonymous with male and female respectively. Here perhaps lies the unconscious root of the nature/culture divide within culture which has been so damaging to women. Freud's association between the father and culture is brought out more clearly in Lacan's idea of the 'place of the father' as we shall see in chapter four.

Let us look finally at what Freud's equation of the father, culture and the boy's source of 'masculine' identity might mean for the boy whose father has been physically or emotionally absent and where there has been no easily available substitute. The danger here, especially if the boy has a controlling and tantalising mother, is that the boy may increasingly experience his identification with her as suffocating and overwhelming, if he has no alternative source of identification to help him separate from her and compensate for her loss. If he is never able to separate sufficiently he may be unable to form satisfying relationships with women because they will always represent potential emotional engulfment. However, the boy may try to compensate for this absence by finding a cultural substitute. He may need to identify strongly with a particular social group, party, institution or leader. The boy's choice of a cultural substitute for an absent father might help to explain the origin and force of such powerful cultural identifications as nationality and ethnicity. Clearly there is the potential for endless forms of cultural mediation of this unconscious need for a substitute father identification. The ideas of God, religion and the church often represent a powerful potential source of a substitute superego. We shall return to a consideration of the question of the church and the significance of the controversy about the ordination of women in the next chapter. Only sometimes does the search for a substitute father express itself in homosexual, or bisexual relationships.

Let us look now at the little girl's experience of the Oedipal situation. This was described by Freud, late in his career, in 'Some Psychical Consequences of the Anatomical Distinction Between the Sexes' (1925), 'Female Sexuality' (1931) and 'Femininity' (1933). Perceiving that she has no penis to lose and that her mother also shares this predicament (although the mother apparently wants an association with one in the form of a relationship with the father), the girl angrily rejects her mother as a love object for not giving her a penis, gives up her clitoral activity (now perceiving it as inferior and irrelevant if it will not get her anywhere with her mother), and moves over to her father for consolation, phantasising him as a new source of identification and later as a love-object. This is motivated by the wild hope that she may perhaps obtain a penis from him. In Freud's view this wish for a penis, what he controversially called *penis-envy*, this 'extra' the little girl feels she lacks but which her mother desires, must for the full achievement of her 'femininity', ideally be transformed into a wish for a baby from her father. This is after she has discovered that a penis is unforthcoming from him also and that only her mother has privileged access to it. With the discovery that she is unable to obtain a baby from her father either (which often coincides with the arrival of a new sibling in the family), her second phantasy is shattered. Eventually, if she is to conform to the demands of patriarchal culture and achieve her 'femininity', the disappointed little girl must console herself with the idea that one day she will be able to get someone like her father who will be willing to give her the *penis/baby* she desires. For the immediate future she must try to re-identify with her mother as a woman in the interest of this future project and her becoming a 'feminine' woman. For Freud, true 'femininity' is associated with identification with the mother and the wish for a baby rather than desire for possession of her, which requires something she does not possess. Freud argues that the penis and the baby are equated in the history of ancient symbolism. Small children believe babies are born through the anus so the baby and the penis are also equated with faeces. He thought this system of symbolic 'stand-ins' or equivalence can be observed particularly in the language of dreams (PFL 7: 296–302). There will be further discussion of this controversial idea in the next section.

So, to summarise: sexual identity or gender rests, for Freud, on what the child 'makes' in its imagination, of sexual difference, of the presence or absence of the penis in early childhood and what s/he unconsciously decides to do about it. In patriarchal cultures children also come to learn retrospectively (after the Oedipal phase) about the power associated with those who possess a penis. Freud describes his view of what needs to happen if the desires or gender-roles of both male and female children are to conform to cultural expectation and in this sense his theory is normative. The castration complex achieves both children's necessary separation from the mother. In the boy it takes the form of castration anxiety in relation to the father and, in the girl, perceiving herself to be already castrated, it expresses itself in penis-envy or envy of what the mother seems to want in her partner. However, Freud also makes it quite clear, as we shall see, that behind the policed gender categories of culture, we are all inherently psychologically bisexual and that women are particularly so because they have to fall in love with both parents or substitutes to achieve 'femininity'. Male bisexuality stems from the fact that little boys phantasise themselves not only as the active lovers of their mothers but also the passive lovers of their fathers. They desire to be loved and 'connected' with both parents. The passive desire for the father is normally more deeply repressed than the girl's corresponding bisexual desire for the mother because of its particular cultural unacceptability within patriarchal, homophobic societies. The repression of desire for both parents resolves the Oedipal crisis for both sexes and results in the creation of the unconscious and the split subject.

Some of Freud's most difficult and controversial concepts relating to the construction of 'femininity' – bisexuality, the significance of the shift from the clitoris to the vagina, penis-envy, the equation of the penis and the baby and heterosexuality are to be found in his lecture 'Femininity' which is reproduced in Part II of this book. These ideas have provoked a great deal of criticism which has largely centred on what has been perceived as Freud's phallocentrism (penis-centredness), his patriarchal attitude to women and his concentration on the father's role in the construction of gender. In the commentary on the essay that follows we shall try to explore some of the meanings of these concepts which may not always have been clearly understood within the context of Freud's whole theory or understood as referring to unconscious rather than conscious processes. The paper 'Femininity' was written towards the end of a career in which Freud seems to have been continually side-tracked away from the recognition of the significance and intensity of the pre-Oedipal mother–daughter relationship. In this paper, which also provides a summary of his theory of the construction of 'femininity', Freud recognises the centrality of the pre-Oedipal mother–daughter relationship in the making of 'femininity' and, in post-modernist mode, the fragility and precariousness of identity.

Commentary on Freud's lecture 33: 'Femininity' (1933)

At the beginning of this paper Freud refers to what he calls 'the riddle of the nature of femininity'. He rejects explanations which derive from the idea of innate biological or psychological characteristics. He raises the important issue of bisexuality and discusses the inadequacy of the terms 'passivity' and 'activity' and their equation, within culture, with 'feminine' and 'masculine' respectively. This issue pre-occupied him throughout his life.

From the outset, in paragraph three of this paper, Freud is at pains to acknowledge that it is social custom and conditions which demand the repression of active sexuality in women, in favour of passivity and what he regarded as a particular version of masochism more prevalent in women than men (female masochism). He never argues or implies that women are passive objects of desire or masochistic by nature. He makes the point that men also display masochistic tendencies, that is, they turn aggressive feelings inwards, against themselves, instead of outwards. In paragraph four he introduces the main psychoanalytic enterprise of this paper. This is not to describe what a woman is or should be but 'how she comes into being, how a woman develops out of a child with a bisexual disposition'. In paragraph six, he makes one of his most controversial statements, 'We are now obliged to recognise that the little girl is a little man'. This particular statement has been energetically rejected by feminists. (Luce Irigaray's critique of this idea is contained in an extract from her work reprinted in this book.) It refers to the fact that girls

[47]

masturbate at this stage using their clitoris, which Freud and most biologists, even today, regard as physiologically comparable to the penis. Rather than being an indication of Freud's phallocentrism, this statement seems to reflect Freud's constant attempts to re-define 'masculinity' as 'activity' in either sex without making his text impossible to understand. Within culture, activity or desire associated with the penis is associated with men's possession of a penis and therefore with 'masculinity'. However, during the girl's clitoral phase, to the extent that the clitoris is a smaller version of a penis, her sexuality is also active and comparable to that of the boy. After she has given up this clitoral activity in relation to her mother and discovered her vagina, her sexuality may be perceived to be passive or receptive. Within culture this passivity is equated with 'femininity', in spite of her earlier phase of activity. In effect, as Mitchell argues, in an excellent discussion of this issue, Freud gave a new meaning to 'masculinity' which includes children of both sexes (Mitchell 1975: 45–8). We shall return to this and related issues later in this commentary.

Freud goes on to argue in paragraphs six and seven that the natural bisexuality in both sexes is particularly prevalent in women because of the active form of the girl's earliest sexuality in relation to her mother, what, for the sake of clarity he continues to call her 'masculine' or, more specifically, sexually active phase which involved pleasure from her clitoris associated with her desire for the mother. It is this bisexual quality which partly explains why Freud controversially referred to women as the 'dark continent'. The idea of the 'dark continent' reflected a popular view of women in the late nineteenth century as irrational, mysterious and ultimately unfathomable, a view which still prevails today in the idea of the 'feminine mystique'. However Freud's perception of women as an enigma is largely based on the conclusions to which his theory logically led him. Women as very young children have to transfer their affections from their mother to their father, unlike boys who are not compelled to make the same kind of dramatic shift in their desires in order to achieve their gender identity. Freud took the view that women's bisexuality is enhanced because they never completely give up their 'masculine', sexually active desire for their mother because the castration complex is never experienced as such a powerful threat as it is for boys. Not having a penis, girls have nothing to lose but their phantasy of total possession of the mother. This means that, unlike boys who must radically separate from the mother in order to achieve their 'masculinity' (and, in phantasy, avoid castration), girls are never compelled by fear to separate from their mother in order to acquire their 'feminine' sexual identity. In fact they must make a secondary identification with her. The fact that women, because they have nothing to lose, suffer less castration anxiety than boys, also explains why Freud suggests that the superego (the father internalised as a moral authority) is less strongly, or rather less rigidly developed, in 'feminine' women.

In paragraph eight, Freud, for the first time in this paper, emphasises the girl's first pre-Oedipal attachment to the mother. He comments that he had never previously recognised that it was 'so rich in content and so long lasting'. This passage really represents the crux of this paper and puts the pre-Oedipal mother, not the father, centre-stage in the girl's development. Freud turns his attention next, in paragraph eleven, to what is the crucial question for him: how is the powerful attachment to the mother brought to an end which results in the small girl's hatred of her mother? After reviewing all the pre-Oedipal deprivations by the mother which might justify and explain this hatred (which he observes is not found in boys), Freud draws his momentous conclusion. He argues once more, that the source of the girl's hatred is that she holds her mother responsible for her lack of a penis. This is the penis-envy which Freud believes will leave 'ineradicable traces on [her] development'.

So, for the sake of clarity, let us review Freud's rather abbreviated theoretical position up to this point (it is perhaps worth bearing in mind that 'Femininity' was a summary of his previous papers, 'Female Sexuality' (1931) and 'Some Psychical Consequences of the Anatomical Distinction between the Sexes' (1925)) and discuss some of his central ideas. In considering the complicated issue of the carving out of 'femininity' from the child's bisexuality, Freud insists that it is not achieved without a struggle and that 'femininity' is rarely completely achieved. He locates two crucial and inter-related tasks for the little girl which do not exist for the boy. The first is that she has to be persuaded to move from the pleasures derived from her clitoris in relation to her desire for her mother to the potential pleasures offered by the vagina after she has discovered it later during puberty. This is symbolised in her subsequent desire for her father. Without this change there would be no reason for a woman ever to become involved in heterosexual relationships with men at all since her clitoris makes her sexually self-sufficient. As Freud recognised, she has two pleasurable sexual organs whereas men have only one. The second task for the girl is to fall out of love with her mother so that she can develop sufficient detachment to fall in love with her father. Freud defines what he sees as the vital question relating to the transformation of the little girl's bisexuality into adult 'femininity': how is the little girl persuaded, in order to achieve what culture defines as her 'femininity', to make the transition from the intense involvement of being in love with her mother and phantasising having a baby with her, to being in love with her father and phantasising having a baby with him, when she has nothing to lose like her male counterpart? This question can usefully be phrased another way. How is the little girl persuaded to give up her position of being the active subject of desire for her mother (what Freud describes as her 'masculine' aim) in favour of becoming a passive object of her father's desire (what Freud calls her 'feminine' aim). The answer Freud produces is his controversial and often misunderstood idea of penis-envy. This emerges directly out of the girl's shattering discovery that she seems to lack what it takes to fulfil her ambitions with her mother. Suddenly she has to confront the reality that she has been living in a fool's paradise. Angrily rejecting her mother, she enviously turns to her father to see if he can love her enough to give her what she wants. It is her envy of the father's penis which achieves this dramatic reversal. However, all is not necessarily what it may seem. Girls are motivated by their penis-envy to cross over to the father initially to obtain a penis but at the unconscious level they want a penis from the father *to make them acceptable to their mother.* Their active love for the mother remains. In Freud's theory of 'femininity' penis-envy provides the motive force for the little girl's switch from her mother to her father as a love-object. For Freud, penis-envy becomes the necessary pre-condition of the achievement of the form of 'femininity' required by patriarchy, women as the passive object of men's desire rather than the active subjects of their own. If a woman can positively wish for a baby as a substitute source of power and identity which puts an end to her penis-envy, so much the better for the 'quality' of her 'femininity', so the truly 'feminine' woman no longer thinks of herself as defective but rather as different but equal to men.

Penis-envy

The concept of penis-envy has been off-putting for many women who resent the idea that, in Freud's theory, gender seems to be structured around the male genital organ and male desire. Let us, therefore, explore for a moment, in more detail, what Freud means by penis-envy. We need to remember that Freud's concept of the castration complex which takes the form of penis-envy in girls and castration anxiety in boys, is an unconscious process based on phantasy. This means it is repressed. This is why most of us could have no conscious access to these feelings in normal circumstances. We do not recognise them as part of our external reality. We also need to remember that the most important meanings of Freud's concepts are at the *symbolic* rather than literal level. In relation to penis-envy this means not just 'I feel castrated and I wish I had a penis like Daddy' but, perhaps more recognisably to women 'Who I am has been found lacking (by the person I loved most who turned out to want someone different from me) therefore there must be something wrong with me: I cannot be good enough as I am.' In the case of the small boy's castration anxiety, 'I am terrified that Daddy will cut off my penis' becomes perhaps more recognisably for men with residual traces of castration anxiety 'I am terrified of the little sense of self I have (I must not be *like* mother although I thought I was being) totally annihilated therefore I must continually be in control and on my guard.' It is these kinds of unconscious meanings lived out in the minds of men and women which Freud's theory suggests we cannot ignore in our analysis of how women's subordination within culture has come about.

Before looking in more detail into the variety of possible meanings of the girl's unconscious penis-envy let us first briefly survey them. Freud tends to stress that penis-envy results from the massive wound to the girl's narcissism and therefore to her sense of identity. In the narcissistic phase she phantasised that her clitoris, and she herself, was perfect. Associated with this idea is the girl's phantasy that having a penis seems to be the only path to the heart of the one who is most important to her, that is it is what the *mother* wants. This is implicit in Freud's theory but not explicitly stressed by him. Grafted onto these unconscious meanings is a further cultural meaning which later becomes entangled with the child's unconscious – the cultural over-valuation of the phallus and 'masculinity' within patriarchal societies. Girls become aware retrospectively that those who have a penis are associated with power. However, the overall structural *function* of the girl's penis envy and the boy's castration anxiety within the unconscious process of the structuring of identity in the family, is to provide the crucial means by which the child is impelled away from the mother so that it can acquire a separate identity from her. So penis-envy which Freud argued lingers in most women throughout their lives, symbolises the extreme difficulties and contradictions, for both sexes, inherent in living out the pure 'masculine'

[51]

and 'feminine' identities sanctioned by culture. It does not represent a patriarchal celebration of the male genital organ for its own sake which is sometimes how it has been understood. Instead, it symbolises many women's lingering disappointment – their continuing phantasy or desire to be what their mother wanted – crucially, someone different from, rather than the same as herself.

Freud's theory of narcissism is important for a fuller understanding of the meanings of penis-envy and castration anxiety. As Elizabeth Young-Bruehl points out, boys' over-valuation of their penis revealed in their castration fear is narcissistic. To give up this confidence, to experience 'castration threat', is to experience a huge threat to their self-love and self esteem and, even more importantly, to their ability to 'connect' and move on (Young-Bruehl 1990: 29). In a sense, in the eyes of both children, the penis provides a bridge, a connection between their auto-eroticism (masturbation) and their future relationship with others but for some girls it may be a source of envy in its own right. Freud's concept of narcissism also explains why the little girl might become so suddenly disenchanted with her clitoris. Young-Bruehl suggests that another way of saying 'penis-envy' is to say 'narcissistic wound'. The penis looks, visibly at least, bigger and better than the girl's clitoris even if it is almost identically physiologically constructed. (Freud's view of the clitoris as a latent penis has been criticised but it is supported by biology. We do not find it difficult to acknowledge that what we call men's chests are a latent form of women's breasts which 'look' less obvious than women's and do not deliver milk.) Young-Bruehl observes that Freud took the view that the boy also experiences another form of the castration complex comparable to penis-envy – envy of his mother's ability to have babies. The feeling of lack behind this is, like that behind penis-envy, experienced as a narcissistic wound which damages his fragile, narcissistic sense of iden-tity. If this sense of lack for some reason, becomes too great, it may then have to be 'split off' and directed elsewhere. (In culture, it looks as if womb-envy is frequently projected back onto women in the form of misogyny. We shall return to this issue later in this chapter.) Building on Freud's idea of womb-envy, we can imagine that the little girl's envy of her mother's creativity can be alleviated a little by the information that she will eventually 'grow' like her mother. However, the girl's narcissistic sense of self-worth cannot be rescued so easily as the boy's is by the penis because the *visible* parts of her which might at least partially rescue her from her penis-envy are not available to her. Her breasts have not yet made an appearance and her womb remains hidden. Her problem, however remains. Mother already has a womb and breasts but the capacity for creativity these confer on her does not seem to be enough. What mother seems to value most is someone with a different kind of body from her own, that is a man. So in the girl's unconscious what mother *wants*, in terms of its desirability and value, seems to transcend what the mother *is*. Interestingly, Freud suggested that the mother's relationship with her son is likely to be more charged than with her daughter because he also represents a sexual 'other', that is, he has a penis. This may, if the little girl has a brother, reinforce the girl's sense of lack and frustration.

In some women, penis-envy, as an enduring narcissistic sense of lack, may be experienced as overwhelmingly as some men's womb-envy. Although it is repressed into the unconscious, symptoms may take the form of the denigration of all men. The female psychical equivalent of the male misogynist or the ultra-patriarchal male is the 'castrating woman'. Both these stances towards the opposite sex appear to spring from what may be viewed as narcissistic dissatisfaction with a self experienced as imperfect or lacking – dominated by the absence of a penis or a womb. The existence of the castrating woman as well as the misogynistic man serves to remind us of something easy for women who suffer real oppression from patriarchal men to forget. If matriarchy had held sway rather than patriarchy, men and women may well have been at the receiving end of powerful castrating women. We can recognise individual instances of this kind of woman in our own societies. A compulsive desire for power and control, and the need to dominate and denigrate the opposite sex may exist equally in both sexes in certain unconscious formations. Freud's concept of narcissism suggests that this may frequently stem from a deep unconscious need to compensate for a sense of imperfection or inferiority beginning in early childhood.

This brings us to the central symbolic function of the girl's penis-envy in Freud's theory. This is the achievement of the small girl's vital need for separation from her symbiotic relationship with her mother so that she can become a viable human being. In a situation where her father or a substitute is physically or emotionally unavailable, it may be much more difficult for the girl to separate from her mother. If, in addition, the mother, lacking a supportive partner, is unconsciously tempted to treat her daughter as a surrogate husband or partner, she may unknowingly feed the child's ultimately impossible incestuous phantasies of being what the mother desires and possessing her for ever. An unconscious identification with her father or a substitute, and her occupation of his place with the mother, may prevent her from experiencing penis-envy (she phantasises that since the mother apparently desires her she must have a penis). Under this delusion she feels no pressure to break away from her mother's needs so that she can lead a life of her own. (This predicament, of course, can and does also arise for a boy.) This situation demonstrates the crucial role of penis-envy in providing the impetus for the girl to separate from her mother and eventually take her father as a new love-object. In the same way, it is castration anxiety which leads the boy away from the mother towards the father who eventually substitutes for his mother but primarily as a source of identity, not a love-object. In children of both sexes, the castration complex in its two different forms, accomplishes the separation from the mother necessary for the achievement of a separate identity as a human subject.

The penis–baby equation

Let us consider next, Freud's idea of a baby being unconsciously experienced by some women, as a substitute penis or source of powerful identity. Freud derived the equation of faeces/baby/penis largely from dream symbolism, jokes, slips of the tongue and pen, random linguistic utterances in everyday life, the things his patients said to him and her extensive anthropological knowledge. A useful summary of the unconscious basis of this unconscious equation may be found in *Psychoanalysis and Feminism* (Mitchell 1975: 101–4). In the final paragraph of her discussion Mitchell elaborates the meaning of Freud's assertion that both a baby and a penis are often spoken of as 'a little one'. 'The little girl, having at least tried to give up her wish for a penis, will nevertheless continue to want it as a gift of a "little one" first from her father, then later from her husband.' It is at this point that another of Freud's contentions enters in: only the birth of a male child really gives the woman the penis she is longing for and, less importantly, a woman will probably only be content with her marriage (as distinct from her maternity) when she can come to mother her husband and turn him into her 'little one' too.

The unconscious idea of the baby as a substitute penis which can confer a certain form of power on women symbolically comparable with the powerful meaning of the phallus might offer a plausible explanation for some women's wish for a baby. The wish for a baby, being entirely

compatible with reality, replaces the culturally unacceptable and unconscious wish for a penis which is incompatible with reality. Let us
consider briefly how this might be 'thought' unconsciously. In physical
terms, the mother may experience the baby as being *like* a penis because
it forms a physical extension of her body, perhaps especially in childbirth.
In this sense of being an extension of herself (and from the very place
where a penis would be located), a baby may be experienced by a woman
as conferring a kind of power on her. A childless woman is often seen as
lacking in cultural status. Certainly, in terms of cultural representation
the mother is elevated in a way other representations of women are not,
especially in Christian and other religious representations. It is as if in
one dimension of culture at least, woman is seen as powerful if she
'extends' herself and produces a child/penis – especially as Freud
remarked, if the baby is a son. Here, in so far as the male baby has
physically been a part of the mother's body and possesses a penis, a
woman may feel herself to have gained a penis of her own with which
she endows her baby. Although she herself lacks a penis she has
apparently miraculously produced one for someone else out of her own
body. Of course there are many other social factors which have traditionally made women value sons more than daughters, but these are
experienced at an ideological rather than unconscious level. In terms of
psychical reality, what Freud seems to be suggesting is that for some
women, having a baby is unconsciously perceived as their restoration to
a position of psychical, if not social, potency. Despite their social
inequality generally, having a baby, and especially a male baby (and
even, as Freud suggests, possibly turning their partner into a baby) blunts
some women's unconscious sense of lack and injustice and makes them
feel, all other things being equal, like 'real' human beings and the equals
of men.

Patriarchal cultures have made having a baby for many women
synonymous with inferiority, restriction and exclusion despite its undoubted pleasures. One of the effects of this situation has been to
persuade some feminists (who may regard any reference to women's
physical difference from men as potentially essentialist) to play down
women's capacity to have children so that it almost disappears from
theoretical view. What seems to have been repressed within some
feminist debate is the significance of the fact that 'masculine' as well as
'feminine' women are capable of having children but men are not.
Although the mother may, in culture, represent the absence of active

desire when compared with men, in a reproductive sense she exudes presence. Envy of women as a potent symbols of life and every kind of creativity may be an important element in some men's misogyny and their attempts culturally to restrict women's creativity exclusively to reproduction.

Freud's paper moves next to another momentous and far-reaching effect of the meaning of penis-envy. This is the unconscious rejection of 'femininity' by many women as well as many men. Freud argues that this is because they continue unconsciously to yearn for a penis and their first love-object, their mother, throughout their adult lives. It is this rejection of the passive psychological stance implicit in 'femininity' which Mitchell regards as the basis of male domination of women (Mitchell 1975). Freud called this repudiation, or casting out of 'femininity' by both sexes, the bed-rock of psychoanalysis (SE 23: 252). After the rejection of the mother for neither having a penis nor being able to bestow one, the girl then unconsciously rejects as inferior not only herself and her mother but all other women. The psychological place occupied by 'femininity' is experienced from that time on as an inferior place to be, as a form of sexual identity. Freud argues that girls frequently regress back to their mothers and their earlier, sexually active 'masculine' period after they have been 'driven away' from their father and their passive 'feminine' aims through disappointment or outright rejection. But he goes further: he argues that most women throughout their lives frequently regress from a position of 'femininity' (being objects of men's desire) to one of 'masculinity' (being the subject of desire for their mother). So here we have the source of the 'disturbance' which Freud considered so character-istic of women's experience of gender. Bisexuality becomes the root of the enigma of women, of his sense of women as 'the dark continent'. 'Femininity', for Freud, is inherently more unstable and impossible to pin down than 'masculinity' precisely because women fluctuate psycho-logically between active and passive sexual aims which make them sometimes what society describes as 'masculine' and, at other times, 'feminine'; sometimes they are the subject of desire (in relation to the mother), sometimes the object (in relation to the father). This idea constitutes the radical force of Freud's description of women which often gets lost in the anger aroused by his insistence that gender is structured around the male genital organ. It is this structuring around the term which represents *difference from the mother*, but what she nevertheless desires, the penis/father, which makes gender for both sexes unstable and precarious, and particularly so for women. This is in a context of a mother who is always female. This means that both the family and culture require the girl to repress her homosexuality, that is half her *sexuality*, and the boy to repress his 'femininity', that is half his *identity*.

The answer therefore to Freud's famous question 'What do women want?' seems to be clear in this paper, although Freud, always open to self-doubt in dealing with the complexity of his subject-matter, was not very satisfied with it. He suggests that, depending on their particular reaction to the discovery that they do not have a penis during their Oedipal crisis, women are constructed unconsciously in at least three different ways. These are described beginning at paragraph eighteen.

One group of women, in response to what they see as their inferiority and the impossibility of their phantasies with their mother previously seen as phallic, withdraw from their sexuality altogether and become sexually inhibited, seeing all women as debased and contemptible. Another group of women unconsciously refuse to give up the pleasures of the clitoris, disavow their lack of a penis (and therefore an important part of reality) and remain in their pre-Oedipal 'masculine phase'. These women may be described as having a 'masculine' gender position and their desire may express itself in lesbian relationships or relationships with male partners who have made a strong 'feminine' identification. The third group consists of those women who fit the patriarchal norm because they abandon their early clitoral pleasure, salvage and cultivate the passive dimension of their desire in relation to their fathers, and have a conscious wish for a baby unconsciously experienced as a substitute for a penis or a means to a powerful identity. Perhaps it is significant that some women say they lose some or all of their desire for their male partner after having a baby. Freud sees the women who reach the final stage of a wish for a baby as representing the most psychologically complete form of 'femininity'. However he became convinced that the majority of 'normal', 'feminine' women never, in fact, arrive at this ideal state of feeling the equal of men because they never lose their unconscious desire for a penis. They continue throughout life to desire what they uncon-sciously regard as the bridge back to the phantasised bliss of unity with their first love, their mother, of being what she desired. So, the conscious, culturally acceptable project of *having* a baby (as opposed to the positive *desire* for a baby) for many women conceals behind it the repressed, unacceptable wish for a penis expressed in a variety of the symptoms of penis-envy. Among these, paradoxically, may be women's desire for heterosexual relationships with men.

In Freud's theory, 'normal' women unconsciously suffering from penis-envy derived from early childhood, may want heterosexual relationships with men primarily as a way of having a share in the penis they lack and symbolically participating in the male power it confers. These women unconsciously but persistently hark back to their active desire to 'be' what their mother wanted. Freud thought that the wound to their narcissism caused by their recognition of what they perceive as a lack, causes women to try to compensate for their sense of inferiority in a quite specific way. They do this by making their entire body into a substitute penis through a pre-occupation with its adornment. This vanity or sexualisation of the whole body, allows them to compete with what they unconsciously feel is the superiority of the penis and at the same time makes them into lovable objects, worthy of the 'pedestal' treatment many of them demand. This occurs in the context of the perceived humiliations of the Oedipal phase when they seemed to be unable to offer either parent anything they valued. Freud's theory draws our attention to the extremely painful feelings of loss associated with the Oedipal stage which are repressed but which underpin all human identity. This dimension of his theory is taken up in chapter four, in Lacan's discussion of women's lack of meaning within culture.

Heterosexuality

Freud's theory of 'femininity' means that, for 'normal' women, heterosexuality would seem to have at least two different, seemingly contradictory meanings, one of which forms a kind of sub-text to the other. It represents two forms of desire at the same time, one of which is a vehicle for the other. The first is the culturally acceptable passive form of women's sexuality as an object for men. The other, at the level of unconscious phantasy, is the active form of women's sexuality in the form of 'becoming' the penis the mother desires through acquiring a share in one with a male partner. Freud's concept of penis-envy taken to one of its logical conclusions suggests that the apparent passivity involved in heterosexuality is unconsciously experienced by many women, very actively, as the route back to the mother, but this time equipped with a share in the penis they lack. Access to a penis can only be achieved by means of a male partner. However, Freud thought that some women's penis-envy was so powerful that it could cause frigidity and did not operate in the interests of heterosexuality.

So, both some women's desire for babies, and heterosexual desire viewed from the perspective of Freud's unconscious, are not quite what they seem. Conscious appearance belies unconscious reality. Freud took the view that for most women, unconscious envy *stands in for* the penis. Envy represents the symbol or metaphor for women's forbidden active desire for their mother. Apart from expressing itself positively in hetero-sexual relationships, Freud thought it could also be expressed, like men's womb-envy, as hostility and contempt for the opposite sex. He thought that depending on their particular unconscious and social circumstances, most women suffered from varying amounts of unconscious penis-envy unless, ideally, they perceived their capacity to have babies as an alternative source of powerful identity equal to those of men.

Freud saw hysteria as the illness which is most directly associated with repressed Oedipal desire. He saw it as a particularly 'feminine' kind of neurosis, whether it occurs in women or men because it is based on the phantasy of being castrated. Symptoms of hysteria involve the un-conscious, symbolic expression of unbearable feelings about the loss of a loved object which is experienced as a kind of castration. It is perhaps easier to understand the castration complex in the girl not as terror of losing something, as with the boy (because she does not have it), but rather terror of losing the special relationship she thinks she has with the mother because of her lack of a connector or bridge to her. A hysterical illness is frequently triggered by the loss, or perceived threat of loss, of a love-object which touches off, in the unconscious of the girl (or feminine-identified boy), potentially overwhelming feelings of rejection associated with the loss of the mother in the Oedipal phase of early childhood. An example of this predicament would be the small girl who experiences the birth of a sibling during her Oedipal phase as a traumatic rejection by her mother. The perceived rejection (which the girl phan-tasises as being due to her apparent castration) may be compounded by a depressed mother who fails to reassure her small daughter of her continuing love. The girl's feelings of helplessness, rage, rejection and loss which have been repressed, may re-emerge in her subsequent life in the form of hysterical symptoms in response to the threat, or perceived threat, of rejection or loss of a significant other (a person who symbolises the mother in the woman's unconscious). At such moments, the painful feelings of the helpless four-year-old child may erupt from the un-conscious incongruously and inappropriately into adult life. 'Old' feel-ings associated with the mother and the birth of a sibling in the past are repeatedly projected onto events in the present and mistakenly ex-perienced as emanating directly from these events in the present. The real source of these feelings remains unconscious. Hysterical symptoms – physical or psychological – may be provoked by the break-up of a relationship, particularly where a third party is involved, but they may also be triggered off by some 'innocent' action by a significant other which re-activates old feelings of exclusion and neglect. For example, a partner or close friend may be pre-occupied with studying for exams or caring for a needy relative and, as a result of her early experience of loss, the woman may irrationally perceive such pre-occupation as rejection and the precursor of another 'abandonment'. Since these feelings refer back to a time when the child's identity was still not separated from the mother, they are experienced as a potential annihilation of the self. The comparable illness in response to castration anxiety in men (which also occurs, to a lesser extent, in women) is what Freud called obsessional neurosis. Because men have to separate so drastically from the mother, they tend to repress vulnerability rather than 'normal' assertiveness (in favour of manipulation), the latter being characteristic of hysteria. Obsessional neurosis expresses itself in symptoms involving an excessive, often compulsive need for order and control. As many people have observed, within modern patriarchal cultures where rationality has a high premium this can be normalised as an acceptable version of 'masculinity' (being a workaholic) whereas hysteria, with its connotations of irration-ality and unfettered emotion, is not considered an acceptable expression of 'femininity'. Frequently, men, and 'masculine'-identified women, respond to loss by 'throwing themselves into their work', whereas women and 'feminine' - identified men tend to 'become hysterical', that is, express intense emotions. An appreciation of Freud's view of hysteria is important for our understanding of the significance of French feminist interest in the girl's pre-Oedipal relationship with the mother before the intervention of the law of the father.

Of course, like all desire in Freud's theory, women's active desire in relation to the mother may be expressed in sublimated forms such as artistic, intellectual, political and social activities. Feminism has been and is one of these arenas for many women. The fact that feminism articulates the culturally prohibited active component of women's desire, which for many women is concealed within their heterosexual relationships with men, is probably why some women, as well as men, still feel so uneasy and ambivalent about it. It articulates what patriarchal societies and many

[60]

men and women find deeply disturbing, the vast realm of unacknowledged desire which does not fit with the norms of patriarchal cultures.
As Freud said 'anatomy is destiny' for those who conform to cultural
demands. But in another sense his theory makes it very clear that for
many whose Oedipal crisis is not resolved ideally, it certainly is not.

For Freud, the girl's secondary identification with her mother after all
the disappointments of the Oedipal stage is what ensures the reproduction of the kind of woman desired by patriarchal societies. However,
this does not mean that everything is then a bed of roses for 'normal'
heterosexual men and women. In the last part of his paper Freud re-
iterates his view that the powerful pre-Oedipal love for the mother which
continually re-surfaces in 'normal' women, also characterises the nature
of women's subsequent relationships with men in many important ways.
But this relationship with her mother, which is so frequently transferred
onto her relationships with men, is almost always ambivalent. It contains,
as well as love, substantial quantities of hostility for all the deprivation
associated with the mother in the past (weaning, toilet-training, prohibitions on masturbation) and particularly for the failure to provide a penis.
Freud suggests that because of this hostility towards her husband, a
woman may only be able to really love her son who can represent both
the mother she loved and with whom she identified and the penis she
coveted. Another possible disappointing scenario is that a man may be
chosen narcissistically as a reflection of a woman's self-love – the man
the woman would have liked to have been – and therefore he is idealised
and later dropped when reality sets in. Of course this also frequently
happens the other way round.

Although the intense, early mother-and-daughter relationship, which
forms the main subject of this paper, was discovered late in his career and
never investigated in more detail by Freud (he regarded it, warily, as an
area best left to women analysts), it forms the core of the subsequent
Object-Relations theory developed by Klein and Winnicott, particularly
in relation to narcissism. Freud's increasing conviction in the later
part of his career, as this paper demonstrates, was that the pre-Oedipal
mother–daughter relationship was of central importance, although he
seems, possibly for unconscious reasons which will be explored later, to
have felt unequal to the task of exploring it more fully himself.

Finally, in a paper which takes as its focus the enormous power of the
mother, we should not overlook the moments in it where Freud does
seem to appear at his most patriarchal and apparently misogynist (see my

references in the explanatory notes after the text of 'Femininity' in Part II). However, his ambivalent attitude seems at odds with what we know of his relationships with women. Appignanesi and Forrester's *Freud's Women* reveals the extent to which Freud enjoyed and depended upon his close relationships with women. All the evidence points to Freud's completely egalitarian professional relationships with his powerful, intellectually gifted female fellow analysts. With the exception of his early fraught and misjudged treatment of Dora, he reputedly related to his articulate female patients with sympathy and respect, rescuing many of those suffering from hysterical conversion symptoms from the still prevalent nineteenth-century view of them as congenitally degenerate. Freud took the very different view that they were frequently unusually intellectually gifted women suffering from the social constraints of their lives and often specifically from repressed sexual feelings. As many people have commented, Freud certainly owed a great deal to the women in his life: his self-sacrificing wife Martha, his beautiful and intellectually powerful colleague and confidante Lou Andreas Salome, his clever daughter Anna and, most important of all, his women patients out of whose 'speaking' bodies Freud conceived his radical theory and his practice of the 'talking cure'. My own view is that Freud's apparent misogyny exists in intermittent moments in a theory which, taken as a whole, is profoundly liberating for women in many ways. In that sense what exactly Freud did or did not feel about women and morality is unimportant beside the momentous implications of his work which in many ways transcends Freud, the man, with a 'masculine' identity to protect. As his theory continually reminds us, he, like the rest of us, was not always perfectly consistent and rational and, consequently, inevitably fails to live up to our phantasies of a perfect father.

Discussion

In spite of the criticisms of Freud's work, his theory of the unconscious and identity represents the monumental leap of the imagination from which all subsequent psychoanalytic theories have grown. This has been the case even when these later developments have evolved into distinctive frameworks of their own with different emphases and incorporating new ideas, often drawing on seeds sown in Freud's work which for reasons of time or inclination he was unable to develop. His revolutionary theory of the unconscious enables us to explain many of those aspects of human identity and culture for which we can find no rational explanation.

The major criticism of Freud's theory has been that it is patriarchal, phallocentric and emphasises the role of the father to the exclusion of the role and importance of the mother. Critics argue that his construction of gender and the inherent inequality within his categories of 'masculine' and 'feminine', seem to centre obsessively around the father and the male genital organ. However, particularly in relation to his later work, Freud suggests that the mother is and continues to be at least as important and potent in the formation of the child's identity as the father. In fact, most girls never give up their mother completely and unconsciously yearn for her for the rest of their lives while boys are compelled to respond to the terror of phantasies of castration in order to tear themselves away from her. 'Masculinity' depends on being 'not mother'. Subsequently, although Freud does not say so, we can infer that many 'masculine' men suffer acutely from an unconscious alienation from the emotional part of their identity associated with the mother and the 'feminine' for most of their lives. Even heterosexuality, the pinnacle of patriarchal sexual achievement favoured by Freud, actually emerges, in his theory, as a vehicle for our phantasised reunion with the mother, for both sexes. Within this perspective, both romantic love and the urgency of sexual passion represent our intense desire for confirmation of our identity and a return to the old bliss of total abandonment within a fused identity of oneness with the mother as our first phantasised lover. These ideas hardly add up to a theory exclusively about the father and the phallus. Freud's theory, whether he intended it or not, is a theory centred around both parents but, in his later work, his theory of 'femininity' depends increasingly on the mother. For the girl, the father and his penis primarily function as being what the mother desires rather than as a celebration of 'masculine' potency. The girl's penis-envy (the female expression of the castration complex) is necessary for her to achieve her separation from the mother and her entry into the world beyond her mother's seductive presence. Penis-envy as a structural concept epitomises the precariousness of identity and the liberating potential of Freud's theory for women.

Another criticism of Freud is that he actually endorsed the gender categories which he described. At one level, in that he was reluctant to commit himself too far, risking alienating too many people from his discoveries, this appears to be true in some of his work. However, he makes his position on gender clear in this statement made late in his career in 1925. 'All human individuals, as a result of their bisexual disposition and of cross-inheritance, combine in themselves both masculine and feminine characteristics, so that pure masculinity and femininity remain theoretical constructions of uncertain content' (PFL 7: 342).

This does not sound like a prescription for culturally acceptable gender categories. It supports the view that Freud's primary concern was to investigate and lay bare the way culturally sanctioned gender positions are lived in the unconscious by men and women. He may, like many after him, have been rather unnerved by what he found. With the benefit of insight provided by his theory, it is possible to suggest that Freud, in common with many men, may also have had his own personal, unconscious agenda to cope with: a lack of confidence in his own 'masculinity' which may have sometimes resulted in an unconscious tendency to over-stress the penis and the father in compensation, especially within a historical and cultural setting which reinforced this view.

Whatever Freud's own personal views about gender, and contrary to many of the criticisms made against him, in his theory pure, binary, biologically determined 'masculinity' and 'femininity' are revealed as fictions although he believed that the gender positions favoured by culture offer us the best defence against neurotic symptoms. He believed that it was the excessive demands of civilisation and cultural prohibition which produced most of our need for repression of unacceptable parts of our sexual identity. In his version of reality, 'masculinity' and 'femininity' emerge as cultural categories saturated with ideology and culturally invested with superiority and inferiority on the basis of our earliest phantasies around our mothers and the discovery of sexual difference. His theory allows us to explain the broad difference between men and women based on the repression of the unacceptable half of their identity and sexuality in order to conform to cultural expectation. We can see that many men, if they want to measure up to the cultural ideal of 'masculinity', have to give up the emotional dimension of who they are by cutting themselves off from 'femininity' and the emotional world of the mother in early childhood. They must identify with the father and relinquish their identification with the mother. Women, on the other hand, must try to cut themselves off from their active desire in relation to the mother and, instead, accept an identity rooted in a sense of unconscious inferiority, lack and desire for the father.

Freud's concepts of the Oedipus complex and bisexuality enable us to explain differences among men and women as well as between them –

why many people, for a variety of reasons, do not resolve their Oedipal crisis entirely in accordance with cultural demands. They end up as complex and varied *mixtures* of what patriarchal societies designate 'masculinity' and 'femininity'. Freud's theory makes possible a view of men and women which corresponds to the reality of the variety of identities we observe around us and the desires, conflicts and contradictions many people feel within themselves. Active women and passive men, and many positions in between, clearly exist as possible gender positions despite their persistent unpopularity within many cultures. 'Masculinity' and 'femininity' are continually situated across the boundaries of the body so that gender can rarely be automatically read off from these bodies. As feminists have suggested, we need to talk about 'masculinities' and 'femininities' to reflect this situation.

Our unconscious identifications and desires for both our parents are often expressed in our adult relationships, both heterosexual and homosexual. However, our variegated gender identities are frequently (but not always) veiled by our conformity with culturally condoned behaviour. Patriarchal societies survive on the basis of 'keeping up appearances' of the pure unequal opposites of 'masculinity' and 'femininity' which frequently mask a much more complex and confused underlying reality. For example, a predominantly 'feminine' identified man may become involved in a homosexual relationship or in a heterosexual relationship with a substantially 'masculine' identified woman where we would say the woman 'wears the pants'. Similarly, a predominantly 'masculine' identified woman may become involved in a homosexual relationship or a hetrosexual one. However, some 'feminine' identified women and 'masculine' identified men may also prefer partners of the same rather than the opposite sex. This situation makes it very difficult to argue that homosexual identities are more likely to be neurotic than heterosexual ones. The crucial difference seems to be that in gay and lesbian relationships, culturally forbidden desires are conscious rather than unconscious and the law of the father, that is culture, is rejected; bodies which are the same are desired rather than bodies which are different. Whether this represents a greater failure to make the transition from phantasy to reality than that involved in the psychological expression of repressed desires in heterosexual relationships remains very controversial and Freud seems to have been highly ambivalent about this matter.

There are, however, some qualifications we need to make to the idea that Freud's theory allows us to dissolve conventional gender categories altogether. There may be some aspects of these categories which represent biologically determined psychological differences which we need to recognise as such, in spite of the fact that they may have been exploited in the interests of power and domination. We also need to take into account situations where extremely painful and damaging experiences in childhood result in sexual identities so precarious that they result in severe neurotic disturbance. These experiences may include sexual and other forms of child abuse, which may have cut the child off from any possibility of a comfortable resolution of its Oedipal crisis or even from being able to enter the Oedipal phase. In this situation these experiences represent only one part of a complex of symptoms of confusion and inhibition which may or may not result in psychological or physical illness.

The significance of Freud's work for our understanding of women's subordination springs directly from his post-modernist de-centring of identity. It is the widespread, if not complete, unconscious rejection of 'femininity' by *both* sexes in early childhood which seems to lie at the heart of the patriarchal domination of women. Our infantile perception of apparent lack gets picked up by culture so that not having a penis comes to represent cultural 'femininity', inferiority and powerlessness. Freud's insight suggests that as adults we live in the deep patriarchal shadow of an infant's narcissistic perception of the meaning of the body as it struggles to discover who it is and where it fits. His work reveals that the ideals of gender within patriarchal societies consist of two opposite or complementary modes of being human, one of which is valued more than the other because of both children's early unconscious rejection of 'femininity'. Ironically it is the *mother* who helps to confer special value on the penis by apparently wanting one from the father. This may provide the linchpin for male power over women. Both male and female children unconsciously want what the mother is perceived to desire in order to fulfil the phantasy of their exclusive possession of her for ever. This wanting to have and be what the mother *desires* rather than what the mother *is*, seems, along with the child's sense of narcissistic wound, an important part of the explanation of the inferior status of 'femininity' and the subordination of women. In men's and women's unconscious imagination, men are superior to women because they represent both what the mother wants and sexual difference. This, paradoxically, makes the mother absolutely central to Freud's theory.

[66]

Let us turn to the significance of Freud's theory for men. It allows us to explain the psychologically crippling effect of patriarchal society on the public and personal lives of many men despite their association with power. Many of those who do not fit the cultural norm feel unconsciously that they fail to measure up to what is expected of them, that they are not 'real' men. The identities of men who emerge from the Oedipal stage closer to the patriarchal ideal are, however, often unconsciously sabotaged by the damage incurred by their radical and premature separation from the mother. The emotional gap in these men make them unconsciously, if not consciously, highly vulnerable and dependent on women to carry their vulnerability. We shall explore this matter further in chapters four and five on Lacan and Irigaray.

The degree of damage boys suffer depends on individual family emotional circumstances, but many may later experience considerable emotional ambivalence towards women. They may never, unconsciously, complete their painful separation from the mother and may be permanently caught up in varying degrees of castration anxiety and compensatory over-valuation of the penis. Since the small Oedipal boy, unlike the girl, is required to separate from the mother before he has been able to disentangle himself from all aspects of her, he suddenly finds himself emotionally marooned in a reality with which he cannot yet cope. Henceforth he is supposed to deny the whole of the 'feminine' dimension of himself and suffer the humiliation of symbolic defeat by his father. How he is supported and encouraged to deal with this potentially terrifying situation varies, depending significantly on the emotional capacities of his parents. If his sense of rupture is too severe, and if a father is emotionally unable to compensate for his loss, he may experience the separation from the mother as a kind of death and, worse still, be convinced that his mother has left *him*. The cultural demand for separation from her may be experienced as the mother's abandonment which may never be forgotten or forgiven. Earlier, the mother has been associated with life and psychical survival. The baby, who still shares an identity with her, feels its existence is endangered every time she goes out of sight, carrying with her its fragile self. Freud's baby grandson, playing the 'fort'/'da'/('gone'/'here') game of repeatedly throwing a cotton reel out of his cot learns to cope, symbolically, with the absence of the mother (PFL II: 284). When, during the Oedipal crisis, the small boy is suddenly compelled to give up the mother completely, he may, if this crisis is not adequately resolved, experience this separation as an emotional trauma from which he may never fully recover. In its most extreme, pathological form, in some men an acute sense of disappointment, betrayal, rage and anxiety manifests itself in violent attacks on women who represent the terror of psychical annihilation.

But for many patriarchal men, the defensive, emotionally deadening effect of separation from the mother frequently expresses itself as emotional withdrawal in subsequent relationships with women. Intimacy may be associated with potential engulfment by a longing for the emotional realm denied them by culture and be perceived as 'feminine' and therefore threatening. Only in the domain of sexuality are some men able, temporarily and often, apprehensively, to regain a phantasised unity with the mother, but even this is frequently associated with a need to dominate and control. Some men, in their attempt to cope with the violent dimension of their feelings about the (m)other, split themselves and the idea of 'woman' in two. They become both the loving husband and the 'bad boy' who sometimes absconds, and women become either de-sexualised Madonnas or whores. To prevent the violent component of their sexuality from contaminating their family life, wives are idealised and de-sexualised as the original phantasy of the perfect mother and prostitutes and pornography provide the split-off place where violent, revengeful phantasies may be 'safely' expressed. This would explain why prostitutes are in particular danger of being attacked or killed.

Freud's work highlights the tragic fact that within all known cultures, at best, the vast range of different qualities which potentially form part of human identity have been divided up into the two unequal and separate, impoverished psychological worlds. The effect of this division, for many women and men, is to cut them adrift from a vital part of what they are. Freud's work draws our attention to the fact that whatever form of 'masculinity' or 'femininity' we end up inhabiting, most of us are compelled to live in a culture which, to differing extents, is controlled by patriarchal institutions and men who are alienated from an essential part of themselves and who often feel hostile, envious and distrustful of women. This suggests that patriarchal culture, and as we shall see in Lacan's and Irigaray's work, in particular, language, may, at an important level, be a massive defence against this emotional void. Many men attempt to master their sense of emptiness and vulnerability through work and alcohol but it is frequently also projected onto women, enhancing women's sense of lack and inferiority. As Christopher Lasch argues in *The Culture of Narcissism*, we all, men and women, live in a narcissistic culture dominated by longing. In this solipsistic, 'me'-orientated world, we continually search for ourselves in the other, relying on the other to sustain and complete us (Lasch 1980). This means that relationships between men and women frequently activate memories of loss and lack and, for many, are also suffused by rage and resentment. Unfortunately, from within Freud's perspective, this predicament, to some degree, seems to be the inevitable price of becoming human.

Freud's concept of the unconscious makes it clear why socialisation theory alone has been unable to provide an adequate explanation for gender difference and inequality. However, although Freud provides a rich analysis of how men and women are unconsciously constructed and live out the contradictions of their gender positions, the question of change remains a fundamental problem. It seems difficult to intervene if gender inequality is unconsciously glued into our identity in early childhood. Perhaps those cultures more tolerant of a variety of sexual identities may be experienced by small children as less repressive, opening the way to different cultural influences on the Oedipal crisis. But, if Freud is right, the penis and men are valued not only for cultural reasons, but because they represent difference and what most mothers continue to desire. As we shall see, Lacan, argues that the Oedipal crisis may not have to involve a real father (or father substitute) at all. In the phantasy of the Oedipal child, culture represents what Lacan calls 'the place of the father' and symbolically, through language and representation, provides the mother with a seductive counter attraction, drawing her away from the perpetual, self-contained unity and bliss the child dreams of having with her. Furthermore, most women, whether or not they are single parents, have sexual relationships and are heterosexual so that simply changing what the child perceives the mother primarily to desire (a woman) is not an option for the majority of women.

As we have seen, Freud's theory raises some fundamental questions not only about 'masculinity' and 'femininity' but also about the nature of heterosexual desire. Patriarchal societies see heterosexual relationships as taking place between unequal opposites who are driven towards each other in a quest for the 'other', complementary part of themselves, someone of the opposite sex. The view of heterosexuality suggested by Freud's work is strikingly different. In this version, heterosexuality seems fundamentally to represent a return to the mother for both sexes, but in a culturally veiled or disguised form. Somewhat confusingly, many women, only when they become the actual objects of men's desire, are

[69]

able to become, in phantasy, the subjects of their own desire for their mothers. This really means that the desire of many women to be the objects of men's desire encapsulates another, deeper, more primary desire for the mother. In a parallel but inverted way, men's involvement in heterosexuality also entails, as well as their acknowledged desire for the mother expressed overtly in their attraction to women generally, also the unacknowledged phantasy of a return to the mother as a form of identity. This is a return to their primary emotional identification with the mother (their homosexuality) which they have had to deny so drastically since early childhood. We are familiar with the idea that men 'marry' their mothers, but less familiar with the notion that women, as Freud's later work suggests, do the same thing. Women consciously acknowledge their deepest emotional identification with their mothers in early childhood but unconsciously disown their desire for her (their active 'masculinity'). Men consciously own their sexual desire for women, their mother substitutes, but disown their primary emotional identification with their mothers in early childhood (their passive 'femininity'). In this context men and women may be seen trying unconsciously to reclaim the homosexual part of themselves culture demands they deny.

So, in Freud's work, we are confronted with a very peculiar situation within patriarchal societies. Women have to deny half of their sexuality (their active sexuality) to conform to cultural demands and then try to regain it through their heterosexual relationships. Men, on the other hand, have to deny half of their identity (their feminine identification) to conform to these same demands and then try to regain this through their heterosexuality. This suggests that ultimately, although men and women need each other, men's need for woman is greater than woman's for men because men need to gain access, in phantasy at least, to their primary identity. This is situated at the positive, angelic end of their binary phantasy of women as either angels or whores. It is this sense of vulnerability or dependency on women for access to their primary emotional identity that is consciously denied in the patriarchal ideal of 'masculinity'. This dependency, coupled with envy, is likely to be a major reason for men's need to control women and for women's cultural oppression in general.

So Freud's theory, with dazzlingly originality in both its modern and post-modern dimensions, suggests some of the reasons why men and women within patriarchal societies live enmeshed within a web of unconscious contradictions. Confusingly, heterosexuality seems to offer

[70]

many women, despite the inequality implicit for them within its conscious meanings, the unconscious satisfaction of the very meanings it denies them in culture, desire for the mother. This is in a culture in which heterosexuality plays such an integral, symbolic part for men's sense of their sexual power. Intriguingly, as we have seen, at one level, heterosexuality seems to be about a return to the primary relationship with the mother for both sexes. However, as we shall see in the chapter on Lacan, at another subterranean level it also functions to prop up men's sense of phallic power which cannot exist without the support of women's desire (even if this is a vehicle for another).

Freud's theory also makes it possible for us to view homophobia, ethnocentricity and racism as well as sexism, as the unconscious expressions of those within patriarchal culture who are unable to cope with the meaning of difference except in terms of 'inferiority' and 'superiority', subjects and objects. What we make of visible physical difference at a highly charged period of our early childhood may represent the first in a chain of cultural responses to difference or the 'other'. Historically, cultures seem have picked up this unconscious discrimination between the sexes by children and transformed it into not only sexual discrimination, but every other kind of discrimination. Within patriarchal cultures, the bearers of different forms of culturally perceived difference are designated inferior, even incompletely human, because they have, in effect, been 'feminised' or manipulated into the other. Certain groups who can be marked out as the 'other' represent for some individuals a sense of inferiority which has been repressed and split off from their own consciousnesses. Those individuals who still retain, from childhood, a deep sense of inferiority and damage to their identity are most likely unconsciously to need to compensate for this through destructive behaviour towards culturally identifiable 'others' whom they phantasise, though identification, are even less human than they feel themselves to be. (The victim/executioner dimension of symbolic castration by the father and its effects on our perception of difference will be explored in chapter six in the section on Kristeva.)

One of the most fascinating aspects of Freud's work is that he eventually produced a theory of identity or subjectivity which both describes and normalises but at the same time subverts, the ideology of patriarchal cultures. Freud's theory as a whole both undermines and transcends what seems to have been his own troubled psychological position. What is remarkable, as many people have observed, is that someone like Freud, who seems, in many ways, to have been con-servative, middle-class and conventionally patriarchal, a man undoubt-edly of his time, was able to produce a stunningly revolutionary theory of how men and women painfully discover who and what they can be. Unfortunately our desire for Freud to be unblemished, our idealised father, something we do not seem to expect of other major intellectual or artistic figures, sometimes blinds us to his enormous achievement.

In the next section we shall look at some of the factors which may have been involved in the theoretical presences and absences in the complex body of Freud's work.

Presences and absences

Our knowledge of Freud is largely dependent on what we know of him from biographers, his letters and what we can perceive between the lines of the texts he produced. I have based my remarks mainly on Peter Gay's excellent biography (Gay 1988), Appignanesi and Forrester's recent book *Freud's Women* (1992), Freud's revealing letters to his friend Wilhelm Fliess (SE 1) and his account of his analysis of the patient he called Dora (PFL 8: 29). I have also drawn on Luce Irigaray's deconstruction of Freud's paper 'Femininity' in her book *Speculum of the Other Woman* (1985); her work is discussed in chapter five. If we look at these sources we find, not unsurprisingly, that it may be Freud's own unconscious entangle-ment with his theory which, although it marred his work in some ways, also provided the spur which allowed him access to the complexity of human identity. He may have needed to unravel this complexity for himself as well as for his 'science'. In this sense, we can see his work, like all discourses, as at one level an exploration of his own psychical reality, his own unconscious 'interests'.

On the basis of the sources of information we have, it seems likely that Freud's identity included a substantial quantity of occasionally acknowl-edged 'femininity' stemming from his 'feminine' identification with his striking and reputedly powerful mother who was only twenty at his birth, while his father was twenty years her senior. This 'femininity' to which he himself referred may have given him the potential for considerable insight into women and particularly into his early women patients who suffered from severe hysterical symptoms, as well as a fear of too great involvement with them. These were women who, it seems, had failed to anchor their sexual identity within the terrain allocated to them by culture.

An unconscious fear about his unresolved femininity may have manifested itself early in Freud's career in his relationship with his friend Wilhelm Fliess. Fliess was a highly eccentric ear, nose and throat specialist to whom Freud confided his latest ideas and insights as he was developing the basic framework for his theory. Bernheimer points out that in a letter written only a few months before their last meeting, Freud alludes to the submerged erotic component of their relationship. Freud wrote 'There can be no substitute for the close contact with a friend which a particular – almost feminine – side of me calls for.' Bernheimer comments, 'This remark suggests that Freud's unconscious transference managed to dissolve what he called in a later essay, "the rebellious over-compensation of the male (that) produces one of the strongest transference resistances"' (Bernheimer and Kahane, eds. 1985: 16) (SE 23: 252).

Freud's early analysis of Ida Bauer, whom he re-named 'Dora' in his case history, also suggests the presence of what Freud referred to as his 'almost feminine side'. The twelve essays collected in *In Dora's Case* (Bernheimer and Kahane 1985) present us with a fascinating elaboration of Freud's unconscious involvement in this case and particularly into its linguistic manifestations in the structure of his text. Dora was a young woman with severe hysterical symptoms and Freud's intriguing but exasperatingly fragmented account of his short four-month analysis of her is revealed as no less full of gaps, detours and omissions than the hysterically fragmented and incoherent discourse of his young patient. What he called a 'Fragment of an Analysis' (1905) seems to have been as much a fragment of an analysis of Freud's own hysteria as that of his patient (Lewin 1974). Freud has been criticised for failing to resolve Dora's transference because it entailed her identification with him not only as a man, or even a passive 'feminine' woman (with which he might have been able to cope), but with one whose sexuality consisted of multiple bisexual inclinations. Clare Kahane comments that Freud's text of *Dora* reveals 'masculinity and femininity to be wholly unmoored in the psychic life of hysterics', but she also observes 'that the place of the analyst was opened to as much uncertainty as that of the analysand' (Bernheimer and Kahane 1985: 23). Freud himself, earlier, in the account of his analysis of his own dreams in 1897, refers directly, with his usual insight, to his search for a resolution of 'my own hysteria' (SE 1: 262).

One particularly noticeable 'symptom' of Freud's possible unresolved 'femininity' in his work as a whole is his ambivalence towards women. There is a sense in which his entire theoretical output exhibits, at one and the same time, both a fascination with what he saw as the 'disturbance' in women, and also a deep need to keep his psychological (and theoretical) distance from them. This suggests an unconscious preoccupation with the sources of his own unconscious 'femininity', but at the same time a fear of being overwhelmed by it. This would explain the patriarchal, even misogynistic, tone which sometimes creeps into his texts (including his lecture 'Femininity'). His unconscious predicament seems to have been that if he allowed himself to become too deeply involved in the unconscious reality of women in his theory, he risked being 'suffocated' by his own unconscious, 'feminine' engagement with his material which always potentially threatened to 'unman' him. This would partly explain his severe reaction to his father's death in 1896 and his 'compensatory' emphasis on the role of the father until late in his life when perhaps the need to protect his own unconscious fragility had diminished. It may also indicate his marked ambivalence towards homosexual identities. His own sense of 'femininity' probably allowed him to view homosexuality as a normal sexual identity like all others at some points in his work. However, at other moments he backed away from this position and included homosexuality under the heading of 'perversions'.

What may have been Freud's unconscious fear of a too-close identification with women perhaps helps us to explain why he had such difficulty in identifying with the political aspirations of feminism when he encountered them. However, his ambivalent attitude seems at odds with what we know of his other relationships with women. Appignanesi and Forrester's *Freud's Women* reveals the extent to which Freud enjoyed and depended upon his close relationships with women.

So, the gaps, absences, contradictions and inconsistencies in Freud's theory seem to reflect a man, like many others, unconsciously struggling to keep in place his precarious 'masculine' identity and perhaps also, as a Jew, his European identity. Freud's sexual identity, like all other identity, was not entirely coherent and fixed because of the potential for disruption from his unconscious desire. This means that the knowledge he produced, like all other knowledge, could never be totally complete, coherent or consistent. He both knew and did not know at the same time. This is the focus of Lacan's development of Freud's work. It is perhaps the sense of inner struggle within the broad sweep of Freud's theory which gives it not only its compelling power and originality, but also its epic quality. In my view, Freud's stunning originality, imagination, and insight, emotional and theoretical, even as it threatened to undermine his own sense of who he was, transcends the criticisms made of it.

Suggested reading

Theory

FREUD, S. (1892–99) Extracts from the Fliess Letters, SE 1: 175–279.

FREUD, S. (1895) *Studies on Hysteria*, SE 2, PFL 3 [Freud's initial ideas on the relationship between unconscious ideas and sexuality inspired by the treatment of women patients suffering from hysterical symptoms].

FREUD, S. (1900) *The Interpretation of Dreams*, SE 4–5, PFL 4 [the symbolic relationship between the unconscious and dreams].

FREUD, S. (1905a) *The Three Essays on the Theory of Sexuality*, SE 7: 123–245, PFL 7 [Freud's theory of infantile sexuality and the early theory of the drives].

FREUD, S. (1905b) 'Fragment of an Analysis of a Case of Hysteria', SE 7: 1–122. PFL 8 [Dora: a case-study of a young girl which links hysteria and bisexuality].

FREUD, S. (1908) 'On the Sexual Theories of Children', SE 9: 205–26, PFL 7 [infantile sexuality].

FREUD, S. (1909) 'Analysis of a Phobia in a Five-Year old Boy', SE 14: 1–149, PFL 8 [Little Hans: a case-study which illustrates the central role of the Oedipus complex and castration anxiety].

FREUD, S. (1914) 'On Narcissism: An Introduction', SE 14: 67–102, PFL 11 [Freud's later theory of identity based on projection].

FREUD, S. (1917) 'Mourning and Melancholy', SE 14: 237–58, PFL 11 [the role of narcissism in mourning and depression].

FREUD, S. (1920) *Beyond the Pleasure Principle*, SE 18, PFL 11 [Freud's later dual instinct theory consisting of both life and death instincts].

FREUD, S. (1922) *Group Psychology and the Analysis of the Ego*, SE 18: 64–143.

FREUD, S. (1923) *The Ego and the Id*, SE 19, PFL 11 [Freud's most sophisticated structural theory of the unconscious and sexuality].

FREUD, S. (1924) 'The Dissolution of the Oedipal Complex', SE 19: 173–9, PFL 7 [the Oedipus complex and the superego].

FREUD, S. (1925) *An Autobiographical Study*, SE 20.

FREUD, S. (1925) 'Some Psychical Consequences of the Anatomical Distinction between the Sexes', SE 19: 241–58, PFL 7: 323–43 [feminine sexuality and penis-envy].

FREUD, S. (1925) 'Negation', SE 19.

FREUD, S. (1926) *The Question of Lay Analysis*, SE 20, PFL 15 [the concept of the unconscious].

FREUD, S. (1928) 'The Future of an Illusion', SE 21: 1–56, PFL 12: 212.

FREUD, S. (1930) *Civilisation and its Discontents*, SE 21, PFL 12 [The relationship between the unconscious, sexuality and culture; aggression and the superego].

FREUD, S. (1931a) 'Female Sexuality', SE 21: 223–43, PFL 7 [Freud's theory of feminine sexuality].

FREUD, S. (1933) *New Introductory Lectures on Psychoanalysis*, SE 22, PFL 2 including 'Femininity', SE 22: 112–35 [a summary of the theory of feminine sexuality and the importance of the pre-Oedipal mother – reprinted in Part II].

FREUD, S. (1940) *An Outline of Psychoanalysis*, SE 23, PFL 15.

Juliet Mitchell's *Psychoanalysis and Feminism* (1975) provides an excellent summary of the chronological developments of Freud's major concepts in Part One. Part Two, section 2: 295–356 covers the main criticisms of Freud's work made by feminists during the nineteen-sixties and early nineteen-seventies.

Laplanche and Pontalis's *The Language of Psychoanalysis* (1985) provides authoritative and readable definitions and interpretations of psychoanalytic terms, aimed at students and researchers.

General

APPIGNANESI, L. and FORRESTER, J. (1992) *Freud's Women*, London, Weidenfeld.

FREUD, A. ed. (1986) *Sigmund Freud: The Essentials of Psychoanalysis*, Harmondsworth, Penguin.

GAY, P. (1988) *Freud: A Life for Our Time*, London, Macmillan.

GAY, P. (1991) *Reading Freud*, New Haven, Yale University Press.

JACOBS, M. (1992) *Sigmund Freud*, London, Sage.

LAPLANCHE, J. and PONTALIS, J.B. (1985) *The Language of Psychoanalysis*, London, Hogarth Press.

LASCH, C. (1980) *The Culture of Narcissism*, London, Sphere Books.

MILLER, A. (1991) *Banished Knowledge*, London, Virago.

ROBINSON, P. (1993) *Freud and His Critics*, Berkeley, University of California Press.

ROITH, E. (1987) *The Riddle of Freud*, London, Tavistock.

STORR, A. (1990) *Freud*, Oxford, Oxford University Press.

WOLLHEIM, R. (1971) *Freud*, London, Fontana [Modern Masters].

YOUNG-BRUEHL, E. (1988) *Anna Freud*, London, Macmillan.

YOUNG-BRUEHL, E. (1990) *Freud on Women*, London, Hogarth Press.

Feminist interpretations

BERNHEIMER C. and KAHANE, C. eds. (1985) *In Dora's Case*, London, Virago.

BRENNAN, T. (1992) *The Interpretation of the Flesh: Freud and Femininity*, London, Routledge.

IRIGARAY, L. (1985) *Speculum of the Other Woman*, trans C. Gill, Ithaca, Cornell University Press.

MITCHELL, J. (1975) *Psychoanalysis and Feminism*, Harmondsworth, Penguin.

MITCHELL J. (1982) 'Introduction 1' in J. Mitchell and J. Rose, eds. *Jacques Lacan and the Ecole Freudienne: Feminine Sexuality*, London, Macmillan.

MITCHELL, J. (1986) 'Introduction' to *The Selected Melanie Klein*, Harmondsworth, Penguin.

SAYERS, J. (1986) *Sexual Contradictions*, London, Tavistock.

WHITEFORD, M. (1991) *Luce Irigaray*, London, Routledge.

2
Klein: phantasy and the mother

I hate and I love: why I do so you may well ask. I do not know, but
I feel it happen and am in agony.

(Catullus (84–54 BC, 'Carmina' no. 85)

Biographical background (1882–1960)

Melanie Klein was born in Vienna, the youngest of four children with a
very dominating mother. Although as a child she was ambitious and
wanted to study medicine, she married Arthur Klein when she was twenty-
one without undertaking any medical training. Between 1903 and 1914 she
brought up her three children but in 1914, after the death of her mother,
she went into analysis with Sandor Ferenczi, one of Freud's colleagues, to
help her with depression. This was to be the turning point in her life. In
1919, after becoming increasingly interested in psychoanalysis, she gave her
first paper and was accepted as a member of the Budapest Psychoanalytic
Society although she did not have a medical qualification. After her divorce
in 1926 she went to England with her son Eric and became a member of the
British Psychoanalytical Society in 1927. She began practising in 1931 and
published *The Psychoanalysis of Children* in the same year. Two years later
her first analyst, Ferenczi, died and her son Eric was killed in a climbing
accident. After the outbreak of war in 1939 she moved to Pitlochry in
Scotland and began her well-documented analysis of an autistic boy
'Richard'. Six months later she returned to London and after controversial
discussions at the British Psychoanalytical Society in the early nineteen-
forties, two separate training programmes were set up, one Freudian and
the other Kleinian. Klein continued to publish major books and papers and
practice throughout the late nineteen-forties and fifties. She died in 1960.

An overview of Klein's ideas

With Melanie Klein we move from Freud's view of a psychical reality
suffused with desire to one dominated by anxiety and the experience of

[78]

the very young baby. Through her work with small children, Klein was able to look behind the Oedipal territory with which Freud was pre-occupied, to the period of childhood Freud describes as 'so grey with age and shadowy and almost impossible to revivify' (PFL 7: 373). This is the stormy world of the infant underlying the reality of all of us. She claims that it is the baby's anxiety and emotional ambivalence rather than sexuality or desire which are the overriding problems with which the small baby, and later the adult, have to cope. From the moment of birth, she argues, the baby is plunged into a chaotic conflict between fluctuating emotions of love and hate which are the cause of acute anxiety. These instinctual emotions could, by means of phantasy, be directed towards both the mother and the self. Although Klein's early work was deeply rooted in Freud, her later thinking differs significantly and marks the beginning of Object-Relations theory, a second major strand in psycho-analytic thought. Klein's approach to the construction of identity is sometimes seen as developmental, that is something which happens stage-by-stage in the baby or individual's life. However, Klein writes about 'positions' rather than 'phases' of development to emphasise that both infant and adult can move from one psychical structure to the other throughout life.

Klein was primarily interested in what she perceived as the baby's struggle to relate to other people, or what Klein calls 'objects' (at first the mother) by taking them into its inner world as phantasy objects and then building an identity out of them. It is the primitive, pre-verbal and extra-verbal language of these internalised objects – Klein called them 'phan-tasies' – which is the major focus of her work.

By 'phantasy' she means a kind of primitive thinking consisting, in the first place, of what the baby 'makes' of experiences, both inside and outside itself and by which it communicates with itself. Klein thought the perceptions of external reality by young babies, but also children and even adults, were influenced by their emotional state. Klein found that her four- or five-year-old son, Eric, when feeling anxious and angry saw her as a wicked witch threatening to poison him. But when he was feeling happy and secure, he saw her as a princess he wanted to marry. For Klein, such phantasies of loving and hating form the basis of a rudimentary sense of identity consisting of impulses, defences and relationships. This distinguishes Klein's concept of phantasy from Freud's concept of the unconscious because although, symbolically, Klein's concept represents a drive, it is associated with a primitive form of self which exists much earlier than Freud's, in the very young baby, whereas Freud's ego and the unconscious come into being at the time of the Oedipal crisis. Klein's concept of phantasy, emerging out of primitive defence mechanisms, is crucial to establishing a future relationship and rational ways of thinking. Such thinking evolves from phantasy as the baby gradually gains a more realistic view of the mother and the rest of the world and needs to defend itself less. But Klein became convinced that an identity constructed only out of phantasy objects was a feature of both the mental life of the very young baby and the psychotic child or adult and that phantasy is a precondition of any engagement we can have with reality.

Julia Segal uses the story of Cinderella to illustrate some of Klein's ideas. If we consider how a real girl would feel if her mother died, we can imagine how she might long for her mother to return and a step-mother might be greeted with very mixed feelings; on the one hand, the child wants a mother-figure who will magically make everything better; on the other, she fears a destructive and scheming woman who will be envious of her and jealous of her relationship with her father. These characteristics are ones we might expect a stepdaughter to sense in herself so that she projects in phantasy a hope for a fairy godmother with magical abilities to make everything right again and fears of her own envy and jealousy towards her father's new wife become embodied in a phantasy of a wicked stepmother (Segal 1992: 29–32).

Klein's primitive phantasies are based on the baby's early instincts and this partial reliance on biology is reflected in her assumption that 'masculinity' and 'femininity' are also biologically determined but re-inforced during early childhood. This returns to the idea that there is some underlying biological component in gender formation which, for Klein and her contemporaries, seems to have been inspired by a wish to establish 'femininity' in its own right and detach it from the dependence on the penis proposed by Freud. We shall focus on the specific issue of the construction of gendered identity in Klein's work later in this chapter but, first, let us look back at Freud's concept of the life and death drives from which Klein derived her own theory of the baby's earliest instincts of love and hate.

Freud's dual instinct theory

Freud first revised his theory of the drives in his paper *Beyond the Pleasure Principle* in 1920. In this paper Freud subsumes the sexual drive as he originally conceived it into a life-drive which includes his earlier concept of a drive for self-preservation. In seeking to find an explanation for aggression as well as sexuality (at a time when the First World War had just finished tearing Europe apart) Freud introduced an idea which he himself regarded as highly speculative but theoretically necessary – a death drive. He became convinced of the existence of a special kind of unconscious pleasure in painful experiences which was much more fundamental than he had imagined in his earlier work on childhood sexuality. He argued that the evidence for such a drive could be seen in masochism, the self-destructive opposite to sadism, a drive for control and mastery characteristic of the anal phase. He linked masochism with what he called 'repetition compulsion', the driving unconscious compulsion to repeat painful or traumatic experiences.

Freud's idea of a repetition compulsion grew partly out of his recognition that certain people repeatedly become enmeshed in destructive and abusive relationships because of an unconscious compulsion to re-enact early childhood experiences which they hope might be resolved differently. Freud thought evidence of a death drive could also be perceived in the unconscious sense of guilt characteristic of severe depression and in the wish not to recover from illness. He argued that these conditions contradicted his earlier idea that the self always attempted to maximise pleasurable experience and minimise the unpleasant in so far as this was compatible with external reality, ideas he termed the pleasure principle and the reality principle. Drawing on biology for scientific support, Freud decided that since drives must have an aim, the death drive had as its aim the longing to return to a state of inertia or state of no pain; 'the Nirvana principle'. But because the organism fears the death instinct whose effects are frequently painful, it deflects it outwards in the form of aggression. 'I must die' becomes 'you must die'. Freud also speculates that the life and death drives did not exist independently of each other but were fused together. When the death instinct is dominant, it gives rise to sadism and masochism, both of which Freud had previously associated with the drive for mastery or control. But when the life drive has the upper hand, aggression acts on behalf of the ego in the form of ordinary sexual feelings and normal assertiveness. In *The Ego and the Id* (1923), Freud associates aggression with the superego which explains the superego's potential for savage attack in the form of a sense of guilt. In the severely depressed person, a condition Freud described as melancholia, the individual, dominated by a sense of guilt coming from a punishing superego, lives within what he described as 'a culture of pure hate'.

Freud saw masochism as an example of behaviour in which aggression becomes eroticised because of its fusion with sexuality. He claimed that normally aggression is projected outwards in acts of self-assertion or defence. However, traces of this aggression remain as part of the sexual/ life instincts, creating a basis for an eroticised form of aggression sometimes turned destructively inwards. He suggested that masochism is most evident in people whose childhood aggression has been inhibited in some way, perhaps through prevention of free movement, messy play, self-assertion or expressions of anger by over-controlling parents. Such children lack the experience of learning to control their anger so that they unconsciously repress their hostility, experienced as unacceptable, by turning it against themselves in the form of masochism. Because this is so closely bound up with sexual feelings, Freud argued that although people like this may consciously *feel* like victims and suffer in a very real sense, they also experience a degree of unconscious pleasure in their pain which derives partly from managing to conceal their own hostile feelings. Leaving aside social and economic factors, this could explain why some women find themselves psychologically paralysed, unable to leave abusive, violent partners, or, if they do manage it, are later compelled to repeat the experience with someone equally abusive. Freud argued that masochism can be found in both men and women but that it was especially prevalent in women because the patriarchal form of the 'feminine' requires the repression of anger and assertiveness. However, in the sense that in the repeat situation the victim is trying to get the original parent to make some kind of reparation, the response of the new partner (the substitute parent) can never be enough to overcome the pain caused by the gap in the victim's sense of being. This means that the repeat situation is almost inevitably doomed to fail.

Phantasies of love and hate

Klein took Freud's idea of a life and death drive and converted it into instincts of love and hate by means of which the baby first constructs a sense of the mother and itself. For Klein, the baby's first fragile identity is forged from its anxiety in relation to these instincts resulting from its extreme helplessness and dependence on the mother at the beginning of its life. Although the struggle between these conflicting emotions produces huge anxiety, Klein sees this as the crucial and eventually humanising trigger for the child's potential to develop an identity of its own. Loving and hating phantasies of the breast, are the baby's first experience of relating to the mother and, because the baby's identity is fused with the breast (since it does not have an identity of its own), of filling itself up with a good or bad phantasy of the breast, thus creating a primitive sense of having a self. Whether the baby can incorporate or 'introject' a good or bad phantasy of the breast and later whole mother depends on whether the mother is present or absent. For Klein, the young baby's earliest task is to allow its love for the mother to overcome its hate, so that it can incorporate her and everything she represents (the breast, but also other internal objects such as the father's penis, siblings) as good objects and therefore experience itself as substantially good rather than bad. This idea develops Freud's idea of the mother as the baby's first distinct, psychological object, which it internalises or introjects when she is perceived to be missing. He had linked this to the baby's sensations of anxiety and helplessness whenever the mother's breast is removed for too long. At such times the baby recreates the external mother, the object, for itself in phantasy inside its inner world. By hallucinating a good feed within its imagination it creates a phantasy of the breast/mother which then becomes a part of the baby's own fragile, residual self over which it has some control, unlike the external breast (SE 1: 319). This capacity to internalise at first phantasies of part objects such as the breast or penis (also contained in the baby's phantasy of the mother) but later, as a sense of external reality sets in, whole objects or people out of which the baby then fabricates its self, lies at the heart of Object-Relations theory.

So, as well as developing her own version of Freud's life and death drives, Klein also took Freud's idea of the imaginary incorporation of objects into the baby's inner world and turned it into a theory of how the baby creates a primitive identity through the psychical internalisation of other people and, initially, parts of these people. For Klein, the object is the mother and the baby's relatedness to her through phantasy, and not the object of desire which is incorporated by Freud's baby. In Klein's theory, when the baby feels full, in a state of bliss and therefore 'good', it introjects the idea of a good breast out of which it then constitutes a positive, pleasing identity. When the baby feels hungry, insecure and empty, it introjects the idea of a bad breast and, since it still shares its self with the mother, it experiences both her and its self as 'bad' and frightening. In the first months of life the baby needs to maintain an inner 'good' breast with which it can build a self which will be able to keep it safe from the 'bad' breast or 'bad' object which in phantasy, both externally and internally, threatens to annihilate it. The baby's aggression or hostility towards its bad internalised objects (parts of the self) is experienced as so dangerous that it has to be projected out of the baby's self onto other people. This then means that these other people are experienced as very dangerous because they contain hostile, split-off parts of the baby's own identity (this is the mechanism of paranoia). Although Klein built on Freud's idea of the life and death instincts and the idea that potentially wounding aggression could be deflected outwards, she was much more interested in the detailed nature of the unconscious mechanisms by which the ego or self protects itself from being overwhelmed and annihilated by its own internalised aggression in the form of bad phantasy objects.

So, there are two poles to Klein's theory, both involving the construction of a phantasy world. The first is the self or ego's relationship, through phantasy, to the *external* world of objects at first seen as the mother's breast which includes other part objects, and later as the mother seen both as a whole and as a combined object containing the idea of the father. These objects are either idealised or denigrated through the mediation of love or hate. The second pole is the self's relationship, through phantasy, with its *inner* world containing instincts, impulses, bodily sensations and, most importantly, the baby's anxiety. This fundamental anxiety is the fear of being psychically annihilated by its own internalised aggression and not Freud's much later Oedipal fear of the loss of the penis (castration anxiety) by the father seen as a rival in love. Taken as a whole, Klein's work is concerned primarily with how the child copes with what it assumes as the loss of the mother when she is absent, by dividing her and the external world by means of phantasy. Significantly, the breast replaces Freud's phallus as the object of most importance to the formation of the child's sexual identity.

Unconscious mechanisms

In her clinical practice with disturbed young children, instead of using Freud's method of free association, Klein used her own celebrated 'play technique' which she used to construct an unprecedented picture of the child's internal world. Klein describes the technique in her paper 'The Psychoanalytic Play Technique' (1955). It involved play with specially made toys which the children used as a way of representing their phantasy life, as a form of language about their inner world. Using this technique Klein perceived a special system of organisation of feelings and impulses based on love and hate through which the baby (and later 'normal' adults and, in extreme forms, psychotics) try to protect their inner worlds from annihilation. This includes four central unconscious mechanisms based on phantasy: *splitting, projection, introjection* and *projective identification.* As we have seen, these mechanisms or defences against acute feelings of fragmentation of identity and emptiness represent a kind of unconscious, non-verbal language. However, they are not part of another separate, psychical domain as the unconscious is for Freud. Let us look at what each of these means in a little more detail.

Splitting involves the baby in unconsciously separating the 'good' phantasy object from the 'bad' one in its internal world. It does this by splitting itself into two; usually it is the 'bad' part of this self which, is disowned and projected onto something in the external world. This is initially the mother's breast which consequently becomes 'bad' because it now carries part of the baby's 'bad', anxiety-ridden identity.

Projection, as Freud had discovered, is the baby's unconscious device for pushing both good and bad feelings within its inner world out onto something or somone in the external world (FPL II: 187–8). Initially this included pushing the split off part of itself which it experiences as 'bad' (its inner bad objects) onto the external object, the mother, in order to preserve its own feelings of goodness and security. (In a child or adult we call this kind of behaviour looking for someone else to blame for our own feelings of vulnerability.) As a result of this, it feels hated and persecuted by its split-off feelings lodged in the mother who is now contaminated and experienced as 'bad' and hostile. This then produces more bad feelings of anxiety which also need to be split-off and projected and so on. However, since in this nightmare cycle so much of the self becomes split-off, this leads inevitably to feelings of acute emptiness and impoverishment. Sometimes, if the mother conveys to the baby that she cannot tolerate its hatred, only its love or idealisation, the baby may project only its good feelings onto the mother retaining only its bad feelings within itself. This is a feature of depression in adult life where an individual feels all 'goodness' exists outside him or her self leaving them, 'inside', worthless and bad. In this situation the individual is being attacked by a part of their own ego, or self, constituted by the bad, destructive objects inside them without any possibility of rescue from the good ones. This may, as Klein suggested, form the basis for psycho-somatic illness where the bad objects attack the self represented by the body. The projection of our 'good' feelings onto an idea of God, an ideal parent, may explain the pre-occupation Christianity has with man's unworthiness as a 'miserable sinner' in need of redemption. (As we shall see Klein's concept of reparation in what she calls the 'depressive position' fits this analysis.) Projection is also likely to be an unconscious factor in certain forms of racial or ethnic hatred and in some men's hatred of women. The people onto whom these projections have been made have to be severely controlled because, like human psychical dustbins, they contain rejected parts of the self.

Introjection is the means by which the baby takes in, or internalises, everything it perceives or experiences in relation to the object (breast or whole mother), both its 'goodness' and its 'badness'. It is the basic building block of the baby's self and, for Klein, the introjection of sufficient 'good', loved objects is the essential requirement for an autonomous self capable of both giving and taking in love.

Projective identification is Klein's version of what Freud calls narcissistic object-relationships and of an internalised narcissistic structure where the object is re-internalised after the initial identification. This means that the individual becomes very heavily dependent on the love-object. Klein distinguishes between narcissistic states where the self is taken as the love-object (which Freud termed auto-eroticism) and those states and the relationships based on them where the self is projected onto the other and then re-introjected. This is what Klein called projective identi-fication. Initially, with the mother, this involves the baby's projection of good as well as bad parts of the self onto her having already imaginatively filled itself up or identified with her as part of its fused self. In some adult relationships between couples based on projective identification, both partners tend to lose sight of who each of them is because there is only one shared identity based on mutual identification and each partner then re-introjects or takes back into the self the other who already contains part of that self. Usually both partners are unaware of how dependent they are on each other. In some cases unconscious feelings of being potentially enslaved by a partner may mean such people try to avoid close relationships because they inevitably find them too suffocating and psychically exhausting. The problem with relationships based on love-objects who carry projected parts of the self is that there is a constant need to control the object and, conversely a persistent fear of being controlled by it. When bad parts of the self are projected the partner may become a feared persecutor and when good parts are projected there may be a huge sense of dependence. The partner has to be controlled because of what their loss might mean to the self while at the same time there is a fear of being controlled because the object contains a valued part of the self.

Unconscious positions

Klein describes two fundamental ways in which our psyche may be organised. She refers to these as positions rather than stages because anyone, as an adult, can find themselves operating within one or other position at any time. They each represent a kind of unconscious system of thinking based on phantasy. The first is what she calls the *paranoid–schizoid position* which is primarily based on persecutory anxiety (fear of attack) and the defences of splitting and projection characteristic of the baby's first three months. The baby, totally vulnerable and dependent on the mother, fears retaliation from her (being devoured, poisoned, having its internal organs scooped out) because of its own destructive phantasies which have been projected outwards onto her. In the case of a severely paranoid adult, splitting and projection create a terrifying persecutory, external world which in a psychotic state might take the form of hearing hostile voices, for example, which lead to further persecution from an equally fragmented inner world. We talk about 'going to pieces' and 'getting ourselves together'. This seems to reflect this unconscious experience of potential fragmentation characteristic of the paranoid–schizoid position.

Klein sees the paranoid–schizoid position as, ideally, a developmental step in the construction of identity. The baby can gradually overcome its fear of disintegration through its first identification with an ideal breast. As the baby develops in the second quarter of the first year, it is able to perceive and take in a whole person, normally its mother. It learns that both loving and hating experiences can be integrated and co-exist in the same person, in both its mother and itself. Although the baby may continue to feel empty and hostile about the frustration caused by the mother's independent existence (the demands, for example, of its father and other children), its fear of retaliation from the mother is gradually replaced by feelings of guilt and anxiety about its phantasies of destroying her. These are very painful. For Freud, guilt is associated with the much later Oedipal period, and with desire and phantasised murderous attacks on the *father*. In Klein's theory, painful feelings of guilt and anxiety result from the baby's phantasised, murderous attacks on the *mother*. They occur much earlier, at between three and six months, but they represent a major turning point for the baby as it enters what for Klein is the all-important *depressive position*. This, not Freud's Oedipal crisis, represents the crux of her theory and the child's entry into its humanity. If the baby can repair the damage to its external world (the mother) and its internalised bad objects through loving, reparative feelings, its inner world can be transformed by re-populating it with good objects – a restored and repaired mother whose loss can be endured. In other words, if, through positive, loving experiences with the mother, the baby can come to trust and internalise an external world of goodness and the possibility of reparation and integration rather than persecution and annihilation, it will have negotiated the depressive position successfully. It will also have achieved the necessary separation from the mother. On the basis of this experience it will be able to form an identity which creatively constructs and repairs rather than destroys, denies or om-nipotently seeks to control parts of the self projected onto objects in the external world. In other words, *blaming* the (m)other as a way of defending against feelings of helplessness and dependence, and the accompanying anxiety, is replaced by an ability to own these 'bad' feelings so that they can be integrated within the self instead of disowned and projected onto the outside world. By learning to integrate good and bad qualities in the same person, in its own developing self and in its perception of the mother, the baby is able to make the vital transition from its crude binary phantasies of love and hate to the recognition of a more complex reality. In Freud's theory the child makes this transition from phantasy to reality much later, in the Oedipal stage, through its successful separation from the mother by means of the intervention of the father (or symbolic father). Klein took the view that most of us never entirely resolve the depressive position throughout our lives.

Defences in the depressive position

The two characteristic defences of Klein's depressive position are *denial* and *omnipotence*. These are less violent than those of the paranoid–schizoid position. Denial is primarily of dependency (feelings of help-lessness) and ambivalent feelings towards the mother. Omnipotence expresses itself in feelings of triumph and contempt which conceal the pain associated with the inevitable loss of the mother as well as the phantasy of total control over her. Freud's concept of repression begins much later in the Oedipal crisis. But, like repression, denial of reality, and the phantasy of having omnipotent control over the mother (the excessive feeling of being in control sometimes described as mania) are the ways in which the baby excludes its painful feelings of loss from consciousness. In the depressive position the still helpless baby's anxiety causes depression rather than fear of attack (persecution). This emotional pain is induced by *guilt* caused by anger turned against the self rather than as before, against someone in the external world. Guilt has replaced hate or blame. In the depressive position the baby's identity, which has been based only on phantasy, is gradually transformed, through the emotional suffering (depression) involved in owning all its feelings, including painful ones of vulnerability and anxiety, into one based on reality and the possibility of creative reparation and change. (This process seems to be reflected in religious ideas of redemption through suffering.)

Most of us, at certain times, employ some of the defences identified in Klein's two kinds of psychical organisation; they are part of what we call normal behaviour. For Klein, the psychoses are psychical predicaments which occur because the depressive position has been so unsuccessfully negotiated that one or other of the defences takes over and dominates over any other forms of communication. The individual's perception of what we call reality may become so distorted by phantasies – projections and introjections, denials and ideas of omnipotence – that internal and external reality can no longer be differentiated and negotiated. No common ground exists to enable normal communication. Freud describes this closed system of reflections detached from reality as an extreme form of narcissism. In a less severe form it may express itself in adults as a psychical inability to tolerate or take responsibility for feelings of vulnerability or being out of control (denial) so that others are blamed for the feelings of anxiety which result. Often, to avoid such feelings, there is an obsessive need for power and control of others to avoid conscious contact with these split-off parts of the self.

Juliet Mitchell suggests that Klein, unlike Freud, argues that, from a very early age, people and even part-objects are perceived to have personalities rather than just bodies and that these are the psychical objects with which the baby peoples its world and, at the same time, constitutes itself (Mitchell 1986: 25–30). Klein's version of the unconscious seems to be modelled as a container of biological predispositions to feelings, impulses and defences rather than a dynamic, potentially subversive system of thought with its own symbolic language, as the unconscious is in Freud's theory. Unlike Freud's concept of identity, a stable, authentic identity *is* possible in Klein's theory through the internalisation of good objects, but only if the child manages to negotiate the pain of the depressive position. It has to acknowledge the potentially overwhelming discovery that it cannot be omnipotent and have complete control over the mother, and it must painfully come to terms with that loss. If a unified identity is achieved in this way, in Klein's theory, there is no separate, unconscious place from which this identity can be subverted.

The role of the father in Klein's theory

In Klein's work the father is included in the baby's early phantasies of the mother. Whereas in Freud's theory the child takes in the father as a crucial parental figure in the shape of the superego during the Oedipal crisis, Klein expands and backdates this idea so that the baby incorporates the rival father as part of its phantasies about the mother. Like the early phantasy of the mother's breast, the phantasy of the father's penis contained in the idea of the mother, is also exposed to splitting and projection but it, too, is capable of being integrated more realistically as the child becomes aware of external reality within the depressive position.

In Klein's later work, the baby's working through of the depressive position virtually replaces Freud's much later resolution of the Oedipal crisis. Klein transforms the child's guilt and fear of castration by the father in Freud's theory into the child's guilt and fear of losing both parents in the depressive position as a result of its persecutory phantasies. Here fear of loss is primarily about generalised loss of good internal objects in the form of the mother and father; what Klein describes as the 'combined object'. Klein's focus on the mother as ultimately a more powerful figure than the father might well make her theory very attractive to feminists put off by the dominance of the phallus in Freud's theory. However, the cost, in theoretical terms, of this return of the mother to what many women might consider her proper place is that we lose touch with desire and the intervention of the father which, in Freud, is the catalyst for castration anxiety and the creation of an unconscious which potentially destabilises all our identities.

Symbolisation

Finally, in this section, let us look at Klein's concept of symbolisation. This is different from Freud's view of symbolisation as the representation of repressed desire – the language of the unconscious – as it is expressed in symptoms and dreams. In Klein's analysis of children's play Klein demonstrated that symbolism using toys rather than words enabled the child operating in the paranoid–schizoid position to project not only its interests but also its unconscious, unspoken phantasies, anxieties and guilt towards the mother (the object). Here, the symbol and object are experienced as the same thing just as, in this phase, the child experiences its mother and itself as the same person. Dick, one of the children with whom Klein worked, equates a little toy coal-cart he has damaged with the body of his mother and throws it out. In doing this he expels both the mother he has damaged and his own destructive aggression. In the depressive position the omnipotent, possessive relationship to the mother is gradually given up and mourned in favour of concern for the mother, and a different kind of symbol is needed to replace it and represent the lost mother with whom the child is no longer fully identified. This symbol Klein regards as non-psychotic and it is capable of being used creatively in language and other forms of representation. For Klein, therefore, all creative activity can be seen as an attempt to recreate the lost object, the mother. Klein took the view that the development of the child's phantasy life through the two kinds of symbolisation was crucial to its development of an identity. Symbolisation through play is the way in which the child bridges and negotiates inner and outer reality. Without this bridge the child is blocked off from the external world. This is an area which is taken up and developed in the work of the other important Object-Relations theorist, Donald Winnicott, in his concept of 'play' and the 'transitional space' which we will come to in the next chapter.

Commentary on 'Envy and Gratitude'

In this paper Klein introduces envy into the range of the child's aggressive feelings towards the mother as the baby envies the limitless riches the mother is perceived to possess compared with its own poverty and helplessness. At the same time Klein extends her idea of reparation to include gratitude. She also raises an issue fundamental to the study of gender and the relationship between the sexes – womb-envy.

At the beginning of the paper Klein re-asserts the view she held for most of her life that the mother and baby relationship from its first moments contains all the fundamental elements of future relationships, and this is based on an innate instinct in the baby which sees the mother not only as the source of nourishment but also of life itself. This is the basis of the life instinct. Pleasure is a source of psychical as well as physical well-being because the baby takes in or 'introjects' the breast as the representation of total love, wisdom, understanding and creativity, capable of turning all distress into complete contentment and bliss. The problem is that envy of the mother is provoked by all these riches which lie frustratingly beyond the baby itself. In other words, although there is a biological factor in the baby's capacity to love, this is modified by the baby's experience with the mother.

Klein makes an important distinction between envy, jealousy and greed. Envy is the most primitive and purely destructive emotion. Jealousy involves a relationship with at least two other people and is concerned with the fear of being deprived of someone we love by another. Greed seems to lack the component of malice implied in envy where the desire to spoil the good object is achieved by splitting off and projecting feelings of being bad onto the object. Greed, however, uses introjection, envy uses destructive projective identification. Greed may conceal envy – if we have everything we don't need to envy anyone.

In this paper, Klein sees envy as the single most dangerous ingredient in the baby's capacity to work through the depressive phase and internalise a good, uninjured and unspoilt breast. She sees the mother's breast, uncontaminated by the baby's phantasised envious attacks as the core of the baby's healthy sense of identity. It is the foundation for an internal world in which the baby's love outweighs its hate so that in its future life it can establish other good object-relationships with which to identify and stock its inner world. A good experience of the breast, Klein argues, forms the basis for the second subject of this paper, gratitude. For Klein, gratitude rests on the belief and trust in good objects, the capacity to love without the interference of envy, and the wish to reciprocate pleasure. Gratitude is bound up for Klein with generosity – a capacity for gratitude allows the baby in later life to share its gifts freely, to take in other people's goodness and share its own around.

After distinguishing between her own view of the life and death instincts and that of Freud, Klein turns to the paranoid–schizoid position and to what she sees as the universal problem of idealisation in this position. Some people still operate unconsciously within the confinement of a world where they are able to relate to other people only through idealising or denigrating them (projecting good or bad phantasies of themselves onto them). The idealisation of someone else, as with the mother, inevitably involves a parallel idealisation of the self; it enables those who idealise to introject or fill themselves up with a good reflection of the self. (This is close to what Freud describes as narcissism – falling in love with one's own reflection in the 'other'.) The problem is that, under the weight of reality this idealisation must collapse and both the lover and the self are then perceived without the rosy tint of the 'good' phantasy. The previously idealised person perceived as the 'perfect partner', is now likely to be experienced as totally bad. An internal bad object is substituted for the internal good object and the identity of the one who idealises suddenly feels terrifyingly precarious. This could explain those people who, unable to sustain a relationship after the phase of idealisation has broken down, compulsively move from one relationship to another in search of their identity. Sometimes the previously idealised person is subsequently experienced as a hated persecutor which indicates the origin of idealisation in persecution. The subject now projects all their envy and hostility onto someone who was formerly their ideal self, the apple (breast) of their eye. For such people, love and hate have never been sufficiently integrated unconsciously in the depressive position to allow for the acceptance of the reality that good and bad qualities exist together in the same person. Others cannot be experienced with love and generosity for what they are, because primitive fantasies of good and evil make idealisation and denigration the only possible emotional stances.

There are many cultural examples of this mechanism of idealisation, the most striking of which probably forms the unconscious basis for much hostility towards women. The cultural representation of women by patriarchal men as 'Madonna', 'goddess', 'whore', 'chick' or 'witch', as either infinitely powerful or utterly helpless, suggest the presence of idealisation and denigration and an ambivalent relationship between patriarchal men and women which is saturated with male dependency projected onto women. If integration in the depressive position has not occurred, a more realistic perception of women is unavailable. We shall pursue this issue later in the 'Discussion' section. Similarly, the apparently blind adulation of deities, political leaders or national heroes are also forms of idealisation. If the object becomes excessively elevated because all the good parts of the one who idealises have been projected onto it, the discrepancy between them and those who idealise them may become so great that comparison becomes impossible and envy is alleviated. This looks very much like the Christian version of the relationship between God and man – the omnipotent perfection of God is split off from man who is so immersed in sin, guilt and unworthiness that envy cannot become an issue. In Kleinian terms, the Christian idea of redemption through suffering and forgiveness may be seen, at some levels at least, as a religious representation of the depressive position.

Klein's distinctive version of the Oedipus complex emerges clearly from her discussion of the difference between envy and jealousy. Jealousy, Klein argues, is based on rivalry with the father who is seen as having frequently monopolised the mother and her breast thus depriving the baby of exclusive possession. However, in dramatic contrast to Freud, Klein sees the Oedipus complex emerging very early at the age of between three and six months at the time of the onset of the depressive position. This is the period of development when, earlier in her career, on the basis of phantasies described to her in her analyses of children, she had formulated the idea of the combined parent figure. At this time this idea replaces the mother as the object of the child's phantasies, its projections and introjections. The mother's breast is now seen as also containing the idea of the father's penis and all it represents as a rival focus of interest for the mother. This view of the Oedipus complex (which initiates the Oedipal crisis) and the role of the father represents a major theoretical difference between Klein and Freud. The father, culture, the law against incest, all so central to Freud, are subsumed in Klein's work in the all-powerful figure of the mother and the central role of the depressive position associated with her. The moment when the child becomes a full-blown human being is no longer the successful resolution of the Oedipal crisis but the successful emergence from the depressive position, and the mother, rather than the father, occupies the central role.

Klein moves next to the process of working through the depressive position, which she argues many of us spend our lives trying to achieve.

At certain moments, particularly of loss, most of us are vulnerable to depressive guilt and the pain of trying to make reparation for the destructive phantasies we have harboured about the one we have lost. The state of bereavement is the commonest form of this kind of experience, where the lost object at some level represents a parent or sibling figure and thus re-activates the conflicts of the depressive position. As we have seen in the discussion of narcissism in the previous chapter, when we lose someone, because of our increased hatred towards them for having left us, we have to face both their loss in external reality, but also the loss of the good object in our internal world. We are exposed again to feelings of emptiness and our primitive, underlying paranoid and depressive fears. If we have not managed to rid ourselves of early phantasies of omnipotence and denial of the loss of the mother, the death in external reality may be experienced as a death of the actual 'self'. Bereavement may then turn into more prolonged depression or even psychosomatic illness. It is striking that partners frequently die within a very short time of the death of their spouses.

The next part of Klein's paper takes up the issue of envy and jealousy in relation, specifically, to the Oedipal period and raises the issues of both penis-envy and womb-envy. As we have seen, Freud saw the girl's envy of the penis as being of far more significance than male envy of the womb. Even in her early work, Klein, like Karen Horney and Hélène Deutsch and other women analysts, disagreed with Freud and saw penis-envy in girls as a secondary and not primary reaction. Like Freud, Klein saw it as eventually constituting a girl's bisexuality (her gender-precariousness) but, for her, this is the result of envy of the mother not the father. The girl first envies her mother's body because this is felt to contain everything – father, future babies, the world. This envy, according to Klein, is then at a later stage projected onto the father's penis when the girl's phantasy of being her father's lover is also frustrated.

Unlike Freud, Klein sees the girl's penis-envy and the boy's similar envy of the riches and creativity of his mother's body as of equal importance. In both sexes, Klein sees envy as primarily envy of the *mother's breast* and body during the paranoid–schizoid position. For her, penis-envy pales into insignificance compared with the envy of the mother as the all-creating, life-giving force. She outlines the repercussions of this phase in adult relationships if it is not adequately resolved in the depressive process of reparation and gratitude. If the girl who has turned to her father still feels dominated by envy of her mother, and her mother's relationship with the father, her desire to spoil the father as a valuable object for her mother will undermine her relationship with him and all other men; in Klein's view this may lead to frigidity. (Freud thought that it was women's excessive penis-envy directly in relation to the father which led to frigidity.) This is Klein's version of Freud's phallic, castrating woman who, like the misogynist, feels the need constantly to ridicule and symbolically castrate the opposite sex. The reason, Klein stresses, is that the girl's powerful envy of her mother and her relationship with her father, compels her in phantasy to spoil and denigrate her father and all men *for* her mother, her rival, and therefore inevitably, for herself also. Female envy for Klein is not primarily envy of the penis, of what the mother is thought to *want* but rather primitive unresolved envy of what the mother *has*. She argues that it is this envy that may destroy some women's potential for fulfilling relationships with men.

Klein turns next to the boy's relationship with the mother, significantly left undeveloped by Freud. If envy prevails in the boy's relationship with his mother and of course with himself (because envy spoils the inner world as well as the outer), the boy will feel unable to experience successful relationships with women. As in the case for the girl, envy and anxiety will interfere with feelings of intimacy. This is most likely to occur in a situation where the boy has been unable to resolve his castration anxiety by an identification with his father. A boy's excessive envy of his mother, emanating originally from the very early paranoid–schizoid position, will leave him in an essentially 'feminine' identification with her. His unconscious envy will, Klein warns, extend to all feminine characteristics and, in particular, women's capacity to bear children. This envy of the womb of course may be omnipotently denied and projected onto women so that only women's penis-envy is acknowledged as a possibility. In this way womb-envy disappears from patriarchal view.

Envy of the breast, Klein argues, amounts to envy of creativity, of fullness and richness in life generally because the breast, and the milk it gives, is experienced as the source of life. This, frustratingly for babies of both sexes, means life's source lies outside the self. In both sexes, Klein argues, envy of the breast and an unsatisfactory object-relationship with it, leads to a wish in both sexes to spoil, take away and denigrate the attributes of the other sex. As we shall see later in this chapter, women's envy of the mother is more likely to be resolved in the realisation that they will eventually have the same capacity for creativity, whereas boys cannot take comfort in this knowledge. 'Masculine' women can have babies but 'feminine' men cannot. The wish to spoil the good object, the mother and later all women, may explain some men's violence against women in phantasy in the form of pornography and the violent 'acting out' of spoiling phantasies in rape and other forms of violence against women. Of course, we need to remember that envy does not only exist *between* the sexes. Any kind of success or perceived 'richness' in an individual tends to provoke envy from other people – our family, friends, colleagues at work – whether they are the same or the opposite sex. We shall return to the importance of womb-envy and its relationship with both public and private patriarchy and misogyny later, in the 'Discussion' section.

As Juliet Mitchell emphasises, Klein describes integration 'horizontally' in the present rather than on a 'vertical' of past and present more characteristic of Freud's perspective (Mitchell 1986: 26). In therapy, destructive, envious, split-off parts of the self can be accepted and drawn back into the self which has been emptied and impoverished by splitting off so much of itself. Like the young baby, the patient comes to see that both the world and she or he, themselves, are not simply one thing or another but a complex mixture of 'good' and 'bad', loving and hating aspects which have to be acknowledged and integrated as part of the same complex whole. This idea is not the same as an acceptance of the *status quo* or the dominant ideology as is sometimes claimed. It is concerned with the development of the capacity to appreciate the complexity of reality, not to accommodate it, but to convert destructive projection into the creative capacity for empathy, and the acceptance of responsibility. This involves the need for action and change rather than adaptation.

Discussion

In many ways Klein's theory significantly expands the scope of Freud's work. She focuses attention on the vital symbolic importance of the breast in the organisation of identity and confronts us with a primitive, raw, psychotic undertow of feelings, impulses and phantasies which she argues lies behind the rationality of all of us – both in the personal and the public sphere – because we have all been helpless, anxiety-ridden babies. For Klein, phantasy prepares the way for our capacity to engage with reality. Historical contingency can offer us an explanation of how the apparently psychotic touchpapers of destructive behaviour come to be ignited. However this, alone, cannot explain the tendency in some people to idealise certain groups and demonise others, and their capacity for apparently mindless cruelty and destruction. Klein's theory helps us to begin to understand the emotional roots which may lie behind this kind of behaviour in a primitive 'thinking' system of binary phantasies of 'good' and 'evil', projected starkly onto the infinite complexity of what we call reality.

But Klein's theory suggests that if our earliest experience as helpless infants was of loving care by our mother (or a substitute), then we will have been able to construct a sufficiently integrated sense of identity to allow us to break away from this primitive, binary mode of thinking to appreciate the complexity of ourselves and others and have the capacity to feel genuine concern for them as well as ourselves. The work of Mike Rustin explores this idea in relation to the aspirations of socialism (Rustin 1991). Rustin agrees that Klein's work suggests that some people's desire for a caring society, is, at the unconscious level, the cultural expression of our desire to introject or internalise caring 'maternal' institutions alongside 'paternal' authority to create a sense of social integration, concern and reparation which mirrors the individual's successful resolution of the depressive position. Klein's and, as we shall see, Winnicott's work suggest that, in the many contexts of deprivation and violence, all societies, whatever else they do, need to pay attention to the well-being of those who mother. They need to create social circumstances where normal human needs are not pathologised within social discourses as 'dependency' and in which mothers (and fathers) can feel sufficiently emotionally secure and free of frustration to be able to share power with their children and help them acknowledge and resolve primitive emotions. Unemployment, ill-health, inadequate food, housing and other social provision inevitably work against women's and men's ability to give their children what they need. Klein's work suggests that children who develop without the capacity to experience genuine concern for other people or take responsibility for their feelings and actions may, as adults, continue to live within the arid and dangerous confinement of the paranoid–schizoid position unconsciously dominated by primitive oppositions of love and hate, 'good' and 'bad', power and powerlessness. This means that in situations which provoke feelings of helplessness and anxiety, without the psychological experience of integration and acceptance of responsibility for these 'bad' feelings, some individuals or groups may, like the deprived young baby, act out powerful phantasies of destruction experienced as the only means to ensure their own psychical survival. Caught up in powerful phantasies of omnipotent control, such people or groups may be unable to experience the world realistically or to 'think' unconsciously in anything other than simplistic, life-denying oppositions. In these circumstances all those who are perceived as different and potentially vulnerable, are transformed, through identification, into split off parts of the self (containing feelings of vulnerability and anxiety) who then need to be rigidly controlled and, often, victimised. Unfortunately, because power and control is of such importance to these individuals, this kind of behaviour is widely visible in political as well as social and personal life and may be an important factor in destructive political behaviour and the creation of conflict. Acceptance of feelings of helplessness is ruled out as a psychological option because reparation in the depressive position, which entails the development of guilt, has never been experienced and blame, in the form of projection, is still the predominant defence against anxiety. In Kleinian terms, emotional development has been inhibited.

Nowadays, some Kleinians who want to rescue Klein's theory from a reliance on biological instincts, re-define anxiety and helplessness as a state of mind which is at least partly socially constructed. This means that what Klein calls paranoid–schizoid behaviour is seen as a response to feelings of helplessness induced by *society*. Primitive binary thinking and sadistic behaviour on the part of individuals and social and political groups are frequently transformed within social discourses into so-called rationality or common sense. In this view, such behaviour shares many of the characteristics of the emotionally shallow, omnipotent, 'blaming' responses to unacknowledged feelings of dependency in the seriously disturbed paranoid–schizoid or narcissistic patient. In political life, this behaviour, which unconsciously seeks to alleviate feelings of helplessness through projections onto vulnerable, scapegoat others (for example, women, single-mothers, ethnic and national groups, homosexuals, recipients of social welfare, trade-unionists) is frequently concealed in the social discourses of moral panics. Psychologically unable to tolerate feelings of helplessness within the self, individuals and groups who display this kind of behaviour may be caught up in a web of primitive attempts at psychic survival which entail the blaming and obsessive control of others, if not their destruction. The need for psychical survival becomes the dominant value. Fascism, Stalinism, violent forms of nationalism look like extreme social examples of this kind of psychological phenomenon. David Bell's study of changes in the National Health service in Britain, 'Primitive Mind of State' (Bell 1993) is an example of the usefulness of this kind of Kleinian analysis when it is embedded in a particular social, historical moment.

Klein's concept of womb-envy is very important for our understanding of male misogyny. From a Kleinian perspective, patriarchal power and control may be seen as fuelled substantially by male envy of 'femininity', of what is perceived as the creative, life-giving power that 'woman' originally symbolises for the infant. In this context, let us look in a little more detail at the implications of Klein's concept of womb-envy, beginning with the situation of the little girl, since children of both sexes experience this kind of envy. As we observed briefly in the previous chapter, if little girls experience envy of the mother's breasts and womb they are soon in a position to dispel these feelings through the growing awareness that they too are female; they will grow breasts and wombs like their mothers whether they choose to use them for reproduction or not. They will have as one option this potentially creative and life-giving identity. Boys, also envious of their mothers, have to accept that no matter how hard they try they can never have breasts or a womb or produce children, even if they retain an emotional identification with her. In this specific sense boys/men are not creative and have to create other things outside themselves to compete with the potent symbol and actuality of women's biological and emotional creativity. Unresolved, unconscious male envy (and we need to remember that this does not necessarily apply to all men) may be a critical reason why women have been debarred from so much cultural creativity and been confined predominantly to the private sphere, to their biological capacity to bear children. It may also, paradoxically, help to explain the willingness by some, to blame single mothers specifically, for increased crime, homelessness and what is perceived as social and moral disorder and crisis. In her earlier paper 'Early stages of the Oedipal Conflict', written when she was still very much influenced by Freud, Klein suggested that boys mask and over-compensate for their womb-envy by both an over-estimation of the penis and a displacement onto the intellectual plane (Mitchell 1986: 75). An identification with reason, knowledge and culture becomes a way in which men control their envy, an issue which is taken up in the work of Lacan and Irigaray. Klein writes that what she calls the 'femininity complex' in men (which may exist in many patriarchal men) goes with an attitude of contempt and 'knowing better' and is highly asocial and sadistic. Unconscious womb-envy helps to explain the familiar, value-laden opposition between 'nature' (identified with women) and 'culture' (identified with men). Men have no choice but to opt for culture because nature, in the sense of giving birth to and feeding children from their own bodies, is simply unavailable to them. In addition, the experience of reparation and gratitude in relation to the mother may be more difficult to achieve for boys because of the cultural requirement for early separation from her in order to achieve the patriarchal version of 'masculinity'.

However, as I have argued elsewhere (Minsky 1995), the *sight* of the culturally valued penis compared with the *insight* into the power of the life-giving mother rescues the small boy from his psychical predicament. Sight, the culturally prized capacity for observation (the basis for science), triumphs over insight which is never valued to the same extent. The boy can deny the terrifying sense of loss in relation to the powerful meaning of his mother's body, which he can never emulate, and take refuge in the power of the meaning of the symbolic penis/phallus which is then culturally inflated out of proportion. The penis then becomes the misrecognised symbol or sign of unresolved male envy of the mother. The womb remains *insignificant*, that is, it doesn't count as a sign of meaning.

It is interesting in this context to consider the controversy about the exclusion of women from the priesthood. Psychologically, one of the factors involved in this exclusion of women may be the substantial amount of male womb-envy on the part of many men who enter the church. As Luisa Accati suggests this envy may be expressed differently within Catholicism and Protestantism. Within the Catholic church, men who become celibate priests may unconsciously seek a 'feminine' identification with the mother, personified in the elevation of the Virgin Mary as the supreme mediator between God and man. In this sense, in denying women access to the priesthood, 'femininity' is appropriated from real women to female-identified men (Accati 1993). A male God and an all-male priesthood may, within Protestantism, particularly, function as the desired but absent third term – the father – for some men. As Freud suggested (PFL 12: 212), the small boy's relationship with his father is at some level homoerotic (under the influence of the father complex, the boy initially takes his father as well as his mother as a love object in phantasy), so that if this relationship has been absent or unresolved, an all-male priesthood which represents a male God as Father may offer an unconscious opportunity to satisfy unmet homoerotic needs as well as a mechanism for separating from the mother. In this way the church may, for some men, become a sanctuary from the mother and women in general. Protestantism, in contrast to Catholicism, offers a direct, un-mediated, emotional relationship between man and God. This might explain the anguish felt by some male priests about women entering the priesthood and becoming part of the male 'body' of the church. When women are included in this body, its symbolic value as an unconscious source of male, phallic 'rescue' from womb-envy and the mother must be radically and permanently undermined. A similar psychoanalytic explanation may explain attempts to exclude women from other power-ful cultural institutions.

Let us return now to Klein's description of two distinctive modes of unconscious organisation or 'thinking' which may be important for an understanding of the differences between some men and women. The French feminist, Hélène Cixous, following Lacan, argues that the binary oppositions by which we categorise reality in language and culture are based, in the first instance, on the meaning of the phallus and sexual difference, the binary opposition between 'masculinity' and 'femininity'. However, in Klein's work, these binary divisions of meaning seem to stem from the primary oppositions of love and hate which, for her, characterise the paranoid–schizoid world of the baby. From within this perspective there is the possibility that a tendency to think unconsciously in this binary way may represent a tangible difference between patriarchal men and women. This kind of mental organisation may be more characteristic of men than women because men have such a major biological obstacle to resolving their envy of the mother. They may also be prevented from resolving this envy because of their need to separate from the mother much earlier than women to achieve their 'masculinity'. This suggests that many men may be less able to fully achieve the integration of their love and hate because their continuing envy of the mother/'woman' prevents them. This in turn would mean that some men may then project this binary-dominated reality onto women so that women are perceived either as ultimately all-powerful, the source of all wisdom and goodness or as weak, simple-minded and childlike, incapable of complex thought and amoral. Perhaps psychological confinement in a binary mode of thinking prevents certain kinds of men (and the cultural institutions through which their power is mediated) from recognising that power-sharing exists within the space between power and powerlessness and that difference can be celebrated and enjoyed rather than controlled or eradicated. As we shall see in the next chapter, Donald Winnicott highlights the capacity to share power in his concept of the 'good enough' mother who is able to gradually transfer her own power to her child.

Klein's theory also sheds light on the destructive dynamics specifically within the realm of sexual relationships. If, as a small child, rage continues to be provoked by any failure of the mother to meet our demands, a life-long pattern may be established in which we continually search for the primordial lost object, the other who can complete us. However, when we think we have found it, our demands may be so excessive that our partner may feel unable to cope. This is likely to make both partners feel deeply disappointed and helpless.

Children's fairy tales support Klein's view that many of us, as small children continue, in phantasy, to experience the mother, and significant female others, as hateful and frightening some of the time. They provide us with the opportunity to express these feelings in our response to the wicked female represented in figures such as, for example, the wicked stepmother and the ugly sisters in Cinderella, the wolf in Red Riding Hood, the wicked witch in Hansel and Gretel and the bad fairy in Sleeping Beauty.

This brings us to the limitations of Klein's theory. From a Freudian perspective, Klein's work has been criticised because gendered identity is seen as largely biologically determined rather than constructed out of the child's perception of difference. Her version of the unconscious in the form of phantasy is also seen as heavily dependent on biological dispositions to feelings, instincts and defences which although it yields important and fascinating new insights, loses a connection with the idea of the unconscious as a separate, dynamic and potentially subversive system of thought based on desire, with its own language. Desire, the castration complex and the significance of difference are marginalised if not excluded. However, the child's intense early relationship with the pre-Oedipal mother, highlighted only in Freud's later work, is brought out into the open in Klein's theory and its role in the construction of identity explored to great theoretical effect. In this sense, it can be argued, the mother is restored to her rightful place in theory, even though this largely entails her loss as an object of desire and the virtual disappearance of the father as the symbol of difference. In Klein's theory the penis is firmly put in the shade of the all-encompassing and powerful breast, thus eclipsing its power as the symbol of desire and loss.

So, in Klein's theory the mother is the object of relatedness rather than desire, and the father, at best, exists as a part of the mother or a combined parent figure. In Klein's later work the father disappears completely as the divisive but 'humanising' third term. He, and the desires of the Oedipal crisis, have effectively been replaced by the depressive position and guilt and anxiety stem from murderous phantasies in relation to the mother and the father rather than castration anxiety exclusively in relation to the father. All this has important consequences for the theorising of gendered identities. The virtual exclusion of desire means that the range of gendered identities made available to men and women by the unconscious in Freud's work – differences among women and men as well as between them – are not theoretically available in Klein's later work. Overall, in the context of these issues, in Klein's theory we seem to have gained enormous insight into the power of the pre-Oedipal mother and the symbolic breast – and access to a whole new way of thinking about psychical reality as phantasy – but, as a consequence, we have lost the father, desire and the richness of the castration complex as a structural concept in the construction of identity.

Klein's theory has also been criticised from a different perspective by Winnicott who developed the second powerful strand of Object-Relations theory discussed in chapter three. He argues that Klein provides us with a rich picture of the psyche of the maternally *deprived* baby but not, as she claims, of the majority of ordinary babies whose mothers have been what he calls 'good enough'. Winnicott argues that the ordinary baby is not mad and that Klein has pathologised the ordinary infant; only the child with a tantalising mother who has been deprived of adequate mothering will experience the terrors of the paranoid–schizoid position. However, the global evidence of wide-spread adult behaviour which seems to derive from this position would suggest, from within Winnicott's perspective, that many people experience inadequate mothering which leads to the conclusion that many people's social and psychological experience prevents them from being able to mother adequately so that this situation is continuously repro-duced. This issue is taken up by the feminist Object-Relations writer Nancy Chodorow.

The centrality of the powerful mother in Klein's theory of identity provided the inspiration for the perceptive, thought-provoking feminist psychoanalytic writing of Dorothy Dinnerstein. Dinnerstein brings a social and historical dimension to her development of Klein's theory which is lacking in Klein's own theory. She suggests that the 'female monopoly of early child-care' determines the adult emotional patterns of behaviour which support patriarchal societies. As Connel argues, Dinnerstein manages to catch the 'ambivalences of men and women towards each other, and the way childhood resonances in their inter-actions lock the participants into patterns they would not rationally choose' (Connel 1987: 203). Drawing on Klein's description of the pre-Oedipal mother, Dinnerstein deals with women's sexuality, men's hatred of women, women's acceptance of exclusion from 'world-making' in the public arena and, finally, the ecological crisis in contemporary culture based on what she sees as the insatiable attempt to pillage and ultimately destroy the earth (a symbol of the mother). This last concern has led to a brand of feminism known as eco-feminism. Dinnerstein's work has been criticised for being normatively based and therefore unable to account for contradictions and, at times, in its predictions of global disaster as a manifestation of a deadly, potentially suicidal symbiosis between men and women, in danger of undermining the effects of the social order altogether. However, her work is very suggestive and shows the rich potential for analysis at both the individual and social level which Klein's theory has made theoretically possible.

Since the mid-nineteen-forties, Klein's distinctive development of Freud's theory has formed the basis of a separate training programme within the British Psychoanalytical Society. As a result of what were known as 'controversial discussions' of Klein's theory in the British Psychoanalytical Society during 1943–4 which centred around the ques-tion of how far Klein's work was consistent with Freud's, particularly in relation to the issue of phantasy, two distinct kinds of psychoanalytic training were set up. One group consisted of Kleinians and the other of Freudians led by Anna Freud, Freud's daughter. (Freud had died five years earlier.)

Klein's clinical technique has also sometimes been considered contro-versial. She had a reputation for frequent and penetrating interpretations risking what Winnicott called an 'impingement' on her patients' already often over-compliant and fragile selves. This rather phallic side of Klein seems, as Mitchell has pointed out, to belie her emotional capacities for identification and intuition (Mitchell 1986: 30–1). Intriguingly, Klein's theory seems to have grown out of both these aspects of her identity. This seems an appropriate moment to consider some of the important events in Klein's life and some possible reasons why Klein might emphasise and explore certain aspects of identity and marginalise or exclude others, including those dimensions of Freud's theory which many would argue, are the most creative and dynamic.

Presences and absences

On the basis of her autobiography, family letters and Phyllis Grosskurth's biography (Grosskurth 1985), there are a number of features of her life and experience which seem relevant to the focus of her interests and the gaps and omissions in her work. Klein's theory revolves around pre-Oedipal passions: irrational feelings and impulses of intense ambivalence, envy, guilt and reparation in relation to the mother. She herself grew up in a family steeped in narcissism where every relationship seems to have been permeated with intense feelings of envy and guilt. The family was dominated by a mother who from her letters is revealed as immensely powerful, controlling and manipulative despite what appears to have been Klein's life-long idealisation of her. Her father, a doctor, appears to have been academically gifted but, within his family, weak and in-effectual in comparison with the mother. Klein describes him as an 'old fifty' at her birth, and he was twenty-five years her mother's senior. Her work seems to address unconsciously the question of how she could make sense of this family and herself. Her experience of her father may explain why her theory revolves around the all-powerful mother, to the virtual exclusion of the father. Since ideally children need to fall in love with both parents to rehearse the whole range of their sexuality in phantasy, the absence of desire in Klein's theory may relate directly to what she perceived as her emotional neglect and even rejection by her father. For Klein, he apparently never represented a third dimension, capable of interrupting the symbiotic, dependent relationship with her mother which seems to have continued until her mother's death. In her un-published autobiography she wrote 'I have no memories of his ever playing with me. It was a painful thought to me that my father could openly state, and without consideration for my feelings, that he preferred my older sister, his first-born' (Grosskurth 1985: 11). This family drama may be reflected in her theoretical concept of the combined parent figure: the father, the Oedipal crisis, and desire swallowed up by the potency of the object-relation with the mother. All the passionate feelings in Klein's theory seem centred around the earliest relationship with the life-giving mother. Everyone else pales beside this potent figure just as they did in Klein's own life.

Klein's relationship with her much admired, elder brother Emmanuel seems rather unusual. Letters between Emmanuel and herself suggest that the relationship was emotionally more that of lovers than brother and sister. The fact that he was regarded as the academic genius of the family, and that he singled her out as the object of his intense emotion, may have offered an Oedipal substitute for her father, although Emmanuel seems to have been more like his mother in character.

Klein's early experience of grief and the death of close relatives – an older sister when she was four and her brother when she was twenty, the deaths of both parents by her late thirties, and later the death of her own son Eric – may well underlie her intense, life-long interest in mourning and depression. She herself suffered frequent bouts of depression throughout what she later perceived as her early 'self-destructive' and unsuccessful marriage. The connection between guilt, depression, mourning, creativity and reparation in terms of the relationship between inner and outer good and bad objects pre-occupied her throughout her psychoanalytic career and the depressive position forms the mainspring of her theory. Her own creativity seems to have burst into life after her mother's death and her analysis first by Sandor Ferenczi and later by Karl Abrahams, both of whom formed part of Freud's inner circle.

Like that of Freud, Klein's theory seems inevitably to reflect the unconscious interests of its creator. Her own, by many accounts, controlling personality as well as her experience of her mother, seems to have given her insight into the creation of a form of early identity which seems particularly characteristic of the way a baby feels in relation to a mother whose narcissism prevents her adequately relating to the baby's needs and who unconsciously demands the baby's exclusive attention to her own.

Suggested reading

Theory

KLEIN, M. (1931) *The Psychoanalysis of Children*, London, Hogarth Press.

KLEIN, M. and RIVIERE J. (1937) 'Love, Guilt and Reparation' in *Love, Hate and Reparation*, London, Hogarth Press [on the depressive position].

KLEIN, M. (1957) *Envy and Gratitude*, London, Tavistock [an elaboration of the ideas found in her paper 'A Study of Envy and Gratitude'].

KLEIN, M. (1961) *Narrative of a Child Analysis*, London, Hogarth Press [an account of her war-time analysis of an autistic child, Richard, in Scotland].

MITCHELL, J. (1986) *The Selected Melanie Klein*, Harmondsworth, Penguin. [This is a collection of Klein's most useful theoretical papers printed in chronological order. It has an excellent general introduction and each paper is introduced with a clear statement of its context and content. Accounts of Klein's child analysis can be found in 'Psychological Principles of Infant Analysis' (1926) and 'Symbol Formation in Ego Development' (1930). Material which relates to the paranoid–schizoid position can be found in 'Infantile Anxiety Situations Reflected in a Work of Art and in the Creative Impulse' (1929) and 'Notes on Some Schizoid Mechanisms' (1946). Material on the depressive position can be found in 'A Contribution to the Psychogenesis of Manic-Depressive States' (1935) and 'Mourning and Manic-Depressive States' (1940). All are reprinted in this selection.]

General

BELL, D. (1993) 'Primitive Mind of State', paper given at the conference *Psychoanalysis in the Public Sphere*, London, University of East London and Free Association Books.

BERKE, J. (1989) *The Tyranny of Malice*, London, Simon and Schuster.

BREEN, D. (1989) *Talking With Mothers*, London, Free Association Books.

GROSSKURTH, P. (1985) *Melanie Klein*, London, Maresfield Library.

HERMAN, N. (1988) *My Kleinian Home*, London, Free Association Books.

HINSHELWOOD, R.D. (1989) *A Dictionary of Kleinian Thought*, Free Association Books.

HOGGETT, P. (1993) *Partisans in an Uncertain World: The Psychoanalysis of Engagement*, London, Free Association Books.

JUKES, A. (1993) *Why Men Hate Women*, London, Free Association Books.

MCDOUGALL, J. (1989) *Theatres of the Body*, London, Free Association Books.

MELTZER, D. (1978) *The Kleinian Development: Part 2, Richard Week-by-Week*, Perthshire: Clunie Press.

RICHARDS, B. ed. (1984) *Capitalism and Infancy: Essays on Psychoanalysis and Politics*, London, Free Association Books.

RUSTIN, M. (1991) *The Good Society and the Inner World*, London, Verso.

SEGAL, H. (1979) *Klein*, London, Fontana [Modern Masters].

SEGAL, H. (1986) *Delusion and Artistic Creativity and Other Psychoanalytic Essays*, London, Free Association Books.

SEGAL, J. (1985) *Phantasy in Everyday Life*, London, Pelican.

SEGAL, J. (1992) *Klein*, London, Sage.

Feminist Interpretations

ACCATI, L. (1993) 'Explicit Meanings: Catholicism, Matriarchy and the Distinctive Problems of Italian Femininism', *62nd Anglo–American Conference of Historians*, University of London, Institute of Historical Research.

DINNERSTEIN, D. (1978) *The Rocking of the Cradle and the Ruling of the World*, London: Souvenir Press.

MINSKY, R. (1994) 'Reaching Beyond Denial – Sight and In-sight – A Way Forward?', London, *Free Associations*, 34.

RICH, A. (1976) *Of Woman Born: Motherhood as Experience and Institution*, New York, Bantam.

ROSE, J. (1993) *Why War?*, Oxford, Blackwell.

SAYERS, J. (1986) *Sexual Contradictions*, chapter 5: 49–63, London, Tavistock.

SAYERS, J. (1991) *Mothering Psychoanalysis: Hélène Deutsch, Karen Horney, Anna Freud and Melanie Klein*, London, Hamish Hamilton.

WEATHERILL, R. (1994) *Violence and Privacy: Psychoanalysis and Cultural Collapse*, London, Free Association Books.

3
Winnicott: the 'good enough' mother

You can put your principles into a match-box but what fills the whole room is your instinctive responses.

(John Berger, 'A Painter Of Our Time')

Biographical background (1896–1971)

Donald Winnicott was born in Plymouth into a Methodist family, the youngest of three children with two older sisters. His father was a corsetry merchant. He studied medicine at Cambridge and completed his clinical studies in London. During his second year as a student in London, he read Freud's *The Interpretation of Dreams* which made a great impression on him. In 1920 he began to specialise in paediatrics and three years later he became a consultant paediatrician at Paddington Green Children's Hospital and Queen's Hospital, Hackney. He married Alice Taylor, a potter in the same year. At the beginning of the war he was appointed consultant to the government evacuation scheme for children in Oxfordshire and during this period made frequent radio broadcasts giving advice to mothers. At this time, while he was setting up hostels for evacuees, he was able to put many of his psychoanalytic ideas into practice. In 1949 he was divorced from his first wife, and two years later married Clare Britton, a psychiatric social worker with whom he had worked on setting up children's hostels. Within the British Psychoanalytic Society, he was a member of the Middle Group, occupying the space between the Freudians and Kleinians. He was made President twice, from 1956–9 and from 1965–9. Throughout his career he worked as a psychoanalyst and paediatrician – indeed he was the first paediatrician to train as an analyst and published many books, papers, broadcasts and talks to lay audiences. He died in 1971.

Overview of Winnicott's ideas

In some ways it seems inappropriate to include Donald Winnicott in a book about psychoanalytic theory when he himself was so deeply sceptical about the theoretical parcelling up of a reality which, like identity, he believed was always elusive and fundamentally unknowable. He was particularly critical of the kind of psychoanalytic practice which relies heavily on interpretations based on what he regarded as erudite, but potentially imprisoning, dogma. Allied to this distaste for certain kinds of psychoanalytic writing, is Winnicott's preference for simple, homely language rather than difficult jargon. As Phillips emphasises, Winnicott repeatedly uses a handful of idiosyncratic terms to communicate his ideas: holding, using, playing, feeling real, illusion and disillusion, true and false self, going on being (Phillips 1988). However, despite his reservations about the uses of theory and the homely directness of his language, Winnicott's work represents a distinct and very important developmental theoretical approach which makes the baby's relationship with the actual rather than the phantasised mother of central importance.

For Winnicott the coming into being of identity involves the gradual development from the baby's initial dependency to what he calls a 'personal way of being'. He sees this way of being as a sense of 'bodily aliveness', of feelings of being real for one's self, of 'life being worth living' and of being in touch with one's own creativity and spontaneity. But Winnicott thought that this sensation of personal authenticity could only be achieved through a special kind of reliable, creative, non-compliant relationship with the mother in early childhood. His frequent use of words like 'holding' and 'handling' reflect the importance he attached to issues of reliability. He insisted that an individual's potential for a creative sense of what he called 'aliveness' could be damaged if, as a baby, their sense of continuous 'going on being' was broken by a traumatic 'waiting too long' or if the baby was emotionally compelled into a pattern of compliance with the needs of a depressed mother. Winnicott's highly individual re-working of Freud's and Klein's ideas (often until they were barely recognisable) produced a powerful, alternative view of psychical reality which nowadays forms the basis of much eclectic psychoanalytic practice. Although Winnicott believed that anyone could get in contact with their own personal potential for creativity, if they had the right kind of maternal environment, he also took the view that this creative self was always ultimately elusive, unknowable and incommunicable. He wrote of the self, 'A word like "self" naturally knows more than we do; it uses us and can command us' (Winnicott 1965: 158). This idea conflicts with

Freud's belief in the centrality of language within psychoanalytic practice in which the subject 'speaks' a hidden part of the self into existence.

In contrast with Klein's idea that the baby's major task is to achieve a victory over its feelings of hate, for Winnicott, it is to get to the stage when it feels it inhabits its own body. He sees the body and psyche as an essential psychosomatic partnership and took the view that the developmental process must involve the negotiation of this relationship. This is in the context of what he calls the 'good enough' mother, who is able to act as a kind of ultra-sensitive co-ordinator of the baby's chaotic emotions. In his paper 'Primitive Emotional Development' (Winnicott 1958), he describes the baby's earliest predicament as a bundle of disparate emotions or what he calls a condition of 'primary unintegration'. This includes the wish greedily to love the mother but, later, the wish also to hold her off and test her resilience. However, he argues that the baby has a natural developmental tendency to integrate the disparate parts of its self, which is made possible by the mother's special kind of care. The baby, Winnicott insists, is a creature who from its moment of birth, enthusiastically wishes to participate in its own development. Winnicott distinguishes between ordinary care and instinctual experience which is repeated over and over again. This involves the mother in continually gathering together the many bits of the baby's self into a potentially whole person, whilst allowing the baby to feel *it* has been responsible for this creative experience. If the mother, who represents the 'holding environment' cannot enable the baby to integrate its self completely, Winnicott thought that the unintegrated part would be split off or 'disassociated' resulting in a blank or blind spot in the baby's sense of being alive. Whenever the mother moves away she takes with her the baby's identity as well as her own. It is at this stage that we learn to equate loss with our own extinction. Winnicott saw maturity as a condition in which the individual could return sometimes to a state of what he called unintegration, such as day-dreaming, for example, or being absorbed or pre-occupied, but always with the freedom of such an individual to move back into a state of integration again.

Winnicott's work as a whole is not directly concerned with issues of gender difference or sexuality. Like Klein, he took the view that at some level gender difference exists from birth but is reinforced during early childhood. However, his work is of great significance in the study of the construction of 'masculinity' and 'femininity' because of the enormous importance he attributes to the role of the mother in the creation of all identity. His perspective offers us important insight into the reasons for the subordinate position of women. Winnicott argues that the mother, and hence all women, are unconsciously associated with the early terror of psychical annihilation by babies of both sexes. For Winnicott everything hangs on the mother's capacity to relate to her baby which, for him, means the ability to allow the baby to create reality for itself rather than having it imposed on it. As the baby's first contact in life the mother is the primary agent for the achievement of its potential, unique identity. In contrast to Freud and Klein, Winnicott always emphasises the qualities of the *actual* mother rather than the *phantasised* mother. He also emphasises the baby's initial powerlessness in relation to her. Winnicott believed one of the mother's most important tasks is to transfer her power to the developing baby through her ability to empathise with its evolving self.

For Winnicott, Freud and Klein's concepts of life and death instincts are transformed into one single instinct, a single, uncontaminated life-force containing love. If our love is accepted we feel creative, alive and strong but, when it is rejected, we feel as if we have been psychically annihilated. Freud's conception of the death instinct as an innate destructive drive drawing us (by means of our sadism or masochism) towards dissolution and disintegration, is, for Winnicott, based on Freud's confusion between what we normally mean by death, and the creative limitless state we are all in at the beginning of life. This is when the baby feels it is part of an unending whole with the mother and the rest of the holding environment. Winnicott takes the view that all our lives we are mesmerised not by death and destruction, but by a longing for this first unintegrated state of unity with the mother – the original bliss of total acceptance, recognition and plenitude. Only in a situation where there is a lack of love, where the mother is depriving, do we find the creative assertiveness contained within the life-force transformed into a sadistic projection against others or turned against the self in the form of masochism.

The 'good enough' mother

In contrast with Freud's theory of desire and Klein's theory of phantasy, Winnicott's theory of identity is based on the idea of emotional nurture. He was convinced that all babies have the potential from birth for enrichment, creativity, integration and, eventually, a successful separation from the mother provided she can be what he called 'good enough'.

Ideally, *the good enough mother* actively adapts to the needs of the infant rather than the other way round. Her relationship with her baby is one of reciprocity, mutuality, recognition and acknowledgement of whatever the baby takes itself to be at any time. Through what Winnicott calls an 'attentiveness', free of anxiety, the mother allows the baby to create, for itself, a feeling of being real within its own body, a sense of life being worth growing up for. The 'good breast' is Winnicott's way of describing the good mother whose undemanding presence allows the baby to build up 'the basic stuff of the inner world that is personal and, in fact, constitutes the self' (Winnicott 1958: 101). The baby brings to this state of 'meaningfulness' between itself and its mother what Winnicott calls its primary, potential for being. Rather than seeking sexual pleasure, the baby clamours above all for intimacy, sociability and a relatedness which goes beyond the satisfaction of instinct suggested by Freud. Winnicott always sees instincts within the context of the relatedness between the baby and its mother. The Freudian baby's phantasy of sexually penetrating the mother is transformed, in Winnicott's account, into the idea of the baby's wish to emotionally penetrate the mother who, if she can be good enough, is ready and willing to be penetrated.

For Winnicott, the baby, from the very beginning, has an innate authenticity, an awareness of its 'true self'. It makes this available to the relationship with the mother if the mother can facilitate the baby's desire to find it. By keeping the world she presents to the baby simple, the mother gives it the capacity to move freely between its inner and outer world. In this perspective, the baby is seen as an agent in its own creative development who longs to be understood and recognised, and waits for acknowledgement in the mother's face which, through its capacity for responsiveness, he argues in 'Mirror-role of Mother and Family in Child Development', reflects the baby's self back to itself like a mirror (in Winnicott 1971). Drawing on Freud's theory of narcissism, Winnicott argues that it is the quality of the mother's responsiveness that endows the baby with its identity. The child sees itself mirrored in the mother's gaze and voice, in the way she holds it in her mind as well as in her arms, in her touch and in the quality of unspoken understanding and empathy she brings to her responses to the baby's needs and the way she communicates to it that it is lovable, full of potential and a person who gives joy and pleasure to the beholder. Any serious interruption or disruption in this relationship – the baby waits too long for the mother, becomes traumatised and gives up hope – interferes with the baby's lifeline, what Winnicott calls its 'going on being' so that it loses its sense of coming into existence, its sense of a continuous self. This is replaced by feelings of deadness rather than aliveness (feelings we associate with depression) and, in its extreme form, psychosis. It is this primitive pain of excessive deprivation, of a kind of emotional blackout, that leads to serious disturbance in later life and even serious physical illness. For Winnicott, the unconscious is the place where these early deprivations are kept.

Illusionment

In Winnicott's conceptual world the mother provides the creative opportunities for the baby's *illusionment* (what Freud called phantasy) before its later confrontation with reality or *disillusionment*. Winnicott's emphasis of the importance of the baby's capacity for illusionment draws directly on Freud's description of the baby's ability magically to conjure up a phantasy or hallucination of the mother's breast before it 'eats' it. In 'Primitive Emotional Development' (in Winnicott 1988) Winnicott focuses on how the good enough mother can make this act of personal creativity possible for the baby. The baby imaginatively conjures out of its desire for the mother an idea of the breast it wants and at the same time, crucially, the mother is 'waiting to be found'. Winnicott suggests that by doing this she allows the baby actively to create its own good breast and realise its phantasy of control and possession. Winnicott sees phantasy, or what he calls 'illusion', as existing earlier than reality and argues that the experience of illusionment allows the baby to enrich its phantasies with positive experiences from the real world as it does when it, apparently magically, conjures up the breast it desires. Phantasy is not a substitute for reality but provides, in the context of the mother's care, the means of finding it. Later, phantasy may be used as a way of escape from the inner world, sometimes, perhaps, in day-dreaming.

Disillusionment

After providing the opportunity for illusionment, Winnicott argues that the mother must then, gradually, create the opportunity for dis-illusionment. This involves her adapting to the baby less exactly so it gradually confronts the fact that it cannot omnipotently control the world. Winnicott argues that the task of the good enough mother, at this stage, is to allow the baby to resolve creatively its gradual separation from her through her ability to contain its ruthless tendencies. For Winnicott, in contrast to Klein, these tendencies are not seen as destructive but related to the baby's impulse for life. They represent the baby's aliveness and capacity for assertiveness and creativity. Winnicott describes the baby's aggression as 'original ruthless virtue' or a 'primitive ruthless love', a form of aggression which he thinks is initially fused in with the baby's primitive impulse to love. Winnicott describes his view of aggression and the concept of 'ruthlessness' in a variety of papers: 'Aggression in Relation to Emotional Development', 'Primary Maternal Pre-occupation', 'The Anti-social Tendency', 'Hate in the Countertransference' (all in Winnicott 1958) and 'The Use of an Object and Relating Through Identification' (in Winnicott 1971). For Winnicott, aggression is vitally necessary for the child to achieve its individuation or separation from the mother as it begins to experience both its love and dependence as sometimes over-whelming. At first this aggression might take the form of biting the mother's breast. In the baby's play, the mother increasingly has to be able to tolerate the baby's 'ruthlessness' as it seeks to symbolise its growing separation from her, to negotiate the route from its inner world to external reality. If the mother is unable to cope with this ruthless play, the child may never make contact with its creative ability to be its self and, as a consequence, there is a risk that it may destructively turn its aggression inwards leading to psychosomatic illness or depression. So, as the baby matures, the good enough mother conceived by Winnicott, has to act as a container for the baby's aliveness even when it takes the form of aggression or non-compliance.

Winnicott also sees the baby's later aggression towards the mother, after its separation from her, what he calls its 'use' of her, as inherently creative. This is the means by which the baby tests the limitations of the environment, after having been part of the mother, rather than the expression of a destructive impulse as it is in Klein. If the baby is not sometimes able to hate, then love will not feel fully real to him or her. Winnicott writes:

> Shall I say that, for a child to be brought up so that he can discover the deepest part of his nature, someone has to be defied, and even at times, hated, without there being a danger of a complete break in the relationship. (Winnicott 1984: 52)

This particular 'use' of the mother is a kind of benign exploitation. The baby's belief in the durability and reliability of an external world beyond its own phantasies of omnipotence depends on the mother's capacity to survive after these destructive attacks. By surviving, she develops her own autonomy and life with which the baby can identity. This is something different from its earlier fusion with her. The proof of the mother's resilience makes possible a shared reality with her in the external world. In Winnicott's world, what we call reality or culture does not inevitably frustrate the child like the reality of Freud and Klein. It is potentially enriching and reassuring even when it takes the form of disillusionment and the way it sets limits to the baby's omnipotent phantasies of control. Winnicott sees the child's vital transition from phantasy to reality as a means to self-realisation and growth, rather than a painful confrontation with the loss of the mother as it is for Freud. As Adam Phillips suggests, in contrast to Klein, the baby's own survival is what creates the subject and not his or her reparation to the mother. The mother must be resilient, but in a non-retaliatory way.

The false self

Winnicott's central concept of the *false self* emerges from his ideas about what happens if there is a failure in the child's 'holding' environment, that is, of adequate maternal provision. In most of the examples Winnicott gives, this takes the form of the depressed mother who, instead of responding to the baby's needs, demands reactions to her *own* needs, forcing adaptation and compliance from the baby. This is what Winnicott describes as 'maternal deprivation'. He writes:

> The feeling of being real is absent and if there is not too much chaos the ultimate feeling is futility. If not chaos there is a false self that hides the true self, that complies with demands, reacts to stimuli, that rids itself of instinctual experiences by having them, but that is only playing for time.
> (Winnicott 1958: 304–5)

As a result the baby's creativity is distorted into an attempt to establish the nurturing environment it needs, but which the mother cannot provide. This means it unconsciously tries to nurse its mother's needs into health so she can then care for it more adequately. This essentially amounts to the baby trying to keep the mother emotionally alive. The child may, at the same time, seek to make reparation to the mother for something it does not understand and has not done. Ultimately, for

Winnicott, the false self (existing to varying extents depending on the degree of deprivation), represents a denial of the reality of a self which has been dissociated or split off. It is a smoke-screen behind which the child and later adult attempts to cope with life without a viable sense of identity.

In 'Reparation in Respect of Mother's Organised Defence against Depression' (in Winnicott 1958), Winnicott stresses the danger of the child having to live reactively to keep the mother cheerful rather than the other way round. Only when the baby does not have to react, can it begin to 'be' for its 'self'. Winnicott argues that at the beginning the child has so little identity that every reaction to the needs of the mother results in a loss of identity.

The idea of *compliance* is central to Winnicott's theory of the false self. If the baby is forced by its separation anxiety out of its own natural mode of creativity into one of compliance with the moods, needs and reality of the mother, it will feel a sense of estrangement from its own self and its body which, as we have seen, Winnicott always sees as constituting a psychosomatic unity, and which have to be felt in relation to each other. A mother whose own needs make it impossible for the baby to penetrate her – in the sense of allowing the baby's psychical being or presence to enter her reality – denies the baby her appreciation of its 'realness', of its existence, not only for herself but also itself. The baby is constantly confronted by what is incomprehensible and the mother is unable to make either the world, or itself, intelligible. The false self which results always lacks its own creative originality and hides the baby's and later adult's 'core self' which has to be protected from the ultimate catastrophe of annihilation. Where for Freud, castration is the ultimate disaster, and for Klein the overwhelming of the psyche by hate, for Winnicott it is annihilation of a central essence, authenticity or core.

In the adult, when compliance remains the dominant way of relating in relationships, the unconscious alienation from the self continues and, if an emotional relationship breaks down, neurotic illness may ensue because he or she has sacrificed too much of the self to the other, made too many life-denying concessions in the interests of maintaining the relationship. Sometimes, in a desperate bid to break out of this inhibiting need to please an often elusive other, an individual may unconsciously go into reverse, so that nothing a partner asks can be complied with. Both of these ways of coping, first with the fear of loss of the relationship and later, with fear of loss of the self, are potentially destructive of relationships and the self. Our determination to survive and maintain a good relationship with those more powerful than ourselves is one of the major characteristics of childhood. As children we all learn to make concessions but if we have to make too many, this denial of our own potential for development may leave a residue of severe loss of self, longing and, in some men, the desire for revenge on women. Of course, in a woman, the desire for revenge may be expressed in relationships with men but this does not take place within a context of cultural acquiescence as it often does for men.

A further problem may arise if the baby is compelled to develop a false self by having to react to the mother's needs too much. In later life as an adult, it may constantly need to surround itself with impingements, a continuous round of demands and situations to which it has to react, in order to make itself feel alive. In 'The Mind and its Relation to the Psyche-Soma' (in Winnicott 1958) Winnicott argues that the child needs to get to the stage where it can mother its own self with its mind. But if the mothering has been inadequate because of the mother's depression or emotional deprivation the child may develop a phantasy of self-sufficiency which means that it can live *entirely* in its own mind. In this situation the mind is used not to continue the mother's care but to displace it altogether. The child's psyche tries to neglect and disown the body which is felt to be a persecutor. What Winnicott calls excessive mental functioning, thinking as a substitute for feeling, may be the baby's, and later the adult's way of dealing with the problem of unreliable mothering, since for Winnicott there should, ideally, be no such thing as the mind isolated from the body, living in the head. An excessive interest in thinking and knowledge for its own sake is a form of splitting off part of the psyche which has been inadequately nurtured, what he calls *disassociation*. Retreat into a mechanical world of the intellect or work becomes an attempt to deaden and blot out painful feelings associated with loss and deprivation. Men may, again, be particularly prone to this kind of defence because of their enforced early separation from the mother experienced as deprivation. Within a Freudian context we could describe this same phenomenon as a form of narcissism. We unconsciously take an identity from something outside our self, as a substitute for the lack of a self gained through successful separation from the mother in childhood.

Winnicott's false self describes the child whose potential aliveness and creativity has gone unnoticed. As a result, it may painfully withdraw from the world, concealing an empty, barren internal world behind a mask of independence and self-sufficiency. As an adult it may only be able to survive by means of this defensive false self and women, in particular, may be perceived, like the mother, as a potential source of psychical death which has only just been avoided. The relationship between an excessive pre-occupation with theory and knowledge is explored further in the work of Irigaray in chapter five.

Transitional phenomena

The question of how the baby makes the transition from dependency to relative independence preoccupied Winnicott throughout his life. As a solution he developed two of his most original concepts, the ideas of the *transitional object* and the *transitional space*, which he sometimes calls the *potential space*. The transitional object is a toy, a piece of rag or any object which becomes, for the child engaged in separation from the mother, a symbol of her, its own self and the external reality it wants to see objectively. It symbolises the child's negotiation of the transition from what Winnicott calls subjectivity to objectivity, from an inner world to an outer one from which its projections and phantasies have been removed. The crucial ingredient of the transitional object is that it is the child's own creative choice, that its status is never challenged, and that it is never interfered with or altered by anyone else, for example, by washing. It represents for the child the state of its psyche in a delicate and fragile balance between intimacy and separation.

In parallel with the transitional object, Winnicott also developed his crucial concept of the transitional space or potential space. This is a psychical space, a place between the baby and its mother, which represents a bridge connecting the subjective to the objective, the inner to outer world where the relationship between phantasy and reality can be explored and negotiated. This replaces Freud's idea of the penis as the same kind of potential connection. Through a quiet, spontaneous playfulness and mutual participation which is pre-verbal, the transitional space offers a creative opportunity for the exploration of what Winnicott describes as 'what life is, itself, about' (Winnicott 1971: 116). The strength of the transitional space compared with language, is that it is creative because it is *provisional and inconclusive*, like artistic experience. These concepts will be discussed further in the commentary on 'Transitional Objects and Transitional Phenomena'.

Winnicott became distrustful of people using knowledge as a defence against emotional pain or as a substitute identity. Always wary of too much interpretation in analytical sessions, he rarely writes about knowing in the formal, non-intuitive sense. He saw much interpretation, however clever or insightful, as potentially an invasion of the child's or patient's core self, of its capacity, given time, for making its own creative sense of itself, and he writes of 'those who fear to wait and who implant' (Winnicott 1965: 100). In describing the ideal condition for awareness he writes enigmatically, 'The object must be found in order to be created' (Winnicott 1965: 189). The mother's, and later the therapist's, relationship with the subject is founded on the mutual involvement in illusionment in which the baby or the patient participates in the creation of its self. Winnicott continually emphasised the intuitive understanding rather than the theoretical knowledge which Klein valued so much. Winnicott's conception of the self became increasingly one of a 'hide and seek self', always ultimately unwilling to be known. He describes invasions by the mother or the therapist as 'impingement', as thefts of the child's or patient's creative ownership of their own knowing, in their own time. The paradox of both wanting to communicate and wanting to hide, lies at the centre of Winnicott's idea of the true self or core of our identity (Winnicott 1965: 179–92).

Being and doing

As many people have observed, Winnicott's preoccupation with the importance of mothering, like Klein's, seems to have resulted in a theory of identity which largely excludes the role of the father and desire, and nowadays most eclectic therapists acknowledge the importance of the role of the father as well as the mother in the transitional space. However, in a fascinating paper 'Creativity and its Origins' (in Winnicott 1971), Winnicott does address the issue of what he regards as male and female psychical components within the identity of both sexes. In this paper he describes how he interprets Freud's concept of bisexuality in both men and women within his own frame of reference. He understands it as representing two different, but vital, aspects of an individual's potential for creative object-relating which he designates 'being' and 'doing'. He equates these with the pure female element and the pure male element which, he argues, exist in everyone.

Winnicott's male and female elements cannot be reduced to the traditional active and passive capacities of gender stereotype because both, he insists, exist only in the pure male element of a person's identity. He calls the male element that part of everyone's identity which is involved in both active relating (or 'doing') and passive being related to. Each of these is supported by instincts or drives in relation to what Freud called the main erotogenic zones (areas which give rise to sexual pleasure or excitement). However, Winnicott argues, the pure female element which consists of the capacity to 'be', to feel alive, must always be in place before 'doing' can begin. The female element is the baby's first relationship to the breast when it imagines its own identity, and that of the breast, are the same. Against Freud, Winnicott argues that in this relationship there are no instincts or drives present. In what he describes as the simplest of all experiences, the baby relates to the first object, which it has not yet repudiated, as a 'not me' phenomenon. Unless the baby has first achieved an identity of being as one with the mother, Winnicott insists, it can never feel at one with anybody. It will always need a false self. By contrast, the object-relating of the male element pre-supposes separateness. (We need to keep in mind here that Winnicott's male and female elements exist in *both* sexes.) Winnicott comments that this may be the reason for male envy of women, whose female element men often take for granted (sometimes in error in the case of a male-identified woman). The mother's ability to allow the baby to create the breast imaginatively, enables it to create a symbol of its own being *before* mother and baby are separated out in the baby's rudimentary mind. If the mother is unable to make this contribution, the baby has to develop without the capacity to 'be' fully. As an adult, such a person may be caught up in a false self and a compulsive cycle of 'doing' to conceal the absence of 'being'. Ultimately, Winnicott makes the female element associated with the mother, the crucial component of all identity. Without it compulsive doing may stand in for spontaneity and creativity which has never been able to develop. Unlike Klein, Winnicott suggests that envy of the breast is not provoked in the child who feels itself to be a *part* of the breast (that is who has created the breast imaginatively) for whom the breast represents self-discovery, a sense of existing, the capacity to develop an inner life, a container, the possession of some degree of interiority. Without this we may, as adults, become involved in destructive or unfulfilling relationships because we have no knowledge of other kinds of relationship. We may also resort to a false self and an adult life dominated and inhibited by compulsive doing and the need for constant control of the self and other people.

Playing and reality

Winnicott's insistence on the role and importance of the *play* shared by mother and baby, is one of the most striking dimensions of his work. In a characteristicly mischievous moment he describes psychotherapy as being 'to do with two people playing' (Winnicott 1971: 44). It is through play, he suggests, that the child – and patient in therapy – go through the process of finding out through pleasure what interests them, and Winnicott took the view that play, and the artistic imagination and enjoyment of art, take place in the same psychical space. For him, the artist is the one who most completely embodies the desire for authenticity and the kind of personal integrity that he values most. Describing artistic ability he writes: 'Through artistic expression we can hope to keep in touch with our primitive selves whence the most intense feelings and even fearfully acute sensations derive, and we are poor indeed if we are only sane' (Winnicott 1958: 150).

Like Klein, Winnicott took the view that the baby was born in a state of initial 'unintegration' dominated by its primitive greed for its mother and desire for total control of her. After the war, he made some interesting speculations about the pychical sources of fascism which revolve around the idea of how the baby resolves its anxiety about the contradiction between its primitive greed and its need to be independent (Winnicott 1987: 210–20). The question which preoccupied him was how does a person grow from their earliest state of primitive greed and total helplessness to a sense of relative autonomy in which they can relate to other people without too much loss of spontaneity and desire? Importantly, in the context of fascism, he asked how this growth is achieved without the false solution of a rigid set of self-controlling convictions or a strong leader by whom they are controlled and made compliant. On the basis of his later work, Winnicott's answer to this question seems to have been the vital importance of what happens in the transitional space between the mother and child. Here, the issue of intimacy and separation, can be resolved by the child in an emotional climate of provisionality and the *absence of absolute values*. Thus compliance with an internal set of rigid convictions, or with an external leader, are never perceived as a viable, creative option. In his paper 'Some Thoughts on the Meaning of the Word Democracy' (in Winnicott 1964b) he suggests that there is a precarious but innate democratic tendency in the developing baby, given the right kind of maternal environment. This seems to be another way of expressing the idea explored earlier that a 'good' experience in early infancy lays the ground for a wish to repeat the same kind of creative experience in the wider culture.

Winnicott belonged to what is known as the British school of psychoanalysis which was represented by the Middle Group within the British Psychoanalytical Society. (The other two groups were the supporters of Freud and Klein.) Winnicott's group was in favour of an eclectic approach within a more empirical tradition. Its members emphasised observation, empathy, the provision of a 'holding' environment, a confidence in people's ability to make themselves known and to be understood. They distrusted too much abstraction, interpretation and dogmatism. Fundamentally, they believed that the most certain aspect of the construction of human identity, including the capacity for each sex to have access to both its 'masculine' and 'feminine' dimensions, was its gradual development and that it would happen spontaneously, given the right kind of maternal environment.

Commentary on 'Transitional Objects and Transitional Phenomena'

In this paper Winnicott is concerned with what he sees as a crucial issue in the formation of identity. This is the means by which the baby manages to separate from the mother and become a creative, imaginative individual who is able to participate in relationships and enjoy a variety of cultural experiences. Winnicott starts by focusing on the baby's first use of what he calls a 'not me' object. This ranges from its own fist which it pushes into its mouth soon after birth, to its later use of soft and hard toys. He argues that the importance of these objects lies not primarily in their capacity to give oral pleasure, but in their ability to provide a vitally important intermediate area of experience. This experience lies somewhere between the baby's fused identity with the mother and its later capacity for a relationship between two, objectively perceived, separate people. He calls these objects 'transitional objects'. As objects in the external world which are invested with meaning from the inner world, they are able to represent an area between what Winnicott sees as the baby's primary creativity based on phantasy or 'illusion', and the projection of this internal good object onto the world so that we can perceive it objectively. (For Winnicott, and most psychoanalysts, objective reality or the external world is always mediated to some extent by the projections we make onto it.) Transitional phenomena represent a psychical space between the baby's experience of being dominated by its omnipotent illusion of total control, without any genuine interchange between itself and the mother, and its later acknowledgement of indebtedness (what Klein had called gratitude) and concern for the mother as a separate person. It is the intermediary state between the baby's ability and lack of ability to recognise and accept reality.

Winnicott identifies the baby's meandering medley of songs and disorganised burblings just before going to sleep as a striking example of transitional phenomena. These create an intermediate space through which the baby comes to terms with its confusing but necessary progress from the external reality of the day to the inner world of sleep, dreaming and phantasy.

Winnicott takes the view that the traditional division within psychoanalysis between inner and outer reality is inadequate as a description of human experience. He suggests that we need to include a third state of intermediate experience to which inner phantasy and outer reality always contribute but which, of itself, is neither of these. This is the place where the subject and the object are able to merge into one (but, importantly, only after the baby has already been able to differentiate between them). It is also a resting place for the individual involved in the continuous task of trying to keep inner and outer reality separate, but interrelated. We experience it when we day-dream or are totally absorbed in listening to music or creating something ourselves. It represents a state of living neither in a perpetual state of phantasy (madness) nor a perpetual state of imprisoning rationality. Winnicott emphasises that the baby can only enter this intermediary area if it has been allowed the experience of illusionment in the earliest stages of its life by a good enough mother. It is essential for the baby's future identity that it is allowed a phase in which it imagines that it has omnipotently created everything, especially the mother's breast. If the baby has been allowed this initial illusionment, it is in a position to use the transitional object to help it connect this early identity based on illusion to its recognition of the external world. Winnicott gives another example of the baby's first use of transitional phenomena. This is its use of a corner of its blanket, an external object, which it takes into its mouth together with its fingers or thumb.

Winnicott suggests that the use of a full-blown transitional object emerges anywhere between four and twelve months. As we saw earlier, this may be a piece of material or a soft toy which is carried around and considered absolutely necessary at times of loneliness or depression. To the outsider it appears only as an external object, but the baby experiences it as saturated with inner reality. The particular texture of the transitional object is all-important for giving it a tangible sense of 'aliveness' and resonance. Eventually, Winnicott suggests, the object is relegated to limbo but not lost or mourned. It simply loses meaning as the baby's transitional areas are spread over a much wider domain, particularly in what Winnicott regards as the crucial area of play. Winnicott goes on to define some areas of intermediate experience in the child or adult: artistic creativity, religious feeling, day-dreaming, fetishism, lying and stealing, falling in and out of love, drug addiction and symbolic objects involved in rituals. For Winnicott, all these represent a psychological space between inner and outer reality where the interplay between the two may be negotiated and recognised.

Winnicott turns next to the idea of the transitional object as a symbol. He assumes that it must be a symbol of the breast but argues that, just as importantly, it is also a symbol of the process by which the baby comes to accept both difference from itself (external reality) and similarity to itself (inner reality) at the same time. It is therefore a symbol of objective perception and subjectivity simultaneously. But, Winnicott emphasises again, the baby must, already, be able to distinguish between phantasy and reality before it can successfully embark on the intermediate area where the creative interplay between these apparent opposites can be delicately negotiated.

Winnicott next offers some clinical evidence to illustrate the vital importance of the transitional object for an individual's future relationships as an adult. For a viable sense of identity, the baby has to progress from its love or need of the actual mother to a transitional object during the first year. But, Winnicott insists, the child is only in a position to employ a transitional object if its internal object, the mother, is 'alive', 'real' and good enough, that is if the child's first environment has been adequate. The transitional object is not under magical, omnipotent control as the phantasised breast has been (which the baby experiences as a part of the self). But neither is it outside control as the actual mother proves to be. It symbolises the recognition of the interplay between the two.

At this point, Winnicott reminds the reader of what the vital process of illusionment–disillusionment entails. The vital enrichment of the baby's residual self depends on an initial period of almost exact adaptation to its needs by the mother. Only this allows it to establish confidence in its own creative, if illusory, power. Enrichment consists in the baby being allowed to imagine that it has been able to recreate the breast over and over again. It is up to the mother to give the baby the illusion that there is an external reality which corresponds to the baby's own capacity to create. There must be an overlap between what the mother supplies, and what the baby might wish for. Later the mother adapts less, but the baby copes because, on the basis of its good experiences, it is aware that its frustrations will not last for ever. Its cognitive abilities are also beginning to develop, it has learned to gain pleasure from its own body and to remember, relive, phantasise and dream, which all involve an integration of the past with the present. If the disillusionment progresses well, the infant will learn from its frustration. It recognises that it feels more 'real' if it is hated, as well as loved, by the mother. It gains a sense of being able to have more than one effect on the mother, and when the love is apparent again, it has the experience of unconditional love which continues in spite of the hate or irritation.

Winnicott sees the mother's tacit acceptance of the status of the baby's use of the transitional object as a matter of vital importance. He suggests that the task of accepting reality is never completed, so that there is always a strain involved in our negotiation of the successful interplay between phantasy and reality in our relationships with future objects. For Winnicott, intermediate experiences provide relief from this strain which, like the child's transitional object, is never challenged in terms of its status as reality. At first, this is the baby's play with the mother which Winnicott sees as of central importance. Later it is the participation in, and enjoyment of, culture generally. For Winnicott, there is a direct continuity between creative play with the mother and the enjoyment of artistic and cultural experience. Here, knowledge is provisional and inconclusive and the interplay between phantasy and reality remains undefined and unchallenged. Winnicott always believed that intuition and knowledge through spontaneous (not imposed) play – which for him includes art, and psychotherapy – is ultimately of more importance than knowledge in the form of statements and direct interpretation where the opportunity for shared illusion is absent. (This absence, in the context of the mother–baby relationship, is what creates the need for the false self.) He wrote:

> Should an adult make claims on us for our acceptance of the objectivity of his subjective phenomena we discern or diagnose psychosis. If, however, the adult can manage to enjoy the personal intermediate area without

making claims, then we can acknowledge our own corresponding inter-mediate areas, and experience pleasure in finding a degree of overlapping, that is to say, common experience between members of a group in art or religion or philosophy. (Winnicott 1971: 14)

In play and artistic experience, he argues, no claims to objective 'truth' can ever be made. What is important in these activities is the shared enjoyment of the interplay between our inner subjectivity and external reality in a context where their meanings may be explored and negotiated.

Discussion

Despite Winnicott's attempts to distance himself from classical analysis, especially in the homespun quality of his language, in many ways his work is a development of Klein's ideas and Phillips compares Winnicott's relationship with the psychoanalytic tradition generally to the baby's 'benign exploitation of the mother' (Phillips 1988: 86). Like Klein, Winnicott emphasises the importance of the inner world, the complexity and power of phantasy, the central ideas of primitive greed and an initial state of unintegration which somehow has to be turned into integration. All these ideas were taken over by Winnicott who shares Klein's fundamental belief in development but not a development based on a conflict between instincts of love and hate. For Winnicott, as we have seen, both love, and what he describes as a primitive ruthless love rather than aggression, are both harnessed to the baby's capacity to relate (Winnicott 1988: 70).

For Winnicott, the rapport with the mother has to happen before there can be any satisfaction of the instincts; 'It is not instinctual satisfaction that makes the baby begin to be, to feel that life is real, to find life worth living', he writes (Winnicott 1971: 116).

Winnicott's originality lies in his conception of transitional phenom-ena and the idea of play as the intermediate space in which the child integrates inner and outer reality. As we have seen, he sees play as the direct precursor of an individual's capacity for self-realisation in artistic and creative, cultural experience. Winnicott described the creative and imaginative identity as one which lies between the isolation of madness and the impoverished futility of objectivity and reason alone.

Marion Milner (who also used the pseudonym Joanna Field) in her books *A Life of One's Own* (1986) and *On Not Being Able To Paint* (1971), uses Winnicott's concept of transitional phenomena to explore the nature of genuine happiness, creativity and art. In *On Not Being Able To Paint*, she suggests that painting, and by implication all artistic experience, takes place in the intermediate space where 'body and mind meet in expressive action' in the kind of state of absorption which we normally associate with day-dreaming. She describes painting as finding a bit of the outside world, whether in chalk or paper, which is willing to temporally fit in with our dreams or inner world, where a moment of illusion is made possible in which inner and outer reality seem to coincide and merge. Like Winnicott, Milner sees this creative intermediary space as involving a process of reciprocity between phantasy and the external world, as an attempt to express the wholeness of certain attitudes which logic and science, on their own, can never do. Art brings subject and object together in a special kind of unity. It is a way of trying to create ourselves, make sense of our loves and hates, and at the same time, the world outside. Our view of ourselves inter-penetrates with the view of the external world because of our capacity to project. This is why a grey day sometimes makes us feel bleak or sad. She suggests that creative expression in art sometimes makes the internal chaos we all feel easier to face because we can combine it with the external world – paint, paper – and give it a life in the world. For Milner, embodying the experience of illusion in artistic activity provides the vital basis for 'realising, making real, for feeling as well as knowing the external world', for what she describes as 'contemplative action', a state of combining both being and doing (Milner 1950: 140). Art can allow the individual to think without being drowned in feeling. Always concerned with the nature of creativity generally, she differentiates between two kinds of creativity within culture: creativity in art is about making symbols for feeling and creativity in science is about making symbols for knowing. Insisting that these must be complementary even though our culture encourages us to value one to the exclusion of the other, Milner argues for an education which integrates feeling and reflective thinking, never one based on reason and logic alone.

So, for Milner, like Winnicott, art provides the opportunity for us to give up the apparent certainty of logic and reason for an experience which like play, is a state where dream and the external world are fused. She likens it to an active stillness of waiting and watching that includes inner and outer in a unity which, crucially, also recognises that these dimensions are separate (Milner 1971: 93). She, like Winnicott, sees the artist as engaged in what everyone is doing all the time. The freedom to do this in art is derived from having entered into an active relationship with the 'other', external reality, which we can do only if we have been able to do this early in our life with the mother or her substitute. She describes this as 'spreading out the Imaginative body in wide awareness' (Milner 1971: 107). Like Winnicott, imagination and creativity must always be integrally linked to the experience of the self as embodied, the sensation that we exist inside our own body and not outside it.

Winnicott's perspective is an inherently optimistic one. For Winnicott, both Freud's and Klein's theories, entailing a death instinct, smacked of theories of original sin. He replaced them with a theory of what looks much more like original innocence. In Winnicott the emphasis is always on the need for a creative mother-and-baby relationship, whereas Freud highlights the role of the father as the one who breaks in on the mother–baby couple, symbolises difference and thus helps the child separate from the mother. The violence of this scenario is in contrast with the quiet self-sufficiency of the mother–baby couple in the transitional space in which the child, ideally, never has to repress the pain of its loss. In Freud, in the face of what are experienced as hostile cultural demands, the child is thrown into mourning and trauma which establish, all at once, the formation of the unconscious, gender and subjectivity.

Winnicott's work, as well as being the most optimistic, is perhaps also the most humane and accessible of all the approaches discussed in this book. He took the view that every baby has the innate potential to blossom without complication into a creative human subject if it has the right kind of emotional environment. However, his critics argue, that he places an enormous responsibility on the instinctive sensitivity and imagination of the mother. (Nowadays, however, in the context of men's increased involvement in early child-care, therapists usually include the father in their notion of the transitional space so that much of what constitutes Winnicott's idea of the 'good enough' mother now also applies to the father.) Some feminists have perceived Winnicott's emphasis on the importance of the good enough mother as mother-blaming. However, Winnicott thought that the mother's responsibility arose specifically from her physical capacity to have children, if she chose, and from the early bodily and emotional connection between mother and baby. In his autobiography he wrote that his career was informed by 'the urge to find and appreciate the ordinary good mother – for me, it has been to mothers that I have so deeply needed to speak' (Winnicott 1987: 123). We shall explore Winnicott's relationship to his own mother in the next section. Winnicott's insistence on the baby's need for substantial contact with a good enough mother or mother substitute (which may include nursery carers as well as fathers) in the earliest years of childhood has been widely accepted, although it has been used ideologically by those who have wanted to coerce women to stay in the home, particularly in the immediate postwar period. But, like Klein, Winnicott's insistence on the importance of a certain kind of responsive, creative mothering in the baby's earliest years also suggests the need for social arrangements which allow women and men to look after their very young children if they choose to, supported by high-quality nursery provision and adequately paid maternity and paternity leave without substantial loss of earnings or prospects in the future.

Unlike Klein, Winnicott makes the mother's depression, and not the child's 'depressive position' central to his approach. His account of the 'deadening' effects of the depressed mother on the development of her baby's identity seem of considerable significance for societies where the incidence of depression in women is almost twice that of men. This aspect of Winnicott's work which has been taken up by the feminist writers Nancy Chodorow, Luise Eichenbaum and Susie Orbach who locate needy and often depressed mothers firmly at the centre of patriarchal societies. They see depression in women as the inevitable outcome of women's lives within these societies. Winnicott suggests that this may have a devastating effect on their children's potential development.

Winnicott's work has been described as a flight from the erotic. It is certainly true that, even more than in Klein, his work largely excludes the idea of the baby's desire, either for the father or the mother. The drive is seen not as pleasure or desire but rather as a relational element in the developmental process. The baby's love for the mother is relational, a source of its being and potential for being rather than sexual as it is in Freud. Even in Winnicott's conception of the psyche as a psychosomatic unity, the body is rarely associated with desire or eroticism. However, Winnicott does acknowledge the father's role in the Oedipal phase when he refers to the need for the father's intervention during the later stages of the child's primitive ruthlessness as a way of containing the child's excited, aggressive love for the mother. He suggests that up until that time 'the child is not yet advanced enough to make use of the idea of a father intervening, and by intervening making the instinctual ideas safe'.

In the next paragraph, still on the subject of ruthlessness, Winnicott also alludes to the importance of the father as a source of support for the mother:

> In this way the healthy infant is at first, with the mother accepting a high degree of dependence as natural, independent of the father who is otherwise needed to protect the mother, unless the infant is to become inhibited, to lose the capacity for excited love. (Winnicott 1988: 70)

As we shall see at the end of this section, Winnicott had a difficult and humiliating relationship with his own father. Perhaps this has some bearing on why, in his theory, in all the crucial stages of the child's development, the mother quietly reigns supreme.

Although Winnicott sees the construction of gender identity as at least in part biologically determined, he does make specific reference to what he thinks may be an important factor in women's subordinate position within culture. He argues that it is the baby's earliest dependency on the mother, inevitably entailing some compliance, which underlies both men and women's attitude to the idea of 'woman' (Winnicott, 1958: 304–5). Winnicott suggests that it is the massively unequal power relationship between mother and baby, rather than the baby's envy (as suggested by Klein), which leads to the unconscious association of the idea of the mother, and women generally, with the fear of annihilation. Unless the mother is able to transfer her power to her child by sensitively fostering the experience of illusionment, the child, whatever gender it is, will associate the mother, 'woman', with the terror of non-being. So as Winnicott and Klein suggest, the oppression of women may involve a mixture of both envy and the fear of annihilation inspired by the mother's power. (In Freudian language this is the perception of the mother as phallic or all-powerful before the revelations of the Oedipal crisis). For Winnicott, those mothers who, for a variety of reasons, cannot be 'good enough', may be experienced as particularly controlling and powerful. This association with power would again help to explain why patriarchal societies have needed to control women so energetically and restrict their power so systematically. The mother's association with phantasies of potentially overwhelming power might also help to explain why some men feel the need for degraded images of women stripped of their connotations of the mother and her power. This is true of many kinds of pornography where women may be seen as exclusively passive, often child-like sexual objects beyond the terrors of a real relationship with a potentially powerful woman. For such men, pornography seems to represent the hostile flight from the all-powerful mother and, at the same time, the need to dominate women shorn of this connotation. Of course, some sexual images which involve unequal power are those based on sado-masochistic phantasies where the 'victim' is a man and not a woman. Here, there seems to be a desire for a return to phantasies of the helpless baby, and the all-controlling, eroticised and sadistic mother.

Presences and absences

If we look at Winnicott's life and work there are certain features which might explain his focus on the mother and his 'flight from the erotic'. His unpublished autobiography, begun in the last years of his life, provides us with some helpful information. He describes himself as the only son of Wesleyan Methodist parents with two older sisters and therefore 'multiple mothers and with a father extremely preoccupied in my younger years with town as well as business matters'. His father was over forty when he was born, as also, interestingly, were the fathers of Freud and Klein. Winnicott's father seems to have been a rather emotionally remote but powerful and humiliating figure towards whom he seems to have adopted a surprisingly tolerant and compliant attitude. However, in the autobiography, he does accuse him of letting him down as a father. 'He left me too much to all my mothers' (Phillips 1988: 28). As we have seen in Winnicott's work it is not the father who separates the child from its mother but the mother's sensitive use of the transitional space. Instead, as Phillips points out, the child is free of the father but always subject to the potentially disabling effects of the demands of the mother.

Winnicott's own mother seems to have been a rather insubstantial figure in his life. However, Phillips identifies a rather telling poem in a letter to his brother-in-law written when he was sixty-seven (Phillips 1988: 29). This poem, entitled 'The Tree', seems to encapsulate what lies at the centre of Winnicott's work. Winnicott used to do his homework in a tree in his garden before he was banished to boarding school. It is this tree to which the poem probably refers.

The Tree

> Mother below is weeping
> weeping
> weeping
> Thus I knew her

Once, stretched out on her lap
as now on dead tree
I learned to make her smile
to stem her tears
to undo her guilt
to cure her inward death
To enliven her was my living.

Phillips suggests that an identification with Christ on the cross, and the anonymous dead wood (Woods, interestingly, was his mother's maiden name), seem to refer to the absence of what became, in Winnicott's theory, the formative experience in the child's life – the way the mother in the fullest sense 'holds' the child in her mind as well as her arms. In other words, the idea of the crucifixion is equated with the child's (and mother's suffering). The poem also seems to refer to the way children attempt to deal with the mother's depressed or withdrawn mood which makes her attention unreliable. A child with a seriously depressed mother could, Winnicott wrote, 'feel infinitely dropped' (Winnicott 1964c: 75). This poem seems to suggest that form of deprivation which lies at the heart of his work, where the child is compelled into an attempt 'to enliven an inaccessible mother at the cost of his own spontaneous vitality' (Phillips 1988: 30). On this account, his work seems to stem directly from his own early childhood experience of trying to make 'my living' by keeping his mother alive. It seems likely that Winnicott's awareness of his own potential for growth and its early inhibition because he had to look after a depressed and frequently emotionally 'absent' mother, acted as the spur to his particular way of understanding the formation of identity and the cause of psychical distress.

Finally, as Phillips suggests, Winnicott's early experiences of dissent in a Wesleyan Methodist family may explain both his unwillingness to identify with existing orthodoxies or institutions, including the British psychoanalytic institutions, and his lifelong concern to speak directly and accessibly in an effort to communicate beyond what he regarded as the merely intellectual. One of Winnicott's major reservations about psychoanalytic theory was that, in emphasising the inner world of phantasy, it was in danger of underestimating the significance of the actual maternal environment, what the child really experiences or fails to experience. Winnicott places the actual mother, 'good enough' or depressed, at the heart of his theory.

[134]

Suggested reading

Theory

WINNICOTT, D. (1957) *The Child and the Family: First Relationships*, London, Tavistock.

WINNICOTT, D. (1958) *Collected Papers: Through Paediatrics to Psychoanalysis*, London, Tavistock and New York, Basic Books.

WINNICOTT, D. (1964a) *The Child, the Family and the Outside World*, Harmondsworth, Penguin.

WINNICOTT, D. (1964b) *The Family and Individual Development*, London, Tavistock.

WINNICOTT, D. (1964c) *The Effect of Psychotic Parents*, London, Tavistock

WINNICOTT, D. (1965) *The Maturational Processes and the Facilitating Environment: Studies in the Theories of Emotional Development*, London, Hogarth Press and The Institute of Psychoanalysis.

WINNICOTT, D. (1971) *Playing and Reality*, London, Routledge.

WINNICOTT, D. (1977) *The Piggle: An Account of Psychoanalytic Treatment of a Little Girl*, Harmondsworth, Penguin.

WINNICOTT, D. (1987) *Home is Where We Start From: Essays by a Psychoanalyst*, Harmondsworth, Pelican.

WINNICOTT, D. (1988) *Human Nature*, London, Free Association Books.

General

BOLLAS, C. (1987) *The Shadow of the Object: Psychoanalysis of the Unthought Unknown*, London, Free Association Books.

BOLLAS, C. (1989) *Forces of Destiny: Psychoanalysis and the Human Idiom*, London, Free Association Books.

GOLDMAN, D. (1993) *In Search of the Real: The Origins and Originality of D.W. Winnicott*, Aronson.

GROLNICK, S. (1990) *The Work and Play of Winnicott*, New York, Aronson.

KAHR, B. (1993) *Winnicott*, London, Sage.

KHAN, M.M.R. (1974) *The Privacy of the Self*, London, Hogarth Press and The Institute of Psychoanalysis.

KHAN, M.M.R. (1975) 'Introduction' to Winnicott, D. *Through Paediatrics to Psychoanalysis*, London, Hogarth Press and The Institute of Psychoanalysis.

KHAN, M.M.R. (1981) *The Case for a Personal Psychotherapy*, Oxford, Oxford University Press.

KHAN, M.M.R. (1983) *Hidden Selves*, London, Hogarth Press and The Institute of Psychoanalysis.

KOHON, G. (1986) *The British School of Psychoanalysis: The Independent Tradition*, London, Free Association Books.

GUNTRIP, H. (1975) 'My Experience of Analysis with Fairburn and Winnicott', *International Review of Psychoanalysis*, 2: 145–56.

LOMAS, P. (1973) *True and False Experience*, London, Allen Lane.

LOMAS, P. (1987) *The Limits of Interpretation: What's Wrong With Psychoanalysis?* London, Penguin.

MILLER, A. (1987) *The Drama of Being a Child*, London, Virago.

MILLER, A. (1990) *The Untouched Key*, London, Virago.

MILLER, A. (1991) *Banished Knowledge*, London, Virago.

MILNER, M. (Joanna Field) (1971) *On Not Being Able To Paint*, Oxford, Heinemann Educational. [The first edition (1950) was published under the pseudonym Joanna Field.]

MILNER, M. (Joanna Field) (1986) *A Life of One's Own*, London, Virago. [The first edition (1934) was published under the pseudonym Joanna Field.]

PHILLIPS, A. (1988) *Winnicott*, London, Fontana [Modern Masters].

PHILLIPS, A. (1994a) *On Kissing, Tickling and Being Bored*, London, Faber.

PHILLIPS, A. (1994b) *On Flirtation*, London, Faber.

RYCROFT, C. (1985) *Psychoanalysis and Beyond*, London, Chatto and Windus.

Feminist theory influenced by Winnicott

BENJAMIN, J. (1990) *The Bonds of Love*, London, Virago.

BRENNAN, T. (1992) *The Interpretation of the Flesh*, London, Routledge [chapter two].

CHODOROW, N. (1978) *The Reproduction of Mothering: Psychoanalysis and the Sociology of Gender*, Berkeley, University of California.

CHODOROW, N. (1989) *Feminism and Psychoanalysis*, Cambridge, Polity Press.

CHODOROW, N. (1994) *Femininities, Masculinities, Sexualities*, London, Free Association Books.

CRAIB, I. (1989) *Psychoanalysis and Social Theory*, Hemel Hempstead, Harvester Wheatsheaf.

EICHENBAUM, L. and ORBACH, S. (1982) *Outside In, Inside Out*, Harmondsworth, Penguin.

EICHENBAUM, L. and ORBACH, S. (1985) *Understanding Women*, Harmondsworth, Penguin.

KELLER, E.F. (1985) *Reflections on Gender and Science*, London and New Haven, Yale University Press.

TONG, R. (1989) *Feminist Thought: A Comprehensive Introduction*, London, Routledge.

4
Lacan: the meaning of the phallus

I am not where I think and I think where I am not.
>   (Jacques Lacan, *Ecrits*)

In [Lacan's] account, which insists upon speech at every turn, the essential day-to-day facts about human beings are these: they address each other and affect each other by what they say; they say what they mean and what they don't mean simultaneously; whatever they get they always want more, or something different; and at any one moment they are consciously aware of only some of what they want.

>   (Malcolm Bowie, *Lacan*)

Biographical background (1901–81)

Lacan was born in Paris where he spent most of his life and trained in medicine and psychiatry. In the early nineteen-thirties he became involved with the French Surrealist movement, joined the Paris Psychoanalytic Society and in 1936 presented the first version of his famous paper on the 'Mirror Stage'. Becoming a member of the French psychoanalytic establishment, he continued to practise as an analyst in Paris until 1952. In 1953, after his controversial presentation known as 'The Rome Discourse', he left the Paris Psychoanalytic Society and founded what he called the French Society of Psychoanalysis. At the same time he began his celebrated series of seminars in which he presented his evolving ideas to enthusiastic supporters. From 1953 until the early nineteen-sixties he continued to develop his ideas, particularly those involving the combination of psychoanalysis and linguistics. In 1963 he was expelled from the International Psychoanalytic Association because of his unorthodox practice and teaching methods. A year later, he reformed his analytic society, calling it L'Ecole Freudienne de Paris. In 1966, the publication of *Ecrits*, a collection of his essays, led to success among innovative 'structuralist' and 'post-structuralist' intellectuals who then dominated the Parisian scene. In 1968, although he did not actively participate in the May Revolution in Paris he addressed the students. At this time he also became President of the Psychoanalytic department of the University of Vincennes. However, in 1980 he suddenly and unilaterally dissolved the Ecole Freudienne and formed La Cause Freudienne, expelling many of his closest colleagues. He died in 1981.

An overview

Psychoanalysis as the analysis of language

With Lacan we are firmly back on Freudian territory in a post-structural context which feels very remote from the comforts of Winnicott's plain language and the possibility of a coherent, stable identity. In a dramatic re-modelling of Freud's central concepts, Lacan's post-structuralist theory transforms identity into precarious subjectivity, the unconscious into language and psychoanalytic theory into the study of language. Since Lacan sees language as the vehicle for unconscious desire, psychoanalytic theory becomes inevitably the study of the construction of the subject.

For Lacan, the unconscious has no existence within the individual outside the range of speech and writing and no structure other than that which language provides. Lacan develops Freud's interest in symbolisation in *The Interpretation of Dreams* and in the clinical technique of free association in a more thoroughgoing way. His application of a theory of language to basic psychoanalytic categories reformulates the basic premises of Freud's theories and has been enormously influential on recent post-structuralist theory. While remaining dedicated to the strangeness and inconceivability of Freud's conception of the unconscious, Lacan draws on modern Saussurean linguistics to re-conceptualise the unconscious as part of an endless chain of unconscious meanings driven by desire. Lacan adopts Ferdinand de Saussure's (1857–1913) concept of the *sign* (a physical object which has meaning like a word) which consists of two interdependent parts, the *signifier* and the *signified*, to construct his model of language as the home of the unconscious. The signifier is the physical part of the sign, such as a mark on paper or sounds in the air and the signified is the meaning attached to the signifier. However, characteristically, Lacan alters these linguistic concepts to suit his own theoretical purposes (which will become clear later in this chapter) making the signifier much more powerful than the meaning itself. Using his own version of Saussure's structural model of meaning, Lacan argues that all meanings, including those of the unconscious, can be represented as a continuous signifying chain in language. These reach down from the rationally chosen words of consciousness into the deepest most inaccessible parts of our unconscious, present in language as gaps, slips, hesitations or silences, all of which, words and gaps, interdependently endow each other with meaning. No signifier can signify independently of other signifiers (for example 'crowd' depends for its meaning on not being 'crown') and where meaning and signification end there is nothing except the intractable, unsymbolisable quality of the materiality of the world, trauma, psychosis and death; what Lacan calls the realm of the Real. Again drawing on concepts from structural linguistics, Lacan converts Freud's two major unconscious symbolic processes described in *The Interpretation of Dreams* – condensation and displacement, which he used to interpret the meanings of dreams – into the linguistic categories of metaphor and metonymy. These are the concepts which organise and connect the signifying chains of meaning and make the structure and cohesion of language possible.

Metaphors are based on similar or associated meanings which exist on different planes of meaning so that their use often stimulates the imagination. For example, we use spatial dimensions from one plane of existence, high and low, near or far, as tools to think with so we can grasp what we experience as more complex or abstract ideas such as feelings from another plane of reality. We say we feel in 'high' or 'low' spirits, 'over the moon', 'under a cloud', 'under the weather', 'on top of everything' or as if things are 'getting us down' or we are at 'at the end of our tether'. When we begin to feel hopeful, we say that we can 'see light at the end of a tunnel' or that we have 'turned a corner' after having been 'on the edge' or 'walking a tight-rope'. We can see metaphors even more deeply embedded in the fabric of everyday language when we speak of waking 'up', 'falling' asleep or of someone 'letting us down'. Metonyms, on the other hand, make a part of reality stand in for the whole in a fluid, unbroken chain of meaning and tend to emphasise the realistic dimensions of an idea. For example, we may talk about the 'green wellies brigade', the 'chattering classes', or the 'crowned heads of Europe', to evoke a much more elaborated conception of the different lifestyles, philosophies and attitudes of different groups of people. However, Lacan, distorting Roman Jakobsen's (1896–1982) original concepts, re-defines metaphor simply as 'one word standing in for another' and metonymy as 'word to word connections or associations in a signifying chain'.

So for Lacan, armed with the insights of modern linguistics, the unconscious as well as consciousness is conceptualised as a linguistic structure based on endless strings and loops of interconnecting meanings. Identity becomes subjectivity within language – no more than the endless versions of the world and ourselves that we can create in the structures and meanings of language. The subject, no longer the ego of classical psychoanalysis, is inhabited by what Lacan calls the Other, those others who lie outside, within the inter-subjectivity of language. The Other-infested subject possesses no substance of its own in the form of personal qualities, aptitudes or dispositions or a definable personality. Nor is it, as Object-Relations theory argues, a container which waits to be inhabited by its relationships with other people as objects. At its starkest, it is a series of events – signifying processes – within language of which the individual is a part. For Lacan these events are the procession of fluctuating meanings with which we are compelled to interpret the world which confronts us. We can never look 'purely' at the world because we cannot resist the flood of meanings which pour into our minds in the very act of perceiving it. We cannot view the world without the mediation provided by language which silently directs how we think about external reality. We are subjects without any subject-matter or stuffing of our own. In that sense, for Lacan, we are like dead creatures who can only be enlivened by the force of our own repressed desire. Although the meanings of language which represent us rest on arbitrary signs and the absence of those things to which they refer, the powerful dynamo of our Desire brings them to life, making inter-subjectivity through language possible.

In Lacan's post-structural theory, sexuality no longer exists as the pursuit of pleasurable experience, as other theorists have assumed. Lacan eroticises both language and the linguistic concepts we use to analyse it, by linking their meanings to the body and sexuality. Language becomes the means by which repression is achieved by driving our unconscious desire underground into the spaces between words and using its energy to propel us from one meaning to another. We can regain access to our repressed desire for the mother only in language where desire becomes the driving force behind the signifiers that propels all acts of speech, all refusals to speak and all other conscious and unconscious representations. Both the subject and the Other to whom we speak within the inter-subjectivity made possible by language, come into being simultaneously and under pressure from each other. But, for Lacan, Desire is the direct effect of the loss produced by symbolic castration or its failure, the moment when someone bars our way to what we desire. 'It is the assumption of castration that creates the lack upon which desire is instituted' (Lacan 1966: 852). In other words, it is the loss of the mother to the father which leaves the space in identity which installs Desire as a permanent feature of who we are. In one sense, language which is dependent for its meaning on arbitrary signs, represents both the curtailment and castration of possibility and the lack of fulfilment that each child must accept before it can become a human subject. But, at the same time, language, in its fullest form, offers to the subject an infinity of richness and potentiality of meaning with which to interpret experience. For Lacan, this plenitude, consisting of unconscious as well as conscious meanings, indeed of the free-play of the unconscious, is the only authentic form of freedom, sexuality, identity and 'truth' we can ever expect.

Identity in the imaginary and the symbolic

In striking contrast with Object-Relations theorists, Lacan rejects the idea that our identity can ever be coherent or authentic. All our identifications lead only to a *sense* of identity, not an actual identity and this sense of having an identity is always unjustified and based on a misrecognition. For Lacan, identity is inevitably fragile and unstable because the power of our unconscious desire continually threatens to throw us off balance. Drawing on Freud's theory of narcissism, he thought that, as babies, in the realm of what he calls the *Imaginary,* our identity is always based on an image of ourself which is reflected back from someone else, like the reflection from a mirror. (He in fact called this the 'Mirror Stage'.) This person, with whom we first 'identify', is usually our mother. Lacan calls this early and very fragile kind of identity an Imaginary one because, although it feels real to us, it unconsciously depends on someone or something outside ourselves, from which we are separated, for its support. This self or ego is never our own because it depends on our identifications – it is always fused with other people or things, who then form a part of us. However, Lacan argues, we also establish another kind of identity – what he calls subjectivity – when we begin to acquire language in what he calls the realm of the *Symbolic.* Here, the apparently fixed meanings offered us in language based, like the meaning of the phallus on difference, give us an alternative, ostensibly stable *sense* of identity, a psychological place where we can discover what appears to be the 'real' meaning of who we are. Through our identification with the certainty and coherence these meanings seem to represent, we can gain a sense of having a coherent identity. We feel defined and buoyed up by these meanings.

However, Lacan argues that even in the Symbolic, all is not as safe and coherent as it appears. Language both places us and displaces us as subjects. We can never get a sure footing in it. The desire for our mother which reappears in the language we speak is returned to us in the spaces between words, in the hesitations and stumbles which frequently gives the lie to the meanings our words try to convey though never where we can know it directly. So our identity in language, which at first sight seems so seductively stable, is always potentially de-stabilised by our unconscious desire and loss, the part of us that feels a sense of longing, an emptiness lying like a shadow behind the confidence of the 'I' we use in our sentences. Lacan argues, therefore, that our conscious identity expressed through language is always bogus. Our Desire can disrupt any of the meanings we build up in our discourse, at any moment. Ultimately, he argues, the identity we achieve in language in the Symbolic – consciousness – is only another reflected identity without substance, like that with our mother and all subsequent identifications. It is no different in structure from the one we gained by looking into our mother's face (or Lacan's mirror) in the Imaginary. The difference between these two reflected identities is that the Imaginary one is part of the personal, bodily, pre-Oedipal world we shared with our mothers, and is pre-verbal, whereas the Symbolic is part of the social, cultural world where we are supposed to be able to achieve an authentic identity and become independent, speaking human subjects. With this kind of argument, Lacan's theory sets up a challenge to all identity and the meanings we build on them in the knowledge we create. The fact that *both* identities are inherently unstable lends Lacan's ideas their sophistication and complexity. His stress on the importance of the fictional element in these processes (the fact that we psychologically invest in false images of ourselves) and on the role of language in the formation of adult identity, are two sources of his originality which have been very influential on much recent psychoanalytic thinking.

So Lacan replaces Freud's three-cornered structural model of identity based on the id, ego and superego with his own system of concepts which represent not so much opposing parts of the self within identity but determining, inter-subjective structural orders. The three realms of the Imaginary, Symbolic and Real position us in a field of forces and make possible the analysis of the ordinary construction of identity and the therapeutic treatment of neurosis and psychosis.

Lacan took the view that the subversive power of the unconscious in Freud's work had been drastically diluted and 'tamed' by the generation of analysts who followed him. This was the origin of his quarrel with the psychoanalytic establishment. He saw what he called the 'universe' of language as the fundamental component of psychoanalytic theory and practice and he believed meaning and identity were primarily communicated not by statement but by denial, ambiguity, slippages and ignorance of intentions, in the margins of what we say. Distinguishing between what he called 'empty speech' and 'full speech', he suggested that while conscious knowledge is ignorant, the apparently unknowable in the unconscious speaks (Lacan 1977a: 40–6). 'It says what it knows, while the subject does not know it', or, as Freud put it, the individual 'speaks more than he knows' (SE 20: 189). For Lacan, the world starts to exist for an individual only in the projection of the self into that world, in our relations first with our mother and later within culture itself. (Lacan 1977a: 2–3). The world, therefore, is always permeated with ourselves preventing us from ever knowing it directly. This is the basis of Lacan's rejection of prevailing psychoanalytic norms which resulted in his career becoming so volatile and controversial.

Many classical and Object-Relations analysts conceptualise the ego as potentially strong, authentic and stable. Lacan, however, sees it as always fictitious and precarious because it is divided by loss and Desire. Lacan rejects both a developmental, stage-by-stage model of the construction of human identity and one resting on biology. He wants to replace both with one all-at-once-structure (such as the Imaginary) which gives way to another (the Symbolic) and a determining structure which lies outside individual experience. He thought Klein should have explained the structural causes of the interaction between the good and bad part-objects which are so central to her theory. Lacan wants to free psychoanalysis from what he see as the myth of identity as plenitude, fullness and stability. For him the task of therapy is to resist both the patient's wish to create what he or she perceives as a genuine identity through making an Imaginary identification with the analyst, as she or he did first with the mother, and the temptation, in the analyst, to strengthen the patients identity by gradually removing its defences (the aim in much conventional therapy). Rather, Lacan wants to throw the creation of subjectivity into the realm of language and signification, so the patient speaks her or himself into a sense of identity from within language (rather than from an outside object in the person of the analyst), thus gaining, at the same time, access to unconscious Desire and loss while not being potentially overwhelmed by it.

But before looking any further at what Lacan has to say about language, let's begin at the beginning with the very young baby and with Lacan's most accessible idea.

The Mirror Stage and the Imaginary

As Freud first suggested, at the earliest stage of its life the baby is unable to distinguish between itself and other objects in the external world. The baby lacks a sense of self, or any defined sense of a centre, and imagines itself to exist in the objects (including people) in its environment. In this early period of total dependence, the baby lives in an undifferentiated and symbiotic relationship with the mother's body so that it never knows who is who, or who is dependent on whom.

For Lacan this early narcissistic infant world is rather like a soup of ingredients for a later identity: phantasies of love and hate circulating around the mother's body; phantasies of fragmentation; inchoate, inexpressible emotions and lack of boundaries. It is a world which for the baby seems to be an unpredictable mixture of heaven and hell, plenitude and emptiness. But into this hotbed of raw emotion and phantasy Lacan introduces his own very distinctive idea of the beginnings of a sense of identity – of becoming something separate from the mother which he calls the *Mirror Stage*. He uses the metaphor of the mirror to describe how the baby, at around the age of six months, first comes to perceive itself as a 'self', because it gains an integrated, coherent image of itself in the mirror. The child who experiences itself as physically uncoordinated and overwhelmed by emotions and phantasies over which it has no control – in fact, as 'all over the place' both physically and psychically – suddenly finds in the specular image reflecting back from the mirror, a satisfying and seductive image of itself as a coherent whole – a thing with edges. At this moment, the chaotic, unintelligible being that the baby up to then has experienced itself being, is magically transformed into a unified whole, though, of course, this is still of a very blurred, undefined and imaginary kind. The mirror image both is and is not the baby; the baby is both subject and object at the same time. But this experience is the baby's first encounter with a process of constructing or mastering itself – its identity – a sense of being centred in its own body, and Lacan argues that this taking of an identity from outside itself forms the basis for all its other identifications. The baby narcissistically and jubilantly arrives at some sense of 'I' only by finding an 'I' reflected back by something outside itself which includes its mother who also acts like a mirror. Lacan's description is very like Freud's description of the narcissistic stage when the child experiences itself, projected onto the mother, as its own love-object. The baby falls in love with its own image reflected back to it from the other, outside itself.

So we first discover a unified identity from outside ourselves – an image of ourselves – yet one which we feel to be an intrinsic part of what we are. We identify with something which looks like what we want to be, but this is also alien and separate from us. For Lacan, the formation of the ego begins at this point. The mirror image splits us in two. We misrecognise ourselves in the alienated image of what we want to be because this ideal image denies the chaos we feel in our own being. Lacan calls this realm of images, of imaginary identifications, the 'Imaginary'. It is a world where our mother is the first most available object and reflects back to us the kind of image we want. We are given a sense of identity, but we think we are given an authentic identity. For Lacan, drawing on Freud's work on primary narcissism, the ego, our sense of self, contains this narcissistic process by which we bolster our sense of ourselves with a fiction – a visual story which we show ourselves – an illusion of an organised self which depends on the view of ourselves that we obtain from other people and objects throughout our lives. Unlike Klein's view of identity, Lacan sees the ego, identity, as purely Imaginary and based on what he perceives as a defensive refusal to accept the actual, much more unstable, state of affairs. In Object-Relations theory the mother's mirroring of the baby to itself creates an authentic identity, whereas for Lacan it creates an entirely illusory and unstable one although it is often rigid and armour-like.

So the child in the Imaginary, contemplating itself in the mirror, can be seen as something that creates meaning. The clearly defined image of the child in the mirror is for the child apparently the meaning of itself although it is only an image or reflection. The mirror images are ones of fullness, wholeness, totality, complete identity although they are mis-recognised. Objects in the Imaginary repeatedly reflect themselves in a kind of sealed unit where everything is an extension of the self which has been projected onto the external world so there are no apparent dif-ferences or divisions. The world of the Imaginary is a world based on the incorporation of sameness where there is no separation or gap between the experience of the child and the world it inhabits, with which it is still fused. But it is also where, through identification with the other as the same, the potential subject is actually annihilated while imagining itself complete, full and defined. However authentic or 'real' the baby feels, its identity is still completely dependent on the mother. If we remain in the Imaginary as adults, it holds us without our knowledge in a realm of identifications with chosen fragments of the world which deriving from ourselves, foreshortens our perception of the world and puts us into a blind alley in which difference cannot exist.

The realms of Demand and Desire

Lacan is interested not only in the construction of identity in the pre-Oedipal world of the Imaginary but also in the nature of the baby's love which accompanies it, what he calls Demand and Desire, in relation to the mother. He describes the baby's experience of love for the mother in the Imaginary as the realm of Demand. This is the realm in which, although the baby longs for satisfaction, its mother can never completely satisfy it. She can satisfy its needs but never its Desire. Something is always missing in terms of what the baby really yearns for (to be what the mother desires and, therefore, to control her for ever and isolate her from all other calls on her potential to satisfy, such as father, other children). Lacan seems to be implying that the baby yearns for the total unity it had with the mother before its birth so that being born represents the initial loss of what it always longs to regain.

In the realm of Demand, the baby's needs can be satisfied in terms of its daily nurture but it always wants more than this. Desire is the result of subtracting satisfaction from Demand. It is what remains and exceeds Demand. For Lacan, what the baby really wants can only be satisfied elsewhere, in another realm of meaning, what he calls the realm of Desire or the Symbolic. For Lacan this realm exists only in language and the unconscious which for Lacan become the same thing. To enter language is to become subject to unconscious Desire rather than Demand. Only there can the missing Desire which we have repressed be given back to us although it can never be grasped consciously because it exists not in the words themselves but in the spaces and energy between them in the unconscious. But the satisfaction of our Desire always eludes us. Because Desire must always exceed satisfaction it forces us continually to chase after it within and between the conventional meanings of language and cultural representation. For Lacan, the drive is no longer biological but the searching movement of language, an endless appeal to the Other for the meaning to end all meaning. Having lost access to the mother's body during the Oedipal crisis we are, henceforth, caught up in a constant search for linguistic substitutes for it, words with which we try to paper over the cracks, plug the gaps at the core of our being, never able to regain the paradise of unity and self-completion which we phantasised with our mothers in the Imaginary. Civilisation rests, as Freud first suggested, on the impossibility of our Desires. Lacan, too, thinks this is the essential human predicament, part of what distinguishes us as human subjects. Both symbolic castration by the father in the sexual world and the symbolic constraints in the world of language, set limits to our phantasies and Desires in the Imaginary by coercing us into culturally acceptable behaviour and conventional meanings. At the heart of both the meaning of the father and language is Desire, 'the power of pure loss'. In language, we shall never be able to find the 'truth' an ultimate meaning from which all meanings flow because in language we are permanently cut off from the object of our Desire (the mother and later substitutes for the mother) which for Lacan exists only in the realm of the *Real*. (The third of Lacan's determining psychoanalytic domains, along with the *Imaginary* and the *Symbolic*.) By the Real, Lacan refers to everything which lies outside or beyond the symbolic process, the superseding power of totality, the 'all'. This is not the same as 'reality' as it is usually understood in psycho-analysis which refers to the external world outside the mind. For Lacan, the Real exists in both the mental and physical world. It includes the inexpressible pre-Imaginary moment of excess and impossible plenitude to which both the Imaginary and the Desire refer (but which they cannot bestow), lying inviolate and out of reach of all Imaginary identity and the subjectivity offered by the language, the Symbolic order (perhaps the womb we once inhabited when we *were* part of our mother – the 'lost object' for which we always yearn). For Lacan, as well as the idea of impossible, super-abundant plenitude, the Real also includes everything else which cannot be symbolised. This includes the materiality of actual objects, the experience of trauma when we are thrown back into the baby's earliest experience of helpless speechlessness, the state of psychosis where the controlled perceptions available in the Symbolic are rejected so that subjectivity collapses into phantasy completely, and finally death, the triumph of the Real, which puts a physical end to subjectivity and meaning.

But while language, unlike the Imaginary, cuts us off from the objects of our Desire (our mother and substitutes for her), at the same time, it returns Desire to us as we move, with a new sense of identity as a human subject, from one meaning to the next in a lifelong search for a perfect fit between language and our phantasy of plenitude. In this way, for Lacan, our entry into language becomes the site for the Oedipal crisis rather than the actual father. Language becomes the Other, the symbolic 'place of the father' which insinuates itself between us and the objects of our Desire and makes Desire insatiable by continually de-stabilising and moving these objects so they always elude us. Thus, Lacan ties the individual's repressed Desire and yearning into the very stuff of language and inter-subjectivity. Language, says Lacan, 'is what hollows being [Imaginary] into desire [Symbolic]'. It bridges the gap between Demand and satisfaction. Contradictorily, although it revolves around emptiness and absence, language *articulates* the richness and fullness of the Imaginary and the idea of total oneness with the mother.

Lacan argues that since Freud, psychoanalysts had frequently reduced Freud's desire to bodily need when quite clearly individuals do not only experience this form of Desire. In contrast to need, Desire is always 'parodoxical, deviant, erratic and eccentric even scandalous' (Lacan 1977a: 690). As clinical literature makes clear, many people desire to be or stay ill or unhappy or wish for their own failure or suffering. As Bowie points out (Bowie 1991: 136) we all make a continual appeal to the other to say 'yes' but the satisfaction of Demand is never enough. The parodox is that the Other to whom the demand is being made is never in a position to answer with an unconditional 'yes'. They and us are only justified in saying 'perhaps' or 'to some extent'. We shall look again at the realms of Demand and Desire in the commentary on 'The Meaning of the Phallus'.

The Father and the place of the Father

As we have seen, for Freud, in the pre-Oedipal world of what Lacan calls Imaginary identifications, we are in a world inhabited by only two people.

Here, the child has phantasies that it is omnipotent and the mother's response seems to support this view most of the time. As the Oedipal drama approaches both boys and girls begin to see their mother as a whole person and fall passionately in love with her. But the Oedipal moment brings a rupture, a dramatic intrusion of a third term which breaks in on the child's phantasy of omnipotence. The father represents something external and potentially annihilating intruding upon the child's idyll with the mother. In recognising the father for what he is – an insurmountable obstacle to the fulfilment of its passionate wishes – the child is brought into contact with the constraints of the wider external world of culture and language. This is the social scenario in which it must in future take its place. As we saw in the chapter on Freud, this shattering of the child's illusions forces the repression of its longing to have the mother for ever and creates the unconscious. It splits the newly created subject, now encapsulated within the social domain beyond the mother-and-child couple, into consciousness and the unconscious.

Lacan, elaborating on Freud's concept of the father, distinguishes between the actual, what Lacan sees as Imaginary father, and what he calls the 'paternal metaphor' or 'the place of the father'. These last two terms refer to what the father represents to the child symbolically rather than the Imaginary, idealised father with whom Lacan thinks the Symbolic father is easily confused (Mitchell and Rose, eds, 1982: 39). Lacan argues that even in the absence of an actual father, the child experiences the place of the father and the Oedipal crisis through cultural substitutions, that is primarily language and other systems of representation. These symbolically represent an intrusion by culture into the fused, bodily world of the mother and child and, crucially, a severing of the child from the object of its desire. The law of the 'name of the father', of what meanings are permitted in language, takes up the space left empty by the loss of the mother. The rational categories of language represent the cutting off (castration) of the child from its phantasies but they also represent the conversion of the child's need (to be the phallus for the mother) into Desire (which can never be satisfied) but which subsequently provides the searching, dynamic energy for knowledge and 'truth' which characterise language and reason. For Lacan the only 'truth' is that lack and Desire, the 'want to be', underlie and undermine all identity and knowledge.

[149]

The phallus: the first sign of difference

As we have seen, at the same time that the child is transformed into a subject of language and history through its obedience to the law of the father, as well as becoming a split subject with an unconscious, it also becomes a gendered subject. It is the child's ability to recognise sexual difference that allows it to take on a sexual identity for the first time. The father, or the symbolic father, signifies this sexual difference by means of his association with the phallus. The phallus, a sign of power within patriarchal societies which is not to be confused with the visible penis (although this is presumably what the child does at one level) is the central term in Lacan's theory. It symbolises to the child that there is a division between the sexes, and later that those who 'have' rather than 'lack' it are privileged. It also, crucially, signifies another division within identity in the formation of the unconscious. The need for the unconscious as a container for the loss of the mother and the desire associated with her is provoked by the recognition, in both girl and boy, that they do not or cannot have the phallus the mother wants. The girl has nothing that visibly compares with the phallus and the boy phantasises the loss of his at the hands of the father if he pursues his Desires. So the phallus symbolises both Desire and loss. The child has probably been dimly aware of sexual difference before the onset of the Oedipal crisis. But once the crisis is in full swing, sexual difference and the sexual identities based on it, operate like a law and the child is required to line up behind the phallic meanings of 'having' or 'lacking' in order for its construction as a 'masculine' or 'feminine' human being to be completed. The phallus represents the moment when the father's prohibition of the Desire for the mother must function. It signals to the subject that having a viable identity can only be achieved at the price of loss (of the mother) and that being human can only come about as the direct consequence of a division (into consciousness and the unconscious) (Mitchell and Rose, eds, 1982: 40). It is at this point that Lacan introduces his most original reworking of Freud's Oedipal drama through his introduction of the dimension of language.

Language and the Symbolic

With the entry of the father onto the scene, the child is precipitated into a crisis. The crucial thing it has to recognise is that identities which are not fused with the mother in the Imaginary can only come into being in language, the Symbolic, as a result of the perception of sexual difference. The phallus represents this difference. The father or what Lacan refers to as the 'name of the father' symbolised by the phallus, legislates to the child that it must take its place within a family which is defined by sexual difference, by the phallus. In future it must recognise that it is different from some people and the same as others. But the difference represented by the phallus also entails, as part of its meaning, exclusion (the child cannot be its parents' lover) and absence (the child must give up its relationship with the mother). So the child's identity as a viable human subject, capable of operating within the family and in society, in Lacan's theory, significantly depends on its unconscious recognition of difference, exclusion and absence.

At this point Lacan makes the vital link between the sexual world dominated by the phallus and the Symbolic world of language. At around the same time that the small child discovers sexual difference, it acquires language. And in the discovery of language the child unconsciously learns that the units of language only have meaning because they are different from other units, and that signifiers in general, like the phallus, can represent things that are absent. Words stand in for objects, and in this sense they operate like metaphors. This is perhaps the central moment in Lacan's theory. As the child learns, unconsciously about the meaning of sexuality – in the discovery of sexual difference – it is also learning about meanings based on difference in the social domain, especially in language. Through its recognition of the pre-determined social fact that meaning depends on difference, the child is able to move from a bodily world of sexual phantasy into the cultural world of language and symbolic systems. So, the recognition of the law of the name of the father, or the meaning of the phallus, in the sexual world anticipates the recognition of the cultural law about what means what in language and symbolic representation in the world at large.

The intrusion of the third term (father, phallus, the Symbolic) into the child's world turns out to be, in Lacan's theory, the law of how we perceive the world within language and culture. The third term which divides the child from the mother is at the same time both the father *and* the cultural meanings which pre-exist us in language. Both these acquire their meaning through the operation of difference and have the power to set limits to our phantasies. They achieve our symbolic, if not real castration, by cutting us off from what we most desire but at the same time they allow us to become human subjects. In this way Lacan manages to link the sexual, psychical world with the social dimension of language and culture. In the same way, perception and thinking become both sexualised and gendered.

So the child unconsciously recognises the phallus as a sign (as something which bestows meaning) like the signs in language. Only this recognition of the phallus as a sign of difference with the power to shatter the child's relationship with the mother allows the child to enter into the cultural system of meaning containing other signs based on difference, language. Here words can be seen as a chain of empty signifiers which, like the phallic signifier, in spite of their arbitrariness and emptiness, convey meanings which are vital for the achievement of our humanity, and our subjectivity is woven into these chains of meaning. For Lacan, the phallus is the first sign which the child encounters, whose meaning, if understood, allows the child access to all the other meanings symbolised in the same way in language. The recognition of the power of the phallic signifier within the context of the fear of castration – picked up and made significant by the undeniable visibility of the penis as the only mark of significant difference between the little girl and little boy – facilitates the acquisition of language by operating in the same symbolic way. By means of this joint entry into language and at the same time sexual ordering and identity, the small child gains an identity and becomes a human being capable of identifying with, seeing itself reflected in, the 'I' of language. ('He', 'him', 'she', 'her' are positions which pre-exist and lie in wait to receive the child when it 'steps into' language.) The child finds the idea of its gendered self awaiting it within language and can then identify with that sense of coherence and self it bestows, just as it did with the image in the mirror in the Imaginary. However, although both children can become human beings, Lacan's theory suggests that only boys can become human subjects because the apparently gender neutral 'I', and the phallus on which it is based, is associated with the male body.

However, Lacan insists that there is always a *misrecognition* in the perceived power of the phallus as there is a misrecognition of the mirror image (Lacan always refers to the 'seeming' value of the phallus). The meaning of the phallus is, in this sense, always bogus and since the phallus is the first signifier on which all other symbolic meanings are built, what follows also involves a misrecognition of the identity within language which the child puts on to cover the pain of its loss of the mother, almost like symbolic clothes. Lacan insists that the power symbolised by the phallus is unjustified because it is based on *symbolic castration*. He reminds us that within the sexual sphere, sexual difference, our gender, is achieved only at a devastating price for the boy, the one who possesses the phallus. This is the acceptance of symbolic castration by the father who humiliatingly retains the desired and desiring mother. Fundamentally, the actual meaning of the phallus is therefore not power but powerlessness, that is defeat by the superior power of the father and the loss of the mother as an object of Desire as well as identification. Likewise, the girl's achievement of her gender identity is only gained at the price of a catastrophe – the acceptance of a lack of what her mother wants and what bestows cultural/social identity and power. The girl therefore, as *the lack*, is constituted, as it were, as a negative. Both children lose their sense of union with the mother's body – the object of what Lacan calls Imaginary Desire – but the girl also loses all sense of the validity of her own body and being since she lacks the legitimising primary signifier, the phallus. For the boy, the pain of the loss of the mother and symbolic castration, and for the girl the loss of her mother and her sense that she has already been castrated, is repressed into the newly formed un-conscious at this moment of sexual division.

Meanwhile, the repressed unconscious desires are returned to us in the language with which we attempt to bridge the gap between Demand and satisfaction. Lacan suggests that at an unconscious level we understand the bogusness of the phallus and the falseness of all the identities based on it. It is from this that he – and several writers following him such as the feminists Hélène Cixous, Julia Kristeva and Luce Irigaray (see chapter five) – derive Freud's original idea that there is a drive from the unconscious which continually destabilises and subverts the intended meanings and rationalities of language. In this way, Lacan's theory is a study of *both* the unavoidable power of conformity (with the conventional meanings in language) *and* the half-articulated desire to resist incorporation into what, for him, is the arid world they represent.

Language, therefore, has an ambiguous status in Lacan. It both forces the abandonment of the full, passionate world of the Imaginary, but it is also the best source of identification the child has had yet apart from the mother. It receives the post-Oedipal child exhausted by its loss and unsatisfied Desire, picking it up and putting it on its feet by constituting it as an apparently convincing human being, both to itself and to other people who will recognise it as such. By means of this step into language the child can achieve some mastery over its otherwise unbearable emotions of Desire, humiliation and loss of the loved object. It does this within a pre-existing system of meanings which, although they represent emptiness, absence and loss compared with those associated with the mother, also offer rationality, objectivity, coherence and meanings which the child perceives as fixed certainties – as linguistic pegs on which it hangs its identity. Through the reassuring anchorage of language and understanding, the child can identify itself with the apparent stability it finds there. Language serves to cover the nakedness of painful experience with its rational linguistic clothes. Ironically, we need to be recognised as precisely what we are not. However, from the point of view of gender, for Lacan, the task for the little girl is much more complex and difficult than that of the little boy, for it may be in patriarchal societies that she has no connection with these linguistic clothes, they don't fit her properly. However, she has to try to live in culture with her unconscious lack of the phallus as if her lack of any significance, of her capacity to be a human subject, were her natural destiny. Lacan would argue that this destiny is entirely socially constructed. It is because it is *so* easy to confuse the most obvious sign of difference for the child – the visible, physical penis – with the phallus, the cultural sign of power, that the construction of 'femininity' can never be on the basis of anything other than lack, of 'not having' and therefore 'not being'.

For Lacan, the phallus seems to offer the only possibility of grounding an endless longing and yearning for completion, for the lost object of Desire which he locates in language. It functions as a structural concept which is an absolute guarantor of all meaning. But, in fact, as Lacan recognises, the phallus has no status in reality, certainly not in the actual male organ. It is an empty symbol of castration and loss, a sign which has the power to insert us into the phallic order of language, but which only gains its meaning from the fact that in patriarchal societies those who bear the sign of the phallus represented by the penis have the power to define all other meanings, and therefore the material power to dominate women. Once again, therefore, there is a crucial bifocal quality to Lacan's ideas. He is concerned both to explain the ruthless psychological dynamics of 'the law of the phallus' and to highlight their limitations. As we shall see, this ambiguity is crucial to the way in which his work has been subsequently used.

The unconscious and language

In Lacan's structural theory the unconscious *is* Desire and Lacan directly equates the structure of language with desire and the unending search for fulfilment in the form of absolute meanings and truth. The unconscious, he says, is structured like a language. Both are structured by signifiers that usually bestow meanings in the absence of the objects to which they refer. The system of meaning we call language, rather than representing certainty and coherence, is constantly shifting and changing its meanings depending on who is using a particular word and what she or he intends in using it. Like the meanings of the unconscious which we can only try to grasp in dreams, slips of the tongue, jokes (all described by Freud as the language of the unconscious) – the meanings of words are never fixed and safe, although they may appear to be so. For Lacan, the language of consciousness is set in motion and driven by our repressed Desire returned to us in language but in a laundered and veiled form. Through the veil we can see its actual content only in the slips and gaps and incoherences which 'poke' through it as we try to speak, or name, what we feel. Psychoanalysis and analytical psychotherapy use language as the means to gain direct access to our unconscious desire by making sense not of its coherences, but of its slippages, excesses, silences and gaps. And if we look hard at the articulations and Desires for our lost mothers which language, according to Lacan, represents, we can see the soft blurred outlines of what is really behind it – unconscious Desire and the symbolically castrated phallus which, despite appearances, represents the loss and absence as well as the energy of Desire. In the unconscious there is a constant sliding and concealment of meaning like the confused meanings we encounter in dreams. Lacan describes the unconscious as a 'sliding of the signified beneath the signifier' – as a constant dissolving and evaporation of meaning (Lacan 1977a: 154). This idea has been very influential in the interpretation of literary texts where Desire, the veiled unconscious meanings which set up a challenge behind the surface meanings, is explored and made explicit.

Quite clearly, if language and consciousness really reflected this turbulent, chaotic, enigmatic unconscious directly to us we would never be able to communicate with anyone. It is because Lacan is trying to mirror his own theory in his writing, to uncover the unconscious in his own language, and avoid mastery, that much of his work is unclear and difficult to understand. However, in conscious life, in the whole body of consciousness which is represented by the different disciplines, scientific and humanistic, it could be argued that we do manage to achieve some sense of ourselves as coherent and unified, and some sense of having created valuable bodies of knowledge which reflect this centredness. But Lacan maintains that all this is purely at the level of the 'Imaginary ego'. If we believe in the stability and 'truth' of language and knowledge, we have simply made another Imaginary identification with an image of ourselves reflected back to us from words whose meanings are as fleeting and illusory as the identities we build on the basis of them (Lacan 1977a: 70–7). In this context our theories become like psychological life-rafts to which we are tempted to cling to avoid being submerged by Desire.

There is, therefore, a radical split in our identity between what we are and what we take ourselves to be in consciousness. When we say 'I will have another cup of coffee', the 'I' that is the subject of the sentence is an immediately accessible and understandable point of reference. But this 'I' veils the shadowy outlines of the much more precarious 'I' who is doing the speaking. In the normal process of speaking and writing these two 'I's seem to refer to one unified self, but Lacan argues that this unity is still only of an Imaginary kind. The subject of the enunciation – the psychological person trying to communicate in language – is impossible to represent; there is no sign which can sum up my entire being. Most of what I am can never be expressed in language. I cannot 'mean' and 'be' at the same time. To emphasise this departure from Descartes' famous equation of consciousness and thinking with identity, Lacan rewrites the well-known 'I think therefore I am' as 'I am not where I think and I think where I am not'. For Lacan the subject is always constructed through a series of paradoxical, fantastic inversions. But what is crucial for becoming a viable human subject is the transfer of difference from the illusory world of the Imaginary where identity has been based on the search for the same, to the Symbolic where subjectivity is based on difference. This is a transfer from the world we see, of the senses, to the world we speak, of the signifier, from the domain of the specular to the domain of the social.

The phallic signifier

As we have seen in Lacan's theory of the construction of identity, the phallus is the primary signifier of the name of the father which sets in motion the endless signifying chain which makes the Symbolic and subjectivity possible. If this particular signifier is repudiated and expelled as it is in psychosis, Lacan suggests that the whole signifying network is thrown into chaos and all meaning is foreclosed. This collapse of meaning acts in direct opposition to subjectivity, producing a gap in the symbolic universe and throwing the fragmented subject catastrophically into the realm of the Real. The child's acceptance of the name of the father, that is the symbolic castration represented by the phallic signifier, opens the way to a system of metaphors or meanings which, however arbitrary and unstable, provide an anchor for the subject, protecting him or her from the delusional horrors of the Real. Without these signifying anchorages derived directly from acceptance of the phallic signifier, delusionary meanings from the Imaginary in the form of hallucinations may overwhelm the individual and feel terrifyingly real because their meanings have not been subjected to the control of the Symbolic.

The inter-subjective character of language means that it becomes the continually flowing space in which meanings, the subject and the Other are created simultaneously and under mutual pressure, and then dis-solved and re-created within the labyrinth of the endless possibilities of the signifying chain. The subject, through the identifications he or she makes in the statements, questions, and demands of language, is in-evitably saturated with the Other. So, if I say 'I don't mind at all' or 'I think it's time we had a comfortable sofa' or 'Let's go away for the week-end' I am creating myself as someone in a particular mood, asking a question or making a demand through the identity I have established in language. This may have nothing to do with the identity I feel outside what I say (I may be trying to appear polite, patient or adventurous). And what I say always implies that I am potentially heard by someone else also created by what he or she says in language, whether or not he or she responds and whether or not what they say is sincere.

In Lacan's linguistic version of psychoanalysis, identities and Freud's 'psychical apparatuses' are wiped out by the signifier which invades every corner of what we know and do not know, silently propelled by the Desire of the subjects it both creates and out of which it is created. Because the signifier is arbitrary and indifferent to any particular context or meaning, the chains and inter-connecting strings of meanings in language – both imprison and liberate us, holding back our Desires but at the same time allowing infinite excursions into possible meanings and interpretations of the world. On the one hand the signifier unrelentingly organises and pre-packages all experience, but on the other, because its signifiers are arbitrary and rest on the absence, it continually withdraws from and strangles these meanings and the identities based on them. In contrast to the foreshortened, narcissistic meanings and identities created in the Imaginary which revolve around the same rather than difference in a self-enclosed system of identifications devoid of insight, the signifying chains within language are inherently outward looking and social. But for Lacan the overriding strength of the signifier is that although it turns us into desiring human subjects (in his view the best we can expect) it also, by continually cancelling meaning, crucially keeps us in touch with the reality that we all have to die.

But in spite of the deathly quality of absence and loss inherent in all signifiers (because the underlying meaning of the phallus is lack) making their status in consciousness bogus, signifiers are paradoxically the vehicles, powered by Desire, for the only freedom available to us. But the coherence of Lacan's Symbolic stands or falls on the structural flexibility of the phallus. Lacan's elevation of the visible penis to the structural concept of the phallus, derived from the ancient emblem of power, and undercut by loss and symbolic castration, creates a primary signifier of Desire on which all other meaning can be built, albeit precariously. Bowie, reflecting on the precise structural antecedents of Lacan's phallus, writes mischievously on the suitability of the penis, unelevated to the symbolic heights of the phallus, to be the foundation stone for a system of signification and subjectivity characterised by disappearance and return, entity and non-entity, sense and non-sense, concentration and dispersal, being there and being gone; a system whose signifieds are constantly slipping, sliding, fleeing, expiring and dispersing. Yet, as Bowie goes on to comment, Lacan steadfastly refuses to adopt these promising lines of argument because he wants to 'maintain the coherence of structure and, more paradoxically, to maintain the neutrality of that structure in relation to gender' (Bowie 1991: 125).

Woman: the lack?

Let us move from Lacan's theory of language and signification to what it means for the child who begins to become an adult by entering language during the Oedipal crisis. According to Lacan, the price for the boy of being able to be a human subject is to accept the loss of his mother to the symbolic father and the symbolic castration implied in this humiliation. This means that he must, paradoxically, spend the rest of his life justifying his right to the power and status that possession of the phallic sign bequeaths to him. According to Lacan, he does this by making sure that he is always the object of desire for one or many women. To be unloved or undesired is to risk being reminded of the rejection by his mother and the symbolic castration by the father and the place of the father which accompanied it. For Lacan, this is primarily the symbolic castration involved in the constraining power of language.

In the case of the little girl, however, perceiving her total lack of what has value and power, she enters language negatively, as one who lacks the sign of essential, full subjectivity, however much she feels it in herself. She has to enter a culture which is driven by a form of Desire which is not her own, as the 'other', a defective version of a human subject. *Having* becomes the requirement for *being*, for a viable identity. For Lacan the only way a woman can obtain a phallus is by 'being' the phallus for her lovers in the realm of Demand where the satisfaction of need is the best thing available; that is, by being what the phallus needs and signifies, a substitute for the mother. Only in this way, through her heterosexual relationships and by becoming an object of Desire for men, can she reach the phallus and therefore have a kind of identity. By doing this she also allows men to feel themselves to be the objects of *her* Desire. And this fulfils the vital patriarchal requirement of bolstering men's identity – their sense of potency and phallic power which cannot be sustained without women. For Lacan, the absence of the penis in women only matters because it makes meaningful the father's prohibition on her desire for the mother. Within this context, females appear retrospectively to have been castrated. A girl has not got what is required to be her mother's lover, and – to add insult to injury – neither does she seem to have what is required to be an active, self-determining subject in the world. She is the *lack* itself. In Lacan's theory, heterosexuality seems to be the only way she can gain a share in male power. This seems unpromising ground for a feminist approach to questions of gender.

However, in this account of the coming into being of men and women's subjectivity within culture, Lacan is not consciously supporting the inequality of gender categories. To begin with he emphatically pulls the theoretical rug from under the comfortable power of the man, within language and culture. He makes it clear that the phallus only *seems* to have power because it has value as a signifier. But since signifiers are arbitrary, lacking any value in themselves, its status is bogus because it lacks any justification for the power it confers. It is, moreover, a phallus which has been symbolically castrated. However, its bogusness, Lacan argues, is transferred to all other meanings. The phallus, in provoking the chain of meanings 'having' and 'not having', positive and negative, power and lack, 'masculinity' and 'femininity', opens the way to the meanings of all other signifiers. In this way the meaning of the phallus is carried over into all the other binary oppositions we use to categorise and differentiate what we call reality (for example, nature/culture, light/ dark, good/bad). If the status of the phallus is false and arbitrary, then so are all these other oppositions modelled on the binary meanings of the phallus and the lack, 'masculinity' and 'femininity', by which we structure our world. So the boy's entry into language is based on a hoax at the very centre of the subject's identity and therefore that of patriarchal culture and knowledge.

So male identity, from Lacan's point of view, begins to look in-creasingly precarious. Based on a false estimation of the power of the phallus, and a use of this power to coerce female desire to bolster male needs, Lacan opens up male sexuality to the kind of criticism which has appealed to some feminists. As Toril Moi wryly puts it: 'woman as defective becomes a defence against the thinking male subject's potentially devastating insight into his own lack' (Moi 1989: 195). Reduced to a projection of male lack and having no meaning except as an object of phantasy in language, woman as herself cannot exist. She is subjected in language only to become a passive spectacle of male phantasy, contradictorily, either denigrated as worthless, the male bad phantasy of himself – the witch woman, unruly monster or whore – or idealised as the male good phantasy of himself and destined to become the Absolute Other, the site of all knowledge, wisdom and truth – the Madonna, the Wise Woman from the Mountains, the unattainable Goddess. Woman, therefore reflects back to men, like the Imaginary mother, a good or bad dimension of himself. The idea of woman being complementary and different is, for Lacan, a myth. In falling in love with women, patriarchal men only fall narcissistically in love with projections of themselves.

But denigration of woman, says Lacan, is the precondition of man's belief in his own soul; without her to project onto he is nothing. She becomes a symptom of male lack. In other words, without the constant availability of woman as a foil, representing a place where he can unconsciously project everything of himself that he doesn't want to acknowledge, his vulnerability, his powerlessness, his sense of uncertainty, chaos and emptiness, man would never have enough room to construct and believe in his own viability and goodness. Woman as nothing, as the site of man's unconscious in language, allows man in contrast to look like something – positive, potent and meaningful.

So, for Lacan all meanings and identities based on the meaning of the phallus are false. The meaning and identity of women – the ones who ostensibly represent the lack – in fact begin to look significantly more solidly based than those of men because, in all of Lacan's work, the mother, 'woman', as the one who inspires all desire is never in question. Women may lack the phallus, but they have something else on which to base their identity even though it has been repressed. The desire for reunion with the mother is what both drives language and produces the dislocations and subversions which are enacted in it. It is this aspect of Lacan's work which has appealed to feminists like Kristeva, Irigaray and Cixous.

However, we must recognise that to deny the Symbolic – language – is, for Lacan, to deny our humanity, however bogus the grounds on which our sense of it rests. To totally refuse to be 'subjected' within language and culture is to remain the prisoner of Imaginary phantasy of an undifferentiated existence with the mother where there can be nothing available to the adult but psychosis. The acceptance of patriarchal language, and therefore male power, paradoxically, in the context of Lacan's theory, becomes the only condition of sanity for both sexes. Once again we recognise the ways in which Lacan's complex work seems to turn in several directions at once.

Masquerade and jouissance

How, then, might women cope with their catastrophic predicament? Since 'woman' within patriarchy is constructed only with reference to the male sign, the phallus, her life is lived as a *masquerade*, playing the part man has assigned to her – the 'not man', 'the lack', a fictional complement to himself (Lacan 1977a: 290). So, according to Lacan, what society takes to be 'natural' 'feminine' behaviour is an acting out of the role of what patriarchal societies requires of women: wife, mother, little girl, housewife, mother-in-law, baby doll, femme fatale, scarlet woman, iron lady, shrinking violet, blue-stocking, bitch, bimbo, single mother. Women, therefore, can represent male phantasies, but never themselves, and cannot exist as subjects within the patriarchal social order even in the bogus sense in which men can. In Lacan's world, where no one has a genuine identity, woman represents a double lack – her own lack of the valued phallus, and as a projection of male lack produced by his symbolic castration by his father. So women are doubly powerless.

Building on Freud's concept of penis-envy, and what he called secondary narcissism which can develop in the girl at the time of the Oedipal crisis, Lacan's notion of the masquerade can illuminate something of the ways in which many women 'package' themselves as objects in response to the demands of male phantasy. In their desire for a phallus – for the power to be a human subject – they make their whole body and being over to attracting an 'Other', through whom they think that they may become potent and whole. In this masquerade, determined entirely in relation to phallic Desire, women effectively annihilate any possibility of a self of their own. In fact, Lacan sees a woman's entire involvement with heterosexual activity as masquerade, as a participation in a phallic sexuality which has nothing to do with her or her body. At the same time, in an attempt to suggest a more positive role for women, he develops the concept of *jouissance* (an untranslatable French word signifying sexual bliss) to suggest a form of sexual pleasure peculiar and specific to them. He describes *jouissance* mysteriously as being 'something more' – what escapes or is left over from the phallic function, and exceeds it (Mitchell and Rose, eds., 1982: 147). Here he refers to other forms of pleasure not 'summed up' and subsumed in phallic activity which he thinks takes place only in the realm of Demand. These are sources of pleasure which, like the unconscious meanings which exist between words, lie beyond the reach and meaning of heterosexual physical satisfaction based on the phallus and are perhaps those forms of pleasure which are associated with the search for an alternative identity through the re-union with the mother, the originator of all Desire. Lacan offers St Theresa, as depicted in Bernini's statue, as an example of a woman experiencing a form of bliss entirely separate from the phallic function (Mitchell and Rose, eds., 1982: 147). He suggests that women, lacking the capacity necessary for the phallic function have access to a greater capacity for undulating and overspilling sexual diversity such as that expressed in St Theresa's apparent mystically inspired orgasm. Once again, these ideas are explored further by the French feminists influenced by Lacan some of whose work we shall examine in the next chapter.

Commentary on 'The Meaning of the Phallus'

Lacan's writing

One of the inherent problems in reading Lacan is the difficulty of his style. This difficulty results directly from Lacan's belief that meaning, including theoretical meaning, always hangs on a knife edge, continually punctured out of existence. He deliberately cultivates obscurity and mystification rather than clarity because, for him, clarity misrepresents the nature of the subject-matter of his theory. Since meaning and identity are immensely complex and fluid concepts, any theory which attempts to describe them must reflect this complexity and fluidity. No meanings can be privileged over any other meanings and theoretical language can have no more value than ordinary, desiring speech. Lacan introduces unconscious Desire into his own texts in a way no other psychoanalytic writer had done before. He insists that his texts should be self-authenticating in the sense that they constantly refuse the settled position of any single identity or meaning in favour of a deluge of semantic multiplicity and fluidity. For Lacan, this kind of writing represents the only notion of identity, 'truth' or pleasure he will accept – the 'truth', ideally, of desiring speech in all its potential fullness, multi-layeredness and mobility as its signifying chains are driven by the movement of desire. Lacan, determined to show the infinite possibilities of originality and expressiveness within language, continually uses wit, word-play, conceits, jokes, parodoxes, puns, irony, extravagant imagery, proverbs, aphorisms, slang and exclamations to convert his theoretical ideas into what are generally considered their opposites – literary texts. He persistently undercuts any meanings he creates by demonstrating the semantic opportunities inherent in those meanings and the possibilities for fakes, evasions, withdrawals, subterfuges and mimicry so that any single, stable meaning comes apart, evaporates or dissolves under a welter of associated meanings or play on meanings, always available to the writer in the continuous signifying flow of language. It is this endlessly inventive excursioning into the labyrinthine super-abundance of poten-tial meaning – of desire in movement – which Lacan sees as the risk-laden freedom and satisfaction open to the desiring human subject. But his style also underlines the unstable, empty impossibility of lack and restriction within a pre-existing circuit of meaning from which the human subject must always interpret the world. Language can never tell us the 'truth', theoretical or otherwise, about anything except its own potential for both the liberation of desire and its structural constraints in a process of continual unveiling and re-veiling of meaning. This process reveals – re-veils – not only the potential for life but also the continuing death of the subject in language as meaning continually collapses.

Even with forewarning and insight, however, Lacan's writing can still be extremely frustrating and unrewarding for the reader trying to make sense of his persistent attempts to include non-sense in his sense and one of Lacan's major projects was constantly to reproduce the moment when surface meaning fails, stumbles or falls apart. As a result, his essay needs to be read with some patience and attention. Like the human subject itself, one never quite knows where one is in a Lacan text.

'The Meaning of the Phallus'

This dense and often difficult paper is typical of Lacan's theoretical writing. It is also Lacan's clearest description of the role of the phallus in his account of sexuality. It is this issue – the fact that, in Freud's theory femininity is structured in relation to the male genital organ – which lay at the centre of the debates about the construction of femininity in the 1920s and 1930s.

In the first part of the paper Lacan energetically takes issue with those followers of Freud – Abraham, Jones and Klein – who, in his view, abandoned the phallic phase altogether in their attempts to produce a more egalitarian account of the construction of 'femininity'. Lacan accuses them of abandoning Freud's central concepts of the castration complex and the unconscious which cause the fundamental division within human identity. This, Lacan argues vehemently, amounts to a repression of what is most radical and innovative in Freud's work; it represents the pursuit of a laundered theory in which feminine identity is not structured in relation to the phallus. The paradox at the centre of the debate on 'femininity' was Freud's insistence on a phallic phase in which the girl does not recognise that she has a vagina, and which culminates in the drama of the Oedipal crisis. If the child recognised the equal role of the vagina, the phallus would no longer be a determining factor in the construction of gender of both sexes. In Lacan's view, Klein and others had reconstructed gender as biologically determined from birth in order to resolve this problem for women. It is at this point that Lacan introduces the idea of the penis not simply as a biological organ, but as a sign. The phallus, Lacan insists, is not an actual organ or a phantasy; it is a potent sign which in psychoanalysis, through language, can reveal its other veiled function – its status as a phallus but a symbolically castrated and therefore bogus one.

On the basis of his distinction between the penis and the phallus Lacan moves next to what he regards as the two psychical realities which reflect this distinction – the realm of Demand and the realm of Desire. Lacan argues that the child and the client in analysis must achieve the move from the realm of Demand, represented by the penis, to the realm of Desire, signified by the phallus.

According to Lacan, Demand functions at the level of the baby's needs and can be satisfied by the mother's adequate care. Desire, however, operates in a separate realm and is that which exceeds Demand. It can never be satisfied – it is the baby's longing for total possession of the mother, to be loved better than all its siblings, and its father and anyone else, for all time. Demand revolves around presence and absence in the space between the mother and baby. It brings the other – the mother – into the presence of the baby, but this presence is never enough because there is always something about her which is absent because she belongs to others too. Desire, says Lacan, is the result of subtracting satisfaction from Demand. It is what remains as a residue which can never be satisfied and the only place where it can be returned to us is in language – the place of the Other beyond the (m)other to which the child addresses its Demands. The problem of modern Object-Relations psychoanalysis, Lacan repeats, is that Desire has been reduced simply to need or the frustration of need, that is, to the requirement for adequate mothering. He argues that at the Oedipal stage and always afterwards, the phallus signifies ineradicable Desire. This Desire extends beyond the level of sexual need which can be satisfied by the penis. It can be represented only in the place of the father, in the Symbolic or language.

The satisfaction of Demand which the baby achieves turns out to be no more than a smothering of this Desire for perpetual possession of the mother. It is this longing for paradise which language helps us to forget but which also, in the gaps it reveals between words, cannot help but be expressed. It is the phantasy of paradise – the satisfaction of Desire – which constitutes the subversive power of the unconscious. It is our potential for being reminded of this which makes all identity unstable. Lacan stresses that the energy of Desire (the 'force of pure loss') expressed in language arises contradictorily from its obliteration at the level of sexuality in relation to the mother, who can only satisfy the baby's Demand.

The enigma for the subject, to which Lacan refers in 'The Meaning of the Phallus' is the fact that its Demand is referred back only as the satisfaction of need, not in terms of the satisfaction of Desire. Therefore its relation to the mother becomes ambivalent. She has not delivered satisfaction of the Desire she has provoked. For both the subject and other (mother), it is not enough for Lacan that they should be involved together only at the level of need or as love objects. So he makes the phallus stand for that place in language where reason is connected to Desire. This idea is very different from the Kleinian concept of the mother–baby relationship which stresses the experience of good care (at the level of need) and the resolution of ambivalence, as the basis for a stable identity and an awareness of morality.

In the remaining part of the paper Lacan describes what he sees as the comedy of sexual relations between men and women based on the false idea of complementarity. Fundamentally, the comedy of heterosexuality for Lacan lies in the fact that 'having' the phallus in the realm of Demand (heterosexual satisfaction) is confused by both sexes with 'being' (or an identity) in the realm of Desire. In what Lacan regards as a farcical roundabout of Desire, the man desires a woman whose own Desire is also constructed around the phallic term. However, although her penis-envy makes her want to have a phallus, she can only do this by being the phallus – supporting the status of the man's phallus through involving herself in the masquerade. So she inevitably ends up giving the man a phallus (to confirm his phallic power) which she herself does not actually possess, although her Desire is constructed in relation to the phallic term. Conversely, she can only gain from the man what he thinks he is, which turns out to be only what he *has* – a penis – because the phallus he and she think he is, in reality, is bogus. The meaning of the phallus in the realm of Desire turns out to be, behind the veil, only the penis and a symbolically castrated one at that! The identity of the heterosexual couple is divided so that nothing, including desire, is what it seems.

Within this bleak view of heterosexual love Lacan has created a farce. Love turns out not to be the mutual complementary encounter of opposites described by patriarchy, but the meeting of two 'lacks' each trying to give each other what neither of them actually has! Heterosexuality represents only the satisfaction of need via the penis in the realm of Demand, in the phantasy of the Imaginary, and only appears to be mediated by the phallus in the realm of Desire. Desire, which goes beyond anything the actual penis can satisfy, can only be experienced sexually in *jouissance* – something which is in excess of anything hetero-sexuality could provide. The gap between Demand and Desire, having and being, which the child first feels in relation to the mother – is what makes splitting and division inevitable because Desire must be repressed. In the heterosexual relationship of substitute others beyond the mother, 'having' is transformed into 'appearing', which then veils the bogus status of the relations signified by the phallus. Lacan is so convinced of the bogus meaning of the phallus – the collapse of 'masculinity' unveiled as symbolic lack – that he describes the penis on the body of the Other – the one the woman loves – merely as a fetish, something which stands in for the penis that the child originally believed was embodied in its first other – the mother. This harks back to the picture of heterosexuality implicit in Freud's work where it emerges as the vehicle for the phantasised reunion with the mother for both sexes.

Lacan concludes this paper with some observations on the relative toleration of lack of sexual satisfaction in men and women and on the issue of sexual infidelity. Because of her symbolic alienation from her own Desire (because it is structured in relation to the phallus rather than a sign based on her own body), Lacan argues that women tolerate frigidity and repressed Desire more easily than men because their Desire is not symbolised. However, men's repressed Desire, because it is never satisfied beyond the level of Demand (the women can only give in love what she cannot have, the phallus), makes them wish for endless self-confirmation in the form of other women who can signify the phallus in another phantasised form. This, Lacan argues, makes impotence harder to bear for men because they need constantly to try to justify the false status of the phallic signifier through recourse to phantasy manifestations of it in different women all of whom, despite the fact that their Desire is constituted in relation to the phallus, can only return him to original emptiness.

Lacan's concept of the phallus resists any naturalistic account of sexuality. For him, what we usually mean by sexuality is only the satisfaction of need in the realm of Demand. He relegates sexuality to two entirely different dimensions – to language where it drives a system of ordering and to the unconscious where, in the spaces between words, meaning continually fails. On the other hand, love belongs to the Imaginary ego which disguises the failure and impossibility of Desire in

[167]

the reflection of like to like. In this view love becomes the ultimate form of self-recognition or narcissism.

Discussion

Lacan's theory of the construction of 'masculinity' and 'femininity' in culture is compellingly coherent in many ways. He offers us an account of how 'masculine' and 'feminine' identity in the form of consciousness comes into being within patriarchal cultures and a map of the patriarchal mode of organisation of values and ideology which is integral to this process. He confronts us with a consciousness shot through with the unconscious or, to put it the other way round, with a socialised unconscious anchored in language and culture – in the way we 'think' the world. Perhaps the most striking feature of Lacan's theory is that the very process of thinking is sexualised and gendered. The male, not the female, Imaginary forms the linchpin of rationality, language and subjectivity. With the boy's entry into the Symbolic, the mind takes precedence over the body so that the order of the Symbolic cuts into and re-shapes his original emotional, bodily way of being with the mother. This means that our identities, our ways of perceiving the world are managed not only by the conscious meanings of the multitude of discourses through which we are constituted but also by the underlying painful emotions of loss and desire which produce these discourses and give them their power.

In making the phallus into the central term of his theory, Lacan builds a convincing bridge between the unconscious *psychical* processes related to the body and the conscious *social* processes involved in language and culture. The phallus straddles both the unconscious and conscious domains as the sign of difference – of sexual difference within the psyche of the Oedipal child and as the first sign of difference within the chain of signs which we call language. So, in Lacan's ingenious theory, the psychoanalytic and the social, the unconscious and consciousness, seem at some level at least to have been integrated by the presence of the phallus and desire within both of these dimensions. For some feminists, Lacan's claim to have produced a theory of the social construction of 'masculinity' and 'femininity' in language (rather than simply treating them as biological givens), seems to offer at least a theoretical possibility for change. The presence of unconscious desire within language where it may be available as another form of identity which is currently repressed, seems to suggest language as a potential site for change and for setting up a challenge to patriarchal identity and knowledge. We shall be discussing the psychoanalytic work of the French feminists Kristeva and Irigaray in this context.

On the face of it, Lacan's work does seem immensely phallocentric, which has been initially off-putting to feminists. Despite Lacan's attempts to convert the penis into the phallus, a gender neutral symbol of power, it still looks like a theory of male subjectivity, power and order and female absence, lack and disorder which fixes male power irrevocably in all identities. But, in Lacan's defence, it only looks like a theory of male privilege if we ignore Lacan's overall understanding of symbolic castration and its power to undermine the status of all identity, knowledge and thinking. The power which Lacan accords to those who are represented by the sign of the phallus is, he insists, always fraudulent and based on symbolic castration, humiliation and loss. This is something Freud, who may have been familiar with similar linguistic ideas, was less able consciously to acknowledge. The price of male power, therefore, is a split subjectivity and an identity which is inevitably fragile and precarious. 'Masculine' men are constantly under threat of sabotage from the re-emergence of their Imaginary, their repressed Desire and powerlessness which always threatens to expose and overwhelm them. This particular aspect of Lacan's theory helps to explain why many men need to keep their psychological 'visors' down, especially in the company of other men and why change is so difficult to achieve at both the individual and institutional levels. As has already been suggested, for psychical survival men have to appear as powerful and different, 'not woman', 'not the lack'. To become significantly less culturally 'masculine' and more like women for many men is to expose them even more to the bogus nature of 'masculinity' and potential psychical annihilation. It evokes the unconscious knowledge of symbolic castration on two counts – the sense of the loss of identity and emptiness after the discovery, as small children, that they were not like the mother and therefore could not, like her, have babies and their painful loss of her to the father, a further heavy blow to their earliest attempts to find an identity.

So, the vulnerability of male identity implicit in Lacan's theory means that women's desire to share power with men inevitably confronts many of them with potential annihilation. If women increasingly resist the position of the lack by expressing the active as well as passive dimensions of themselves, Lacan's work suggests that many men are threatened with not simply loss of power but with psychical disintegration. This is something which has not always been recognised by feminists. Women who express their psychological bisexual nature openly, who are active and self-determining, who feel that they *are* subjects, threaten many men who are unconsciously dependent on women to support their bogus identities (the only ones available to them), with women's passive desire and their silence. If women increasingly own the active as well as passive dimensions of themselves, many men risk having to confront their own lack (their symbolic castration and powerlessness) which unconsciously they have always projected onto women. Women can no longer represent what Girard describes as the 'monstrous double' (Girard 1979). This situation, if Lacan is right, explains why the acceptance of difference as equal has been and is so hard to achieve beyond a certain point, at both the public and personal levels. If patriarchal male identity depends for its existence on unconscious dependence on women as the symbolic bearers of loss and lack, women's refusal to accept this position threatens some men with psychical extinction.

Lacan's theory of language poses problems for both men and women in that, amongst other things, it insists that the justification for, and confidence in, male power on which culture rests, is fraudulent. Since women as well as men think in and use reason and language they are implicated in this fraud. However, a greater problem for women in Lacan's theory is his positioning of women as the cultural representation of the lack, that is the excess, the indecipherable, the uncategorisable outside meaning, an ever-present foil to men's rationality and search for knowledge and 'truth'. If, according to Lacan, woman within patriarchal societies has no place outside language and if within language she can represent only man's unconscious, his instability and disorder, we are compelled to wonder who is the 'I' or 'me' who speaks in language from a female body? Lacan's reply, as we have seen, is that she can only be woman in masquerade – in a kind of psychical fancy dress – which does not offer grounds for much optimism for feminists. Lacan seems to condemn women to being an unconscious symptom of men's hysteria over their symbolic castration by their fathers and their fear of being 'feminine'. And Lacan's own position on women is rather uncompromising. There are no means apparent by which women can change their position from negativity and powerlessness. Many feminists have taken issue with Lacan in this respect. They argue that his work doesn't equate with how women feel, with women's experience of what they are or what they could become, and that many women do not feel disempowered within language or society in the way he seems to describe. Feminism has emphasised that women can be active, self-determining, autonomous subjects who can and have united with other women to analyse their predicament within patriarchal societies and initiate both cultural and material change. The question, therefore, is whether we can theorise this other way of being a woman within a Lacanian framework? Lacan himself rejected the idea of French feminists such as Cixous that there could be some essential form of the feminine 'behind' language within the girl's pre-Oedipal phantasised relationship with her mother. Without the Symbolic, he argues, there can be no human subjectivity, only psychosis. Entry into language – the intellectual mastery of unbearable emotion – is the *condition* of sanity. The only way for a woman to enter the Symbolic without representing the lack, as Irigaray argues, is as a man, which means she therefore becomes disembodied. From a Lacanian point of view, this kind of identity is based on an identification with male power and the phallus and is therefore equally fraudulent.

There is also a problem for some women in Lacan's de-centring of subjectivity. At a time when feminists are trying to win acceptance for the idea that women too are subjects, the political equals of men even if that means equal in a different way, Lacan argues that not only are women not subjects, but the subjects that men take themselves to be are fraudulent and based on a fallacy (phallusy). As far as Lacan is concerned men, stripped of their rational categories, remain dependent babies, chaotic, polymorphously perverse (that is, driven by a variety of oral, anal and phallic aims like the pre-Oedipal child), and still living in the Imaginary. How can women affirm female subjectivity at a time when a significant part of modern philosophy challenges the very concept of subjectivity? In other words the goal of being a full, political subject which is desired by feminists for women, must be understood as a phantasy. If we have reached a theoretical position where *no one* can be a subject, where might this leave women who have never been subjects? If feminists are trying to re-think the situation of women and speculate on another path leading away from the pre-Oedipal fused identity with the mother, it seems an irony to many that the intellectual rug seems to be being pulled from under them. Men may be de-centred, chaotic, polymorphously perverse and lacking access to any authentic meaning beyond the pain and loss of their mother. They may be unconsciously still dependent on the mother and possessed by a yearning to retrieve a paradise lost for which they search endlessly in language. However, it is women who are culturally categorised as simple-minded, innocent, helpless 'little girl', 'baby', 'doll', 'chick'. The question therefore becomes: if men are desiring babies, who or what are women – are they babies too but without the obscuring veil – or are they something else? If they are mothers – the creators – of these veiled babies, does this make women the real subjects because the equivalent of symbolic castration has never happened to the womb? Lacan's work suggests, inadvertently it has to be said, that we have to entertain again the possibility that the womb is the power which men unconsciously envy and fear. His work perhaps, hints that what Freud called penis-envy, is for him, a disguised inversion of womb-envy, as Klein, in a very different framework, also implies. (This is not to argue that penis-envy does not exist but that it is unconsciously emphasised to obscure a form of envy which is much more threatening to men.) So male identity, founded in symbolic castration is experienced, unconsciously, as absence and void. This experience of emptiness and lack of meaning is then projected onto women by means of the signifying power of the phallus so that women, in spite of the overwhelming presence entailed in their capacity literally to double themselves, emerge, magically, through what looks like a gigantic linguistic conjuring trick and against all the odds, as the representation of lack. In this context, an anti-essentialist feminist appropriation of Lacan's work might look to the womb rather than the phallus as a centre for its ideas.

In a recent paper I have argued, using Lacan's theory of how meanings are initiated in the child's early bodily world, that patriarchal culture may rest on the repression of a female signifier based on the womb (Minsky 1995). However, although both children may first recognise this hidden signifier of powerful creativity through their *in-sight*, it is subsequently repressed in favour of the *sight* of the visible phallus which, furthermore, the mother apparently wants. For boys, the phallus provides a much-needed rescue from the consequences of their terrifying realisation that, although they, like girls, at first identify with the creativity and power of the mother, only girls can eventually 'be like mummy' and have babies. No matter how hard boys try this will never be an available identity for them as mothers have to try to explain. This might explain why knowledge based mainly on observation is culturally valued much more than knowledge based on 'in-sight and in-tuition' and why men are compelled to construct and experience their identity primarily through work and 'doing' whereas, ideally, most women have the capacity for two identities. If womb-envy is, after all, the unconscious source of women's domination within patriarchy, to what extent could this situation be changed? In focusing on signification and the sexed human subject, Lacan raises these kinds of questions but within a radically different conceptual framework from that of Klein and Winnicott.

Perhaps taking the most positive view of Lacan's ultimately 'masterful' theory of signification, the most important insight Lacan offers both men and women is that we cannot achieve a language, a mode of knowledge or a creative and imaginative way of living which is not bogus and destructive of the 'other' without a willingness, as Julia Kristeva suggests, to question and challenge all meaning. This challenge to meaning has been the project of much modern literary criticism based on her ideas. This thinking seeks to reveal the unconscious desire and the hidden meanings which often lie behind the apparent surface meanings of a text, rather as Lacan seeks to reveal the desire which underpins the subject. Lacan's work also suggests that we need to try to tolerate some gaps and slippages, some uncertainty in the knowledge we create. We cannot expect to be able to produce a totally coherent knowledge when we know that our own identities can never be totally coherent. His theory also suggests that we need to try to engage with what Kristeva describes as the marginal within culture, which includes insight and intuition as well as reason and logic, to produce a form of knowledge which is not reducible to control and mastery. Such knowledge, reflecting a new definition of rigour, would make no illusory claims to have mastered the world and may produce new meanings of which culture needs to take account. On the other hand, Irigaray's work suggests that we need to pay attention to the sex of the bodies which support our speech. She argues that women suffer from the fact that the unconscious phantasies associated with women's bodies (what she calls the female imaginary) are not symbolised in language and that a feminine challenge to male language must come first from those with women's bodies who, as she sees it, have been 'buried alive' in culture. For her, freeing the repressed 'feminine' in men is of secondary importance to the disinterring of women.

Despite the undeniable value of Lacan's work in challenging identity and meaning perhaps we need to recognise that a perpetual awareness of the potential fragmentation of our identities and the bogusness of all identity is, beyond a certain point, an unliveable position. In ordinary life we cannot constantly confront the idea that much of what we think we understand is fiction, based on the potentially overwhelming emotions of desire and loss which we then attempt to control through the rationality of language. We have to cope, to communicate, to live much of the time *as if*, everything, including ourselves, were much more coherent and stable than it is, *as if*, if Lacan is right, the phallus were not the primary but empty, signifier of power and identity. We, and women in particular, have to live as if we can be authentic subjects even if Lacan's theory, and post-structuralism generally, convinces us that this is, theoretically at least, an impossibility, since subjectivity exists in a continual state of flux.

Lacan's theory of language and signification has sometimes been criticised for separating its concepts too radically from their context in everyday existence and for having little to say about suffering and death. The signifier seems oblivious to the ordinary dramas of inter-subjective life. The very scope and complexity of Lacan's model of what 'is', conceptualised in the interlace between the Real, the Symbolic and the Imaginary, seems to entail a loss of theoretical and emotional contact with the fact that, as Bowie argues, 'there are causes to defend, suffering to alleviate, pleasures to pursue' which cannot be eradicated by a kind of 'word magic' (Bowie 1991: 203). As Jacoby has commented, recently there seems to have been a retreat from politics into theory where the world has come to be seen only as a vast text on which there is nothing left for us to do except write endless secondary texts and commentaries (Jacoby 1987). In spite of erecting a theory which describes the patriarchal construction of woman as the lack, Lacan did not identify himself with feminism because causes smack of some alliance with notions of 'truth' and justice which Lacan, believing he had uncovered the bogusness of all knowledge and identity, could not accept. For Lacan 'truth' can exist only in the 'full speech' of the speaking subject where the action of the unconscious on language makes any given chain of signifiers inescapably 'true'. Somewhat parodoxically, Lacan identifies himself most closely with the 'truth' of 'jouissance', the form of pleasure he argued was most characteristic of women but which given the appropriate signifying aspirations, could be achieved by men and women.

A practical response to Lacan's work might involve finding a way of integrating his post-modernist awareness of the precariousness of identity and knowledge with our persisting insight and intuitive sense, both of which seem to lie outside signification, that some meanings still seem to have more value than others, and our continuing commitment to them. As we have seen this modernist, humanistic way of thinking clearly runs against the tide of Lacan's thinking which is that to want to live by some meanings and not others is, in linguistic terms, simply to conflate the signifier with the signified, to over-identify with a particular meaning and lose the sense of its arbitrariness. We shall explore some of these ideas further in the next chapter which includes the work of two women influenced by Lacan, Julia Kristeva and Luce Irigaray.

However, despite reservations about aspects of Lacan's theory, his achievement has been to de-mythologise identity and patriarchal culture. It is perhaps Lacan's suggestion that, at some level, illusion lies at the heart of our lives, and of the provisionality of cultural knowledge, which is his most distinctively modern and valuable contribution to psycho-analytic theory and theory generally.

Presences and absences

Finally in this chapter let us look briefly at aspects of Lacan's career and ideas in the context of the presences and absences in his theory. Despite his undoubted insights, his formidable creativity and breadth of knowledge and the usefulness of his theory for our analysis of patriarchal ideology, there are aspects of his practice and his writing which have been controversial. Many of those who knew him have testified to his seductive appeal amongst those (including many women) who flocked to his seminars in Paris, which began in the early nineteen-fifties and continued until his death in 1981. But this appeal is certainly not apparent in the notorious difficulty of his writing and he seems not to have been interested in clear communication. His desire to maintain the purity of his ideas about language, that it should be continually subject to the subversion and disruption of the unconscious, seems to have been more important to him than accessibility for those suffering from the effects of the patriarchal ideology his theory exposed. Certainly there is no evidence in Lacan's writing of a wish to communicate with women, despite the cultural cage with which his theory, at one level, confronts them. It is tempting, therefore, to conclude that his uncompromising anti-humanist theoretical position, at some level, veils a narcissistic enjoyment of mystification as a form of omnipotent power, particularly with the awareness of both his institutional relationships with colleagues and his analytic practice.

In the context of the castration complex which Lacan makes central to his theory, the abrupt and autocratic closing of his school of psycho-analysis, the Ecole Freudienne, in 1980 without consulting his colleagues, may again suggest phantasies of narcissistic omnipotence and castration in the form of the abrupt curtailment of whatever shows any sign of a settled identity. In his now notorious clinical practice he is reputed regularly to have 'cut off' the session whenever he felt a patient showed signs of slipping into what he regarded as an 'Imaginary' identification with him, even if the session had only just begun. He took the view that this behaviour had the effect of a symbolic castration in the transference and threw the patient out of the realm of Demand and into that of Desire, language and the reality of separation from the world of the mother. These two examples seem to reflect a kind of glorification of the 'cut' which come close to a form of sadism. This celebration of symbolic castration also, as we have seen, expresses itself in his discourse where his conscious intention is to show the continual play of the unconscious in language. But for the reader, this, perhaps, requires just too much continual severing of our understanding, a too persistent undermining of any accumulating coherence so that we are always thrown back into the realm of Desire and frustration. In Lacan's work, despite its literary inventiveness, we find a contradictory celebration of the very patriarchal qualities he criticises and exposes.

However, despite what may have been Lacan's unconscious short-comings, he manages to produce insights into the relationship between men and women and patriarchal cultures which are difficult to ignore. Perhaps insight into the status of his own 'masculinity' made him acutely sensitive to its existence within culture and it is this which fuelled the development of his theory. In the sense that all writers are writing about themselves at some unconscious level, Lacan, like Freud, Klein and Winnicott probably also inscribed his own unconscious desire onto the 'body' of his theory. But if we are tempted to use this as a reason to reject his work we need to remind ourselves that all of us do much the same thing, not only as writers, but also as readers. What we understand, what we remember, what we 'make' of a text, or indeed any representation, depends not just on our conscious interests, but also on our unconscious ones over which we have very little control.

Suggested reading

Theory

LACAN, J. (1966) *Ecrits*, Paris, Seuil.
LACAN, J. (1977a) *Ecrits: A Selection*, trans. A. Sheridan, London, Tavistock.

LACAN, J. (1977b) *The Four Fundamental Concepts of Psychoanalysis*, ed. J. Alain-Miller, trans. A. Sheridan, London, Hogarth Press and the Institute of Psychoanalysis.

MITCHELL, J. and ROSE, J. eds. (1982) *Jacques Lacan and the Ecole Freudienne: Feminine Sexuality*, London, Macmillan.

Lacan's writing is often very difficult to follow. The following includes fairly accessible introductions and/or discussions.

General

BENVENUTO, B. and KENNEDY, R. (1986) *Jacques Lacan: An Introduction*, London, Free Association Books.

BOOTHBY, R. (1991) *Death and Desire: Psychoanalytic Theory in Lacan's Return to Freud*, London, Routledge.

BOWIE, M. (1991) *Lacan*, London, Fontana [Modern Masters].

BRENNAN, T. (1991) *History After Lacan*, London, Routledge.

FORRESTER, J. (1991) *The Seductions of Psychoanalysis*, Cambridge, Cambridge University Press.

GALLOP, J. (1985) *Reading Lacan*, Ithaca and London, Cornell University Press.

GIRARD, R. (1979) *Violence and the Sacred*, trans. P. Gregory, Baltimore and London, Johns Hopkins University Press.

JACOBY, R. (1987) *The Last Intellectuals*, New York, Basic Books.

ROUDINESCO, E. (1990) *Psychoanalysis in France 1925–1985*, London, Free Association Books.

SCHNEIDERMAN, S. (1983) *Jacques Lacan: The Death of an Intellectual Hero*, Cambridge MA, Harvard University Press.

TURKLE, S. (1978) *Psychoanalytic Politics*, New York, Basic Books.

Feminist interpretations

BRENNAN, T. ed. (1989) *Between Feminism and Psychoanalysis*, London, Routledge.

GALLOP, J. (1985) *Reading Lacan*, Ithaca and London, Cornell University Press.

GROSZ, E. (1990) *Jacques Lacan: A Feminist Introduction*, London, Routledge.

LEMOINE-LUCCIONE E. (1987) *The Dividing of Women or Woman's Lot*, London, Free Association Books.

MINSKY, R. (1992) 'Lacan' in *Knowing Women*, ed. H. Crowley and S. Himmelweit, Milton Keynes, Open University and Cambridge, Polity Press.

MINSKY, R. (1995) 'Reaching Beyond Denial – Sight and In-sight – A Way Forward?' *Free Associations*, 35.

MITCHELL, J. and ROSE, J. 'Introduction' in J. Mitchell and J. Rose, eds. (1982) *Jacques Lacan and the Ecole Freudienne: Feminine Sexuality*, London, Macmillan.

SARAP, M. (1992) *Jacques Lacan*, New York, Harvester Wheatsheaf.

SILVERMAN, K. (1988) *The Acoustic Mirror – The Female Voice in Psychoanalysis and Cinema*, Bloomington: Indiana University Press.

5
Feminist interpretations

Or is it that having started with the idea of difference, feminism will be able to break free of its belief in Woman, her power, her writing, so as to channel this demand for difference into each and every element of the female whole, and, finally, to bring out the singularity of each woman, and beyond this, her multiplicities, her plural languages, beyond the horizon, beyond sight, beyond faith itself.

(Julia Kristeva, 'Women's Time')

Overview

This chapter will explore the uses made of psychoanalytic theory by two feminist writers who have made distinctive contributions to recent debate about the construction of gendered identity. Work by the psychoanalytic feminists (sometimes called post-modern feminists) Julia Kristeva and Luce Irigaray illustrates not only a much more directly politicised version of psychoanalytic theory which has been influential over recent years, but also the eclectic reach of these developments across the various international psychoanalytic traditions. Kristeva and Irigaray's work draws on the Lacanian symbolic, linguistic development of Freud, whereas in America Nancy Chodorow's more sociological work, drew primarily on the Winnicottian version of Object-Relations theory and explored how the experience of being mothered by a woman affects children of both sexes.

The two feminist perspectives discussed in this chapter belong to the second debate on 'femininity' in the nineteen-seventies and eighties. The first, in the nineteen-twenties and thirties was conducted largely by psychoanalysts in response to Freud's work and focused mainly on the issues of penis-envy. The second debate centred on the issues of whether the family, and in particular, motherhood and marriage within it, was responsible for women's subordinate position in society; the construction of gendered identity; the relationship between identity and sexuality and the relationship between the unconscious and language. The second debate benefited from the awareness of two new major theoretical developments since the first debate. One was the Object-Relations theory developed by Klein which had resulted in two strands of Object-Relations theory, both of which made the mother centrally important: the more sociological approach of Winnicott and Klein's own theory which was primarily concerned with the inner world of phantasy. The second new current of thought came from France in the form of work by Lacan and Derridà. This was concerned primarily with theories about language and meaning and its potential for disruption by the unconscious.

This work has been taken up with enthusiasm by French feminists such as Hélène Cixous, Julia Kristeva and Luce Irigaray. Although these writers are often grouped together by others, the work of each is very distinctive. Cixous, though she uses psychoanalysis, is primarily a literary theorist as well as a creative writer, Kristeva is a specialist in linguistics and literary theory and, more recently, has trained as a psychoanalyst, and Irigaray is a philosopher and psychoanalyst who was formerly a member of Lacan's Ecole Freudienne de Paris. However, what appeals to these very different writers, confronting Lacan's development of Freud's work from very different perspectives, is the way his work overtly opens up the possibility of thinking about sexuality and identity within the sphere of language and thought where desire and the unconscious become accessible. The very process of thought itself is discovered to be gendered and oppressive because, in the patriarchal Symbolic order, man is the self and woman the, or his, other, having her existence only in relation to him and meaningless without him. But, as Lacan makes clear, the meanings of language are always potentially vulnerable to the unconscious disruption made possible by the presence of desire, so that meanings and identities, including those of 'man' and 'woman', are never fixed and change is always possible.

French feminist writers (nowadays often referred to as post-modernist feminists) suggest that unconscious desire, associated with the mother and imprisoned between the rational, binary categories of language, can be freed from patriarchal control through the use of a specifically poetic language which, because of its close involvement with the unconscious, must always challenge the arbitrary, male-defined categories through which we experience the world, with which men must identify but which are imposed on women. This poetic approach has been emphasised particularly by Cixous. Many French feminists have been particularly interested in Lacan's insistence that 'masculinity' and 'truth' are bogus cultural constructions, and also in the distinctive pre-Oedipal realm, of the Imaginary which might be thought of as a pre-patriarchal realm, of particular importance to women. This realm is emphasised in much of this work because it seems to offer a sphere of psychical experience in which woman can articulate herself before cultural inhibitions and distortions come into play. Cixous, Kristeva and Irigaray see women's position as the lack as marginal, dislocated, excluded, despised, abandoned and rejected but also a position which, because it lies in the unconscious, allows a way of thinking and speaking to women and men beyond the reach of phallic control, in a domain which potentially offers meanings based on openness, plurality, diversity and genuine difference. In other words, this position may offer women and men the opportunity to become themselves. The work of Kristeva, Irigaray and Cixous, therefore, often revolves around the issue of the place or position from which women can speak. Can women speak from the place of the father, the mother, or both? The problem they tackle is that if women speak from the place of the father they will be alienated from their own identity and desire. But if they speak from the place of the mother in the Imaginary, outside the Symbolic, they risk being engulfed in what is normally considered an infantile realm whose form in adult experience is hysteria and madness. Alternatively, if the Imaginary and the pre-Oedipal mother is simply revalued as positive, they risk being caught up in and promoting another category of 'truth' which simply reflects, as a reverse image, the phallic position they oppose.

Let us look in more detail at the distinctively psychoanalytic writing of Julia Kristeva and Luce Irigaray whose work grew directly out of Lacan's strand of psychoanalysis.

Julia Kristeva: ending the 'fight to the death'

Julia Kristeva, as a Bulgarian woman who experiences French culture from its margins, sees Lacan's work as potentially liberating. But, unlike her contemporary, Hélène Cixous, she takes an emphatically anti-essentialist view of 'femininity'. As a result, Kristeva does not place her hopes for women in the body and the pre-Oedipal, phallic mother beyond the authority of the phallus. For her this Imaginary position is as bogus as the position of male authority because any position, even that of the powerful phallic mother, can be absorbed into language so that its meaning becomes rigid and potentially oppressive. All positions can be assimilated into the Symbolic, no settled experience or identity can guarantee a challenge to the phallic ordering of meaning. As Kristeva aptly puts it

> once represented, be it under the aspect of a woman, the truth of the unconscious passes into the phallic order. The vulgar but oh how effective trap of 'feminism': to recognise our selves, to make of us The Truth so as to keep us from functioning as [the order's] unconscious truth.
>
> (Kristeva, 1974: 42)

Here Kristeva warns against feminists simply making women into the symbol of 'the truth' instead of men, thus giving up their power to challenge language as the *unrepresented*, unstable, fluid truth of the unconscious.

Kristeva takes the view that the meaning of the pre-Oedipal mother actually encompasses both 'masculinity' and 'femininity'. By this she means that the mother in the Imaginary is 'masculine' in the sense that the baby sees her as all-powerful before the intervention of the father/ phallus, and 'feminine' because she lies outside the phallic imposition of meaning which asserts itself during the Oedipal crisis. For Kristeva she is never a 'feminine' essence and we can never totally avoid the phallus because we experience the mother as phallic and all-powerful in the Imaginary, however vulnerable mothers, in themselves, may frequently feel. Children phantasise that the mother is all-powerful until they are seduced by the desirability of having not just what she is but what she apparently wants, that is, the father. Kristeva sees phallic power based on the male phallus, or an idealised phallic mother as equally fraudulent. However, acknowledging the contradictions within any position for women, she argues that women need both the Imaginary and Symbolic positions in order to speak with authority and a meaningful identity (Kristeva 1986b: 155–8). She warns that women need the language of the paternal, Symbolic order to protect themselves from the merged identity with the mother. It is vital for the achievement of a viable, independent self. For these reasons, Kristeva argues that women should employ a *double* discourse which reflects the real state of all identity which must always be fluid – at the same time both 'masculine' and 'feminine' – both inside and outside the boundaries of the Symbolic. She argues that women should be active and assertive (which inevitably must incorporate them into the patriarchal domain of the phallus) but at the same time they should relentlessly challenge, question and refuse these assertions which must never rigidify into oppressive patriarchal certainties. Women's position should be a continual vacillation between order and disorder.

So Kristeva rejects any essentialist idea of woman as revolutionary 'feminine' essence. Rather, she takes a vigorously anti-essentialist view which stresses women's position within culture rather than their bodies (although as we shall see she does not want to leave these out). Always insisting on a fluid, multiple view of 'femininity' (which can exist in men as well as women), she refuses to use the category of woman at all since she sees it as an entirely patriarchal construction which is oppressive even in the very act of naming 'women' as a separate category. Instead she wants to re-define the concept of 'femininity' as marginality, as that which is unconscious, repressed, unspoken and which perpetually challenges, refuses and disrupts any one meaning. She urges women to ally themselves with anything which is marginalised by the patriarchal order, anything which is dissident and disruptive of the traditional categories of thought and language (Kristeva, 1986: 298–9). In this identification with marginality, she shares the position of Cixous who was born and brought up as both a woman and as a Jew in Algeria and therefore experienced both French colonialism and anti-semitism as well as sexism. Like Cixous, Kristeva advocates that women, in their practice, should ally themselves with avant-garde artists like the Surrealists who work in an unconscious space outside conventional, patriarchal culture. For Kristeva, these artists represent a fluidity of sexual identification, whether they are men or women. This enables them to turn consciousness inside out and challenge the normal values of intelligibility, rationality and coherence in their art, literature and music. She argues that innovative male artists such as James Joyce, John Cage or Karlheinz Stockhausen are like 'honorary' women in that they inhabit the same space in culture, representing the free unmastered ingredient of the human subject which exists beyond the boundaries of conventional meanings, collapsing and sabotaging the rationality of consciousness.

Kristeva takes the view that women are part of a wider group consisting of those in society, such as the Jews in the Third Reich, who become cultural scapegoats. She grounds this in her concept of the 'abject', that is an unconscious sense of disgust which harks back to the baby's pre-Oedipal experience of its own and its mothers bodily products. Only later with the onset of the castration complex and the discovery of sexual difference does this disgust become translated into a connection with the feminine as the 'abject'. For Kristeva the 'abject' comes to represent what is marginalised and repressed in society in the pre-Oedipal stage she calls the 'semiotic'. She contrasts the semiotic (Lacan's Imaginary) with the Symbolic of the post-Oedipal stage, arguing that male-dominated thought rests on the repression of the semiotic and therefore the pre-Oedipal but sexually unidentified mother.

In her provocative essay 'Women's Time', a part of which is contained in Part II of this book, Kristeva focuses specifically on feminism, women's experience and the symbolic order. In the earlier part of this fascinating paper, Kristeva defines different identities, patriarchal and feminist, as structured within different notions of time. She distinguishes between three conceptions of time – linear, monumental and cyclical – and relates them to three different strands of European feminism. Linear time refers to our place within what she calls the prospective unfolding of *history*. Kristeva associates this particularly with patriarchal 'masculinity', defining it as civilisational or obsessional time (it can make slaves of us), and with liberal feminism which has sought women's assimilation and equality with men. But she also associates it with socialist feminism which has also failed to emphasise women's bodies and desire. Monumental time, which cuts diagonally across linear time, refers to non-subjective or *eternal* time – our structural place in the mode of reproduction and representation which, although culturally specific, also refers to *universal* traits such as maternity. Cyclical time (such as that involved in menstruation) which Kristeva sees as particularly involved in the experience of female subjectivity, is essentially structured in a way that retains the ideas of *repetition, cycles, gestation and biological rhythms* in unison with eternal or monumental time. She links both these notions of time with the radical feminism of the nineteen-seventies which focused on the symbolic. Although she sees both monumental and cyclical time as traditionally linked to female subjectivity, she also emphasises that these are the fundamental and often the sole conceptions of time in numerous civilisations and experiences, particularly mystical ones.

Kristeva rejects all existing forms of feminism as based on single definitions of time and identity. She wants, in her analysis of women's position, to highlight the interwoven meanings of the sexual, the symbolic and linear time. The sexual and symbolic, she argues are present within monumental and cyclical time, but repressed and denied in the linear time of history and patriarchal culture. This is the central concern of the extract from the concluding section of 'Women's Time' which we will look at now in a little more detail.

Commentary on an extract from 'Women's Time'

At the beginning of this extract, Kristeva focuses on the two forms of women's creativity evident in the current generation of feminists at the time of writing (1979): motherhood and women's writing. She suggests that as a result of increasing numbers of women combining motherhood with employment, there has been a new appreciation of the complexity of female experience which has been revealed as a confusing mixture of joy and pain rather than the uncomplicated achievement of maternal plenitude. But Kristeva is dismissive of those lesbian women and single mothers who have refused the role of men. For her, this is one of the most violent forms of the lie of what she calls 'Woman as Truth'. She argues that without the law and the Symbolic, life for women and children would be violent and essentially unliveable, unless, that is, women could develop alternative legislation to check violence. But the question of whether they would be able to do this, she argues, is not addressed by women possessed by the same rage with which they were originally victimised by dominant men.

In the next paragraph Kristeva argues that it has become clear that the mass refusal of motherhood advocated by an earlier generation of feminists is impossible, because the majority of women experience children as a source of pleasure and fulfilment. The question of what this widespread desire for children means in terms of women's specific nature, she argues, is the crucial question for the current generation of feminists, if not the preceding ones. Here, Kristeva returns to a familiar theme in her work – the idea that only the church has provided women with a discourse which satisfies 'the anguish, the suffering and hopes of mothers'. This position is elaborated in 'Stabat Mater' (in Kristeva 1986b).

She moves next to a reference to Freud's view that, for women, babies represent a substitute penis. She suggests that even if this is only partly true, we should attend to what women have to say about their experience of pregnancy. They say, she tells us, that they experience it as a splitting of identity, a re-doubling of the body, as both separation from and co-existence of the self with another, as part of both nature and culture, biology and language. In other words, they experience pregnancy as both a major challenge to identity and yet something which is also accompanied by a phantasy of completeness and totality – what Kristeva calls a kind of institutionalised, 'natural' psychosis. In addition, she argues, the arrival of a baby is accompanied by something women rarely encounter, love for another. (Here Kristeva is referring to Freud's idea that women tend to love narcissistically, wanting to be loved rather than to love.) She movingly describes what she thinks this involves for a woman: 'the slow, difficult and delightful apprenticeship in attentiveness, gentleness, forgetting oneself'. Success on this path, without succumbing to masochism or the annihilation of the rest of what one is as a woman, Kristeva suggests, is a rare form of 'guiltless maternity' which for most women is still a Utopian dream. She then says something about the nature of women's creativity which, although a dimension of women played down by feminists in the past, is of fundamental importance for her, 'It then becomes a creation in the strong sense of this term.' Here she is emphasising the powerful creativity involved in the activity of mothering rather than only the biological capacity for reproduction. Empathy, the delicate and subtle process of conferring an identity on a baby, while maintaining one's own in this relationship of unconditional love, remains, Kristeva suggests, the form of creativity which lies at the heart of what is specific to women's experience. However, she concludes in this section, that this form of creativity is evidently not how many women wish to affirm themselves. Their dominant aspiration is artistic expression.

Why, Kristeva asks in the next section, are women so concerned with writing literature? She answers that it is because writing enables women to reveal what is an 'otherwise, repressed, nocturnal, secret and unconscious universe', that is their own denied experience. The identification with the powerful pre-Oedipal mother in the Imaginary, in women's writing, testifies to women's desire to dissociate themselves from what she describes as the 'sacrifice' at the centre of patriarchal culture. By 'sacrifice' Kristeva means the loss of the mother, the acceptance of which is the patriarchal requirement for entry into this culture. In writing from an identification with the mother, women refuse this sacrifice of a crucial dimension of what they are. In writing they continue to want to attest to what culture denies them, 'the enigma of the body, dreams, secret joys, shames, hatreds of the second sex'.

However, in the next paragraph Kristeva seems unimpressed with the actual achievements of recent women writers whom she criticises for their contempt for the male writers they imitate, for naivety, romanticism and, particularly, for their attacks on patriarchal culture from a silent, semi-mystical assertion of the body whose 'truth' can only be witnessed through gesture and tonality. (She might have had Cixous in mind here.) And yet, she comments with more optimism, women *are* writing and we have yet to see what they will eventually produce.

At this point Kristeva returns to her idea of religion as the only practice which has expressed the human need for symbolic representation of ourselves. Is feminism in its present form, she asks, in danger of becoming the new religion in the first epoch of history when human beings have tried to live without it. Or will feminism be able to resist this development by breaking new ground? Will it be able to break away from its belief in 'Woman' as another version of 'Truth' so that the unavoidable demand for the acknowledgement of difference can be channelled where it really belongs – into every part of every woman to bring out their singularity and the multiplicity and plurality of their experience and language? Is this idea, she asks, the basis for future action and analysis?

The 'truth' of her question, Kristeva argues, belongs to a different terrain from its statement. This is within what she calls a new 'signifying space, a both corporeal and desiring mental space' which is in the process of forming, which can interweave all three feminist temporalities described above (linear, monumental and cyclical) in a new parallel existence in the present. Men and women can no longer continue to represent opposing forms of a 'Truth' which are bogus and destructive. She proposes therefore, an abandonment of the 'fight-to-the-death' response to difference found in both men and women. Rejecting the idea that she is advocating mere reconciliation, she argues that she is proposing an even more 'intransigent struggle' but not between oppressors and their victims, but between the victim and oppressor we internalise within 'personal and sexual identity itself' – in other words the difference, the 'other' in ourselves.

Here Kristeva refers to the destructive effects of the castration complex if it remains unresolved in the adult. She wants a retreat from what she sees as male and female sexism based on a capacity to internalise 'the cutting edge' (the father responsible for our symbolic castration, that is our conversion in phantasy into the inferior, the lack, the 'feminine') on which she believes sexism is founded, into the interior of 'every identity whether subjective, sexual [or] ideological'. In place of the usual resort to the fabrication of a scapegoat as the basis of every identity, society or counter-society (that is the projection onto different others of our unconscious sense of victimisation by the father – the symbolic castration which we cannot bear to acknowledge in ourselves) Kristeva proposes an analysis of the potential of both the victim and executioner which is constructed out of this unconscious which is part of the psychical make-up of all of us, 'each identity, each subject, each sex'. For her, it is artistic practices which must demystify the increasingly technologically dominated, patriarchal Symbolic which totalises and equalises, denying the difference between people, the multiplicity of their identifications, the variability of their capacity for expressing themselves – as well as their biological variation. For Kristeva, the abolition of the oppression of women (and that of other groups perceived as different), rests on the conscious recognition of symbolic castration. This would mean individual or collective acknowledgement, within ourselves, of the unconscious painful Oedipal feelings of loss, anger and humiliation which resulted from our being the victims of symbolic castration and, at the same time, our perception of sexual difference. If these are not resolved adequately they remain repressed and potentially destructive. Kristeva sees the conscious acknowledgement of the difference within ourselves, what elsewhere she calls the 'stranger in ourselves' rather than its unconscious denial, as the modern answer to the search for value (Kristeva 1991). She insists that we must rid ourselves of the destructive impulse to establish our identities on the basis of a subtle undermining or open attack on those who are different from ourselves, in the form of the projection of our own difference; that which we need to disown because it feels alien to our consciousness. She argues that the painful unconscious recognition of guilt involved in the process of the acknowledgement of our unconscious capacity for destruction of the other, and the precariousness of a life where we must challenge all meaning, is more than adequately compensated for by our access to different forms of pleasure or 'jouissance' which can be enjoyed by both sexes.

In the last paragraph of this extract Kristeva rejects the versions of morality defined in classical philosophy. Women's morality, she argues, is in the form of a demand which does away with the fixed, stable identities posturing as 'Truth', formed in a moment of history when identity was constructed on the basis of making victims of those perceived as different. We can only answer Spinoza's question about whether women are subject to ethics, she suggests, if we are prepared to see not only patriarchal identity as a temporary moment in history, but also feminist identity which often also shuts us all off from what we could be.

Discussion

Kristeva's work highlights what she sees as the need for women to make language their own so that they can communicate their 'feminine' experience. Where the existing categories and binary structures do not reflect this experience, she suggests, like Cixous, that women should find new ones, inventing different styles of explanation and arguing for new criteria for evidence which take into account their specific ways of being. Both these feminist writers suggest that women should experiment with new ways of structuring experience which have more in common with certain forms of artistic expression than prevailing rationalistic norms. Without the need for mastery and control, these new forms and directions can make available a space for a freer play of the unconscious in the form of insight, intuition and pleasure (*jouissance*) and the expression of those multiple emotions and desires which patriarchal societies have compelled women to disown and repress. In the context of the womb-envy which emerges as a recurring theme in the present text, a language celebrating sexual identities and forms of pleasure which are denied in culture may offer many men as well as women a site for the expression of a form of creativity unassociated with control or work, which produces the forms of sexual pleasure and fulfilment that Kristeva associates with childbirth as well as writing. This access to *jouissance*, and a form of creativity free of mastery, may be what are necessary to undermine the unconscious male need to project their womb-envy onto women as the lack.

The problem about Kristeva's work for some women – for example, Rosi Braidotti (Brennan ed. 1989: 92–104) – is that, although she has transformed Lacan's 'woman' into a positive, critical category which represents the unconscious, marginal meanings beyond the surface meanings of any text, she has left her somehow divorced from her material, bodily existence and effectively outside politics. As such she represents a mirror version of the problem of essentialism she highlights in Cixous's more essentialist work. With both Cixous and Kristeva, in their different ways, it is sometimes argued, we lose sight of the essentially mundane world of social relationships. However, the criticism that Kristeva has abandoned flesh and blood political action in favour of a rarefied world of artistic practices is, I think, a misreading of her position, which is in many ways psychoanalytically much richer than that of Cixous.

Kristeva's argument is that all forms of fixed identity, whether those of individuals or groups, have their basis in symbolic castration and projection. Coinciding with the discovery of sexual difference, repressed parts of the self experienced as vulnerable and 'feminine' (as a result of symbolic castration in the Oedipal crisis), are projected onto those who are different, who then, as a result of their victimisation, free their oppressor of this 'femininity' which cannot be acknowledged as belonging to the self. In such circumstances, in relation to the oppression of women and all groups who are victimised, Kristeva argues that political change within linear time, cannot, on its own, bring about a solution. Since it operates at the level of consciousness, it cannot intervene in the unconscious mechanisms of projection involving 'scapegoating' and idealisation because they lie outside the control of the political subject. Kristeva sees action at the level of the Symbolic – in the language we use and in artistic practices generally – as of crucial importance because the repressed fluidity and multiplicity of sexual identity can be freed within this sphere in both sexes. Difference – victim/executioner, 'femininity'/masculinity – can be acknowledged within our own psyche. Kristeva reminds us that, in the context of the feelings of castration, anger and humiliation cultivated in women by patriarchal societies, some women and feminists may be as prone to projection of these feelings in the form of extreme penis-envy (the female version of the castration complex) as patriarchal men. She argues that men and women need a more integrated, emotionally mature and honest way of being which depends on recognising painful feelings associated with loss and symbolic castration. The owning of these often destructive feelings, she admits, involves personal suffering (the coming to terms with unconscious guilt in relation to the mother as well as loss). Kristeva does not deny the importance of political action which she acknowledges has undeniably achieved significant changes for some women, but she does attempt to explain the limitations of such change.

At the moment, apart from the process of writing advocated by Kristeva, individual and group psychotherapy are the only other practices based on language in which individuals and groups can gain access to their unconscious 'other' and ensure that this is neither projected into the external world nor turned against the self in the form of masochism. However, neither of these activities are, or are likely to be, available on a mass scale.

Womb-envy, explicitly and implicitly, has been a recurring theme in the different theories explored in this book and it is again implicit in Kristeva's distinctive development of Lacanian theory. For some, perhaps many, men the pain of symbolic castration is unconsciously compounded by the knowledge that there is nowhere to go beyond this castration. This predicament of lack, of 'femininity' as we have seen, has to be defended against unconsciously, in some men, to the death. Women also find themselves symbolically castrated but they know they have another source of identity available to them beyond the lack – the special pleasure and power involved in motherhood, despite culture's lack of recognition of this experience. The small boy's womb-envy is never entirely overcome because, after the rescue of his self-esteem by the phallus, he has at the same time to suffer symbolic castration and loss of the mother in order to enter culture as a man. So he suffers humiliation and loss on two counts. This means that the quantity of painful, chaotic feelings that some men repress is likely to be greater than that repressed by women. These are then unconsciously projected onto women who then represent lack and disorder. The female form of the castration complex, penis-envy, may be mitigated in many women, as Freud suggests, by the pleasure and sense of power motherhood confers, something Kristeva highlights in 'Women's Time' (although women have to pay dearly for it in other ways). However, the understatement or even denial of many women's enjoyment of motherhood (as well as their other activities) by some feminists, has obscured the perception that widespread, unconscious womb-envy may be fundamental to patriarchal culture and language.

In many ways Kristeva's conclusions in 'Women's Time', although expressed within a Lacanian theoretical framework, draw together central ideas and themes explored in this book. The unconscious phenomena underlying Freud's concepts of castration and narcissism, Klein's concepts of phantasy, splitting, projection, the paranoid–schizoid position and the integration and reparation of the depressive phases, Winnicott's concepts of the transitional space, creativity and artistic activity all permeate this paper though the experiences to which they refer are expressed in Kristeva's own Freudian/Lacanian language. Her paper incorporates the central issue within psychoanalysis which lies at the heart of each of its theories although they conceptualise it in different terms. How can the child separate from the mother and make the transition from phantasy to reality, without inflicting damage on itself or others (through masochistic or sadistic behaviour)? Kristeva asserts the fundamental value encapsulated within Freudian psychoanalysis, and its distinctive political moment. This is the achievement of the conscious recognition of the unbearable feelings associated with loss and symbolic castration which, together with the acknowledgement of sexual difference, seem to lie at the centre of our identity. This acknowledgement of our 'masculinity' and 'femininity', of executioner and victim, Kristeva stresses, is what genuinely empowers in the non-oppressive sense. It seems that if too much painful, unconscious experience remains outside who we think we are, many of us are unconsciously tempted to denigrate, attack or even destroy these 'bad' aspects of ourselves we have embodied within others perceived as different. We repeatedly act out the unacceptable 'execution' of ourselves on vulnerable others who symbolically stand in for us as victims. Genocide must be one of the most terrible examples of this behaviour.

Theoretically, Kristeva tries to achieve what Moi sees as a difficult balancing act. As Moi recognises, on the one hand she wants to deconstruct subjectivity and identity to demonstrate the fragility of these meanings in language, but at the same time she wants to recognise that these are both connected to the body and social reality. Subjectivity must always be precarious but nevertheless, at the same time, necessary and real. The symbolic and sexuality are always inseparable but the difficulty is how to act in both spheres at once (Kristeva 1986b: 13). This, as we shall see, is an issue which is central to Irigaray's work. In 'Women's Time', Kristeva, while recognising the transformative nature of art and writing, does not discuss directly how the problem of difference might be tackled at source – how parents can ensure that their children, and especially boys, can be emotionally supported and helped to bear the separation and loss of their identification with the mother (involving womb-envy for boys) and sense of humiliation in relation to their symbolic castration by the father, and also their loss of the mother as an object of desire. In some men, this double loss may, as we have seen, be unconsciously orchestrated into a massive projection of rage towards women.

Alice Miller, writing from the perspective of humanist therapy rather than psychoanalysis, attempts to provide an answer to why so many children emerge from childhood in a damaged state. Arguing from a position much closer to Winnicott's than that of Freud and Lacan, Miller argues that many of us have suffered from an emotional form of abuse which is no less damaging than sexual abuse. She argues that this is the result of the socially sanctioned emphasis on 'firmness' and discipline in child-rearing which is inflicted on many of us in childhood, 'for our own good', at a time when many of us are struggling desperately to negotiate our multiple losses. Miller argues that this kind of 'normal' child-rearing has never been seriously questioned and is the legacy of parents who were themselves abused in this way (Miller 1987). Her work suggests the need, in parents and all those who care for children, for the kind of creative parenting practices characteristic of Winnicott's 'good enough mother'. If this kind of emotional deprivation is what underpins our reaction to women and difference (what Kristeva describes as 'the fight to the death') Miller's attention to the real circumstances of our childhood which become enmeshed with our phantasies, perhaps offers us a line of action at a societal level which might go a considerable way to achieving a fundamental change in our unconscious response to difference (especially for those for whom 'writing the feminine' is not a realistic option). This is a crucial area in which the different strands of psychoanalytic and humanistic thinking about gender come together.

Luce Irigaray: 'two lips touching and re-touching'

Irigaray is both a philosopher and a psychoanalyst. She was once a member of Lacan's Ecole Freudienne and but was expelled from Lacan's department of psychoanalysis at Vincennes in 1974 because of her openly feminist psychoanalytic stance. Her work focuses on two issues which she thinks are of central importance to women: the analysis of the unconscious and the analysis of the cultural assumptions which underlie Western philosophy and psychoanalysis. This large project looks towards a radical transformation in language and culture because, she insists, women's specific difference is not represented in mainstream cultural forms. One of the interesting features of her work is that, although she is heavily influenced by Freudian psychoanalysis, she is also openly critical of it and her work has become of increasing interest to women recently, largely as a result of Margaret Whitford's mediation of it.

Irigaray psychoanalyses the work of a range of major Western philosophers (including Plato, Descartes, Hegel, Nietzsche, Kant and Derridà) as well as the theory of Freud and Lacan. She agrees with Lacan that women have been aligned with the lack in culture but goes even further, arguing that what Lacan calls subjectivity in the Symbolic is simply the representation of the male Imaginary. Because of the assumptions which accompany the apparent visibility of the phallus, she contends that the potential for the girl's female Imaginary based on her concealed female genitals and her capacity for pleasure from her entire body, is submerged. But Irigaray also suggests that subjectivity based on the male Imaginary is a neurotic, immature form of male identity which defensively over-values the phallus and feels a compulsive need for control. In particular, she argues, it is an identity which while denying the importance of the mother and women, remains unconsciously dependent on them. So for Irigaray, what she sees as the symptoms of a neurotic male Imaginary become the defining characteristics of Western philosophy and psycho-analysis and are based on unconscious denial of the mother.

Irigaray thinks that because patriarchal men still unconsciously iden-tify with the mother and the 'feminine', male culture is governed by men's love of the same (other men) rather than difference (women). In what she describes as a culture of the same, woman, instead of being able to represent difference – what she calls 'the other of the other' – can only represent reflections of men, which she describes as 'the other of the same'.

Irigaray suggests that women have been buried alive in culture. She argues that since patriarchal men are still unconsciously merged with the mother, woman has been allotted everything in culture that men have to deny in themselves – nature, biology, the body – to protect them from knowing about their continued unconscious dependence on the mother and women generally. Male lack, therefore, has been unconsciously projected onto women (who, as partners and wives, function symbolically as mirrors, as their substitute mothers), thus making them the symbolic representations of what men cannot bear to acknowledge in themselves, their symbolic castration or lack of identity. Irigaray thinks that for men, women represent not only nature, the bodies from which they were born, but the continuing spectre of castration. Women appear particularly suited to this unconscious role because they already appear, in phantasy, as castrated. To the extent that for men the castration complex is about fear of loss of identity, women threaten men with potential disintegration. So, for Irigaray, men see women as a kind of black hole in being, an abyss equated with death which cannot be mastered within language. This echoes Lacan's notion that death lies outside the Symbolic in the realm of the Real. She argues that this explains why women have to be kept outside language and knowledge as the literally unthinkable. If woman functions in the Symbolic by means of projection, as the un-thought, as the dark continent, the 'feminine mystique', men are able to sustain the illusion that they have mastered death. By making death the other which women then merely represent, patriarchal men are able to control the unthinkable (Irigaray 1985a: 27, 53, 72, 94).

Margaret Whitford suggests that we can understand Irigaray's interpretation of the idea of 'truth' within philosophy in the context of the castration complex. The illusion of 'truth', the phallus, becomes an endless way of blocking women's subjectivity in order to maintain a fragile barrier against unthinkable psychical disintegration and collapse. This state of affairs means that men, in a very literal sense, cannot hear women. To hear would mean facing their own anxiety, fragility and mortality, the psychical as well as symbolic death of the subject (Whitford 1991a: 117).

Using the language of bodily phantasy which she insists underpins all language, Irigaray argues that the woman may be seen as either a 'hole' or absence within discourse or an unsymbolised residue or excess which lies outside the apparent phallic wholeness of culture. Irigaray sees women's sexuality as in excess of phallic sexuality because her sexual pleasure, in the form of *jouissance*, is multiple and diffuse rather than centred on her genitals. Outside culture the undifferentiated female represents the indefinable formlessness which underlies all possible identities, all the possible shapings and mouldings which might allow us to 'grasp' the world in different ways. So although theoretically hidden from view, Irigaray argues, the mother and woman lead a kind of double existence: they are denied but nevertheless ceaselessly nourish and supply the material and symbolic conditions of male culture. This exclusion of the mother from culture as the unthought male unconscious leaves women in what Irigaray graphically describes as a state of 'dereliction', without a home or protective covering in the Symbolic and therefore outside normative subjectivity, reason and ethics (Irigaray 1993a).

Irigaray argues that women are condemned to a cultural wilderness unless the female imaginary – consisting of phantasies around the female body – can be symbolised, thus allowing women to become subjects in their own right rather than simply objects of symbolic projection. Meanwhile, unless they enter the Symbolic as ersatz men, she thinks women continue to experience the destructive immediacy of phantasies and death drives associated with the female imaginary. This is because the mother–daughter relationship (as opposed to the mother–son) is not represented in mainstream cultural forms thus damaging relationships between women. Without shelter in the Symbolic, women are inevitably outlawed in society. Irigaray argues that the male Imaginary inevitably becomes the social Imaginary, an area of power and authority. This is, like the male Imaginary, also taken to be reality although it is equally illusory.

In her influential book, *Speculum of the Other Woman* (1985) Irigaray asserts that Western thought is founded on a structure of what she calls 'specularisation'. This means that the male philosopher or psychoanalyst projects his own Imaginary onto the world thus seeing his own reflection wherever he looks. For Irigaray, women are the screen for the projection of male phantasy as embodied in theory and, as we have seen, Irigaray's work distinguishes sharply between the male and female Imaginary. She insists that Lacan's concept of the Imaginary is a male one. His theoretical mirror cannot reflect anything back to women except their absence or their defect. This situation, Irigaray argues, leads to a sterile impasse in thought which, perceiving women as defective men, consequently silences her. Irigaray argues that the destructive effects of modern technology, based almost exclusively on reason, testify to the effects of this repression of the woman, symbolised in the earth and the natural world, and point to the urgent need for a different way of conceptualising the world. No matter how far-reaching and innovative its insights and products, theoretical knowledge goes on perpetuating the denial of women and therefore exists in a permanent theoretical and social tomb. In other words, men and women as the same are prevented from creatively producing symbolic offspring which might be capable of addressing the pressing problems which confront the world.

But, Irigaray argues, if a theoretical curved mirror or speculum (a curved mirror used by doctors mainly for internal vaginal examinations) replaced Lacan's mirror in the Imaginary (which can also be understood as the mirror of male theory) the female genital would be seen as an image just as suitable as a signifier in the Symbolic as the phallus. She suggests that Lacan's theory is a prescription rather than a description of patriarchal culture, while her vision of a transformed Symbolic containing what a female Imaginary might be like, suggests this Symbolic would be associated with women's specific difference, repeatedly described as 'two lips touching' and 're-touching' (Irigaray 1985b: 24–9). Here, however, Irigaray is suggesting that women's experience of sexuality is not genitally centred but spreads across their whole body as multiple and diffuse pleasure which is radically unlike men's pleasure focused on the phallus. A female Symbolic would, therefore, reflect female bodily sensations and the phantasies they generate: openness, associativeness, multiplicity and fluidity. For Irigaray, male phantasies, based on male bodily sensations, take a more binary form than women's; things are either one thing or the other, and rest on assertion and control.

Like Cixous, Irigaray sets great store by the bodily difference of women. If women enter the male Symbolic they become disembodied and she argues that this has allowed classical philosophers and psycho-analysts to control women's place in language and knowledge. She argues that even the deconstruction of the male subject by post-modern male philosophers such as Jacques Derridà, has, despite appearances, still not broken the tradition of denial and sameness because it omits the embodiment of women in the Symbolic and social order. She argues that although Derridà recognises the illusory nature of wholeness of the male subject, and the violent hierarchy between men and women implicit in all binary oppositions in Western thought, his concept of '*différance*' as the unconscious or 'the repressed feminine' functions merely as a figure in language and has nothing to do with a wish to end the plight of real women (Irigaray 1985b: 157). Deconstruction, whether by a man or a woman, is separated from the female body and female Imaginary because women have to become disembodied when they enter language. Irigaray makes a radical distinction between 'speaking as a woman'; what she sees as the 'feminine feminine' and 'speaking like a woman'; what she perceives as the 'masculine feminine'. The quality of the repressed feminine when spoken by male writers is undermined because men have a privileged speaking position which makes people pay attention to them. For Irigaray, the kind of body we speak from makes all the difference. Men speak what Irigaray sees as a phallic 'feminine' from a male body whereas women speak the 'feminine' from a woman's body which is habitually silenced or unheard. To equate the 'masculine feminine' with the 'feminine feminine' is, for Irigaray, to confuse identity (which involves bodies) with identification.

Irigaray regards men speaking 'as woman' (their 'repressed feminine') as an appropriation of 'femininity' by male writers who no longer want to be identified with the desire for mastery, and the claim for an illusory 'truth' characteristic of the traditional 'masculine' stance. She argues that some male philosophers now use a 'feminine' language because it allows them access to meanings which are more shifting and elusive; but she criticises them for often failing to support women's claims for symbolic and social power. This, she thinks, is as an unconscious attempt by men to colonise the space which might, in a projected future, belong to women. Men's 'repressed feminine', she maintains, perpetuates the 'other as the same' and denies the 'other as the other' because its tools for subversion are borrowed from the same male Imaginary underlying the Western classical tradition. For this reason Irigaray prefers to emphasise woman as *potential* subjects in the Symbolic and society rather than as participants in what Cixous calls an 'écriture feminine'. And she insists that women, as well as creating themselves in the Symbolic, must be actively involved in the creation of a social and political reality which recognises women's specificity, that is in their social lives as well as their potential role within language.

Irigaray's main complaint is that many men have become involved in what has been described by Susanne Moore as 'gender tourism' (Moore 1988: 165–92). Such men use the concept of the 'repressed feminine' to erect another phallic theoretical structure around 'femininity' which denies the crucial embodiment of women and simultaneously fails to share power with them (Todd 1983: 243). As Margaret Whitford comments, in this situation, a paradoxical scenario arises in which assertive feminists, in speaking the only language available to them, are deemed to be less 'feminine' and more phallocentric than men who identify with the 'feminine' (Whitford 1991a: 128–9). Irigaray sees this competition beween varieties of the 'feminine' as, yet again, a means whereby men incorporate the figure of the repressed mother on which they un-consciously depend at the expense of real women with bodies. Irigaray wants to restore the passionate links with the body within philosophy and psychoanalysis which can put philosophy and psychoanalysis back in symbolic touch with the unacknowledged body of the mother. For Irigaray the male 'repressed feminine' cannot do this.

Irigaray insists that women as both mothers and as desiring women could emerge to speak in their own right and as radically different from men because their bodies are associated with their own distinctive Imaginary, consisting of phantasies and desires which emerge in the context of the mother–daughter relationship. (Little girls desire the mother as well as little boys.) However, Irigaray pushes her concept of the female Imaginary beyond unconscious phantasy to form a vision of the future. Unlike Lacan, she does not see the dominant male Imaginary (as the Symbolic) as unchangeable. This, she thinks, limits the potential of the Symbolic to the current masculine accounts of it. She argues, in a visionary mode, that women need to use their imaginations and creativity

[197]

to construct a future Imaginary of their own with which they might create a new Symbolic. She argues that a radical transformation of the Symbolic and the social order could replace existing ways of thinking with a previously unimagined configuration of categories and syntax generated by two different Imaginaries, one related to the mother and women as themselves, and one related to men who would have abandoned their projections onto women. A 'double syntax', she suggests, reflecting both a transformed male and a newly discovered female Imaginary, would allow women to become subjects, 'the other of the other' instead of the 'other of the same' (Irigaray 1985b: 33).

Irigaray argues that the Symbolic stands in urgent need of what she calls the 'amorous exchange', the symbolic representation of fertile, creative intercourse between men and women both recognising each other as the other of the other. This, Irigaray suggests, would bring about undistorted, mutually enriching, creative relationships among women, and between women and men in which they would, together, be able creatively to produce a new kind of knowledge which could lead out of what she regards as a sepulchre of narcissistic reflections in which men are imprisoned and women buried (Irigaray 1993a). She thinks men's insistence on immobilising and controlling the meanings of the mother block their own as well as women's creativity. The consequent failure to recognise sexual difference neutralises heterosexual relationships in the social and Symbolic and creates a sterile culture. In a future Symbolic, embodying and benefiting from the female imaginary, men would be able to acknowledge openly the origins of their identities in the body and their passionate motivations in relation to the mother. The unconscious could henceforth operate within each individual without the ideological projections by men onto women.

Irigaray's own writing underlines her belief that women need, not only to try to understand their position theoretically, but also to try to evoke the flavour and possibility of a way of being and thinking which acknowledges the origin of conceptual thought and expression in women and men's bodily phantasies (that is, phantasies which interpret bodily processes symbolically). This process lies at the heart of psychoanalysis but is often misunderstood. The Imaginary, resting on the passionate relationship with the mother, for both sexes, is what fleshes out the Symbolic which is only an empty structural possibility without it. Irigaray insists that subjectivity is not identity. The speaking subject in the Symbolic is carved out of the richness of an identity in the imaginary which, however illusory, is rooted in love and the body of the mother, despite her subsequent murder in culture.

Although Irigaray recognises that her ideas refer to a Utopian future in which each sex could creatively shelter the other, she argues that there is something women can do in the short-term to keep a space open for themselves in the symbolic and social world. Although aware of the risks of implying women are irrational or culture's unconscious, she argues that women, lacking any other form of representation, should adopt a strategy of mimicry. She suggests that women should deliberatly assume a 'feminine' role in an attempt to direct attention to the place where patriarchal men project their phantasies (angel, goddess, little girl, slag). She wants to make this place visible by means of a playful exaggeration of how woman is summed up in male reason, and of what is supposed to remain invisible/Irigaray argues that, through mimicry, the intentional assumption of the content of male metaphors and images of women, women can unveil the destructive power of these projections (Irigaray 1985b: 76)./The danger of this strategy, of course, is that it may confirm rather than de-stabilise men's phantasies of women.

Irigaray suggests that the female Symbolic must emerge simultaneously with the symbolisation of the currently unsymbolised mother–daughter relationship and the emphasis on women as desiring subjects distinct from their existence as de-personalised mother substitutes for men without any individuality or desire of their own. She argues that the present situation causes distorted relationships between women based on destructive rivalry and cruelty which she attributes to women's difficulties in separating from the mother without a home to go to in the Symbolic. This results in a confusion of identity, and a role as the representative of men's loss and lack frequently expressed in women's depression and self-deprecation. She argues that women's emergence in the Symbolic and that of sexual difference will depend upon their ability to love their mothers, other women, and therefore themselves as subjects. For Irigaray, creative, constructive relationships between men and women will depend first on both sexes being able to express their love for themselves and each other. (Irigaray 1985b: 143).

Irigaray's interest in language focuses on embodied individuals communicating with each other. She dislikes traditional scientific and academic language which uses passive constructions and syntactical structures which obscure bodies and sexual difference. She associates a 'feminine' Symbolic with fluid, metonymical relationships which she sees as 'touching and re-touching' rather than the metaphorical separations characteristic of male discourse. For her knowledge must always be linked to love. She argues that contrary to traditional assumptions, love should not have to be abandoned in order to become learned or wise. In other words, we need not abandon our original passionate relationship with the mother and her body. It is 'love which leads the way and is the path of the mediator par excellence', she writes (Irigaray 1993a). For her philosophy and reason has gone astray because, in order to sustain the illusion of the strength and power of male identity, it has resolutely denied its passionate origins in love and bodily closeness symbolised by relations with the mother. A new Symbolic would put language and knowledge back in touch with this dimension of who we are. In contemporary society, she sees women as the main source of love within language and the social world and as the focus of hope for the future.

Commentary on an extract from *Speculum of the Other Woman*

At the begining of this extract Irigaray draws our attention to the number of places in Freud's lecture 'Femininity' which betray a pre-occupation with establishing the little girl's similarity to the little boy, what she calls 'blind reversals'. Freud, she argues, in the sway of the male Imaginary, has felt unconsciously compelled to make these reversals in order to sustain his identity as culturally 'masculine'. In other words, like many male philosophers, Freud betrays the symptoms of an over-controlling identity still unconsciously fused with the mother which continues to desire the same, woman as mirror rather than the woman as the other. But it is boys, insists Irigaray, who, because of their symbolic castration and their denial of their origin in the mother, have the more painful evolution.

She continues with an elaboration of her indictment of Freud's theory of 'femininity'. For Freud, she insists, a normal woman is a defective man. She is thus placed in a hopeless situation in the culture of the same where only death represents difference. Developing this theme, she suggests that in projecting symbolic castration onto women, men can feel they have triumphed over death when they have heterosexual intercourse, if, that is, they manage to sustain their pleasure in spite of having to confront the horror of proximity to female lack which has, in phantasy, the power to humiliate and terrify because of its association with loss and death. This trial of strength will be given added piquancy, she writes ironically, because of the possibility that it might result in the production of a son (the same) who will carry on the great tradition of defying death during intercourse with women.

In the next section Irigaray turns to the cultural assumptions embedded in psychoanalysis. She suggests that the old male phantasy of the same comes in such a variety of theoretical disguises that even the most talented psychoanalysts (such as Freud and Lacan) have been unable to detect their own unconscious investment in it. This, she suggests is because they have never questioned the cultural assumptions on which psychoanalysis is based. But, Irigaray comments with mock innocence, these psychoanalytic discoveries, although suffused with the illusions of the male Imaginary, apparently achieve some clinical success with patients. However, she insists, this is because psychoanalysts can only see what they want to see. Such 'success' is only a confirmation of the same. But, Irigaray suggests, when a genius such as Freud turns his attention to an issue as central and fundamental as the construction of sexual difference, he is genuinely taking a risk in thinking through such definitions and exposing their formulations. Irigaray suggests that Freud, by venturing into the dangerous terrain of sexual difference, makes himself vulnerable because he fails to question the cultural, ideological assumptions inherent in the concepts he uses to found his theory. She concludes this section of her book with the claim that Freud's theory of sexual difference is merely a modern re-working of an old theme. However, as she knows very well as an analyst, Freud (like others who spend much of their lives in search of knowledge, constructing theories), combines the conscious objective of investigating the crucial question of sexual difference with the unconscious need both to discover himself and, at the same time, protect himself from his discoveries. This sometimes involves unconsciously presenting concepts upside down and inside out. In fact, elsewhere, Irigaray praises Freud as an honest scientist and for his capacity to listen even when he was hearing things which contradicted his own theoretical stance (Whitford 1991: 79–104).

Discussion

For Irigaray, women's bodies and the multiple pleasures associated with them, make all the difference (although she recognises that at one level gender crosses the boundaries of the body). This differentiates her from Kristeva who often takes the view that the kind of bodies which underpin 'femininity' are less important than the fluid, multiple genders that inhabit them. Indeed both she and Cixous cite a variety of male writers and artists who represent the 'feminine' as models for women, in the sense that they attempt to challenge and overturn what Kristeva sees as traditional 'masculine' logic. This project is less radical than that of Irigaray who thinks it makes a crucial difference whether we speak from a male or female body.

Irigaray has frequently been criticised for being essentialist, that is for assuming an unmediated relationship between 'masculinity' and 'femininity' and the body. However, since Margaret Whitford's wide-ranging and perceptive reappraisal of her work it seems that she has often been misunderstood on this point (Whitford 1991). To begin with, she is not suggesting a direct and unmediated relationship between women's bodies and a female Symbolic. Whitford makes it clear that Irigaray's central concern is to unearth the potential female Imaginary associated with the multiple and fluid pleasures of women's bodies which she thinks is currently buried by the male Imaginary and work towards incorporating it in the Symbolic as part of a dual way of understanding the world shared by both men and women.

Irigaray has also been accused of reproducing traditional gender categories used so effectively throughout history to withhold power from women, because of her view that women are lacking, powerless and outside culture. But this objection seems to confuse gender difference with the ways in which it may be interpreted unconsciously by small children and used to exploit women by oppressive systems. Irigaray's work suggests that the problem for women is one of locating and transforming the conditions which make it possible to deny her difference. She wants women to begin to bring themselves to life, as subjects, within a male Symbolic which she perceives as stuck in a blind alley of the same. Irigaray's project is to try to keep a space open for women to represent her as she might be if she were free.

Irigaray focuses our attention on what may be a common form of male identity, especially among intellectuals who spend their lives trying to theorise human existence. Her work re-thinks psychoanalysis while continually grappling with what she perceives as an alienating, male language to formulate and communicate her ideas, though this difficulty, and her visionary and Utopian style has led to some misinterpretation. One of the intriguing aspects of Irigaray's work is that while criticising psychoanalysis and philosophy she also uses them in her analysis. Her work demonstrates that even if Freud and Lacan were prey to the distortions of a male imaginary, this does not invalidate the depth and scope of their conceptual imaginations. By putting some of psycho-analysis into reverse or putting something else alongside it (womb-envy alongside penis-envy, mother beside father) we can gain dramatic insights into the construction of identity and knowledge in a gender-conscious context.

At the same time we can understand the need of some male intel-lectuals to evolve theories or systems of interpretations which have as their unconscious goal the satisfaction of their unconscious desires and their need for control and denial. Paradoxically, reason may be un-consciously experienced as a surrogate mother while at the same time its categories represent the territory of the father and the phallus, so that women are denied. For such people, theorising and intellectual work may be an important means of psychical survival. Fascinating and useful as theories can be, in one sense they are also a form of cultural dreaming whose desires seem to resonate in the unconscious of other men and women in the social world as well as in the domain of knowledge.

Finally, Irigaray's vision of change raises the same problem as any other which threatens to confront patriarchal men with their projections onto women. Irigaray does not seem to be concerned with what might happen to men if women's hidden cultural support for them were withdrawn. Indeed, some think the first signs of this may have already started. If women increasingly insist that men should acknowledge the content of their projections (which includes the lack of a womb as well as the lack of power brought about by symbolic castration), many men's sense of having any viable identity at all might collapse. Would a new female Imaginary resting on the 'truth' afforded by insight and made available in a transformed Symbolic, be enough to rescue men also? In a therapeutic situation, a patient confronted by such a threatening situation would be emotionally supported by the therapist until he (or she) had managed to come to terms emotionally with what had previously been projected. Shared speech would allow the patient to construct another more open, less defensive identity. The Utopian prospects of Irigaray's work needs to confront such potential collapses.

Suggested reading for Kristeva

JARDINE, A. (1981) 'Introduction to "Women's Time"', *Signs*, 7, 1: 13–15.
JARDINE, A. (1985) *Gynesis: Configurations of Women and Modernity*, Ithaca, Cornell University Press.

JARDINE, A. (1986) 'Opaque Texts and Transparent Contexts: The Political Difference of Julia Kristeva' in N.K. Miller, ed. *The Poetics of Gender*, New York, Columbia University Press.

KRISTEVA, J. (1980) *Desire in Language*, trans L.S. Roudiez, Oxford, Blackwell.

KRISTEVA, J. (1981) 'Women's Time', trans. A. Jardine and H. Blake, *Signs*, 7, 1: 13–15.

KRISTEVA, J. (1984a) *Revolution in Poetic Language*, trans. M. Waller, New York, Columbia University Press.

KRISTEVA, J. (1984b) 'Julia Kristeva in Conversation with Rosalind Coward', *ICA Documents*, special issue on Desire, ed. Lisa Appignanesi, 22–7.

KRISTEVA, J. (1984c) 'Two Interviews with Kristeva', *Partisan Review* 51, 1: 128–32 [with E.H. Baruch].

KRISTEVA J., (1985) 'The Speaking Subject' in M. Blonsky, ed. *On Signs*, Baltimore, Johns Hopkins University Press.

KRISTEVA, J. (1986a) 'An Interview with Julia Kristeva', *Critical Texts* 3: 3 [with I. Lipkowitz and A. Loselle].

KRISTEVA, J. (1986b) *The Kristeva Reader*, Toril Moi ed., Oxford, Blackwell.

KRISTEVA, J. (1987) *Tales of Love*, trans. L.S. Roudiez, New York, Columbia University Press.

KRISTEVA, J. (1991) *Strangers to Ourselves*, trans. L.S. Roudiez, New York, Columbia University Press.

LECHTE, J. (1990) *Julia Kristeva*, London, Routledge.

OLIVER, K. (1993) *Reading Kristeva*, Bloomington and Indianapolis, Indiana University Press.

PAJACZKOWSKA, C. (1981) 'Introduction to Kristeva', *m/f* 5, 6: 149–57.

PAJACZKOWSKA, C. (1985) 'On Love and Language', *Free Associations*, 2, 5: 94–109.

Suggested reading for Irigaray

IRIGARAY, L. (1981) 'When the Goods Get Together', trans. C. Reeder, in E. Marks, and I. de Courtivron, eds. *New French Feminisms: An Anthology*, Brighton, Harvester.

IRIGARAY, L. (1985) *Speculum of the Other Woman*, trans. G.C. Gill, Ithaca, Cornell University.

IRIGARAY, L. (1985b) *This Sex Which is Not One*, trans. C. Porter and C. Burke, Ithaca, Cornell University Press.

IRIGARAY, L. (1992) *Elemental Passions*, trans. J. Collie and J. Still, London, Athlone Press.

IRIGARAY, L. (1993a) *An Ethics of Sexual Difference*, trans. C. Burke and G. Gill, London, Athlone Press.

IRIGARAY, L. (1993b) *Sexes and Genealogies*, trans. G. Gill, New York, Columbia University Press.

IRIGARAY, L. (1993c) *Je, Tu, Nous*, trans. A. Martin, London, Routledge.
MOORE, S. (1988) 'Getting a Bit of the Other – The Pimps of Post-Modernism' in R. Chapman and J. Rutherford, eds. *Male Order: Unwrapping Masculinity*, London, Lawrence and Wishart, 165–92.
TODD, J. ed. (1983) *Women Writers Talking*, New York, Holmes & Meier.
WHITFORD, M. (1991a) *Luce Irigaray: Philosophy in the Feminine*, London, Routledge.
WHITFORD, M. ed. (1991b) *The Irigaray Reader*, Oxford, Blackwell.

General

ANDERMATT CONELEY, V. (1992) *Hélène Cixous*, London, Harvester Wheatsheaf.
CIXOUS, H. (1976) 'The Laugh of the Medusa', trans. K. Cohen and P. Cohen, *Signs*, I, 4: 875–93.
GROSZ, E. (1989) *Sexual Subversions: The French Feminists*, Sydney, Allen and Unwin.
MOI, T. (1985) *Sexual Texual Politics*, London, Methuen.
MOI, T. ed. (1987) *French Feminist Thought*, London, Blackwell.
SELLERS, S. ed. (1988) *Writing Differences: Reading from the Seminar of Hélène Cixous*, Milton Keynes, Open University Press.
SHIACH, M. (1991) *Hélène Cixous: A Politics of Writing*, London, Routledge.

6
Conclusions

One of the criticisms often made of psychoanalytic theory generally is that the theories contained within it – Freudian and Object-Relations, modern and post-modern – are, despite their similarities, fundamentally incompatible. One of the most striking differences between them is that Object-Relations theory sees identity as potentially stable, coherent and integrated, whereas Freudian theory, particularly Lacan's linguistic development of it, sees it as permanently fragile and precarious. However, I hope I have suggested that this theoretical difference is not as divisive as it appears and that we can use both strands of psychoanalytic theory eclectically in our analysis of the complexity of gender.

As we have seen, the idea of precariousness in psychoanalytic theory can be understood in two distinctive ways. One is in the sense that all identity is precarious because of the potential subversion of the unconscious whatever kind of childhood experiences we have had. Psychoanalytic writers, including post-modernists, like Lacan, see this kind of precariousness as part of the normal human condition. The second way in which psychoanalytic theory sees identity as precarious is in the form of particularly troubling neurotic symptoms deriving from an individual's unconscious, unresolved tensions and conflicts in early childhood. This layer of precariousness may be theorised either in the context of a post-modernist condition of precariousness or, from a classical or Object-Relations perspective, within the context of a perception of identity as potentially whole and coherent. Clearly, for many individuals there is yet a further layer of social precariousness beyond the domain of the unconscious which results from an individual's conscious experiences of social power, domination and deprivation.

So psychoanalytic theory allows us to analyse and seek solutions to cultural problems at two unconscious levels of identity. Irigaray's development of Lacan's theory, however, blurs this division. She suggests that the 'normal' precariousness inherent in reason and language is, in fact, neurotic, and arises out of unresolved Oedipal conflicts. Rationality

[206]

itself, and the subjectivity based on it, are not only constructed out of male identity but out of a neurotic form of male identity.

In the context of gender and women's subordination within culture, the French feminists like Irigaray and Kristeva emphasise the need for Symbolic as well as social and political change. But their strategy for resolving the problem of difference within the Symbolic has been criticised for being elitist and remote from the tensions of social reality and the problems of women and those others who have been 'feminised' and oppressed. However, changes in the Symbolic might be more easily achieved by a different route which involves intervention in the way male and female identities are constructed in childhood. In the context of male domination, this approach suggests that we could try to lessen the likelihood of men growing up with ultra-precarious, controlling, potentially women-denying identities which express themselves destructively in both the Symbolic and the social sphere. It argues that we need to bring up boys (as well as girls) to be adult men who would feel as uncomfortable with the existing categories and exclusions in the symbolic and the social as many women because they would be able to acknowledge their 'stranger within'. Such men already clearly exist. Winnicott's concept of the transitional space, Klein's concept of the depressive position and Freud's Oedipal stage, despite their differences, all point in the same direction. They suggest that a greater cultural awareness and attention to the small child's transition from phantasy to reality and the potential for envy, humiliation and a devastating sense of loss in early childhood, might produce adult identities which could resist rather than perpetuate the existing patriarchal meanings, exclusions and projections in language knowledge, and the social sphere.

As we have seen, Winnicott stresses the vital importance of our *actual* as well as phantasised experience of early childhood. His conception of the transitional space suggests a site for intervention in the perpetuation of patriarchal identities which is more generally open than 'writing the feminine' or creating an entirely new Symbolic. His work suggests that men and women can make it possible for their small children to cope creatively with early phantasies and conflicts so that they are able to acknowledge their own 'other' and maintain their emotional dignity and creativity in the face of potentially overwhelming feelings of separation and loss. In this kind of emotional environment, the child is guaranteed the support it needs to make the initial impact of reality (the separation from the mother and the discovery of difference) a source of possibility and creativity rather than a humiliating loss and defeat.

The kind of responsive empathetic parenting advocated by Winnicott characterised by the provision of unconditional love and a non-intrusive, containing and empowering transitional space for children clearly needs a context of 'good enough' social as well as psychological circumstances (a social version of what Winnicott calls a continuous sense of 'going on being'). This means a situation where parents are themselves supported by a culture which values and makes possible a social context sympathetic to this kind of parenting, that is a culture which includes 'feminine' as well as patriarchal institutions and one which makes possible the successful integration of phantasy and reality. If societies reinforce a sense of castration in their members by failing to respond to ordinary human needs and frequently expressing contempt for them, and, instead, induce feelings of deprivation, helplessness, humiliation, frustration and lack of self-esteem in significant numbers of men and women, they destroy much of the potential for 'good enough' parenting. If, at the same time, they also promote parenting discourses which advocate 'firmness', discipline and condemnation rather than responsiveness, sensitivity and containment, then parents may, through a sense of hopelessness, and absence of personal worth and dignity, lack the capacity to be 'good enough'. If the mother and father, when available, and the wider culture make possible the creative and imaginative identity Winnicott believed to be the realisable outcome of every childhood, the resulting individual is less likely to have the unconscious need to repress the 'feminine', emotional dimensions of who they are and to destructively project phantasies of lack onto others. This might mean that destructive cultural forces which subordinate women and others defined as different could be resisted more effectively because they would not be so likely to resonate with widespread, potentially destructive unconscious denials and unresolved conflicts.

It is also significant, in relation to the losses children have to sustain in early childhood, that boys have to sustain a double loss compared with girls, the loss of their identification with the physical and emotional creativity, closeness and expressiveness with their mothers as well as the loss of her as an object of desire, to the father. As I have argued in this sense they lose both their primary sense of identity and their sexual identity in early childhood. This is symbolically a double castration. Thus the problem of difference and, specifically, the unconscious 'masculine' need to deny and obliterate the 'feminine' other may stem from the unconscious perception, in many men, that most women do *not* have to fight for psychical survival as they do. However much culture may deprive women of a cultural identity, the creative and powerful identity of the mother is usually available to them as well as, at least potentially, the other identities available to men. (This is independent of whether women avail themselves of it or even value it themselves.) The identity of the mother, is, of course, intimately involved with the crucial and delicate business of making an eventual identity possible for her sons or daughters. For many men, the unconscious perception of women's experience may be that, in spite of women's difference and their persistent cultural denial and subordination, most women *still* emerge in possession of what really counts. This seems to be at least one creative, emotionally authentic and guaranteed source of identity and value – both the biological capacity literally to double themselves and the capacity for sufficient integration to allow them to respond creatively to another human being's sense of helplessness and need for an identity. This is whether or not women are successful in the achievement of the other identities available to men. The envy and hostility likely to be provoked in some, perhaps many, men by women's capacity for both a culturally 'masculine' and 'feminine' identity – for reason, physical and emotional creativity and a sense of connection with their bodies – might help to explain the need, in patriarchal cultures, to make it as difficult as possible for women to achieve success in *both* her potential identities – as a mother and in a career. It seems that women cannot be permitted to have unencumbered access to both these identities because in doing so their power threatens to run out of control. They become not just men's equals but substantially more than men can ever be. There seems to be a 'real' place for them outside phantasy. Although gender crosses the boundaries of the body, 'masculine' women can have babies but 'feminine' men cannot, whatever they do. In the sense that women may provoke envy in this way, anatomy is destiny. Tragically for men and women, envy in some men may make it a significant factor in their experience of difference and women's subordination. The continual unconscious spoiling and exclusion of women's potential power within discourses and practices then becomes the means of preventing 'masculine' psychical annihalition. The designation of women as irrational, ultra-precarious and even mad is a necessary unconscious manoeuvre to sustain the idea of men as rational and objective and conceal their envy and dependence on them.

An eclectic reading of both Freudian and Object-Relations psycho-analytic approaches suggests that, despite their conceptual differences, they identify the same kind of unconscious phenomena in play in relation to our response to difference. They suggest that destructive responses to identities perceived as different stem from an inability to recognise and reconcile (take responsibility for) our own 'other', the difference within ourselves which we unconsciously hold in contempt. The Freudian-based work of Kristeva refers to the divisive effects of the child's symbolic castration by the father on our identity, as the 'victim and executioner' within us all, whereas Kleinian theory describes the same phenomenon as the splitting and projection of inner 'bad' feelings out into the external world. As Irigaray emphasises, for the boy, the mother and 'femininity' must be symbolically killed in order to achieve a 'masculine' identity and locate him in language and culture.

As we have seen, a destructive cultural response to difference is evident in, for example, the patriarchal 'masculine' response not only to gender but to sexual orientation, race, class, ethnicity and nation. It also extends to cruelty towards those who are particularly vulnerable, such as children and animals. In one sense all these groups may be seen as having been 'feminised', because they come to symbolise weakness and vulnerability – what is unconscious and unacceptable to 'masculine', phallic consciousness – so that they must be disowned and denigrated. The need to externalise a sense of lack seems to lie behind the widespread pre-occupation, particularly among young men, with representations of violence in the media and, more recently, in the form of one-to-one combat in video games. These seem to be the contemporary mani-festations of the same preoccupation with violent combat which char-acterises ancient myths, folk-tales and fairy stories. All of these real or imagined conflicts involve an other onto whom we project and banish rejected parts of the self in the interests of maintaining an identity which feels free of conflict and inferiority.

In the realm of knowledge, as Irigaray stresses, psychoanalytic per-spectives insist that we need to incorporate meanings which reflect and resonate with our unconscious, bodily as well as conscious experience. And, as Kristeva's work emphasises, it suggests we need to cultivate a continual creative vacillation between conscious and unconscious, knowl-edge and insight, order and disorder. But perhaps, most importantly, as Kristeva suggests, we need forms of knowledge which can encompass a suspension of our potentially lethal wish to compete and divide in order to sustain a sense of identity – theories which can encapsulate a suspension of our narcissism which Kristeva describes as that enviable quality specific to many women's experience of motherhood, 'the slow, difficult and delightful apprenticeship in attentiveness, gentleness, forgetting oneself'. In other words, psychoanalytic theory suggests we need to carve out of what is available to us in the Imaginary, a more intuitive form of knowledge based on emotional as well as theoretical insight which is capable of a flexible but empathic response to the diversity of identity. Putting aside our narcissism would mean abandoning our need to identify with certain forms of knowledge simply because they reflect our own defensive need to deny and project. It would mean that we should not reject humanist, biological and essentialist perspectives without first carefully analysing what is at issue, and our personal stake in it. Otherwise, we replicate the very division between body/mind, nature/culture, reason/emotion, masculine/feminine which we criticise in traditional forms of thought. We cannot regard identity as having existence only in the Symbolic because psychoanalytic approaches as a whole suggest that what we call reality is not identical with the structures through which we speak about it. However fashionable that view, the 'reality' is more complicated. Psychoanalytic theory suggests that our analysis of identity must include all the levels of our existence – those aspects which are structurally determined by language, those dimensions which are determined by our biology, our everyday, conscious, lived experience and those constructed out of our unconscious phantasies which are not symbolised and embodied in the structures of language and which therefore remain denied and repressed until we uncover them. In this sense, the connection between knowledge, the body and the unconscious needs to become a commonplace in our assumptions about knowledge without undermining our capacity to challenge the meanings of any of them.

Finally, psychoanalytic approaches emphasise that whatever level of identity we are addressing, we need continually to bear in mind what Irigaray and Kristeva reminds us of: the human subject is always a subject of love whether or not it is consciously acknowledged. All disciplines including the most abstract and conceptual inevitably have their roots in unconscious phantasies around the body of the mother and our inevitable separation from her in order to become human subjects. As psychoanalysis 'knows', as subjects of love, we all, men and women, inevitably, have an unconscious which makes us prone at best to forget, and at worst to deny, this part of our experience. It suggests that while we do this, we remain subjects of love, but also subject to narcissism and unacknowledged rivalry and conflict. In the context of finding a new source of cultural values, psychoanalytic theory suggests that the future depends on making it more possible within culture for our earliest phantasies and experience of love and loss to be mediated in ways which are life-enhancing and creative rather than sadistic and destructive of our own and other identities and meanings, however fluid and precarious these inevitably may be.

PART II

7
Sigmund Freud, 'Femininity' (1933)

This paper was first published in Vienna six years before Freud's death. In it Freud summarises and reworks his most developed ideas on the nature of 'femininity' which he first presented in 'Some Psychical Consequences of the Anatomical Distinction between the Sexes' (1925). The latter provoked considerable discussion and controversy in psychoanalytic circles of which Freud was very aware when he wrote 'Female Sexuality' and 'Femininity'. This probably accounts for the rather defensive tone in some parts of it. In 'Femininity' Freud re-states his perception of what he sees as 'a disturbance' at the heart of femininity, what he regards as the girl's early 'active', 'masculine' love for the mother from which he thought she never entirely breaks free. The paper re-iterates a variety of conclusions which have made Freud's work on femininity controversial among feminists, including the issues of bi-sexuality, penis-envy, passivity and activity in relation to cultural definitions of 'masculinity' and femininity', and the significance of the clitoris and the vagina. However, these ideas need to be understood within the wider context of Freud's writing, as the discussion in chapter two of this book makes clear. What is new in this paper is the link he attempts to make between his description of adult women and his new focus on the intense pre-Oedipal mother–daughter relationship which was not present in his earlier description of 'femininity' in the *Three Essays on the Theory of Sexuality* (1905).

The first paragraph of this paper containing only local details has been omitted. It was translated by James Strachey. Fuller commentary on this paper begins on page 47.

'Femininity'

To-day's lecture too, should have no place in an introduction; but it may serve to give you an example of a detailed piece of analytic work, and I can say two things to recommend it. It brings forward nothing but observed facts, almost without any speculative additions, and it deals with a subject which has a claim on your interest second almost to no other. Throughout history people have knocked their heads against the riddle of the nature of femininity –

> Häupter in Hieroglyphenmützen,
> Häupter in Turban und schwarzem Barett,
> Perückenhäupter und tausend andre
> Arme, schwitzende Menschenhäupter.[1]

Nor will *you* have escaped worrying over this problem – those of you who are men; to those of you who are women this will not apply – you are yourselves the problem. When you meet a human being, the first distinction you make is 'male or female?' and you are accustomed to make the distinction with unhesitating certainty. Anatomical science shares your certainty at one point and not much further. The male sexual product, the spermatozoon, and its vehicle are male; the ovum and the organism that harbours it are female. In both sexes organs have been formed which serve exclusively for the sexual functions; they were probably developed from the same [innate] disposition into two different forms. Besides this, in both sexes the other organs, the bodily shapes and tissues, show the influence of the individual's sex, but this is inconstant and its amount variable; these are what are known as the secondary sexual characters. Science next tells you something that runs counter to your expectations and is probably calculated to confuse your feelings. It draws your attention to the fact that portions of the male sexual apparatus also appear in women's bodies, though in an atrophied state, and vice versa in the alternative case. It regards their occurrence as indications of *bisexuality,* as though an individual is not a man or a woman but always both – merely a certain amount more the one than the other. You will then be asked to make yourselves familiar with the idea that the proportion in which masculine and feminine are mixed in an individual is subject to quite considerable fluctuations. Since, however, apart from the very rarest cases, only one kind of sexual product – ova or semen – is nevertheless present in one person, you are bound to have doubts as to the decisive significance of those elements and must conclude that what constitutes masculinity or femininity is an unknown characteristic which anatomy cannot lay hold of.

Can psychology do so perhaps? We are accustomed to employ 'masculine' and 'feminine' as mental qualities as well, and have in the

[216]

same way transferred the notion of bisexuality to mental life. Thus we speak of a person, whether male or female, as behaving in a masculine way in one connection and in a feminine way in another. But you will soon perceive that this is only giving way to anatomy or to convention. You cannot give the concepts of 'masculine' and 'feminine' *any* new connotation. The distinction is not a psychological one, when you say 'masculine', you usually mean 'active', and when you say 'feminine', you usually mean 'passive'. Now it is true that a relation of the kind exists. The male sex cell is actively mobile and searches out the female one, and the latter, the ovum, is immobile and waits passively. This behaviour of the elementary sexual organisms is indeed a model for the conduct of sexual individuals during intercourse. The male pursues the female for the purpose of sexual union, seizes hold of her and penetrates into her. But by this you have precisely reduced the characteristic of masculinity to the factor of aggressiveness so far as psychology is concerned. You may well doubt whether you have gained any real advantage from this when you reflect that in some classes of animals the females are the stronger and more aggressive and the male is active only in the single act of sexual union. This is so, for instance, with the spiders. Even the functions of rearing and caring for the young, which strike us as feminine *par excellence*, are not invariably attached to the female sex in animals. In quite high species we find that the sexes share the task of caring for the young between them or even that the male alone devotes himself to it. Even in the sphere of human sexual life you soon see how inadequate it is to make masculine behaviour coincide with activity and feminine with passivity. A mother is active in every sense towards her child; the act of lactation itself may equally be described as the mother suckling her baby or as her being sucked by it. The further you go from the narrow sexual sphere the more obvious will the 'error of superimposition[2]' become. Women can display great activity in various directions, men are not able to live in company with their own kind unless they develop a large amount of passive adaptability. If you now tell me that these facts go to prove precisely that both men and women are bisexual in the psychological sense, I shall conclude that you have decided in your own minds to make 'active' coincide with 'masculine' and 'passive' with 'feminine'. But I advise you against it. It seems to me to serve no useful purpose and adds nothing to our knowledge.

One might consider characterizing femininity psychologically as giving preference to passive aims. This is not, of course, the same thing as passivity; to achieve a passive aim may call for a large amount of activity. It is perhaps the case that in a women, on the basis of her share in the sexual function, a preference for passive behaviour and passive aims is carried over into her life to a greater or lesser extent, in proportion to the limits, restricted or far-reaching, within which her sexual life thus serves as a model. But we must beware in this of underestimating the influence of social customs, which similarly force women into passive situations. All this is still far from being cleared up. There is one particularly constant relation between femininity and instinctual life which we do not want to overlook. The suppression of women's aggressiveness which is prescribed for them constitutionally and imposed on them socially favours the development of powerful masochistic impulses, which succeed, as we know, in binding erotically the destructive trends which have been diverted inwards. Thus masochism, as people say, is truly feminine. But if, as happens so often, you meet with masochism in men, what is left to you but to say that these men exhibit very plain feminine traits?

And now you are already prepared to hear that psychology too is unable to solve the riddle of femininity. The explanation must no doubt come from elsewhere, and cannot come till we have learnt how in general the differentiation of living organisms into two sexes came about. We know nothing about it, yet the existence of two sexes is a most striking characteristic of organic life which distinguishes it sharply from in-animate nature. However, we find enough to study in those human individuals who, through the possession of female genitals, are charac-terized as manifestly or predominantly feminine. In conformity with its peculiar nature, psychoanalysis does not try to describe what a woman is – that would be a task it could scarcely perform – but sets about enquiring how she comes into being, how a woman develops out of a child with a bisexual disposition. In recent times we have begun to learn a little about this, thanks to the circumstance that several of our excellent women colleagues in analysis have begun to work at the question. The discussion of this has gained special attractiveness from the distinction between the sexes. For the ladies, whenever some comparison seemed to turn out unfavourable to their sex, were able to utter a suspicion that we, the male analysts, had been unable to overcome certain deeply-rooted prejudices against what was feminine, and that this was being paid for in the partiality of our researches. We, on the other hand, standing on the ground of bisexuality, had no difficulty in avoiding impoliteness. We had only to say: 'This doesn't apply to *you*. You're the exception; on this point you're more masculine than feminine.'

We approach the investigation of the sexual development of women with two expectations. The first is that here once more the constitution will not adapt itself to its function without a struggle. The second is that the decisive turning-points will already have been prepared for or completed before puberty. Both expectations are promptly confirmed. Furthermore, a comparison with what happens with boys tells us that the development of a little girl into a normal woman is more difficult and more complicated, since it includes two extra tasks, to which there is nothing corresponding in the development of a man. Let us follow the parallel lines from their beginning. Undoubtedly the material is different to start with in boys and girls: it did not need the psychoanalysis to establish that. The difference in the structure of the genitals is accompanied by other bodily differences which are too well known to call for mention. Differences emerge too in the instinctual disposition which give a glimpse of the later nature of women. A little girl is as a rule less aggressive, defiant and self-sufficient; she seems to have greater need for being shown affection and on that account to be more dependent and pliant. It is probably only as a result of this pliancy that she can be taught more easily and quicker to control her excretions: urine and faeces are the first gifts that children make to those who look after them, and controlling them is the first concession to which the instinctual life of children can be induced. One gets an impression, too, that little girls are more intelligent and livelier than boys of the same age; they go out more to meet the external world and at the same time form stronger object-cathexes. I cannot say whether this lead in development has been confirmed by exact observations, but in any case there is no question that girls cannot be described as intellectually backward. These sexual differences are not, however, of great consequence: they can be outweighed by individual variations. For our immediate purposes they can be disregarded.

Both sexes seem to pass through the early phases of libidinal development in the same manner. It might have been expected that in girls there would already have been some lag in aggressiveness in the sadistic–anal phase, but such is not the case. Analysis of children's play has shown our women analysts that the aggressive impulses of little girls leave nothing to be desired in the way of abundance and violence. With their entry into the phallic phase the differences between the sexes are completely eclipsed by their agreements. We are now obliged to recognize that the little girl is a little man. In boys, as we know, this phase is marked by the fact that they have learnt how to derive pleasurable sensations from their small penis and connect its excited state with their ideas of sexual intercourse. Little girls do the same thing with their still smaller clitoris. It seems that with them all their masturbatory acts are carried out on this penis-equivalent, and that the truly feminine vagina is still undiscovered by both sexes. It is true that there are a few isolated reports of early vaginal sensations as well, but it could not be easy to distinguish these from sensations in the anus or vestibulum; in any case they cannot play a great part. We are entitled to keep to our view that in the phallic phase of girls the clitoris is the leading erotogenic zone. But it is not, of course, going to remain so. With the change to femininity the clitoris should wholly or in part hand over its sensitivity, and at the same time its importance, to the vagina. This would be one of the two tasks which a woman has to perform in the course of her development, whereas the more fortunate man has only to continue at the time of his sexual maturity the activity that he has previously carried out at the period of the early efflorescence of his sexuality.

We shall return to the part played by the clitoris; let us now turn to the second task with which a girl's development is burdened. A boy's mother is the first object of his love, and she remains so too during the formation of his Oedipus complex, and in essence, all through his life. For a girl too her first object must be her mother (and the figures of wet-nurses and foster-mothers that merge into her). The first object-cathexes occur in attachment to the satisfaction of the major and simple vital needs, and the circumstances of the care of children are the same for both sexes. But in the Oedipus situation the girl's father has become her love-object, and we expect that in the normal course of development she will find her way from this paternal object to her final choice of an object. In the course of time, therefore, a girl has to change her erotogenic zone and her object – both of which a boy retains. The question then arises of how this happens: in particular, how does a girl pass from her mother to an attachment to her father? or, in other words, how does she pass from her masculine phase to the feminine one to which she is biologically destined?

It would be a solution of ideal simplicity if we could suppose that from a particular age onwards the elementary influence of the mutual attraction between the sexes makes itself felt and impels the small woman towards men, while the same law allows the boy to continue with his mother. We might suppose in addition that in this the children are following the pointer given them by the sexual preference of their parents. But we are not going to find things so easy; we scarcely know whether we are to believe seriously in the power of which poets talk so much and with such enthusiasm but which cannot be further dissected analytically. We have found an answer of quite another sort by means of laborious investigations, the material for which at least was easy to arrive at. For you must know that the number of women who remain till a late age tenderly dependent on a paternal object, or indeed on their real father, is very great. We have established some surprising facts about these women with an intense attachment of long duration to their father. We knew, of course, that there had been a preliminary stage of attachment to the mother, but we did not know that it could be so rich in content and so long-lasting, and could leave behind so many opportunities for fixations and dispositions. During this time the girl's father is only a troublesome rival; in some cases the attachment to her mother lasts beyond the fourth year of life. Almost everything that we find later in her relation to her father was already present in this earlier attachment and has been transferred subsequently on to her father. In short, we get an impression that we cannot understand women unless we appreciate this phase of their pre-Oedipus attachment to their mother.

We shall be glad, then, to know the nature of the girl's libidinal relations to her mother. The answer is that they are of very many different kinds. Since they persist through all three phases of infantile sexuality, they also take on the characteristics of the different phases and express themselves by oral, sadistic–anal and phallic wishes. These wishes represent active as well as passive impulses; if we relate them to the differentiation of the sexes which is to appear later – though we should avoid doing so as far as possible – we may call them masculine and feminine. Besides this, they are completely ambivalent, both affectionate and of a hostile and aggressive nature. The latter often only come to light after being changed into anxiety ideas. It is not always easy to point to a formulation of these early sexual wishes; what is most clearly expressed is a wish to get the mother with child and the corresponding wish to bear her a child – both belonging to the phallic period and sufficiently surprising, but established beyond doubt by analytic observation. The attractiveness of these investigations lies in the surprising detailed findings which they bring us. Thus, for instance, we discover the fear of being murdered or poisoned, which may later form the core of a paranoic illness, already present in this pre-Oedipus period, in relation to the mother.[3] Or another case: you will recall an interesting episode in the history of analytic research which caused me many distressing hours. In the period in which the main interest was directed to discovering infantile sexual traumas, almost all my women patients told me that they had been seduced by their father. I was driven to recognize in the end that these reports were untrue and so came to understand that hysterical symptoms are derived from phantasies and not from real occurrences. It was only later that I was able to recognize in the phantasy of being seduced by the father the expression of the typical Oedipus complex in women. And now we find the phantasy of seduction once more in the pre-Oedipus prehistory of girls; but the seducer is regularly the mother. Here, however, the phantasy touches the ground of reality, for it was really the mother who by her activities over the child's bodily hygiene inevitably stimulated, and perhaps even roused for the first time, pleasurable sensations in her genitals.

I have no doubt you are ready to suspect that this portrayal of the abundance and strength of a little girl's sexual relations with her mother is very much overdrawn. After all, one has opportunities of seeing little girls and notices nothing of the sort. But the objection is not to the point. Enough can be seen in the children if one knows how to look. And besides, you should consider how little of its sexual wishes a child can bring to pre-conscious expression or communicate at all. Accordingly we are only within our rights if we study the residues and consequences of this emotional world in retrospect, in people in whom these processes of development had attained a specially clear and even excessive degree of expansion. Pathology has always done us the service of making discernible by isolation and exaggeration conditions which would remain concealed in a normal state. And since our investigations have been carried out on people who were by no means seriously abnormal, I think we should regard their outcome as deserving belief.[4]

We will now turn our interest on to the single question of what it is that brings this powerful attachment of the girl to her mother to an end. This, as we know, is its usual fate: it is destined to make room for an attachment to her father. Here we come upon a fact which is a pointer to our further advance. This step in development does not involve only a simple change of object. The turning away from the mother is accompanied by hostility; the attachment to the mother ends in hate. A hate of that kind may become very striking and last all through life; it may be carefully overcompensated later on; as a rule one part of it is overcome while another part persists. Events of later years naturally influence this greatly. We will restrict ourselves, however, to studying it at the time at which the girl turns to her father and to enquiring into the motives for it. We are then given a long list of accusations and grievances against the mother which are supposed to justify the child's hostile feelings; they are of varying validity which we shall not fail to examine. A number of them are obvious rationalizations and the true sources of enmity remain to be found. I hope you will be interested if on this occasion I take you through all the details of a psychoanalytic investigation.

The reproach against the mother which goes back furthest is that she gave the child too little milk – which is construed against her as a lack of love. Now there is some justification for this reproach in our families. Mothers often have insufficient nourishment to give their children and are content to suckle them for a few months, for half or three-quarters of a year. Among primitive peoples children are fed at their mother's breast for two or three years. The figure of the wet-nurse who suckles the child is as a rule merged into the mother; when this has not happened, the reproach is turned into another one – that the nurse, who fed the child so willingly, was sent away by the mother too early. But whatever the true state of affairs may have been, it is impossible that the child's reproach can be justified as often as it is met with. It seems, rather, that the child's avidity for its earliest nourishment is altogether insatiable, that is never gets over the pain of losing its mother's breast. I should not be surprised if the analysis of a primitive child, who could still suck at its mother's breast when it was already able to run about and talk, were to bring the same reproach to light. The fear of being poisoned is also probably connected with the withdrawal of the breast. Poison is nourishment that makes one ill. Perhaps children trace back their early illnesses too to this frustration. A fair amount of intellectual education is a prerequisite for believing in chance; primitive people and uneducated ones, and no doubt children as well, are able to assign a ground for everything that happens. Perhaps originally it was a reason on animistic lines. Even to-day in some strata of our population no one can die without having been killed by someone else – preferably by the doctor. And the regular reaction of a neurotic to the death of someone closely connected with him is to put the blame on himself for having caused the death.

The next accusation against the child's mother flares up when the next baby appears in the nursery. If possible the connection with oral frustration is preserved: the mother could not or would not give the child any more milk because she needed the nourishment for the new arrival. In cases in which the two children are so close in age that lactation is prejudiced by the second pregnancy, this reproach acquires a real basis, and it is a remarkable fact that a child, even with an age difference of only II months, is not too young to take notice of what is happening. But what the child grudges the unwanted intruder and rival is not only the suckling but all the other signs of maternal care. It feels that it has been dethroned, despoiled, prejudiced in its rights; it casts a jealous hatred upon the new baby and develops a grievance against the faithless mother which often finds expression in a disagreeable change in its behaviour. It becomes 'naughty', perhaps, irritable and disobedient and goes back on the advances it had made towards controlling its excretions. All of this has been very long familiar and is accepted as self-evident; but we rarely form a correct idea of the strength of these jealous impulses, of the tenacity with which they persist and of the magnitude of their influence on later development. Especially as this jealousy is constantly receiving fresh nourishment in the later years of childhood and the whole shock is repeated with the birth of each new brother or sister. Nor does it make much difference if the child happens to remain the mother's preferred favourite. A child's demands for love are immoderate, they make exclusive claims and tolerate no sharing.

An abundant source of a child's hostility to its mother is provided by its multifarious sexual wishes, which after according to the phase of the libido and which cannot for the most part be satisfied. The strongest of these frustrations occur at the phallic period, if the mother forbids pleasurable activity with the genitals – often with severe threats and every sign of displeasure – activity to which, after all, she herself had introduced the child. One would think these were reasons enough to account for a girl's turning away from her mother. One would judge, if so, that the estrangement follows inevitably from the nature of children's sexuality, from the immoderate character of their demand for love and the impossibility of fulfilling their sexual wishes. It might be thought indeed that this first love-relation of the child's is doomed to dissolution for the very reason that it is the first, for these early object-cathexes are

[224]

regularly ambivalent to a high degree. A powerful tendency to aggressiveness is always present beside a powerful love, and the more passionately a child loves its object the more sensitive does it become to
disappointments and frustrations from that object, and in the end the love
must succumb to the accumulated hostility. Or the idea that there is an
original ambivalence such as this in erotic cathexes may be rejected, and it
may be pointed out that it is the special nature of the mother–child
relation that leads, with equal inevitability, to the destruction of the
child's love; for even the mildest upbringing cannot avoid using compulsion and introducing restrictions, and any such intervention in the child's
liberty must provoke as a reaction an inclination to rebelliousness and
aggressiveness. A discussion of these possibilities might, I think, be most
interesting, but an objection suddenly emerges which forces our interest
in another direction. All these factors – the slights, the disappointments
in love, the jealousy, the seduction followed by prohibition – are, after
all, also in operation in the relation of a *boy* to his mother and are yet
unable to alienate him from the maternal object. Unless we can find
something that is specific for girls and is not present or not in the same
way present in boys, we shall not have explained the termination of the
attachment of girls to their mother.

I believe we have found this specific factor, and indeed where we
expected to find it, even though in a surprising form. Where we expected
to find it, I say, for it lies in the castration complex. After all, the
anatomical distinction [between the sexes] must express itself in psychical consequences. It was, however, a surprise to learn from analyses that
girls hold their mother responsible for their lack of a penis and do not
forgive her for their being thus put at a disadvantage.

As you hear, then, we ascribe a castration complex to women as well.
And for good reasons, though its content cannot be the same as with boys.
In the latter the castration complex arises after they have learnt from the
sight of the female genitals that the organ which they value so highly
need not necessarily accompany the body. At this the boy recalls to mind
the threats he brought on himself by his doings with that organ, he begins
to give credence to them and falls under the influence of fear of castration,
which will be the most powerful motive force in his subsequent development. The castration complex of girls is also started by the sight of the
genitals of the other sex. They at once notice the difference and, it must
be admitted, its significance too. They feel seriously wronged, often
declare that they want to 'have something like it too', and fall a victim to

'envy for the penis', which will leave ineradicable traces on their development and the formation of their character and which will not be surmounted in even the most favourable cases without a severe expenditure of psychical energy. The girl's recognition of the fact of her being without a penis does not by any means imply that she submits to the fact easily. On the contrary, she continues to hold on for a long time to the wish to get something like it herself and she believes in that possibility for improbably long years; and analysis can show that, at a period when knowledge of reality has long since rejected the fulfilment of the wish as unattainable, it persists in the unconscious and retains a considerable cathexis of energy. The wish to get the longed-for penis eventually in spite of everything may contribute to the motives that drive a mature woman to analysis, and what she may reasonably expect from analysis – a capacity, for instance, to carry on an intellectual profession – may often be recognized as a sublimated modification of this repressed wish.

One cannot very well doubt the importance of envy for the penis. You may take it as an instance of male injustice if I assert that envy and jealousy play an even greater part in the mental life of women than of men. It is not that I think these characteristics are absent in men or that I think they have no other roots in women than envy for the penis; but I am inclined to attribute their greater amount in women to this latter influence. Some analysis, however, have shown an inclination to depreciate the importance of this first instalment of penis-envy in the phallic phase. They are of opinion that what we find of this attitude in women is in the main a secondary structure which has come about on the occasion of later conflicts by regression to this early infantile impulse. This, however, is a general problem of depth psychology. In many pathological – or even unusual – instinctual attitudes (for instance, in all sexual perversions) the question arises of how much of their strength is to be attributed to early infantile fixations and how much to the influence of later experiences and developments. In such cases it is almost always a matter of complemental series such as we put forward in our discussion of the aetiology of the neuroses. Both factors play a part in varying amounts in the causation; a less on the one side is balanced by a more on the other. The infantile factor sets the pattern in all cases but does not always determine the issue, though it often does. Precisely in the case of penis-envy I should argue decidedly in favour of the preponderance of the infantile factor.

The discovery that she is castrated is a turning-point in a girl's growth.

Three possible lines of development start from it: one leads to sexual inhibition or to neurosis, the second to change of character in the sense of a masculinity complex, the third, finally, to normal femininity. We have learnt a fair amount, though not everything, about all three.

The essential content of the first is as follows: the little girl has hitherto lived in a masculine way, has been able to get pleasure by the excitation of her clitoris and has brought this activity into relation with her sexual wishes directed towards her mother, which are often active ones; now, owing to the influence of her penis-envy, she loses her enjoyment in her phallic sexuality. Her self-love is mortified by the comparison with the boy's far superior equipment and in consequence she renounces her masturbatory satisfaction from her clitoris, repudiates her love for her mother and at the same time not infrequently represses a good part of her sexual trends in general. No doubt her turning away from her mother does not occur all at once, for to begin with the girl regards her castration as an individual misfortune, and only gradually extends it to other females and finally to her mother as well. Her love was directed to her *phallic* mother; with the discovery that her mother is castrated it becomes possible to drop her as an object, so that the motives for hostility, which have long been accumulating gain the upper hand. This means, therefore, that as a result of the discovery of women's lack of a penis they are debased on value for girls just as they are for boys and later perhaps for men.

You all know the immense aetiological importance attributed by our neurotic patients to their masturbation. They make it responsible for all their troubles and we have the greatest difficulty in persuading them that they are mistaken. In fact, however, we ought to admit to them that they are right, for masturbation is the executive agent of infantile sexuality, from the faulty development of which they are indeed suffering. But what neurotics mostly blame is the masturbation of the period of puberty; they have mostly forgotten that of early infancy, which is what is really in question. I wish I might have an opportunity some time of explaining to you at length how important all the factual details of early masturbation become for the individual's subsequent neurosis or character: whether or not it was discovered, how the parents struggled against it or permitted it, or whether he succeeded in suppressing it himself. All of this leaves permanent traces on his development. But I am on the whole glad that I need not do this. It would be a hard and tedious task and at the end of it you would put me in an embarrassing situation by quite certainly asking me to give you some practical advice as to how a parent or educator should deal with the masturbation of small children. From the development of girls, which is what my present lecture is concerned with, I can give you the example of a child herself trying to get free from masturbating. She does not always succeed in this. If envy for the penis has provoked a powerful impulse against clitoridal masturbation but this nevertheless refuses to give way, a violent struggle for liberation ensues in which the girl, as it were, herself takes over the role of her deposed mother and gives expression to her entire dissatisfaction with her inferior clitoris in her efforts against obtaining satisfaction from it. Many years later, when her masturbatory activity has long since been suppressed, an interest still persists which we must interpret as a defence against a temptation that is still dreaded. It manifests itself in the emergence of sympathy for those to whom similar difficulties are attributed, it plays a part as a motive in contracting a marriage, and, indeed, it may determine the choice of a husband or lover. Disposing of early infantile masturbation is truly no easy or indifferent business.

Along with the abandonment of clitoridal masturbation a certain amount of activity is renounced. Passivity now has the upper hand, and the girl's turning to her father is accomplished principally with the help of passive instinctual impulses. You can see that a wave of development like this, which clears the phallic activity out of the way, smooths the ground for femininity. If too much is not lost in the course of it through repression, this femininity may turn out to be normal. The wish with which the girl turns to her father is no doubt originally the wish for the penis which her mother has refused her and which she now expects from her father. The feminine situation is only established, however, if the wish for a penis is replaced by one for a baby, if, that is, a baby takes the place of a penis in accordance with an ancient symbolic equivalence. It has not escaped us that the girl has wished for a baby earlier, in the undisturbed phallic phase: that, of course, was the meaning of her playing with dolls. But that play was not in fact an expression of femininity, it served as an identification with her mother with the intention of substituting activity for passivity. *She* was playing the part of her mother and the doll was herself: now she could do with the baby everything that her mother used to do with her. Not until the emergence of the wish for a penis does the doll–baby become a baby from the girl's father, and thereafter the aim of the most powerful feminine wish. Her happiness is great if later on this wish for a baby finds fulfilment in reality, and quite especially so if the baby is a little boy who brings the longed-for penis with him. Often enough in her combined picture of 'a baby from her father' the emphasis is laid on the baby and her father left unstressed. In this way the ancient masculine wish for the possession of a penis is still faintly visible through the femininity now achieved. But perhaps we ought rather to recognize this wish for a penis as being *par excellence* a feminine one.

With the transference of the wish for a penis–baby on to her father, the girl has entered the situation of the Oedipus complex. Her hostility to her mother, which did not need to be freshly created, is now greatly intensified, for she becomes the girl's rival, who receives from her father everything that she desires from him. For a long time the girl's Oedipus complex concealed her pre-Oedipus attachment to her mother from our view, though it is nevertheless so important and leaves such lasting fixations behind it. For girls the Oedipus situation is the outcome of a long and difficult development. It is a kind of preliminary solution, a position of rest which is not soon abandoned, especially as the beginning of the latency period is not far distant. And we are now struck by a difference between the two sexes, which is probably momentous, in regard to the relation of the Oedipus complex to the castration complex. In a boy the Oedipus complex, in which he desires his mother and would like to get rid of his father as being a rival, develops naturally from the phase of his phallic sexuality. The threat of castration compels him, however to give up that attitude. Under the impression of the danger of losing his penis, the Oedipus complex is abandoned, repressed and, in the most normal cases, entirely destroyed, and a severe super-ego is set up as its heir. What happens with a girl is almost the opposite. The castration complex prepares for the Oedipus complex instead of destroying it; the girl is driven out of her attachment to her mother through the influence of her envy for the penis and she enters the Oedipus situation as though into a haven of refuge. In the absence of fear of castration the chief motive is lacking which leads boys to surmount the Oedipus complex. Girls remain in it for an indeterminate length of time; they demolish it late and, even so, incompletely. In these circumstances the formation of the super-ego must suffer, it cannot, attain the strength and independence which give it is cultural significance, and feminists are not pleased when we point out to them the effects of this factor upon the average feminine character.

To go back a little. We mentioned as the second possible reaction to

[229]

the discovery of female castration the development of a powerful masculinity complex. By this we mean that the girl refuses, as it were, to recognize the unwelcome fact and, defiantly rebellious, even exaggerates her previous masculinity, clings to her clitoridal activity and takes refuge in an identification with her phallic mother or her father. What can it be that decides in favour of this outcome? We can only suppose that it is a constitutional factor, a greater amount of activity, such as is ordinarily characteristic of a male. However that may be, the essence of this process is that at this point in development the wave of passivity is avoided which opens the way to the turn towards femininity. The extreme achievement of such a masculinity complex would appear to be the influencing of the choice of an object in the sense of manifest homosexuality. Analytic experience teaches us, to be sure, that female homosexuality is seldom or never a direct continuation of infantile masculinity. Even for a girl of this kind it seems necessary that she should take her father as an object for some time and enter the Oedipus situation. But afterwards, as a result of her inevitable disappointments from her father, she is driven to regress into her early masculinity complex. The significance of these disappointments must not be exaggerated; a girl who is destined to become feminine is not spared them though they do not have the same effect. The predominance of the constitutional factor seems indisputable, but the two phases in the development of female homosexuality are well mirrored in the practices of homosexuals, who play the parts of mother and baby with each other as often and as clearly as those of husband and wife.

What I have been telling you here may be described as the prehistory of women. It is a product of the very last few years and may have been of interest to you as an example of detailed analytic work. Since its subject is woman, I will venture on this occasion to mention by name a few of the women who have made valuable contributions to this investigation. Dr Ruth Mack Brunswick [1928] was the first to describe a case of neurosis which went back to a fixation in the pre-Oedipus stage and had never reached the Oedipus situation at all. The case took the form of jealous paranoia and proved accessible to therapy. Dr Jeanne Lampl-de Groot [1927] has established the incredible phallic activity of girls towards their mother by some assured observations, and Dr Hélène Deutsch [1932b] has shown that the erotic actions of homosexual women reproduce the relations between mother and baby.[5]

It is not my intention to pursue the further behaviour of femininity

[230]

through puberty to the period of maturity. Our knowledge, moreover, would be insufficient for the purpose. But I will bring a few features together in what follows. Taking its prehistory as a starting-point, I will only emphasize here that the development of femininity remains exposed to disturbance by the residual phenomena of the early masculine period. Regressions to the fixations of the pre-Oedipus phases very frequently occur; in the course of some women's lives there is a repeated alternation between periods in which masculinity or femininity gains the upper hand. Some portion of what we men call 'the enigma of women' may perhaps be derived from this expression of bisexuality in women's lives. But another question seems to have become ripe for judgement in the course of these researches. We have called the motive force of sexual life 'the libido'. Sexual life is dominated by the polarity of masculine – feminine; thus the notion suggests itself of considering the relation of the libido to this antithesis. It would not be surprising if it were to turn out that each sexuality had its own special libido appropriated to it, so that one sort of libido would pursue the aims of a masculine sexual life and another sort those of a feminine one. But nothing of the kind is true. There is only one libido, which serves both masculine and the feminine sexual functions. To it itself we cannot assign any sex; if, following the conventional equation of activity and masculinity, we are inclined to describe it as masculine, we must not forget that it also covers trends with a passive aim. Nevertheless the juxtaposition 'feminine libido' is without any justification. Further-more, it is our impression that more constraint has been applied to the libido when it is pressed into the service of the feminine function, and that – to speak teleologically – Nature takes less careful account of its [that function's] demands than in the case of masculinity. And the reason for this may lie – thinking once again teleologically – in the fact that the accomplishment of the aim of biology has been entrusted to the aggressive-ness of men and has been made to some extent independent of women's consent.[6]

The sexual frigidity of women, the frequency of which appears to confirm this disregard, is a phenomenon that is still insufficiently under-stood. Sometimes it is psychogenic and in that case accessible to influence; but in other cases it suggest the hypothesis of its being constitutionally determined and even of there being a contributory anatomical factor.

I have promised to tell you of a few more psychical peculiarities of mature femininity, as we come across them in analytic observation. We do not lay claim to more than an average validity for these assertions; nor is it always easy to distinguish what should be ascribed to the influence of the sexual function and what to social breeding. Thus, we attribute a larger amount of narcissism to femininity, which also affects women's choice of object, so that to be loved is a stronger need for them than to love. The effect of penis-envy has a share, further, in the physical vanity of women, since they are bound to value their charms more highly as a late compensation for their original sexual inferiority. Shame, which is considered to be a feminine characteristic *par excellence* but is far more a matter of convention than might be supposed, has as its purpose, we believe, concealment of genital deficiency.[7] We are not forgetting that at a later time shame takes on other functions. It seems that women have made few contributions to the discoveries and inventions in the history of civilization, there is, however, one technique which they may have invented – that of plaiting and weaving. If that is so, we should be tempted to guess the unconscious motive for the achievement. Nature herself would seem to have given the model which this achievement imitates by causing the growth at maturity of the pubic hair that conceals the genitals. The step that remained to be taken lay in making the threads adhere to one another, while on the body they stick into the skin and are only matted together. If you reject this idea as fantastic and regard my belief in the influence of lack of a penis on the configuration of femininity as an *idée fixe*, I am of course defenceless.

The determinants of women's choice of an object are often made unrecognizable by social conditions. Where the choice is able to show itself freely, it is often made in accordance with the narcissistic ideal of the man whom the girl had wished to become. If the girl has remained in her attachment to her father – that is, in the Oedipus complex – her choice is made according to the paternal type. Since, when she turned from her mother to her father, the hostility of her ambivalent relation remained with her mother, a choice of this kind should guarantee a happy marriage. But very often the outcome is of a kind that presents a general threat to such a settlement of the conflict due to ambivalence. The hostility that has been left behind follows in the train of the positive attachment and spreads over on the new object. The woman's husband, who to begin with inherited from her father, becomes after a time her mother's heir as well. So it may easily happen that the second half of a woman's life may be filled by the struggle against her husband, just as the shorter first half was filled by her rebellion against her mother. When this reaction has been lived through, a second marriage may easily turn out very much more satisfying. Another alteration in a woman's nature, for which lovers are unprepared, may occur in a marriage after the first child is born. Under the influence of a woman's becoming a mother herself, an identification with her own mother may be revived, against which she had striven up till the time of her marriage, and this may attract all the available libido to itself, so that the compulsion to repeat reproduces an unhappy marriage between her parents. The difference in a mother's reaction to the birth of a son or a daughter shows that the old factor of lack of a penis has even now not lost its strength. A mother is only brought unlimited satisfaction by her relation to a son, this is altogether the most perfect, the most free from ambivalence of all human relationships.[8] A mother can transfer to her son the ambition which she has been obliged to suppress in herself, and she can expect from him the satisfaction of all that has been left over in her of her masculinity complex. Even a marriage is not made secure until the wife has succeeded in making her husband her child as well and in acting as a mother to him.

A woman's identification with her mother allows us to distinguish two strata: the pre-Oedipus one which rests on her affectionate attachment to her mother and takes her as a model, and the later one from the Oedipus complex which seeks to get rid of her mother and take her place with her father. We are no doubt justified in saying that much of both of them is left over for the future and that neither of them is adequately surmounted in the course of development. But the phase of the affectionate pre-Oedipus attachment is the decisive one for a woman's future: during it preparations are made for the acquisition of the characteristics with which she will later fulfil her role in the sexual function and perform her invaluable social tasks. It is in this identification too that she acquires her attractiveness to a man, whose Oedipus attachment to his mother it kindles into passion. How often it happens, however, that it is only his son who obtains what he himself aspired to! One gets an impression that a man's love and a woman's are a phase apart psychologically.

The fact that women must be regarded as having little sense of justice is no doubt related to the predominance of envy in their mental life; for the demand for justice is a modification of envy and lays down the condition subject to which one can put envy aside. We also regard woman as weaker in their social interests and as having less capacity for sublimating their instincts than men. The former is no doubt derived from the dissocial quality which unquestionably characterizes all sexual relations. Lovers find sufficiency in each other, and families too resist inclusion in more comprehensive associations.[9] The aptitude for sublimation is subject to the greatest individual variations. On the other hand I cannot help mentioning an impression that we are constantly receiving during analytic practice. A man of about thirty strikes us as a youthful, somewhat unformed individual, whom we expect to make powerful use of the possibilities for the development opened up to him by analysis. A woman of the same age, however, often frightens us by her psychical rigidity and unchangeability. Her libido has taken up final positions and seems incapable of exchanging them for others. There are no paths open for further development; it is as though the whole process had already run its course and remains thenceforward insusceptible to influence – as though, indeed, the difficult development to femininity had exhausted the possibilities of the person concerned. As therapists we lament this state of things, even if we succeed in putting an end to our patient's ailment by doing away with her neurotic conflict.[10]

That is all I had to say to you about femininity. It is certainly incomplete and fragmentary and does not always sound friendly. But do not forget that I have only been describing women in so far as their nature is determined by their sexual function. It is true that that influence extends very far; but we do not overlook the fact that an individual woman may be a human being in other respects as well. If you want to know more about femininity, enquire from your own experiences of life, or turn to the poets, or wait until science can give you deeper and more coherent information.

Notes for Freud's Lecture on 'Femininity'

1   Heads in hieroglyphic bonnets,
                         Heads in turbans and black birettas,
                         Heads in wigs and thousand other
                         Wretched, sweating heads of humans.
                         (Heine, *Nordsee* [Second cycle, 7, 'Fragen'])
                         [Strachey's note in Standard Edition]

2 Mistaking two different things for a single one. The term is explained in *Introductory Lectures*, SE 16: 304.
3 These fears form the basis of Klein's concept of the paranoid–schizoid phase, a central component of her theory of the pre-Oedipal psychical reality of the very young baby (see chapter three).

[234]

4 These patients who are 'by no means seriously abnormal' provide the empirical evidence on which Freud built his theory.

5 Freud took the view that there is both a biological and psychological factor in the development of a lesbian object-choice. The issue remains controversial among analysts and therapists, though Freud's attempt at a psychological explanation seems able to stand on its own without the support of a 'constitutional' factor.

6 Even if, at some level, what he writes is true, the *way* he writes in this passage makes it sound as if he sees men driven biologically to rape.

7 Freud's unconscious rejection of 'femininity', starting with his own, is reflected in his phrase 'genital deficiency' rather than 'perceived genital deficiency' which is what he actually means, However, the whole of the rest of this paragraph represents Freud at his worst. Despite his many egalitarian, successful relationships with women colleagues and patients, Freud occasionally lapses into a misogyny typical of his period. I discuss the problem of Freud's own unconscious 'femininity' at the end of chapter two.

8 This idea was first introduced by Freud in this footnote to chapter six of *Group Psychology* (1921) (SE 18: 101). He repeated it in his *Introductory Lectures* (SE 15: 206) and in *Civilisation and its Discontents* (1930) (SE 21: 113) [Young-Breuhl's note in Young-Breuhl (1990).]

9 Some further remarks on the subject may be found in chapter twelve *Group Psychology* (1921) (SE 18: 140) [Young-Breuhl's note in Young-Breuhl (1990)].

10 This view of the difference between men and women in analytic practice is not supported by contemporary analysts or psychotherapists. On the contrary, they tend to take the view that it is more likely to be the other way round.

8
Melanie Klein, 'A Study of Envy and Gratitude' (1956)

This paper derives from a lecture given in 1955 at the Nineteenth International Psychoanalytic Congress in Geneva and elaborated in 1956 in a lecture to the British Society of Psychoanalysis where a distinctive Kleinian school had been established after World War II. Later, in 1957, the ideas were expanded into one of Klein's major books, *Envy and Gratitude*. The paper presents Klein's most mature view of the world of the very young baby. She puts forward the idea that the baby's envy of the mother is of fundamental importance to its psychical development. The idea proved immediately controversial rather like Freud's idea of the death drive. Juliette Mitchell comments that, 'the notion was found unobservable' (Mitchell 1986: 211) as envy was perceived as too sophistic-ated an emotion for the very young baby to experience. Klein's parallel introduction of the idea of gratitude as a balancing emotion caused less discussion even though the debate about envy and gratitude still con-tinues today.

Fuller commentary on this begins on page 91.

'A Study of Envy and Gratitude'

From the beginning of life, the infant turns to the mother for all his needs but, in my view, which I have substantiated in other connections, this first bond already contains the fundamental elements of an object relation. Furthermore, this relation is based on an innate factor; for the breast, towards which all his desires are directed, is instinctively felt to be not only the source of nourishment but of life itself. The relation to the gratifying breast in some measure restores, if things go well, the lost prenatal unity with the mother. This largely depends on the infant's capacity to cathect sufficiently the breast or its symbolic representative, the bottle: for in this way the mother is turned into a loved object. It may well be that his having formed part of the mother in the prenatal state contributes to the innate feeling that there exists an object which will give him all he needs and desires.

An element of frustration by the breast is bound, however, to enter into the infant's earliest relation to it, because even a happy feeding situation cannot altogether replace the prenatal unity with the mother. Also, the infant's longing for an inexhaustible and always present breast – which would not only satisfy him but prevent destructive impulses and persecutory anxiety – cannot ever be fully satisfied. These unavoidable grievances, together with happy experiences, reinforce the innate conflict between love and hatred, at bottom between life and death instincts, and result in the feeling that a good and bad breast exists. As a consequence, early emotional life is characterized by a sense of losing and regaining the good object. In speaking of an innate conflict between love and hatred, I am implying that both destructive impulses and the capacity for love are, to some extent, constitutional, varying individually in strength. They are increased by external circumstances. For instance, a difficult birth and unsatisfactory feeding – and possibly even unpleasant experiences in the prenatal state – undoubtedly intensify destructive impulses, persecutory anxiety, greed and envy.[1]

In this paper I wish to draw attention to a particular aspect of earliest object relations and internalization processes. I am referring to the effects of envy on the development of the capacity for gratitude and happiness. The contention I wish to put forward is that envy contributes to the infant's difficulties, in that he feels that the gratification he was deprived of has been kept for itself by the breast which frustrated him.

A distinction should be drawn between envy, jealousy and greed. Envy is the angry feeling that another person possesses and enjoys something desirable – the envious impulse being to take it away or to spoil it. Moreover, envy implies the subject's relation to one person only and goes back to the earliest exclusive relation with the mother. Jealousy is based on envy, but it involves the subject's relation to at least two people. Jealousy is mainly concerned with love which the subject feels is his due and which has been taken away, or is in danger of being taken away from him. In the everyday conception of jealousy, a man or a woman feels deprived of the person they love by somebody else.

Greed is an impetuous and insatiable craving, exceeding what the subject needs and what the object can and wishes to give. At the unconscious level, greed aims primarily at completely scooping out, sucking dry and devouring the breast, that is to say, its aim is destructive introjection; whereas envy not only aims at robbing in this way, but also at putting badness, primarily bad excrements and bad parts of the self, into the mother – first of all into her breast – in order to spoil and destroy her; in the deepest sense this means destroying her creativeness. This process I have defined elsewhere as a destructive aspect of projective identification which starts from the beginning of life. The difference between greed and envy, although no rigid dividing line can be drawn since they are so closely associated, would accordingly be that greed is mainly bound up with introjection and envy with projection.

My work has shown me that the first object to be envied is the feeding breast, for the infant feels that it possesses everything that he desires and that it has an unlimited flow of milk and love which it keeps for its own gratification. The feeling adds to his sense of grievance and hatred. If envy is excessive – which would indicate that paranoid and schizoid features are strong – the result is a disturbed relation to the mother.

We find this primitive envy revived in the transference situation. For instance: the analyst has just given an interpretation which brought the patient relief and produced a change of mood from despair to hope and trust. With some patients, or with the same patient at other times, this helpful interpretation may soon become the object of criticism. It is then no longer felt to be something good he has received and which he has experienced as an enrichment. The envious patient grudges the analyst the success of his work; and if his envious criticism has the effect of making him feel that the analyst and the help he is giving have become spoilt, the patient cannot introject the analyst sufficiently as a good object and cannot accept his interpretations with real conviction. He may also feel, because of guilt about devaluing the help given, that he is unworthy to benefit by analysis.

In these ways envy plays an important part in the negative therapeutic reaction in addition to the factors discovered by Freud and further developed by Joan Riviere.[2] Needless to say, our patients criticize us for a variety of reasons, sometimes with justification. But a patient's need to devalue the very help he has experienced is the expression of envy. This applies particularly to paranoid patients, who indulge in the sadistic pleasure of disparaging the analyst's work even though it has given them relief. On the other hand, some of our patients try to avoid criticism and are, up to a point, very co-operative. And yet we find that their doubts and uncertainties about the value of the analysis persist. In my experience the slow progress we make in such cases has also to do with envy. The patient has split off the envious and hostile part of his self; nevertheless it is bound to influence fundamentally the course of the analysis. Other patients try to avoid criticism by becoming confused. This confusion is not only a defence but also expresses the uncertainty as to whether the analyst is still a good figure, or whether he and the help he is giving have become bad because he has been spoilt by criticism.

All these attitudes are part of the negative therapeutic reaction because they interfere with the gradual building up of a good object in the transference situation and therefore – just as in the earliest situation the good food and the primal good object could not be assimilated – in the transference situation the result of the analysis is impaired.

Thus in the context of the analytic material we can sometimes gather how the patient felt as a baby toward the mother's breast.[3] For instance, the infant may have a grievance that the milk comes too quickly or too slowly; or that he was not given the breast when he most craved for it, and therefore when it is offered, he does not want it any more. He turns away from it and sucks his fingers instead. When he accepts the breast he may not drink enough, or the feed is disturbed. Some infants obviously have great difficulty in overcoming such grievances. With others these feelings, even though based on actual frustration, are soon overcome: the breast is taken and feed is fully enjoyed.

It is in the nature of envy that it spoils the primal good object and gives added impetus to sadistic attacks on the breast, which I have often described in other connections. Excessive envy increases the intensity of such attacks and their duration, and thus makes it more difficult for the infant to regain the lost good object; whereas sadistic attacks on the breast which are less determined by envy pass more quickly and therefore do not, in the infant's mind, so strongly and lastingly destroy the goodness of the object; the breast which returns is felt as an evidence that it is not injured and that it is still good.

When envy is excessive, the infant does not sufficiently build up a good object, and therefore cannot preserve it internally. Hence, somewhat later he is unable to establish firmly other good objects in his inner world.

The contrary situation holds in children with a strong capacity for love. The relation to the good object is deeply rooted and can, without being fundamentally damaged, withstand temporary states of envy, hatred and grievance – which arise even in children who are loved and well mothered. Thus, when these negative states are transient, the good object is regained time and again. This is an essential factor in establishing the good object and in laying the foundations for stability and a strong ego.

The emotions and attitudes I have referred to arise in the earliest stage of infancy when for the baby the mother is the one and only object. How far this exclusive relation remains undisturbed depends partly on external factors. But the feelings which underlie it – above all the capacity for love – appear to be innate. I have repeatedly put forward the hypothesis that the primal good object, the mother's breast, forms the core of the ego and vitally contributes to its growth and integration. We find in the analysis of our patients that the breast in its good aspects is the prototype of maternal goodness and generosity, as well as of creativeness. All this is felt by the infant in much more primitive ways than language can express it.

Strong envy of the feeding breast interferes with the capacity for complete gratification which is of vital importance for the infant's development. For if the *undisturbed* enjoyment in being fed is *frequently* experienced, the introjection of the mother's breast as a good object comes about with relative security. The capacity to fully enjoy gratification at the breast forms the foundation for all later happiness, as well as for pleasure from various sources. It is significant that Freud attributed so much importance to the pleasure–pain principle.

A full gratification at the breast means that the infant feels he has received from this loved object a unique gift, which he wants to keep. This is the basis of gratitude. Gratitude includes belief in good objects and trust in them. It includes also the ability to assimilate the loved object – not only as a source of food – and to love it without envy interfering. The more often this gift received is fully accepted, the more often the feeling of enjoyment and gratitude – implying the wish to return pleasure – is experienced. Gratitude is closely bound up with generosity. For inner wealth derives from having assimilated the good object, and this enables the individual to share its gifts with others.

To clarify my argument, a reference to my views on the early ego is necessary. I believe that it exists in a rudimentary form from the beginning of post-natal life, and performs a number of important functions. It might well be that this early ego is identical with the unconscious part of the ego which Freud postulated. Though he did not assume that an ego exists from the beginning, he attributed to the organism a function which, as I see it, can only be performed by the ego. The threat of annihilation by the death instinct within is, in my view – which differs from Freud's on this point – the primordial anxiety and it is the ego which, in the services of the life instinct, possibly even called into operation by the life instinct, deflects to some extent that threat outwards. This fundamental defence against the death instinct Freud attributed to the organism, whereas I regard this process as the primary activity of the ego.[4]

There are other primary activities of the ego which in my view derive from the imperative need to deal with the struggle between life and death instincts. One of these functions is gradual integration. The opposite tendency of the ego to split itself and its object is partly due to the ego lacking cohesion at birth, and partly it is a defence against the primordial anxiety. I have, for many years, attributed great importance to one particular process of splitting, the division of the breast into a good and bad object. I took this to be an expression of the innate conflict between love and hate and the ensuing anxieties. However, coexisting with this division there appear to be various processes of splitting, such as fragmenting the ego and its objects, whereby a dispersal of the destructive impulses is achieved. This is one of the characteristic defences during the paranoid–schizoid position which I believe normally extends over the first three or four months of life.

This does not of course mean that during that period the infant is not capable of fully enjoying his feeds, the relation to his mother and frequent states of physical comfort and well-being. What it does mean is that when anxiety arises, it is mainly of a paranoid nature and the defences against it, as well as the mechanisms used, are predominantly schizoid. The same applies, *mutatis mutandis*, to the infant's emotional life during the period characterized by the depressive position.

To return to the splitting process which I take to be a precondition for the young infant's relative stability: during the first few months he predominantly keeps the good object apart from the bad one and thus, in a fundamental way, preserves it. This primal division only succeeds if there is adequate capacity for love. Excessive envy, a corollary of destructive impulses, interferes with the building up to a good object and the primal split between the good and bad breast cannot be sufficiently achieved. The result is that later the differentiation between good and bad is disturbed in various connections. On the other hand, if the split between the two aspects of the object is too deep, the all-important processes of ego integration and object synthesis, as well as of mitigation of hatred by love, are impaired and the depressive position cannot be worked through. A very deep and sharp division between loved and hatred objects indicates that destructive impulses, envy and persecutory anxiety are very strong and serve as a defence against these emotions.

I am touching here on the problem of idealization. This is an early process which I take to be universal, but the motive power behind it varies individually. As I discovered many years ago in my work with young children, idealization is a corollary to persecutory anxiety – a defence against it – and the ideal breast is the counterpart of the devouring breast. But I also found that idealization derives from the innate feeling that an extremely good breast exists, a feeling which leads to the longing for a good object. Infants whose capacity for love is strong have less need for idealization than those in whom destructive impulses and persecutory anxiety are paramount. Excessive idealization denotes that persecution is the main driving force. It becomes also an important defence against envy, because if the object is exalted so much that comparison with it becomes impossible, envy is counteracted. The idealized object, which largely replaces the good one, is much less integrated in the ego since it stems predominantly from persecution.

While people who have been able to establish the primal good object with relative security are capable of retaining their love for it in spite of its shortcomings, with others idealization is a characteristic of their love relations and friendships. This tends to break down and then one loved object may have to be frequently exchanged for another; for no such person can fully come up to expectations. The former idealized person is then often felt as a persecutor (which shows the origin of idealization as a counterpart to persecution) and on to him is projected the subject's envious and critical attitude.

There is a direct link between the envy experienced towards the mother's breast and the development of jealousy. Jealousy is based on the suspicion of and rivalry with the father, who is accused of having taken away the mother's breast, and the mother. The rivalry marks the early stages of the positive and negative Oedipus complexes which arise concurrently with the depressive position in the second quarter of the first year. The importance of the combined parent figure, expressed in such phantasies as the mother or the mother's breast containing the penis of the father, or the father containing the mother, have been elaborated by me in earlier writings. The influence of this combined parent figure on the infant's ability to differentiate between the parents and to establish good relations with each of them, is affected by the strength of envy and the ensuing jealousy. For the feeling that the parents are always getting sexual gratification from one another reinforces the phantasy – derived from various sources – that they are always combined. The consequence may be a lasting disturbance in the relation to both parents.[5]

During the period characterized by the depressive position, when the infant progressively integrates his feelings of love and hatred and synthesizes the good and bad aspects of the mother, he goes through states of mourning bound up with feelings of guilt. He also begins to understand more of the external world and realizes that he cannot keep his mother to himself as his exclusive possession. Jealousy is, as we know, inherent in the Oedipus situation and is accompanied by hate and death wishes. Normally, however, the gain of new objects who can be loved – the father and siblings – and other compensations which the developing ego derives from the external world, mitigate jealousy and grievance to some extent. If paranoid and schizoid mechanisms are strong, jealousy – and at bottom envy – remain unmitigated.

All this has an essential bearing on the development of the Oedipus complex. Freud has shown how vital the relation of the girl to the mother is in her subsequent relations to men. I believe that if her first oral gratifications have been disturbed, mainly by internal factors such as strong envy, greed and hatred, her turning away from the breast towards the penis is largely a flight mechanism. If this is so, the relation to the father, and later on to other men, may suffer in different ways.

Freud's discovery of penis-envy in women, and its link with aggressive impulses, was a basic contribution to the understanding of envy. When penis-envy and castration wishes are strong, the envied object, the penis, is to be destroyed, and the man who owns it deprived of it. There are a number of factors contributing to penis-envy which are, however, not relevant to my thesis. In this context I wish to consider the woman's penis-envy only in so far as it is of oral origin. As we know, under the dominance of oral desires, the penis is strongly equated with the breast (as Abraham has shown) and in my experience penis-envy can be traced back to envy of the mother's breast.[6]

Much in the girl's relation to the father depends on whether envy of the mother's possession of the father prevails, or whether she is mainly intent on gaining his love entirely for herself. If envy is the main factor, her desire to spoil the father for the mother makes him into a valueless or bad object, undermines her relation to men and may express itself in frigidity. If jealousy about the father's love predominates, she may combine some hatred against the mother with love for the father.

In men, the envy of the mother's breast is also a very important factor. If it is strong and oral gratification thereby impaired, hatred and anxieties are transferred to the female genital. Whereas normally the genital development enables the boy to retain his mother as a love-object, a deep disturbance in the oral relation opens the way for severe difficulties in the genital relation to women. Excessive envy of the breast is likely to extend to all feminine attributes, in particular to the woman's capacity to bear children.

At bottom, envy is directed against creativeness: what the envied breast has to offer is unconsciously felt as the prototype of creativeness, because the breast and the milk it gives is felt to be the source of life. In both men and women this envy plays a major part in the desires to take away the attributes of the other sex, as well as to possess or spoil those of the parent of the same sex. It follows that paranoid jealousy and rivalry in the direct and inverted Oedipus situations are in both the male and female, however divergent their development, based on excessive envy towards the primal object: the mother and her breast.

I shall now illustrate some of my conclusions by clinical material. My first instance is taken from the analysis of a woman patient. She had been breast-fed, but circumstances had otherwise not been favourable and she was convinced that her babyhood and feeding had been wholly un-satisfactory. Her grievance about the past linked with hopelessness about the present and future. Envy of the feeding breast, and the ensuing difficulties in object relations, had already been extensively analysed prior to the material to which I am going to refer.

The patient telephoned and said that she could not come for treatment because of a pain in the shoulder. On the next day she rang me to say that she was still not well but expected to see me on the following day. When, on the third day, she actually came, she was full of complaints. She had been looked after by her maid, but nobody else had taken an interest in her. She described to me that at one moment her pain had suddenly increased, together with a sense of extreme coldness. She had felt an impetuous need for somebody to come at once and cover up her shoulder so that it should get warm, and go away again as soon as that was done. It occurred to her at that moment that this must be how she had felt as a baby when she wanted to be looked after and nobody came.

It was characteristic of the patient's attitude to people and threw light on her earliest relation to the breast that she desired to be looked after but at the same time repelled the very object which was to gratify her.

The suspicion of the gift received, together with her impetuous need to be cared for, which ultimately meant a desire to be fed, expressed her ambivalent attitude towards the breast. I have referred to infants whose response to frustration is to make insufficient use of the gratification which even the delayed feed could give them. I would assume that though they do not give up their desire for a gratifying breast, they cannot enjoy it and therefore repel it. The case under discussion illustrates some of the reasons for this attitude: suspicion of the gift she wished to receive because the object was already spoilt by envy and hatred, and therefore deep resentment about every frustration. We also have to remember – and this applies to other adults in whom envy is marked – that many disappointing experiences, no doubt partly due to her own attitude, had even beforehand made her feel that the desired care would not be satisfactory.

In the course of this session the patient reported a dream: she was in a restaurant, sat down at a table, but nobody came to serve her. She decided to join a queue and fetch herself something to eat. In front of her was a woman who took two or three little cakes and went away with them. The patient also took two or three little cakes. From her associations I am selecting the following: the woman seemed very determined, and her figure reminded her of mine. There was a sudden doubt about the name of the cakes (actually *petits fours*) which she first thought were *petit fru*, which reminded her of *petit frau* and thus of *Frau Klein*. The gist of my interpretations was that her grievance about the missed analytic sessions related to the unsatisfactory feeds and unhappiness in babyhood. The two cakes out of the 'two or three' stood for the breast which she felt she had been twice deprived of by missing analytic sessions. The fact that the woman was 'determined' and that the patient followed her example in taking the cakes pointed both to her identification with the analyst and at her projection of her greed on to her. In the context of this paper, our aspect of the dream is most relevant. The woman who went away with the two or three *petits fours* stood not only for the breast which was withheld, but also for the breast which was going to feed itself. (Taken together with the other material, the 'determined' analyst did not only represent a breast but a person with whose qualities, good or bad, the patient identified herself.)

To frustration was thus added envy of the breast. This envy gave rise to bitter resentment, for the mother was felt to be selfish and mean, feeding and loving herself rather than her baby. In this analytic situation

I was suspected of having enjoyed myself during the time when she was absent, or of having given the time to other patients whom I preferred. The queue which the patient had to join referred to other more favoured rivals.

The response to the analysis of the dream was a striking change in the emotional situation. The patient now experienced a feeling of happiness and gratitude more vividly than in previous analytic sessions. She had tears in her eyes, which was unusual, and said that she felt as if now she had had an entirely satisfactory feed.

It also occurred to her that her breast-feeding and her infancy might have been happier than it appeared to her in retrospect. Moreover, she felt more hopeful about the future and about the result of her analysis. The patient had more fully realized one part of herself which was by no means unknown to her in other connections. She was fully aware that she was envious and jealous of various people but had not been able to recognize it sufficiently in the relation to the analyst because it was too painful to acknowledge that she was grudging me the success of the analysis on which her hopes were centred. In this session, after the interpretation of it, her envy had lessened; the capacity for enjoyment and gratitude had come to the fore, and she was able to experience a happy feed. This emotional situation had to be worked through over and over again, both in the positive and negative transference, until a more stable result was achieved.

We find that some patients are even quite able to express their dislike and criticism of the analyst; but this differs fundamentally from the realization that at bottom it was they who by their envy spoilt the analyst and his work. The envious part of the self is split off, but exerts its power and contributes to the negative therapeutic reaction.

To come back to the patient under discussion, it was by enabling her gradually to being the split-off parts of her self together in relation to the analyst, and by her recognizing how envious and therefore suspicious she was of me, and in the first place of her mother, that the experience of that happy feed came about. This was bound up with feelings of gratitude. In the course of the analysis envy was diminished and feelings or gratitude became much more frequent and lasting.

In passing I would say that it is not only in children but also in adults that a full revival of the emotions felt during the earliest feeding experiences can come about in the transference situation. For instance, a feeling of hunger or thirst comes up very strongly during the session and has gone after the interpretation which was felt to have satisfied it. One of my patients, overcome by such feelings, got up from the couch and put his arms round one section of the arch which separated one part of my consulting room from the other. I have repeatedly heard the expression at the end of such a session, 'I have been well nourished.' The good object, in its earliest primitive form as the mother who takes care of the baby and feeds him, had been regained.

My next example is of a woman patient whom I would describe as fairly normal. She had in the course of time become more and more aware of envy experienced both towards an older sister and towards her mother. The envy of the sister had been counteracted by a feeling of strong intellectual superiority which had a basis in fact, and by an unconscious feeling that the sister was extremely neurotic. The envy towards the mother was counteracted by very strong feelings of love towards her and appreciation of her goodness.

The patient reported a dream in which she was alone in a railway carriage with a woman of whom she could only see the back; she was leaning towards the door of the compartment and was in great danger of falling out. The patient held her strongly, grasping her by the belt with one hand; with the other hand she wrote a notice and put it up on the window, to the effect that a doctor was engaged with a patient in this compartment and should not be disturbed.

The associations to the dream were as follows: the patient felt that the figure on whom she kept a tight grip was a part of herself and a mad part. In the dream she had an urgent feeling that she should not let the woman fall out but should keep her in the compartment (standing for herself) and deal with her. The associations to the hair, which was only seen from behind, were to her older sister. Further associations led to recognition of rivalry and envy in relation to her, going back to the time when the patient was still a child while her sister was already being courted.

These associations also led to a special dress which her mother wore and which as a child the patient had both admired and coveted. This dress had very clearly shown the shape of the breasts, and it became more evident than ever before (though none of this was entirely new), that what she originally envied and spoiled in her feelings was the mother's breast.

I said that the patient felt that she had to keep a grip on a mad, split-off part of herself, though this mad part was also linked with the internalization of the neurotic sister. The result of this realization, following the dream, on the patient who had reason to regard herself as reasonably normal, was a feeling of strong surprise and shock. An increased feeling of guilt, both towards her sister and her mother, was aroused through this realization, and this led to a further revision of her earliest relations. She arrived at a much more compassionate understanding of the deficiencies of her sister and felt that she had not loved her sufficiently. She also discovered that in her early childhood she had loved her much more than she had realized.

The feeling that she had to keep a firm hold on that figure implied that she should also have helped her sister more, prevented her, as it were, from falling, and this feeling was now re-experienced in connection with an internalized sister. The revision of her earliest relations was bound up with changes in her internal situation, in particular with changes in feelings towards her introjected early objects. The fact that that sister also represented the mad part of herself turned out to be partly a projection of her own schizoid and paranoid feelings on to the sister, but it was together with this realization that both the split in her ego diminished and a fuller integration came about.

In both these cases – and this applies to others as well – the relation to the analyst as an internal object turned out to be of fundamental importance. Generally speaking, when anxiety about envy and its consequences reaches a climax, the patient, in varying degrees, feels persecuted by the analyst as a grudging and envious internal object, disturbing his life, work and activities. When this occurs, the good object is felt to be lost, and with it inner security. My observations have shown me that when at any stage in life the relation to the good object is seriously disturbed, not only is inner security lost but character deterioration sets in. The prevalence of internal persecutory objects reinforces destructive impulses; whereas if the good object is well established, the identification with it strengthens the capacity for love and constructive impulses. This is in keeping with the hypothesis, put forward in this paper, that if the good object is deeply rooted, temporary disturbances can be withstood and the foundation is laid for mental health, character formation and a successful ego development.

I suggested above that the internalized persecuting object, which is felt to be grudging and envious owing to the individual's envy being projected on to it, is experienced as particularly dangerous because it has the effect of hampering all attempts at reparation and creativeness. Envy interferes most of all with these constructive attempts because the object which is to be restored is at the same time attacked and devalued by envy.

[248]

Since these feelings are transferred to the analyst, the incapacity to make reparation, which shows itself in the incapacity to co-operate in the analysis, forms part of the negative therapeutic reaction, in addition to the factors I have mentioned earlier. We have to be prepared for lengthy work if we want to achieve a better and more stable balance in the deep layers, in which envy and destructive impulses originate. I have always been convinced of the importance of Freud's finding that working through is one of the main tasks of the analysis. My experiences in analysing the processes by which a deeply hated and despised part of the personality is split off and my attempts to heal this split and bring about integration have deepened further this conviction.

I can only touch here on the fluctuation and difficulties we encounter when we analyse the splitting processes which are bound up with the analysis of envy. For instance, the patient has experienced gratitude for the appreciation of the analyst's skill, but this very skill becomes the cause of the transformation of admiration into envy. Envy may be counteracted by pride in having a good analyst. But if this pride stirs up possessiveness and greed, there is a return to the baby's greedy attitude which could be described in the following terms: I have everything I want, the good mother belongs only to me. Such a greedy and controlling attitude is liable to spoil the relation to the good object. Guilt about destructive greed might soon lead to another defence, such as: I do not want to injure the analyst (mother); I rather refrain from accepting her gifts. Such an attitude in turn may easily give rise to guilt about not accepting the analyst's help.

Each of the changes I have just enumerated has to be analysed as it comes up in the transference situation. It is by working through a multitude of defences and the emotions which underlie these defences that we can in time help the patient to achieve a better balance. With this end in view we have again and again to analyse the splitting processes, which I now think is the most difficult part of the analytic procedure. Since no anxiety can be experienced without the ego using whatever defences are available, these splitting processes play an important role as defences against persecutory and depressive anxieties. It appears to me that the realization of envy and the harm done by it to the loved object, and the deep anxieties to which this realization gives rise, contributes to the strong resistance we meet in attempting to undo the split and to bring about steps in integration. It is of the greatest importance to observe every detail in the transference situation which throws light on the earliest difficulties. In this way we sometimes discover that even a strong positive transference may be deceptive for it may be based on idealization and a covering up of the hatred and envy which are split off.

I have described how painful it is for the patient to realize his harmful and spoiling envy against the loved mother, and why there is such a strong resistance against such insight. When the patient nevertheless, through the analytic procedure, comes face to face with this split-off hated and despised part of his personality, this is often experienced as a shock and leads to depression. The feeling of guilt resulting from the realization of destructive envy may lead to the patient temporarily inhibiting his own capacities. We encounter a very different line when the undoing of the split is felt as unbearable and the consequent is an increase of omnipotent and even megalomaniac phantasies. This can be a critical stage because the patient may take refuge in increasing his hostile attitudes. Thus he feels justified in hating the analyst and in thinking that he, the patient, is superior to him and undervalued by him. He feels that everything so far achieved in the analysis was his own doing. To go back to the early situation, the patient as an infant sometimes felt superior to the parents; I have also met with the phantasies that he or she created, as it were, the mother or gave birth to her and possessed the mother's breasts. It was thus the mother who robbed the patient of the breast and not the patient who robbed her. Projection, omnipotence and persecution are then at their highest.

I am stressing the difficulties arising at certain points in the analysis in patients whose envy is constitutionally strong; but we should remember that people whose analysis has never been carried into such depths, or who have never been analysed at all, may experience similar difficulties, and even break down, because the underlying envy and anxieties are operative and may come up under certain circumstances.[7] Without being over-optimistic, because I realize the difficulties and limitations of psychoanalytic therapy, I believe that the analysis of those deep and severe disturbances is in many cases a safeguard against potential danger resulting from excessively envious and omnipotent attitudes.

The insight gained in the process of integration leads step by step to the patient recognizing that there are dangerous parts in his self; he becomes able to accept this because with growing integration the capacity for love increases and envy and hatred are mitigated. The pain which the patient goes through during these processes is gradually diminished by improvements bound up with integration. For instance, patients become able to make decisions which they were previously unable to come to make, and in general to use their gifts more freely. This is linked up with a lessening inhibition of their capacity to make reparation. Their powers of enjoyment may increase in many ways and hope comes up again and again.

The enrichment of the personality by integrating split-off parts of the self is a vital process. Together with hatred, envy and destructiveness, other important part of the personality had been lost and are regained in the course of the analysis.

Freud accepted a number of factors as constitutional. For instance, in his view anal-erotism in many people is a constitutional factor.

In this paper I have particularly emphasized envy, greed, hatred and feelings of persecution in relation to the primal object, the mother's breast, as largely innate. I have linked these constitutional factors with the preponderance of the one or other instinct in the fusion of the life and death instincts assumed by Freud. Abraham, too, believed in innate factors. In particular he discovered the constitutional element in the strength of oral impulses, which he connected with the aetiology of manic-depressive illness. He found that envy is an oral trait but – and this is where my views differ from his – he assume that envy and hostility belong to a later, the oral-sadistic stage. Abraham mentioned envy as an anal trait which, however, originates in the oral phase. He did not speak of gratitude but he described generosity as an oral feature.[8] Eisler (1919) had emphasized the constitutional factor in oral erotism and had recognized envy as an oral trait.[9] My concept of envy also includes the anal-sadistic tendencies which express themselves in splitting, projecting and putting badness first into the breast and then into the mother's body. The fact that not only oral-sadistic but also urethral- and anal-sadistic trends are operative from the beginning of life has been suggested by me as far back as my 'Psycho-Analysis of Children'.

The existence of constitutional factors points to the limitations of psychoanalytic therapy. While I am quite aware of them, my experience has taught me that nevertheless we are able in a number of cases to produce fundamental and favourable changes.

I have found that whenever integration has come about more fully and the patient has been able up to a point to accept the hating and hated part of his personality, he has also in retrospect established the primal good object more securely than he had done in infancy. We can, therefore, look from another angle at the aspects of technique which I am trying to convey. From the beginning all emotions attach themselves to the first object. If destructive impulses, envy and paranoid anxiety are excessive, the infant grossly distorts and magnifies every frustration from external sources which he experiences, and the mother's breast turns externally and internally predominantly into a persecutory object. Then even actual gratifications cannot be sufficiently accepted and cannot sufficiently counteract persecutory anxiety. In taking the analysis back to earliest infancy, we enable the patient to revive fundamental situations – a revival which I have often spoken of a 'memories in feelings'. This implies that in retrospect the patient lives more successfully through early frustrations. This means by which this is achieved is the analysis of the negative and positive transference which takes us back to earliest object relations. If we succeed, the patient realizes his own destructive impulses and projections, revises therefore his first object relations and establishes, in retrospect, his good object more securely, in particular by establishing the analyst as a good object in the transference. This can only come about if splitting processes, which have been largely used as a defence against persecution and guilt, lose in strength as a result of analysis. Thus the more integrated ego becomes capable of experiencing guilt and feelings of responsibility which it was unable to face in infancy; object synthesis and therefore a mitigation of hatred by love becomes possible, and greed and envy, which are corollaries of destructive impulses, lose in power. It is on these lines that also the psychoanalysis of psychotics can succeed.

To put it differently: by the consistent analysis of the negative as well as the positive transference, persecutory anxiety and schizoid mechanisms are diminished and the patient can work through the depressive position. When his initial inability to establish a good object is to some extent overcome, his capacity for enjoyment, and the appreciation of the gifts received from the good object, increases step by step and envy is diminished and gratitude becomes possible. These changes extend to many aspects of the patient's personality and range from earliest emotional life to adult experiences and relations. In the analysis of the effects of early disturbances on the whole development lies, I believe, our greatest hope of helping our patients.

Notes for Klein's 'A study of envy and gratitude'

1   Klein believed that the capacity to love and hate were instincts present from the moment of birth but were influenced by the baby's subsequent experience with the mother.

2 'Negative therapeutic reaction' or 'negative transference' refers to a patient's negative rather than positive reaction to the therapist.

3 Here Klein gives the reader some of the flavour of her analytic sessions and of how feelings associated with very early infancy manifest themselves in the therapeutic situation.

4 Klein argues that a primitive form of self deflects primal anxiety (which Klein sees as the death instinct) outwards into the external world, though Freud saw this deflection as a property of the biological organism rather than a rudimentary self. Klein goes on to argue that there are other ways in which this early fragmented 'self' tries to rid itself of the struggle between love and hate which causes it so much anxiety. One is the gradual integration of fragmented bits of the self, the other is to split the self into good and bad.

5 Envy of the 'combined parent figure' involves the idea that the parents are involved in the gratification of each other which excludes the baby.

6 Klein sees penis-envy as originating at the oral stage when it forms part of the baby's phantasy of the mother's breast containing a penis (the idea of the father). In this way penis-envy derives from envy of the mother's breast. Oedipal penis-envy, as we have seen, was regarded by Klein as a secondary rather than primary mechanism.

7 Here Klein assumes that a high degree of envy is innate. Winnicott, the creator of the second strand of Object-Relations theory argued that envy was not innate but always a product of inadequate mothering.

8 Karl Abraham, 'Contributions to the Theory of the Anal Character' (1921) *Selected Papers on Psychoanalysis* (1973: 382–3) [Klein's note].

9 M. J. Eisler, 'Pleasure in Sleep and the Disturbed Capacity for Sleep. A Contribution to the Study of the Oral Phase of the Development of the Libido', *International Journal of Psychoanalysis*, III (1922) [Klein's note].

9
Donald Winnicott, from 'Transitional Objects and Transitional Phenomena' (1971)

This paper is one of Winnicott's most important. It was published first in the *International Journal of Psychoanalysis* in 1953 and later in Winnicott's *Collected Papers: Through Paediatrics to Psychoanalysis* (1958). Like all those published in his later book *Playing and Reality* (1971), the paper focuses on the effect of the baby's experiences with the mother and on its eventual capacity to separate from her successfully. This extract is concerned with how what Winnicott refers to as 'the magic of imaginative and creative living' comes about through the mother's creative use of transitional phenomena or what he later called the transitional or potential space. These concepts are perhaps Winnicott's most original and influential theoretical innovations. In the transitional space the child is enabled to make the delicate transition from its merged identity with the mother to one which is separate from her in the external world.

The clinical material which forms the last part of this paper has been omitted. Fuller commentary on this paper begins on page 124.

From 'Transitional Objects and Transitional Phenomena'

I Original hypothesis

It is well known that infants as soon as they are born tend to use fist, fingers, thumbs in stimulation of the oral erotogenic zone, in satisfaction of the instincts at that zone, and also in quiet union. It is also well known that after a few months infants of either sex become fond of playing with dolls, and that most mothers allow their infants some special object and expect them to become, as it were, addicted to such objects.

There is a relationship between these two sets of phenomena that are separated by a time interval, and a study of the development from the earlier into the later can be profitable, and can make use of important clinical material that has been somewhat neglected.

THE FIRST POSSESSION

Those who happen to be in close touch with mothers' interests and problems will be already aware of the very rich patterns ordinarily displayed by babies in their use of the first 'not-me' possession. These patterns, being displayed, can be subjected to direct observation.

There is a wide variation to be found in a sequence of events that starts with the newborn infant's fist-in-mouth activities, and leads eventually on to an attachment to a teddy, a doll or soft toy, or to a hard toy.

It is clear that something is important here other than oral excitement and satisfaction, although this may be the basis of everything else. Many other important things can be studied, and they include:

1 The nature of the object.
2 The infant's capacity to recognize the object as 'not-me'.
3 The place of the object – outside, inside, at the border.
4 The infant's capacity to create, think up, devise, originate, produce an object.
5 The initiation of an affectionate type of object-relationship.

I have introduced the terms 'transitional objects' and 'transitional phenomena' for designation of the intermediate area of experience, between the thumb and the teddy bear, between the oral erotism and the true object-relationship, between primary creative activity and projection of what has already been introjected, between primary un-awareness of indebtedness and the acknowledgement of indebtedness ('Say: "ta"').

By this definition an infant's babbling and the way in which an older child goes over a repertory of songs and tunes while preparing for sleep come within the intermediate area as transitional phenomena, along with the use made of objects that are not part of the infant's body yet are not fully recognized as belonging to external reality.

Inadequacy of usual statement of human nature
It is generally acknowledged that a statement of human nature in terms of interpersonal relationships is not good enough even when the imaginative elaboration of function and the whole of fantasy both conscious and unconscious, including the repressed unconscious, are allowed for. There is another way of describing persons that comes out of the researches of the past two decades. Of every individual who has reached to the stage of being a unit with a limiting membrane and an outside and an inside,

it can be said that there is an *inner reality* to that individual, an inner world that can be rich or poor and can be at peace or in a state of war. This helps, but is it enough?

My claim is that if there is a need for this double statement, there is also need for a triple one: the third part of the life of a human being, a part that we cannot ignore, is an intermediate area of *experiencing*, to which inner reality and external life both contribute. It is an area that is not challenged, because no claim is made on its behalf except that it shall exist as a resting-place for the individual engaged in the perpetual human task of keeping inner and outer reality separate yet interrelated.

It is usual to refer to 'reality-testing', and to make a clear distinction between apperception and perception. I am here asking a claim for an intermediate state between a baby's inability and his growing ability to recognize and accept reality. I am therefore studying the substance of *illusion*, that which is allowed to the infant, and which in adult life is inherent in art and religion, and yet becomes the hallmark of madness when an adult puts too powerful a claim on the credulity of others, forcing them to acknowledge a sharing of illusion that is not their own. We can share a respect for *illusory experience*, and if we wish we may collect together and form a group on the basis of the similarity of our illusory experiences. This is a natural root of grouping among human beings.

I hope it will be understood that I am not referring exactly to the little child's teddy bear or to the infant's first use of the fist (thumb, fingers). I am not specifically studying the first object of the object-relationships. I am concerned with the first possession, and with the intermediate area between the subjective and that which is objectively perceived.

Development of a personal pattern
There is plenty of reference in psychoanalytic literature to the progress from 'hand to mouth' to 'hand to genital', but perhaps less to further progress to the handling of truly 'not-me' objects. Sooner or later in infant's development there comes a tendency on the part of the infant to weave other-than-me objects into the personal pattern. To some extent these objects stand for the breast, but it is not especially this point that is under discussion.

In the case of some infants the thumb is placed in the mouth while fingers are made to caress the face by pronation and supination movements of the forearm. The mouth is then active in relation to the thumb, but not in relation to the fingers. The fingers caressing the upper lip, or

[256]

some other part, may be or may become more important than the thumb engaging the mouth. Moreover, this caressing activity may be found alone, without the more direct thumb-mouth union.

In common experience one of the following occurs, complicating an auto-erotic experience such thumb-sucking:

(*i*)   with the other hand the baby takes an external object, say a part of a sheet or blanket, into the mouth along with the fingers; or

(*ii*) somehow or other the bit of cloth is held and sucked, or not actually sucked; the objects used naturally include napkins and (later) handkerchiefs, and this depends on what is readily and reliably available; or

(*iii*) the baby starts from early months to pluck wool and to collect it and to use it for the caressing part of the activity; less commonly, the wool is swallowed, even causing trouble; or

(*iv*) Mouthing occurs, accompanied by sounds of 'mum-mum', babbling, anal noises, the first musical notes, and so on.

One may suppose that thinking, or fantasying, gets linked up with these functional experiences.

All these things I am calling *transitional phenomena*. Also, out of all this (if we study any one infant) there may emerge some thing or some phenomenon – perhaps a bundle of wool or the corner of a blanket or eiderdown, or a word or tune, or a mannerism – that becomes vitally important to the infant for use at the time of going to sleep, and is a defence against anxiety, especially anxiety of a depressive type. Perhaps some soft object or other type of object has been found and used by the infant, and this then becomes what I am call a *transitional object*. This object goes on being important. The parents get to know its value and carry it round when travelling. The mother lets it get dirty and even smelly, knowing that by washing it she introduces a break in continuity in the infant's experience, a break that may destroy the meaning and value of the object to the infant.

I suggest that the pattern of transitional phenomena begins to show at about four to six to eight to twelve months. Purposely I leave room for wide variations.

Patterns set in infancy may persist into childhood, so that the original soft object continues to be absolutely necessary at bed-time or at times of loneliness or when a depressed mood threatens. In health, however, there is a gradual extension of range of interest, and eventually the extended range is maintained, even when depressive anxiety is near. A need for a specific object or a behaviour pattern that started at a very early date may reappear at a later age when deprivation threatens.

The first possession is used in conjunction with special techniques derived from very early infancy, which can include or exist apart from the more direct auto-erotic activities. Gradually in the life of an infant teddies and dolls and hard toys are acquired. Boys to some extent tend to go over to use hard objects, whereas girls tend to proceed right ahead to the acquisition of a family. It is important to note, however, that *there is no noticeable difference between boy and girl in their use of the original 'not-me' possession*, which I am calling the transitional object.

As the infant starts to use organized sounds ('mum', 'ta', 'da') there may appear a 'word' for the transitional object. The name given by the infant to these earliest objects is often significant, and it usually has a word used by the adults partly incorporated in it. For instance, 'baa' may be the name, and the 'b' may have come from the adult's use of the word 'baby' or 'bear'.

I should mention that sometimes there is no transitional object except the mother herself. Or an infant may be so disturbed in emotional development that the transition state cannot be enjoyed, or the sequence of objects used is broken. The sequence may nevertheless be maintained in a hidden way.

Summary of special qualities in the relationship
1 The infant assumes rights over the object, and we agree to this assumption. Nevertheless, some abrogation of omnipotence is a feature from the start.
2 The object is affectionately cuddled as well as excitedly loved and mutilated.
3 It must never change, unless changed by the infant.
4 It must survive instinctual loving, and also hating and, if it be a feature, pure aggression.
5 Yet it must seem to the infant to give warmth, or to move, or to have texture, or to do something that seems to show it has vitality or reality of its own.
6 It comes from without from our point of view, but not so from the point of view of the baby. Neither does it come from within; it is not a hallucination.

7 Its fate is to be gradually allowed to be decathected, so that in the course of years it becomes not so much forgotten as relegated to limbo. By this I mean that in health the transitional object does not 'go inside' nor does the feeling about it necessarily undergo repression. It is not forgotten and it is not mourned. It loses meaning, and this is because the transitional phenomena have become diffused, have become spread out over the whole intermediate territory between 'inner psychic reality' and 'the external world as perceived by two persons in common', that is to say, over the whole cultural field.

At this point my subject widens out into that of play, and of artistic creativity and appreciation, and of religious feeling, and of dreaming, and also of fetishism, lying and stealing, the origin and loss of affectionate feeling, drug addiction, the talisman of obsessional rituals, etc.

Relationship of the transitional object to symbolism
It is true that the piece of blanket (or whatever it is) is symbolical of some part-object, such as the breast. Nevertheless, the point of it is not its symbolic value so much as its actuality. Its not being the breast (or the mother), although real, is as important as the fact that it stands for the breast (or mother).

When symbolism is employed the infant is already clearly distinguishing between fantasy and fact, between inner objects and external objects, between primary creativity and perception. But the term transitional object, according to my suggestion, gives room for the process of becoming able to accept difference and similarity. I think there is use for a term for the root of symbolism in time, a term that describes the infant's journey from the purely subjective to objectivity; and it seems to me that the transitional object (piece of blanket, etc.) is what we see of this journey of progress towards experiencing.

It would be possible to understand the transitional object while not fully understanding the nature of symbolism. It seems that symbolism can be properly studied only in the process of the growth of an individual and that it has at the very best a variable meaning. For instance, if we consider the wafer of the Blessed Sacrament, which is symbolic of the body of Christ, I think I am right in saying that for the Roman Catholic community it *is* the body, and for the Protestant community it is a *substitute*, a reminder, and is essentially not, in fact, actually the body itself. Yet in both cases it is a symbol.

[259]

CLINICAL DESCRIPTION OF A TRANSITIONAL OBJECT

For anyone in touch with parents and children, there is an infinite quantity and variety of illustrative clinical material. The following illustrations are given merely to remind readers of similar material in their own experiences.

Two brothers: contrast in early use of possessions

Distortion in use of transitional object. X, now a healthy man, has had to fight his way towards maturity. The mother 'learned how to be a mother' in her management of X when he was an infant and she was able to avoid certain mistakes with the other children because of what she learned with him. There were also external reasons why she was anxious of the time of her rather lonely management of X when he was born. She took her job as a mother very seriously and she breast-fed X for seven months. She feels that in his case this was too long and he was very difficult to wean. He never sucked his thumb or his fingers and when she weaned him 'he had nothing to fall back on'. He had never had the bottle or a dummy or any other form of feeding. He had a very strong and early *attachment to her herself*, as a person, and it was her actual person that he needed.

From twelve months he adopted a rabbit which he would cuddle, and his affectionate regard for the rabbit eventually transferred to real rabbits. This particular rabbit lasted till he was five or six years old. It could be described as a *comforter*, but it never had the true quality of a transitional object. It was never, as a true transitional object would have been, more important than the mother, an almost inseparable part of the infant. In the case of this particular boy the kinds of anxiety that were brought to a head by the weaning at seven months later produced asthma, and only gradually did he conquer this. It was important for him that he found employment far away from the home town. His attachment to his mother is still very powerful, although he comes within the wide definition of the term normal, or healthy. This man has not married.

Typical use of transitional object. X's younger brother, Y, has developed in quite a straightforward way throughout. He now has three healthy children of his own. He was fed at the breast for four months and then weaned without difficulty. Y sucked his thumb in the early weeks and this again 'made weaning easier for him than for his older brother'. Soon after weaning at five to six months he adopted the end of the blanket where the stitching finished. He was pleased if a little bit of the wool stuck out at the corner and with this he would tickle his nose. This very early became his 'Baa'; he invented this word for it himself as soon as could use organized sounds. From the time when he was about a year old he was able to substitute for the end of the blanket a soft green jersey with a red tie. This was not a 'comforter' as in the case of the depressive older brother, but a 'soother'. It was a sedative which always worked. This is a typical example of what I am calling a *transitional object*. When Y was a little boy it was always certain that if anyone gave him his 'Baa' he would immediately suck it and lose anxiety, and in fact he would go to sleep within a few minutes if the time for sleep were at all near. The thumb-sucking continued at the same time, lasting until he was three or four years old, and he remembers thumb-sucking and a hard place on one thumb which resulted from it. He is now interested (as a father) in the thumb-sucking of his children and their use of 'Baas'.

The story of seven ordinary children in this family brings out the following points, arranged for comparison in the table below:

			Thumb	Transitional Object	Type of Child
X		Boy	o Mother	Rabbit (comforter)	Mother-fixated
Y		Boy	+ 'Baa'	Jersey (soother)	Free
Twins	{	Girl	o Dummy	Donkey (friend)	Late maturity
		Boy	o 'Ee'	Ee (protective)	Latent psychopathic
Children of Y	{	Girl	o 'Baa'	Blanket (reassurance)	Developing well
		Girl	+ Thumb	Thumb (satisfaction)	Developing well
		Boy	+ 'Mimis'	Objects (sorting)*	Developing well

* Added note: This was not clear, but I have left it as it was. D.W.W., 1971.

Value in history-taking
In consultation with a parent it is often valuable to get information about the early techniques and possessions of all the children of the family. This starts the mother off on a comparison of her children one with another, and enables her to remember and compare their characteristics at an early age.

The child's contribution
Information can often be obtained from a child in regard to transitional objects. For instance:

Angus (eleven years nine months) told me that his brother 'has tons of teddies and things' and 'before that he had little bears', and he followed this up with a talk about his own history. He said he never had teddies. There was a bell rope that hung down, a tag end of which he would go on hitting, and so go off to sleep. Probably in the end it fell, and that was the end of it. There was, however, something else. He was very shy about this. It was a purple rabbit with red eyes. 'I wasn't fond of it. I used to throw it around. Jeremy has it now, I gave it to him. I gave it to Jeremy because it was naughty. It *would* fall off the chest of drawers. *It still visits me. I like it to visit me.*' He surprised himself when he drew the purple rabbit.

It will be noted that this eleven-year-old boy with the ordinary good reality-sense of his age spoke as if lacking in reality-sense when describing the transitional object's qualities and activities. When I saw the mother later she expressed surprise that Angus remembered the purple rabbit. She easily recognized it from the coloured drawing.

Ready availability of examples
I deliberately refrain from giving more case-material here, particularly as I wish to avoid giving the impression that what I am reporting is rare. In practically every case-history there is something to be found that is interesting in the transitional phenomena, or in their absence.

THEORETICAL STUDY

There are certain comments that can be made on the basis of accepted psychoanalytic theory:

1 The transitional object stands for the breast, or the object of the first relationship.
2 The transitional object antedates established reality-testing.
3 In relation to the transitional object the infant passes from (magical) omnipotent control to control by manipulation (involving muscle erotism and coordination pleasure).
4 The transitional object may eventually develop into a fetish object and so persist as a characteristic of the adult sexual life. (See Wulff's (1946) development of the theme.)
5 The transitional object may, because of anal erotic organization, stand for faeces (but it is not for this reason that it may become smelly and remain unwashed).

Relationship to internal object (Klein)

It is interesting to compare the transitional object concept with Melanie Klein's (1934) concept of the internal object. The transitional object is *not an internal object* (which is mental concept) – it is a possession. Yet it is not (for the infant) an external object either.

The following complex statement has to be made. The infant can employ a transitional object when the internal object is alive and real and good enough (not too persecutory). But this internal object depends for its qualities on the existence and aliveness and behaviour of the external object. Failure of the latter in some essential function indirectly leads to deadness or to a persecutory quality of the internal object.[1] After a persistence of inadequacy of the external object the internal object fails to have meaning to the infant, and then, and then only, does the transitional object become meaningless too. The transitional object may therefore stand for the 'external' breast, but *indirectly*, through standing for an 'internal' breast.

The transitional object is never under magical control like the internal object, nor is it outside control as the real mother is.

Illusion–disillusionment

In order to prepare the ground for my own positive contribution to this subject I must put into words some of the things that I think are taken too easily for granted in many psychoanalytic writings on infantile emotional development, although they may be understood in practice.

There is no possibility whatever for an infant to proceed from the pleasure principle to the reality principle or towards and beyond primary identification (see Freud 1923), unless there is a good-enough mother.[2] The good-enough 'mother' (not necessarily the infant's own mother) is one who makes active adaptation to the infant's needs, an active adaptation that gradually lessens, according to the infant's growing ability to account for failure of adaptation and to tolerate the results of frustration.[3] Naturally, the infant's own mother is more likely to be good enough than some other person, since this active adaptation demands an easy and unresented preoccupation with the one infant; in fact, success in infant care depends on the fact of devotion, not on cleverness or intellectual enlightenment.

The good-enough mother, as I have stated, starts off with an almost complete adaptation to her infant's needs, and as time proceeds she adapts less and less completely, gradually, according to the infant's growing ability to deal with her failure.

The infant's means of dealing with this maternal failure include the following:

1 The infant's experience, often repeated, that there is a time-limit to frustration. At first, naturally, this time-limit must be short.
2 Growing sense of process.
3 The beginnings of mental activity.
4 Employment of auto-erotic satisfactions.
5 Remembering, reliving, fantasying, dreaming; the integrating of past, present, and future.

If all goes well the infant can actually come to gain from the experience of frustration, since incomplete adaptation to need makes objects real, that is to say hated as well as loved. The consequence of this is that *if all goes well* the infant can be disturbed by the close adaptation to need that is continued too long, not allowed its natural decrease, since exact adaptation resembles magic and the object that behaves perfectly becomes no better than hallucination. Nevertheless, *at the start* adaptation needs to be almost exact, and unless this is so it is not possible for the infant to begin to develop a capacity to experience a relationship to external reality, or even to form a conception of external reality.

Illusion and the value of illusion

The mother, at the beginning, by an almost 100 per cent adaptation affords the infant the opportunity for the *illusion* that her breast is part of the infant. It is, as it were, under the baby's magical control. The same can be said in terms of infant care in general, in the quiet times between excitements. Omnipotence is nearly a fact of experience. The mother's eventual task is gradually to disillusion the infant, but she has no hope of success unless at first she has been able to give sufficient opportunity for illusion.

In another language, the breast is created by the infant over and over again out of the infant's capacity to love or (one can say) out of need. A subjective phenomenon develops in the baby, which we call the mother's breast.[4] The mother places the actual breast just there where the infant is ready to create, and at the right moment.

From birth, therefore, the human being is concerned with the problem of the relationship between what is objectively perceived and what is subjectively conceived of, and in the solution of this problem there is no health for the human being who has not been started off well enough by the mother. *The intermediate area to which I am referring is the area that is allowed to the infant between primary creativity and objective perception based on reality-testing.* The transitional phenomena represent the early stages of the use of illusion, without which there is no meaning for the human being in the idea of a relationship with an object that is perceived by others as external to that being.

The idea illustrated in Figure 1 is this: that at some theoretical point early in the development of every human individual an infant in a certain setting provided by the mother is capable of conceiving of the idea of something that would meet the growing need that arises out of instinctual tension.

The infant cannot be said to know at first what is to be created. At this point in time the mother presents herself. In the ordinary way she gives her breast and her potential feeding urge. The mother's adaptation to the infant's needs, when good enough, gives the infant the *illusion* that there is an external reality that corresponds to the infant's own capacity to create. In other words, there is an overlap between what the mother supplies and what the child might conceive of. To the observer, the child perceives what the mother actually presents, but this is not the whole truth. The infant perceives the breast only in so far as a breast could be created just there and then. There is no interchange between the mother and the infant. Psychologically the infant takes from a breast that is part of the infant, and the mother gives milk to an infant that is part of herself. In psychology, the idea of interchange is based on an illusion in the psychologist.

In Figure 2 a shape is given to the area of illusion, to illustrate what I consider to be the main function of the transitional object and of transitional phenomena. The transitional object and the transitional phenomena start each human being off with what will always be important for them, i.e. a neutral area of experience which will not be challenged. *Of the transitional object it can be said that it is a matter of agreement between us and the baby that we will never ask the question: 'Did you conceive of this or was it presented to you from without?' The important point is that no decision on this point is expected. The question is not to be formulated.*

This problem, which undoubtedly concerns the human infant in a hidden way at the beginning, gradually becomes an obvious problem on account of the fact that the mother's main task (next to providing

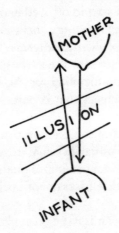

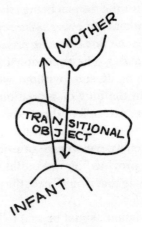

opportunity for illusion) is disillusionment. This is preliminary to the task of weaning, and it also continues as one of the tasks of parents and educators. In other words, this matter of *illusion* is one that belongs inherently to human beings and that no individual finally solves for himself or herself, although a *theoretical* understanding of it may provide a *theoretical* solution. If things go well, in this gradual disillusionment process, the stage is set for the frustrations that we gather together under the word weaning; but it should be remembered that when we talk about the phenomena (which Klein (1940) has specifically illuminated in her concept of the depressive position) that cluster round weaning we are assuming the underlying process, the process by which opportunity for illusion and gradual disillusionment is provided. If illusion–disillusionment has gone astray the infant cannot get to so normal a thing as weaning, nor to a reaction to weaning, and it is then absurd to refer to weaning at all. The mere termination of breast-feeding is not a weaning.

We can see the tremendous significance of weaning in the case of the normal child. When we witness the complex reaction that is set going in a certain child by the weaning process, we know that this is able to take place in that child because the illusion–disillusionment process is being carried through so well that we can ignore it while discussing actual weaning.

Development of the theory of illusion–disillusionment
It is assumed here that the task of reality-acceptance is never completed, that no human being is free from the strain of relating inner and outer reality, and that relief from this strain is provided by an intermediate area of experience (cf. Riviere 1936) which is not challenged (arts, religion, etc.). This intermediate area is in direct continuity with the play area of the small child who is 'lost' in play.

In infancy this intermediate area is necessary for the initiation of a relationship between the child and the world, and is made possible by good-enough mothering at the early critical phase. Essential to all this is continuity (in time) of the external emotional environment and of particular elements in the physical environment such as the transitional object or objects.

The transitional phenomena are allowable to the infant because of the parents' intuitive recognition of the strain inherent in objective perception, and we do not challenge the infant in regard to subjectivity or objectivity just here where there is the transitional object.

Should an adult make claims on us for our acceptance of the objectivity of his subjective phenomena we discern or diagnose madness. If, however, the adult can manage to enjoy the personal intermediate area without making claim, then we can acknowledge our own corresponding intermediate areas, and are pleased to find a degree of overlapping, that is to say common experience between members of a group in art or religion or philosophy.

SUMMARY

Attention is drawn to the rich field for observation provided by the earliest experiences of the healthy infant as expressed principally in the relationship to the first possession.

This first possession is related backwards in time to auto-erotic phenomena and fist- and thumb-sucking, and also forwards to the first soft animal or doll and to hard toys. It is related both to the external object (mother's breast) and to internal objects (magically introjected breast), but is distinct from each.

Transitional objects and transitional phenomena belong to the realm of illusion which is at the basis of initiation of experience. This early stage in development is made possible by the mother's special capacity for making adaptation to the needs of her infant, thus allowing the infant the illusion that what the infant creates really exists.

The intermediate area of experience, unchallenged in respect of its belonging to inner or external (shard) reality, constitutes the greater part of the infant's experience, and throughout life is retained in the intense experiencing that belongs to the arts and to religion and to imaginative living, and to creative scientific work.

An infant's transitional object ordinarily becomes gradually decathected, especially as cultural interests develop.

What emerges from these considerations is the further idea that paradox accepted can have positive value. The resolution of paradox leads to a defence organization which in the adult one can encounter as true and false self organization.

Notes for extract from Winnicott's 'Transitional Objects and Transitional Phenomena'

1 Text modified here, though based on the original statement [D.W.W.'s note].
2 Winnicott's emphasis on the 'good enough' mother highlights the need for society to protect the mother–baby, parent–baby relationship at the early stage of every child's development. In contemporary terms this translates into secure employment and housing, freely available support in the form of nursery provision and health care, adequate maternity and paternity paid leave, protection of employment and promotion rights. Winnicott's work suggests that parents who are treated by society with respect and sensitivity, in a climate where ordinary human need is not pathologised in discourses of dependency, are most likely to be in a position to treat their very young children in the same way.
3 Winnicott is referring to all those professionals who care for very young children – for example, those who work in nurseries, children's homes and hospitals as well as parents.
4 I include the whole technique of mothering. When it is said that the first object is the breast, the word 'breast' is used, I believe, to stand for the technique of mothering as well as for the actual flesh. It is not impossible for a mother to be a good-enough mother (in my way of putting it) with a bottle for the actual feeding [D.W.W.'s note].

10

Jacques Lacan, 'The Meaning of the Phallus' (1958)

This paper was first presented in German at the Max Planck Institute in Munich and was first published in *Ecrits* (1966). Here, building directly on Freud, Lacan gives his clearest description of how the penis within the realm of what is normally called sexuality is transformed into the phallus, the first signifier in the Symbolic order which subsequently determines human subjectivity or consciousness. Lacan also introduces his key concepts of the realm of Demand and the realm of Desire which coincide with those of the Imaginary and the Symbolic. Lacan's work has been of particular interest to French feminist writers such as Cixous, Kristeva and Irigaray.

The following text is a translation by Jacqueline Rose and was first published in *Jacques Lacan and the Ecole Freudienne: Feminine Sexuality* (1982).

Fuller commentary on this paper begins on page 164.

'The Meaning of the Phallus'

What follows is the unaltered text of a paper delivered in German on 9 May 1958, at the Max Planck Institute in Munich where Professor Paul Matussek had invited me to speak.

The vaguest idea of the state of mind then prevailing in circles, not for the most part uninformed, will give some measure of the impact of terms such as 'the other scene', to take one example used here, which I was the first to extract from Freud's work.

If 'deferred action' (*Nachtrag*), to rescue another such term from its current affectation, makes this effort unfeasible, it should be realised that they were unheard of at that time.

We know that the unconscious castration complex has the function of a knot:

(1) in the dynamic structuring of symptoms in the analytic sense of the

term, meaning that which can be analysed in neuroses, perversions and psychoses;

(2) as the regulator of development giving its *ratio* to this first role: that is, by installing in the subject an unconscious position without which he would be unable to identify with the ideal type of his sex, or to respond without grave risk to the needs of his partner in the sexual relation, or even to receive adequately the needs of the child thus procreated.[1]

What we are dealing with is an antinomy internal to the assumption by man (*Mensch*) of his sex: why must he take up its attributes only by means of a threat, or even in the guise of a privation? As we know, in *Civilisation and its Discontents*, Freud went so far as to suggest not a contingent, but an essential disturbance of human sexuality, and one of his last articles turns on the irreducibility for any finite (*endliche*) analysis of the effects following from the castration complex in the masculine unconscious and from *penisneid* [penis-envy] in the unconscious of the woman.[2]

This is not the only point of uncertainty; but it is the first that the Freudian experience and its resulting metapsychology introduced into our experience of man. It cannot be solved by any reduction to biological factors, as the mere necessity of the myth underlying the structuring of the Oedipus complex makes sufficiently clear.

Any recourse to an hereditary amnesic given would in this instance be mere artifice, not only because such a factor is in itself disputable, but because it leaves the problem untouched, namely, the link between the murder of the father and the pact of the primordial law, given that it is included in that law that castration should be the punishment for incest.[3]

Only on the basis of the clinical facts can there be any fruitful discussion. These facts go to show that the relation of the subject to the phallus is set up regardless of the anatomical difference between the sexes, which is what makes its interpretation particularly intractable in the case of the woman and in relationship to her, specifically on the four following counts:[4]

(1) as to why the little girl herself considers, if only for a moment, that she is castrated, in the sense of being deprived of the phallus, at the hand of someone who is in the first instance her mother, an important point, and who then becomes her father, but in such a way that we must recognise in this transition a transference in the analytic sense of the term;

(2) as to why, at a more primordial level, the mother is for both sexes considered as provided with a phallus, that is, as a phallic mother;

(3) as to why, correlatively, the meaning of castration only acquires its full (clinically manifest) weight as regards symptoms formation when it is discovered as castration of the mother;

(4) these three problems culminate in the question of the reason for the phallic phase in development. We know that Freud used this term to specify the earliest genital maturation – as on the one hand characterised by the imaginary predominance of the phallic attribute and masturbatory pleasure, and on the other by a localising of this pleasure for the woman in the clitoris, which is thereby raised to the function of the phallus. This would seem to rule out for both sexes, until the end of this phase, that is, until the dissolution of the Oedipus complex, any instinctual awareness of the vagina as the place of genital penetration.[5]

This ignorance smacks of mis-recognition [*méconnaissance*] in the technical sense of the term, especially as it is on occasions disproved.[6] All it agrees with, surely, is Longus's fable in which he depicts the invitation of Daphnis and Chloë as dependent on the revelations of an old woman.

It is for this reason that certain authors have been led to regard the phallic phase as an effect of repression, and the function assumed in it by the phallic object as a symptom. The difficulty starts when we need to know *which* symptom. Phobia, according to one, perversion according to another – or, indeed, to the same one. In this last case, it's not worth speculating: not that interesting transmutations of the object from phobia into fetish do not occur, but their interest resides precisely in the different place which they occupy in the structure. There would be no point in asking these authors to formulate this difference from the perspective of object relations which is currently in favour. This being for lack of any reference on the matter other than the loose notion of the part object, uncriticised since Karl Abraham first introduced it, which is more the pity in view of the easy option which it provides today.

The fact remains that, if one goes back to the surviving texts of the years 1928–32, the now abandoned debate on the phallic phase is a refreshing example of a passion for doctrine, which has been given an additional note of nostalgia by the degradation of psychoanalysis consequent on its American transplantation.

A mere summary of the debate could only distort the genuine diversity of the positions taken by figures such as Hélène Deutsch, Karen Horney and Ernest Jones, to mention only the most eminent.

The series of three articles which Jones devoted to the subject is especially suggestive: if only for the starting premise on which he constructs his argument, signalled by the term *aphanisis*, which he himself coined.[7] For by correctly posing the problem of the relationship between castration and desire, he reveals such a proximity to what he cannot quite grasp that the term which will later provide us with the key to the problem seems to emerge out of his very failure.

The amusing thing is the way he manages, on the authority of the very letter of Freud's text, to formulate a position which is directly opposed to it: a true model in a difficult genre.

The problem, however, refuses to go away, seeming to subvert Jones's own case for a re-establishment of the equality of natural rights (which surely gets the better of him in the Biblical 'Man and woman God created them' with which he concludes). What does he actually gain by normalising the function of the phallus as part object if he has to invoke its presence in the mother's body as internal object, a term which is a function of the fantasies uncovered by Melanie Klein, and if he cannot therefore separate himself from her doctrine which sees these fantasies as a recurrence of the Oedipal formation which is located right back in earliest infancy.[8]

We will not go far wrong if we re-open the question by asking what could have imposed on Freud the obvious paradox of his position. For one has to allow that he was better guided than anyone else in his recognition of the order of unconscious phenomena, which order he had discovered, and that for want of an adequate articulation of the nature of these phenomena his followers were bound to go more or less astray.

It is on the basis of such a wager – laid down by me as the principle of a commentary of Freud's work which I have been pursuing for seven years – that I have been led to certain conclusions: above all, to argue, as necessary to any articulation of analytic phenomena, for the notion of the signifier, in the sense in which it is opposed to that of the signified in modern linguistic analysis. The latter, born since Freud, could not be taken into account by him but it is my contention that Freud's discovery stands out precisely for having had to anticipate its formulas, even while setting out from a domain in which one could hardly expect to recognise its sway.[9] Conversely, it is Freud's discovery that gives to the opposition of signifier to signified the full weight which it should imply: namely, that the signifier has an active function in determining the effects in which the signifiable appears as submitting to its mark, becoming through that passion the signified.

This passion of the signifier then becomes a new dimension of the human condition, in that it is not only man who speaks, but in man and through man that it [*ça*] speaks, that his nature is woven by effects in which we can find the structure of language, whose material he becomes, and that consequently there resounds in him, beyond anything ever conceived of by the psychology of ideas, the relation of speech.[10]

It is in this sense that one can say that the consequences of the discovery of the unconscious have not been so much as glimpsed in the theory, although its repercussions have been felt in the praxis to a much greater extent that we are as yet aware of, even if only translated into effects of retreat.

Let me make clear that to argue for man's relation to the signifier as such has nothing to do with a 'culturalist' position in the ordinary sense of the term, such as that which Karen Horney found herself anticipating in the dispute over the phallus and which Freud himself characterised as feminist. The issue is not man's relation to language as a social phenomenon, since the question does not even arise of anything resembling that all too familiar ideological psychogenesis, not superseded by a peremptory recourse to the entirely metaphysical notion, underlying the mandatory appeal to the concrete, which is so pathetically conveyed by the terms 'affect'.[11]

It is a question of rediscovering in the laws governing that other scene (*eine andere Schauplatz*) which Freud designated, in relation to dreams, as that of the unconscious, the effects discovered at the level of the materially unstable elements which constitue the chain of language: effects determined by the double play of combination and substitution in the signifier, along the two axes of metaphor and metonymy which generate the signified; effects which are determinant in the institution of the subject. What emerges from this attempt is a topology in the mathematical sense of the term, without which, as soon becomes clear, it is impossible even to register the structure of a symptom in the analytic sense of the term.

It speaks in the Other, I say, designating by this Other the very place called upon by a recourse to speech in any relation where it intervenes. If it speaks in the Other, whether or not the subject hears it with his own ears, it is because it is there that the subject, according to a logic prior to any awakening of the signified, find his signifying place. The discovery of what he articulates in that place, that is, in the unconscious, enables us to grasp the price of the division (*Spaltung*) through which he is thus constituted.[12]

The phallus is elucidated in its function here. In Freudian doctrine, the phallus is not a fantasy, if what is understood by that is an imaginary affect. Nor is it as such an object (part, internal, good, bad, etc....) in so far as this term tends to accentuate the reality involved in a relationship. It is even less the organ, penis or clitoris, which it symbolises. And it is not incidental that Freud took his reference for it from the simulacrum which it represented for the Ancients.

For the phallus is a signifier, a signifier whose function in the intra-subjective economy of analysis might lift the veil from that which it served in the mysteries. For it is to this signifier that it is given to designate as a whole the effect of there being a signified, inasmuch as it conditions any such effect by its presence as signifier.[13]

Let us examine, then, the effects of this presence. First they follow from the deviation of man's needs by the fact that he speaks, in the sense that as long as his needs are subjected to demand they return to him alienated. This is not the effect of his real dependency (one should not expect to find here the parasitic conception represented by the notion of dependency in the theory of neuroses) but precisely of the putting into signifying form as such and of the fact that it is from the place of the Other that his message is emitted.

What is thus alienated in needs constitutes an *Urverdrängung* (primal repression) because it cannot, by definition, be articulated in demand. But it reappears in a residue which then presents itself in man as desire (*das Begehren*). The phenomenology which emerges from analytic experience is certainly such as to demonstrate the paradoxical, deviant, erratic, eccentric and even scandalous character by which desire is distinguished from need. A fact too strongly attested not to have always won the recognition of moralists worthy of the name. It does seem that early Freudianism had to give this fact its due status. Yet paradoxically psychoanalysis finds itself at the head of an age-old obscurantism, all the more wearisome for its denial of the fact through the ideal of theoretical and practical reduction of desire to need.

Hence the necessity for us to articulate that status here, starting with demand whose proper characteristics are eluded in the notion of frustration (which was never employed by Freud).

[274]

Demand in itself bears on something other than the satisfactions which it calls for. It is demand for a presence or an absence. This is manifest in the primordial relation to the mother, pregnant as it is with that Other to be situated *some way short of* any needs which it might gratify. Demand constitutes this Other as already possessing the 'privilege' of satisfying needs, that is, the power to deprive them of the one thing by which they are satisfied. This privilege of the Other thus sketches out the radical form of the gift of something which it does not have, namely, what is called its love.

Hence it is that demand cancels out (*aufhebt*) the particularity of anything which might be granted by transmuting it into a proof of love, and the very satisfactions of need which it obtains are degraded (*sich erniedrigt*) as being no more than a crushing of the demand for love (all of which is palpable in the psychology of early child-care to which our nurse-analysts are so dedicated).

There is, then, a necessity for the particularity thus abolished to reappear *beyond* demand. Where is does indeed reappear, but preserving the structure harbouring within the unconditional character of the demand for love. In a reversal which is not a simple negation of negation, the force of pure loss arises from the relic of an obliteration. In place of the unconditional aspect of demand, desire substitutes the 'absolute' condition: in effect this condition releases that part of the proof of love which is resistant to the satisfaction of a need. Thus desire is neither the appetite for satisfaction, nor the demand for love, but the difference resulting from the subtraction of the first from the second, the very phenomenon of their splitting (*Spaltung*).

One can see how the sexual relation occupies this closed field of desire in which it will come to play out its fate. For this field is constituted so as to produce the enigma which this relation provokes in the subject, by 'signifying' it to him twice over: as a return of the demand it arouses in the form of a demand made on the subject of need, and as an ambiguity cast onto the Other who is involved, in the proof of love demanded. The gap in this enigma betrays what determines it, conveyed at its simplest in this formula: that for each partner in the relation, the subject and the Other, it is not enough to be the subjects of need, nor objects of love, but they must stand as the cause of desire.

This truth is at the heart of all the mishaps of sexual life which belong in the field of psychoanalysis.

It is also the precondition in analysis for the subject's happiness: and to disguise this gap by relying on the virtue of the 'genital' to resolve it through the maturation of tenderness (that is by a recourse to the Other solely as reality), however piously intended, is none the less a fraud. Admittedly it was French psychoanalysts with their hypocritical notion of genital oblativity who started up the moralising trend which, to the tune of Salvationist choirs, is now followed everywhere.

In any case man cannot aim at being whole (the 'total personality' being another premise where modern psychotherapy goes off course) once the play of displacement and condensation, to which he is committed in the exercise of his functions, marks his relation as subject to the signifier.

The phallus is the privileged signifier of that mark where the share of the logos is wedded to the advent of desire. One might say that this signifier is chosen as what stands out as most easily seized upon in the real of sexual copulation, and also as the most symbolic in the literal (typographical) sense of the term, since it is the equivalent in that relation of the (logical) copula. One might also say that by virtue of its turgidity, it is the image of the vital flow as it is transmitted in generation.

All these propositions merely veil over the fact that the phallus can only play its role as veiled, that is, as in itself the sign of the latency with which everything signifiable is struck as soon as it is raised (*aufgehoben*) to the function of signifier.

The phallus is the signifier of this *Aufhebung* itself which it inaugurates (initiates) by its own disappearance. This is why the demon of 'Αἰδώς [*Scham*, shame] in the ancient mysteries rises up exactly at the moment when the phallus is unveiled (cf. the famous painting of the Villa of Pompei).

It then becomes the bar which, at the hands of this demon, strikes the signified, branding it as the bastard offspring of its signifying concatenation.

In this way a condition of complementarity is produced by the signifier in the founding of the subject: which explains his *Spaltung* as well as the intervening movement through which this is effected.

Namely:

(1) that the subject designates his being only by crossing through everything which it signifies, as can be seen in the fact that he wishes to be loved for himself, a mirage not dispelled merely by being denounced as grammatical (since it abolishes discourse).

(2) That the living part of that being in the *urverdrängt* [primary repressed] finds its signifier by receiving the mark of the *Ver-*

drängung [repression] of the phallus (whereby the unconscious is language).

The phallus as signifier gives the ratio of desire (in the musical sense of the term as the 'mean and extreme' ratio of harmonic division).

It is, therefore, as an algorithm that I am going to use it now, relying – necessarily if I am to avoid drawing out my account indefinitely – on the echoes of the experience which unites us to give you the sense of this usage.

If the phallus is a signifier then it is in the place of the Other that the subject gains access to it. But in that the signifier is only there veiled and as the ratio of the Other's desire, so it is this desire of the Other as such which the subject has to recognise, meaning, the Other as itself a subject divided by the signifying *Spaltung*.

What can be seen to emerge in psychological genesis confirms this signifying function of the phallus.

Thus, to begin with, we can formulate more correctly the Kleinian fact that the child apprehends from the outset that the mother 'contains' the phallus.

But it is the dialectic of the demand for love and the test of desire which dictates the order of development.

The demand for love can only suffer from a desire whose signifier is alien to it. If the desire of the mother *is* the phallus, the child wishes to be the phallus so as to satisfy this desire. Thus the division immanent to desire already makes itself felt in the desire of the Other, since it stops the subject from being satisfied with presenting to the Other anything real it might *have* which corresponds to this phallus – what he has being worth no more than what he does not have as far as his demand for love is concerned, which requires that he *be* the phallus.

Clinical practice demonstrates that this test of the desire of the Other is not decisive in the sense that the subject learns from it whether or not he has a real phallus, but inasmuch as he learns that the mother does not. This is the moment of experience without which no symptomatic or structural consequence (that is, phobia or *penisneid*) referring to the castration complex can take effect. It is here that the conjunction is signed between desire, in so far as the phallic signifier is its mark; and the threat or the nostalgia of lack-in-having.

It is, of course, the law introduced into this sequence by the father which will decide its future.

But simply by keeping to the function of the phallus, we can pinpoint the structures which will govern the relations between the sexes.

Let us say that these relations will resolve around a being and a having which, because they refer to a signifier, the phallus, have the contradictory effect of on the one hand lending reality to the subject in that signifier, and on the other making unreal the relations to be signified.

This follows from the intervention of an 'appearing' which gets substituted for the 'having' so as to protect it on one side and to mask its lack on the other, with the effect that the ideal or typical manifestations of behaviour in both sexes, up to and including the act of sexual copulation, are entirely propelled into comedy.

These ideals gain new strength from the demand which it is in their power to satisfy, which is always the demand for love, with its complement of reducing desire to demand.

Paradoxical as this formulation might seem, I would say that it is in order to be the phallus, that is to say, the signifier of the desire of the Other, that the woman will reject an essential part of her femininity, notably all its attributes through masquerade. It is for what she is not that she expects to be desired as well as loved. But she finds the signifier of her own desire in the body of the one to whom she addresses her demand for love. Certainly we should not forget that the organ actually invested with this signifying function takes on the value of a fetish. But for the woman the result is still a convergence onto the same object of an experience of love which as such (cf. above) ideally deprives her of that which is gives, and a desire which finds in that same experience its signifier. Which is why it can be observed that the lack of satisfaction proper to sexual need, in other words, frigidity, is relatively well tolerated in women, whereas the *Verdrängung* inherent to desire is lesser in her case than in the case of the man.

In men, on the other hand, the dialectic of demand and desire gives rise to effects, whose exact point of connection Freud situated with a sureness which we must once again admire, under the rubric of a specific depreciation (*Erniedrigung*) of love.

If it is the case that the man manages to satisfy his demand for love in his relationship to the woman to the extent that the signifier of the phallus constitutes her precisely as giving in love what she does not have — conversely, his own desire for the phallus will throw up its signifier in the form of a persistent divergence towards 'another woman' who can signify this phallus under various guises, whether as a virgin or a prostitute. The result is a centrifugal tendency of the genital drive in the sexual life of the man which makes impotence much harder for him to bear, at the same time as the *Verdrängung* inherent to desire is greater.

We should not, however, think that the type of infidelity which then appears to be constitutive of the masculine function is exclusive to the man. For if one looks more closely, the same redoubling is to be found in the woman, except that in her case, the Other of love as such, that is to say, the Other as deprived of that which he gives, is hard to perceive in the withdrawal whereby it is substituted for the being of the man whose attributes she cherishes.

One might add here that masculine homosexuality, in accordance with the phallus mark which constitutes desire, is constituted on its axis, whereas the orientation of feminine homosexuality, as observation shows, follows from a disappointment which reinforces the side of the demand for love. These remarks should be qualified by going back to the function of the mask inasmuch as this function dominates the identification through which refusals of love are resolved.

The fact that femininity takes refuge in this mask, because of the *Verdrängung* inherent to the phallic mark of desire, has the strange consequence that, in the human being, virile display itself appears as feminine.

Correlatively, one can glimpse the reason for a feature which has never been elucidated and which again gives a measure of the depth of Freud's intuition, namely, why he advances the view that there is only one libido, his text clearly indicating that he conceives of it as masculine in nature. The function of the signifier here touches on its most profound relation: by way of which Ancients embodied in it both the Noῦς [*Nous*, sense] and the λόγος [*Logos*, reason].

Notes for Lacan's 'The meaning of the phallus'

1 Lacan stresses the central role of the castration complex in the unconscious construction of conventional gender categories, heterosexuality and the successful care of children.
2 This is a reference to Freud's view that male castration anxiety and female penis-envy which are both unconscious are rarely totally resolved and that Freud's 'disturbance' within sexuality – actually bisexuality – stems from this lack of resolution.
3 Lacan rejects hereditary factors as the cause of the 'disturbance' in sexuality in the form it takes in Freud's speculative idea of the primal horde. This involves the murder

of the father by the sons to gain the mother and the subsequent development of a primordial law prohibiting incest which is then passed down the generations.

4   This refers to the relation of the subject to the phallus which crosses the boundaries of the body, i.e. a woman may identify with the father and the phallus and a man may identify with the mother and the 'lack'.

5   Lacan agrees with Freud that there is no awareness of the vagina until after the Oedipal crisis.

6   This refers to ignorance of the vagina.

7   A term introduced by Ernest Jones, a follower of Freud, meaning the disappearance of sexual desire. According to Jones the fear of this is greater than the fear of castration in both sexes. See Jones 1948.

8   Lacan rejects Jones's and Klein's idea of the phallus as a part object contained in the idea of the mother's body.

9   Here Lacan introduces the concept of the signifier with which Freud seems to have been unfamiliar.

10 The meaning of the phallus speaks through man. Man as distinct from woman is part of the structure of language whose material he becomes, so language and the meaning of the phallus 'resound' in him.

11 Lacan rejects the idea of the signifier as a social phenomenon, emphasising that it speaks in the unconscious and according to the rules of the unconscious.

12 The subject discovers that it is in language that he finds not only his status as a subject, but also his unconscious and his desire. This is the division within which 'men' are constituted.

13 This originates the entire field of signification or meaning.

II

Julia Kristeva, from 'Woman's Time'
(1981)

This paper was first published as 'Le temps des femmes' in *Cahiers de recherche de sciences des textes et documents*, in 1979. It was translated in *Signs* in 1981 and reprinted in Keohane, Rosaldo, and Gelpi, eds. (1982) and in Moi, ed. (1986).

In this extract Kristeva argues that a new generation of feminists needs to reconcile motherhood (taking place in what she calls monumental and cyclical time) with politics (taking place in what she calls linear time). If we fail to take theoretical account of women's desire for and enjoyment of motherhood, she insists, we lay ourselves open to a resurgence of religion and mysticism, the only places, in the past, where women have been able to express feelings associated with motherhood. She argues that recent feminists, in focusing on feminine subjectivity and the establishment of woman as 'Truth', have been as sexist as patriarchal men. However, she takes the view that the earlier, pre-1968, generation of feminists, in concentrating on entry into the existing social, political and economic structures, simply allowed themselves to be assimilated into the meanings and values of the phallus. Anarchy and a continual 'fight to the death' over difference, she argues, can only be avoided if the three feminist approaches based on different conceptions of time can be allowed to intermingle in a parallel existence. In future, instead of using those who are different as a place to project our unacceptable symbolic castration in the form of blame, we should withdraw these projections and fight out the contradictions between 'good' and 'bad', 'masculinity' and 'femininity' within our own identities. In other words, we must interiorise 'or take responsibility for' the founding moment of our existence, symbolic castration and sexual difference, instead of projecting it destructively into the external world.

The following text is translated by Alice Jardine and Harry Blake. Fuller commentary on this text begins on page 184.

From 'Women's Time'

Creatures and creatresses

The desire to be a mother, considered alienating and even reactionary by the preceding generation of feminists, has obviously not become a standard for the present generation. But we have seen in the past few years an increasing number of women who not only consider their maternity compatible with their professional life or their feminist involvement (certain improvements in the quality of life are also at the origin of this: an increase in the number of daycare centres and nursery schools, more active participation of men in child care and domestic life, etc.), but also find it indispensable to their discovery, not of the plenitude, but of the complexity of the female experience, with all that this complexity comprises in joy and pain. This tendency has its extreme: in the refusal of the paternal function by lesbian and single mothers can be seen one of the most violent forms taken by the rejection of the symbolic outlined above, as well as one of the most fervent divinizations of maternal power – all of which cannot help but trouble an entire legal and moral order without, however, proposing an alternative to it. Let us remember here that Hegel distinguished between female right (familial and religious) and male law (civil and political). If our societies know well the uses and abuses of male law, it must also be recognized that female right is designated, for the moment, by a blank. And if these practices of maternity, among others, were to be generalized, women themselves would be responsible for elaborating the appropriate legislation to check the violence to which, otherwise, both their children and men would be subject. But are they capable of doing so? This is one of the important questions that the new generation of women encounters, especially when the members of this new generation refuse to ask those questions seized by the same rage with which the dominant order originally victimized them.

Faced with this situation, it seems obvious – and feminist groups become more aware of this when they attempt to broaden their audience – that the refusal of maternity cannot be a mass policy and that the majority of women today see the possibility for fulfilment, if not entirely at least to a large degree, in bringing a child into the world. What does this desire for motherhood correspond to? This is one of the new questions for the new generation, a question the preceding generation had foreclosed. For want of an answer to this question, feminist ideology leaves the door open to the return of religion, whose discourse, tried and proved over thousands of years, provides the necessary ingredients for satisfying the anguish, the suffering and the hopes of mothers. If Freud's affirmation – that the desire for a child is the desire for the penis and, in this sense, a substitute for phallic and symbolic dominion – can be only partially accepted, what modern women have to say about this experience should none the less be listened to attentively. Pregnancy seems to be experienced as the radical ordeal of the splitting of the subject:[1] redoubling up of the body, separation and coexistence of the self and of an other, of nature and consciousness, of physiology and speech. This fundamental challenge to identity is then accompanied by a fantasy of totality – narcissistic completeness – a sort of instituted, socialized, natural psychosis. The arrival of the child, on the other hand, leads the mother into the labyrinths of an experience that, without the child, she would only rarely encounter: love for an other. Not for herself, nor for an identical being, and still less for another person with whom 'I' fuse (love or sexual passion). But the slow, difficult and delightful apprenticeship in attentiveness, gentleness, forgetting oneself. The ability to succeed in this path without masochism and without annihilating one's affective, intellectual and professional personality – such would seem to be the stakes to be won through guiltless maternity. It then becomes a creation in the strong sense of the term. For this moment, Utopian?

On the other hand, it is in the aspiration towards artistic and, in particular, literary creation that woman's desire for affirmation now manifests itself. Why literature?

It is because, faced with social norms, literature reveals a certain knowledge and sometimes the truth itself about an otherwise repressed, nocturnal, secret and unconscious universe? Because it thus redoubles the social contract by exposing the unsaid, the uncanny? And because it makes a game, a space of fantasy and pleasure, out of the abstract and frustrating order of social signs, the words of everyday communication? 'Flaubert said, 'Madame Bovary, c'est moi'. Today many women imagine, Flaubert, c'est moi'. This identification with the potency of the imaginary is not only an identification, an imaginary potency (a fetish, a belief in the maternal penis maintained at all costs), as a far too normative view of the social and symbolic relationship would have it. This identification also bears witness to women's desire to lift the weight of what is sacrificial in the social contract from their shoulders, to nourish our societies with a more flexible and free discourse, one able to name what has thus far never been an object of circulation in the community: the enigmas of the body, the dreams, secret joys, shames, hatreds of the second sex.

It is understandable from this that women's writing has lately attracted the maximum attention of both 'specialists' and the media.[2] The pitfalls encountered along the way, however, are not to be minimized: for example, does one not read there a relentless belittling of male writers whose books, nevertheless, often serve as 'models' for countless productions by women? Thanks to the feminist label, does one not sell numerous works whose naive whining or market-place romanticism would otherwise have been rejected an anachronistic? And does one not find the pen of many a female writer being devoted to phantasmic attacks against Language and Sign as the ultimate supports of phallocratic power, in the name of a semi-aphonic corporality whose truth can only be found in that which is 'gestural' or 'tonal'?

And yet, no matter how dubious the results of these recent productions by women, the symptom is there – women are writing, and the air is heavy with expectation: What will they write that is new?

In the name of the Father, the Son ... and the Woman?

These few elements of the manifestations by the new generation of women in Europe seem to me to demonstrate that, beyond the socio-political level where it is generally inscribed (or inscribes itself), the women's movement – in its present stage, less aggressive but more artful – is situated within the very framework of the religious crisis of our civilization.

I call 'religion' this phantasmic necessity on the part of speaking beings to provide themselves with a *representation* (animal, female, male, parental, etc.) in place of what constitutes them as such, in other words, symbolization – the double articulation and syntactic sequence of language, as well as its preconditions or substitutes (thoughts, affects, etc.). The elements of the current practice of feminism that we have just brought to light seem precisely to constitute such a representation which makes up for the frustrations imposed on women by the anterior code (Christianity or its lay humanist variant). The fact that this new ideology has affinities, often revindicated by its creators, with so-called matriarchal beliefs (in other words, those beliefs characterizing matrilinear societies) should not overshadow its radical novelty. This ideology seems to me to be part of the broader anti-sacrificial current which is animating our culture and which, in its protest against the constraints of the socio-symbolic contract, is no less exposed to the risks of violence and terrorism. At this level of radicalism, it is the very principle of sociality which is challenged.

Certain contemporary thinkers consider, as is well known, that modernity is characterized as the first epoch in human history in which human beings attempt to live without religion. In its present form, is not feminism in the process of becoming one?

Or is it, on the contrary and as avant-garde feminists hope, that having started with the idea of difference, feminists will be able to break free of its belief in Woman, Her power, Her writing, so as to channel this demand for difference into each and every element of the female whole, and, finally, to bring out the singularity of each woman, and beyond this, her multiplicities, her plural languages, beyond the horizon, beyond sight, beyond faith itself?

A factor for ultimate mobilization? Or a factor for analysis?

Imaginary support in a technocratic era where all narcissism is frustrated? Or instruments fitted to these times in which the cosmos, atoms and cells – our true contemporaries – call for the constitution of a fluid and free subjectivity?

The question has been posed. Is to pose it already to answer it?

Another generation is another space

If the preceding can be *said* – the question whether all this is *true* belongs to a different register – it is undoubtedly because it is now possible to gain some distance on these two preceding generations of women. This implies, of course, that a *third* generation is now forming, at least in Europe. I am not speaking of a new group of young women (though its importance should not be underestimated) or of another 'mass feminist movement' taking the torch passed on from the second generation. My usage of the word 'generation' implies less a chronology than a *signifying space*, a both corporeal and desiring mental space. So it can be argued that as of now a third attitude is possible, thus a third generation, which does not exclude – quite to the contrary – the *parallel* existence of all three in the same historical time, or even that they be interwoven one with the other.

In this third attitude, which I strongly advocate – which I imagine? – the very dichotomy man/woman as an opposition between two rival entities may be understood as belonging to *metaphysics*. What can 'identity', even 'sexual identity', mean in a new theoretical and scientific space where the very notion of identity is challenged?[3] I am not simply suggesting a very hypothetical bisexuality which, even if it existed, would only, in fact, be the aspiration towards the totality of one of the sexes and thus an effacing of difference. What I mean is, first of all, the demassification of the problematic of *difference*, which would imply, in a first phase, an apparent de-dramatization of the 'fight to the death' between rival groups and thus between the sexes. And this not in the name of some reconciliation – feminism has at least had the merit of showing what is irreducible and even deadly in the social contract – but in order that the struggle, the implacable difference, the violence be conceived in the very place where it operates with the maximum intransigence, in other words, in personal and sexual identity itself, so as to make it disintegrate in its very nucleus.

It necessarily follows that this involves risks not only for what we understand today as 'personal equilibrium' but also for social equilibrium itself, made up as it now is of the counterbalancing of aggressive and murderous forces massed in social, national, religious and political groups. But is it not the insupportable situation of tension and explosive risk that the existing 'equilibrium' presupposes which leads some of those who suffer from it to divest it of its economy, to detach themselves from it and to seek another means of regulating difference?

To restrict myself here to a personal level, as related to the question of women, I see arising, under the cover of a relative indifference towards the militance of the first and second generations, an attitude of retreat from sexism (male as well as female) and, gradually, from any kind of anthropomorphism. The fact that this might quickly become another form of spiritualism turning its back on social problems, or else a form of repression[4] ready to support all status quos, should not hide the radicalness of the process. The process could be summarized as an *interiorization of the founding separation of the socio-symbolic contract*, as an introduction of its cutting edge into the very interior of every identity whether subjective, sexual, ideological, or so forth. This in such a way that the habitual and increasingly explicit attempt to fabricate a scapegoat victim as foundress of a society or a counter-society may be replaced by the analysis of the potentialities of *victim/executioner* which characterize each identity, each subject, each sex.

What discourse, if not that of a religion, would be able to support this adventure which surfaces as a real possibility, after both the achievements and the impasses of the present ideological reworkings, in which feminism has participated? It seems to me that the role of what is usually called 'aesthetic practices' must increase not only to counterbalance the storage and uniformity of information by present-day mass media, data-bank systems and, in particular, modern communications technology, but also to demystify the identity of the symbolic bond itself, to demystify, therefore, the *community* of language as a universal and unifying tool, one which totalizes and equalizes. In order to bring out – along with the *singularity* of each person and, even more, along with the multiplicity of every person's possible identifications (with atoms, e.g., stretching from the family to the stars) – the *relativity of his/her symbolic as well as biological existence*, according to the variation in his/her specific symbolic capacities. And in order to emphasize the *responsibility* which all will immediately face of putting this fluidity into play against the threats of death which are unavoidable whenever an inside and an outside, a self and an other, one group and another, are constituted. At this level of interiorization with its social as well as individual stakes, what I have called 'aesthetic practices' are undoubtedly nothing other than the modern reply to the eternal question of morality. At least, this is how we might understand an ethics which, conscious of the fact that its order is sacrificial, reserves part of the burden for each of its adherents, therefore declaring them guilty while immediately affording them the possibility for *jouissance*, for various productions, for a life made up of both challenges and differences.

Spinoza's question can be taken up again here: are women subject to ethics? If not to that ethics defined by classical philosophy – in relationship to which the ups and downs of feminist generations seem dangerously precarious – are women not already participating in the rapid dismantling that our age is experiencing at various levels (from wars to drugs to artificial insemination) and which poses the *demand* for a new ethics? The answer to Spinoza's question can be affirmative only at the cost of considering feminism as but a *moment* in the thought of the anthropomorphic identity which currently blocks the horizon of the discursive and scientific adventure of our species.

Notes for extract from Kristeva's 'Women's Time'

1   The 'split subject' (from *Spaltung* as both 'splitting' and 'cleavage'), as used in Freudian psychoanalysis, here refers directly to Kristeva's 'subject in process/in question/on trial' as opposed to the unity of the transcendental ego [translator's note].

2   A reference to *écriture feminine* as generically labelled in France over the past few years and not to women's writing in general [translator's note].

3   See seminar on *Identity* directed by Lévi-Strauss 1977.

4   Repression (*le réfoulement* or *Verdrängung*) as distinguished from the foreclosure (*le forclusion* or *Verwerfung*) evoked earlier in the article (see Laplanche and Pontalis 1985) [translator's note].

12

Luce Irigaray, from Speculum of the Other Woman *(1985)*

The first version of *Speculum* was published in French in 1974. An English translation was published in 1985.

The French version of *Speculum* led to Irigaray's expulsion from her post in the Department of Psychoanalysis at Vincennes because her book made it clear that she was both an outspoken feminist and critical of psychoanalysis. In particular, psychoanalysts criticised her for being political, on the grounds that being a psychoanalyst should preclude a political stance.

In the extract from the first part of *Speculum* titled 'The Blind Spot of an Old Dream of Symmetry', Irigaray uses psychoanalysis to psychoanalyse Freud's paper 'Femininity' (contained in this anthology) published in 1933. The main criticisms of Freud which emerge in this extract are that psychoanalysis is not interested in its historical and philosophical determinants, that it is dominated by unacknowledged phantasies and repressions and that it is patriarchal because it refuses to recognise its debt to the mother. As a result, it is blind to its own assumptions and takes the little boy as the model for the development of the little girl. The idea for the notion of a speculum refers to the curved mirror doctors use to conduct internal examinations of the body, most often vaginal examinations. For Irigaray, the book's title therefore epitomises the nature of sameness in Western thought and challenges Lacan's mirror, the mirror of male theory and discourse, which Irigaray thinks can only perceive women as lacking, as a 'hole'. In this context, Toril Moi comments 'Specularisation suggests not only the mirror image that comes from the visual penetration of the speculum inside the vagina' but also 'the necessity of postulating a subject that is capable of *reflecting* on its own being'. Male discourse characterised by narcissistic 'specularisation' can only understand women as a reflection. Irigaray's book titled *Speculum* suggest that only a speculum (a theory written by a woman from a female Imaginary) can reveal, in theory, what is specific to women.

The following text is translated by Gillian Gill. Fuller commentary on this text begins on page 200.

From *Speculum of the Other Woman*

The little girl is (only) a little boy

AN INFERIOR LITTLE MAN

Individuals of both sexes seem to pass through the early phases of libidinal development *in the same manner.* Contrary to all expectations, the little girl, in the sadistic–anal phase, shows *no less aggressiveness than* the little boy.... The aggressive impulses of little girls are *no less abundant and violent* [than those of little boys].... From the onset of the phallic phase, the *differences between the sexes are completely eclipsed by the agreements.*... THE LITTLE GIRL IS THEREFORE A LITTLE MAN.... The little girl uses, with the *same* intent [as the little boy] her *still smaller* clitoris ... a penis *equivalent* ... man *more* fortunate [than she] ... as she passes from her masculine phase to the feminine.... During this (pre-Oedipal, 'masculine') phase, *everything* that will later be found in the Oedipal situation *already exists* and later is *merely transferred* to the person of the father [?!] ... the *ultimate differentiation* of the sexes ... the little girl when she discovers her *disadvantage* ... the little girl who had up till then lived *like a little boy* ... the *comparison with the boy* ... *activity more resembling* that of the male ... regressing toward the *old masculinity complex* ... residual manifestations of the *primitive masculinity* ... the libido suffers a *greater* repression ... nature pays *less* attention to the girl's demands than is the case with masculinity ... *more* developed narcissism ... *more* jealous ... women have *fewer* social interests *than* men and the faculty for sublimating instincts is *weaker* ... as far as social concern goes, the *inferiority* of women [with respect to men] ... When laying *side by side* the development of the little boy and little girl, we find that the latter must, to *become a normal woman*, [?] suffer a *more* painful and *more* complex evolution and surmount two difficulties that have no *equivalent* for boys.

So we must admit that THE LITTLE GIRL IS THEREFORE A LITTLE MAN. A little man who will suffer a more painful and complicated evolution than the little boy in order to become a normal woman! A little man with a smaller penis. A disadvantaged little man. A little man whose libido will suffer a greater repression, and yet whose faculty for sublimating instincts will remain weaker. Whose needs are less catered to by nature and who will yet have a lesser share of culture. A more narcissistic little man because of the mediocrity of her genital organs(?). More modest because ashamed of that unfavourable comparison. More envious and jealous because less well endowed. Unattracted to the social interest shared by men. A little man who would have no other desire than to be, or remain, a man.

THE CARDS TURNED OVER

Thus Freud discovers – in a sort of blind reversal of repressions – certain variously disguised cards that are kept preserved or stored away and that lie beneath the hierarchy of values of the game, of all the games: the desire for the same, for the self-identical, the self (as) same, and again of the similar, the alter ego and, to put it in a nutshell, the desire for the auto . . . the homo . . . the males, dominates the representational economy. 'Sexual difference' is a derivation of the problematics of sameness, it is, now and forever, determined within the project, the projection, the sphere of representation, of the same. The 'differentiation' into two sexes derives from the a priori assumption of the same, since the little man that the little girl is, must become a man minus certain attributes whose paradigm is morphological – attributes capable of determining, of assuring, the reproduction–specularization of the same. A man minus the possibility of (re)presenting oneself as a man = a normal woman. In this proliferating desire of the same, death will be the only representative of an outside, of a heterogeneity, of an other: woman will assume the function of representing death (of sex/organ), castration, and man will be sure as far as possible of achieving mastery, subjugation, by triumphing over the anguish (of death) through intercourse, by sustaining sexual pleasure despite, or thanks to, the horror of closeness to that absence of sex/penis, that mortification of sex that is evoked by woman. The trial of intercourse will have, moreover, as teleological parameter the challenge of an indefinite regeneration, of a reproduction of the *same* that defies death, in the procreation of the *son*, this same of the procreating father. As testimony, for self and others, of his imperishable character, and warranty of a new generation of self-identity for the male seed.

[291]

THE DREAM INTERPRETERS THEMSELVES

Still incomplete is the enumeration, and, of course, the interpretation of the faces, the forms, the morphologies that can be taken on by that old dream of 'the same' which has defied the most prescient diviners, since their *method* did not question the credits that the method itself had already invested in that dream. The interpreters of dreams themselves had no desire but to rediscover the same. Everywhere. And, indeed, it was not hard to find. But was not *interpretation* itself, by that fact, caught up in the dream of identity, equivalence, analogy, of homology, symmetry, comparison, imitation, was it also not more or less *adequate*, that is to say more or less *good*? Since, after all, the most able of the interpreters were also the most gifted, the most inventive dreamers, those most inspired by what was liable to perpetuate, even to reactivate the desire of the same?

But when this same desire comes to speak, and theorize, and prescribe itself in the very name of, in the very place of, the relation between the sexes, of sexual difference, then it seems that the paroxysm of that demonstration, of that exhibition, is equivalent to announcing that the central postulate is in fact being called into question. Required by every figure in the ontology, the a priorism of the same was able to maintain itself only through an expatriation, an extrapolation, an expropriation of a quasi-theological nature. Under the direction of man, but not directly attributable to him. Referred back to some transcendence that was supposed to make capital of the interest of the operation. But if man is explicitly presented as the yardstick of the same, if the underlying and hitherto masked desire of the same – that is, the autoeroticism more or less deferred or differentiated into the autological or homologous representation of a (masculine) 'subject' – if that desire is interpreted overtly, then the representation project is confounded in its detours and in its idealist justifications. The pleasure man can take therein becomes apparent. At the same time as the question is inevitably raised: why should this pleasure be his alone?

Thus Freud would strike at least *two blows* at the scene of representation. One, as it were, directly, when he destroys a certain conception of the present, or of presence, when he stresses secondary revision, overdetermination, repetition compulsion, the death drive, etc., or when he indicates, in his practice, the impact of so-called unconscious mechanisms on the discourse of the 'subject'. The other blow, blinder and less direct, occurs when – himself a prisoner of a certain economy of the logos, of a certain logic, notably of 'desire', whose link to classical philosophy he fails to see – he defines sexual differences as a function of the a priori of the same, having recourse, to support this demonstration, to the age-old processes: analogy, comparison, symmetry, dichotomic oppositions, and so on. When, as card-carrying member of an 'ideology' that he never questions, he insists that the sexual pleasure known as masculine is the paradigm for all sexual pleasure, to which all representations of pleasure can but defer in reference, support, and submission. In order to remain effective, all this certainly needed at the very least to remain hidden! By exhibiting this 'symptom', the crisis point in metaphysics where we find exposed that sexual 'indifference' that had assured metaphysical coherence and 'closure'. Freud offers it up for our analysis. With his text offering itself to be understood, to be read, as doubtless the most relevant re-mark of an ancient dream of self . . . one that had never been interpreted.

Bibliography

ABRAHAM, K. (1922) 'Manifestations of the Female Castration Complex', *International Journal of Psychoanalysis*, 3: 1–29.

ABRAHAM, K. (1973) 'Contributions to the Theory of the Anal Character', *Selected Papers on Psychoanalysis*, London, Hogarth Press.

ABRAHAM, K. (1979) *Selected Papers of Karl Abraham*, London, Maresfield Reprints.

ACCATI, L. (1993) 'Explicit Meanings; Catholicism, Matriarchy and the Distinctive Problems of Italian Feminism', paper given in an abbreviated form at the *62nd Anglo–American Conference of Historians*, University of London, Institute of Historical Research.

ALLINSON, B. (1993) *Eros and Thanatos: The Eroticisation of Female Suffering*, M.A. dissertation, Anglia Polytechnic University Library.

ANDERMATT CONELEY, V. (1984) *Hélène Cixous: Writing the Feminine*, Lincoln, University of Nebraska Press.

ANDERMATT CONELEY, V. (1992) *Hélène Cixous*, London, Harvester Wheatsheaf.

APPIGNANESI, L. and FORRESTER, J. (1992) *Freud's Women*, London, Weidenfeld.

ARCANA, J. (1979) *Our Mothers' Daughters*, London, The Women's Press.

BAKAN, D. (1990) *Sigmund Freud and the Jewish Mystical Tradition*, London, Free Association Books.

BARUCH, E. (1991) *Women Analyse Women*, New York, New York University Press.

BELL, D. (1993) 'Primitive Mind of State', paper given at the conference *Psychoanalysis in the Public Sphere*, London, University of East London and Free Association Books.

BEMPORAD, J. (1990) *Psychoanalysis and Eating Disorders*, New York, Guilford Publications.

BENJAMIN, J. (1990) *The Bonds of Love*, London, Virago.

BENVENUTO, B. and KENNEDY, R. (1986) *Jacques Lacan: An Introduction*, London, Free Association Books.

BERKE, J. (1989) *The Tyranny of Malice*, London, Simon and Schuster.

BERNHEIMER C. and KAHANE, C. eds. (1985) *In Dora's Case*, London, Virago.

BERSANI, L. (1990) *The Freudian Body*, New York, Columbia University Press.

BION, W. (1967) *Second Thoughts: Selected Papers on Psycho-Analysis*, New York, Aronson.

BION, W. (1977) 'Learning from Experience' in *The Seven Servants*, New York, Aronson.

BOLLAS, C. (1987) *The Shadow of the Object: Psychoanalysis of the Unthought Unknown*, London, Free Association Books.

BOLLAS, C. (1989) *Forces of Destiny: Psychoanalysis and the Human Idiom*, London, Free Association Books.

BOLLAS, C. (1992) *Being a Character: Psychoanalysis and Self Experience*, London, Routledge.

BOOTHBY, R. (1991) *Death and Desire: Psychoanalytic Theory in Lacan's Return to Freud*, London, Routledge.

BOTT SPILLIUS, E. (1988) *Melanie Klein Today*, 2 vols., London, Routledge.

BOWIE, M. (1991) *Lacan*, London, Fontana [Modern Masters].

BOWIE, M. (1993) *Psychoanalysis and the Future of Theory*, Oxford, Blackwell.

BOWLBY, J. (1963–80) *Attachment and Loss*, 3 vols., London, Hogarth Press and New York, Basic Books.

BRAIDOTTI, R. (1989) 'The Politics of Ontological Difference' in Brennan, T. ed., *Between Feminism and Psychoanalysis*, London, Routledge

BRAIDOTTI, R. (1991) *Patterns of Dissidence*, Cambridge, Polity Press.

BREEN, D. (1989) *Talking With Mothers*, London, Free Association Books.

BREEN, D. (1993) *The Gender Conundrum*, London, Routledge.

BRENNAN, T. ed. (1989) *Between Feminism and Psychoanalysis*, London, Routledge.

BRENNAN, T. (1991) *History After Lacan*, London, Routledge.

BRENNAN, T. (1992) *The Interpretation of the Flesh: Freud and Femininity*, London, Routledge.

BROWN, J.A.C. (1960) *Freud and the Post-Freudians*, London, Penguin.

BUTLER, J. (1990) *Gender Trouble*, London, Routledge.

BUTLER, J. (1993) *Bodies that Matter*, London, Routledge.

CASTIORADIS, C. (1987) *The Imaginary Institution of Society*, Cambridge, Polity Press.

CHASSEGUET-SMIRGEL, J. (1981) *Female Sexuality*, London, Virago.

CHODOROW, N. (1978) *The Reproduction of Mothering: Psychoanalysis and the Sociology of Gender*, Berkeley, University of California.

CHODOROW, N. (1989) *Feminism and Psychoanalysis*, Cambridge, Polity Press.

CHODOROW, N. (1994) *Femininities, Masculinities, Sexualities*, London, Free Association Books.

CIXOUS, H. (1975) 'Sorties' in *La jeune née*, Paris, Union Générale d'Editions.

CIXOUS, H. (1976) 'The Laugh of the Medusa', trans. K. Cohen and P. Cohen, *Signs*, 1, 4: 875–93.

CLEMENT, C. (1987) *The Weary Sons of Freud*, London, Free Association Books.

COHN, N. (1993) *Cosmos, Chaos and the World To Come*, Yale, Yale University Press.

[295]

CONNEL, R.W. (1987) *Gender and Power*, Cambridge, Polity Press.

CRAIB, I. (1989) *Psychoanalysis and Social Theory*, London, Harvester Wheatsheaf.

CREED, B. (1993) *The Monstrous Feminine*, London, Routledge.

CROWLEY, H. and HIMMELWEIT, S. (1992) *Knowing Women*, Milton Keynes, Open University and Cambridge, Polity Press.

DECKER, H.S. (1991) *Freud, Dora and Vienna 1890*, New York, The Free Press.

DEUTSCH, H. (1925) 'The Psychology of Women in Relation to the Functions of Reproduction', *International Journal of Psychoanalysis*, 6: 405–18.

DEUTSCH, H. (1932a) 'The Significance of Masochism in the Mental Life of Women', *International Journal of Psychoanalysis*, 11: 48–60.

DEUTSCH, H. (1932b) 'On Female Homosexuality', *Psychoanalytic Quarterly*, 1: 484–510.

DEUTSCH, H. (1933a) 'Female Sexuality', *International Journal of Psychoanalysis*, 19: 34–56.

DEUTSCH, H. (1933b) 'Motherhood and Sexuality', *Psychoanalytic Quarterly*, 2: 476–88.

DEUTSCH, H. (1944) *The Psychology of Women*, vol. 1, New York, Grune and Stratton; vol. 2 (1947) London, Research Books.

DINNAGE, R. (1988) *One to One*, Harmondsworth, Penguin.

DINNERSTEIN, D. (1978) *The Rocking of the Cradle and the Ruling of the World*, London: Souvenir Press.

DOANE, J. (1992) *From Klein to Kristeva*, Ann Arbor, University of Michigan.

EICHENBAUM, L. and ORBACH, S. (1982) *Outside In, Inside Out*, Harmondsworth, Penguin.

EICHENBAUM, L. and ORBACH, S. (1985) *Understanding Women*, Harmondsworth, Penguin.

EISLER, M.J. (1922) 'Pleasure in Sleep and the Disturbed Capacity for Sleep', *International Journal of Psychoanalysis*, 3.

FAIRBURN, W. (1952) *Psychoanalytic Studies of the Personality*, London, Tavistock.

FAIRBURN, W. (1954) *An Object-Relations Theory of the Personality*, New York, Basic Books.

FAY, P. (1987) *A Godless Jew*, New Haven, Yale University Press.

FELMAN, S. (1993) *What Does a Woman Want?*, Baltimore, Johns Hopkins University Press.

FLAX, J. (1990) *Thinking Fragments*, Berkeley, University of California Press.

FLETCHER, J. ed. (1990) *Abjection, Melancholia and Love*, London, Routledge.

FOLLETT, M.P. (1930) *Creative Experience*, New York, Longman, Green and Co.

FORDHAM, M. (1993) *The Making of an Analyst*, London, Free Association Books.

FORRESTER, J. (1985) *Language and the Origins of Psychoanalysis*, London, Macmillan.

FORRESTER, J. (1991) *The Seductions of Psychoanalysis*, Cambridge, Cambridge University Press.

FOUCAULT, M. (1981) *The History of Sexuality*, vols 1 and 2, trans. R. Hurley, Harmondsworth, Penguin.

FREUD, A. ed. (1986) *Sigmund Freud: The Essentials of Psychoanalysis*, Harmondsworth, Penguin.

FREUD, S. (1895) *Studies on Hysteria*, SE 2, PFL 3 [with Breuer].

FREUD, S. (1900) *The Interpretation of Dreams*, SE 4–5, PFL 4.

FREUD, S. (1905a) 'Fragment of an Analysis of a Case of Hysteria', SE 7: 1–122, PFL 8 [Dora].

FREUD, S. (1905b) *Three Essays on the Theory of Sexuality*, SE 7: 123–245, PFL 7.

FREUD, S. (1908a) 'Character and Anal Eroticism', SE 9: 167–75, PFL 7.

FREUD, S. (1908b) 'On the Sexual Theories of Children', SE 9: 205–26, PFL 7.

FREUD, S. (1909) 'Analysis of a Phobia in a Five-Year old Boy', SE 14: 1–149, PFL 8 [Little Hans].

FREUD, S. (1910) 'A Special Type of Choice of Object made by Men', SE 11: 163–75, PFL 7.

FREUD, S. (1912) 'On the Universal Tendency to Debasement in the Sphere of Love', SE 11: 177–90, PFL 7 [Contributions to the psychology of love].

FREUD, S. (1914) 'On Narcissism: An Introduction', SE 14: 67–102, PFL 11.

FREUD, S. (1915) 'The Unconscious', SE 11: 1612, PFL 11: 159.

FREUD, S. (1917a) 'The Taboo of Virginity', SE 11: 193–208, PFL 7.

FREUD, S. (1917b) 'Mourning and Melancholy', SE 14: 237–58, PFL 11.

FREUD, S. (1920) *Beyond the Pleasure Principle*, SE 18, PFL 11.

FREUD, S. (1921) *Group Psychology and the Analysis of the Ego*, SE 18: 64–143, PFL 12: 91.

FREUD, S. (1923) *The Ego and the Id*, SE 19, PFL 11.

FREUD, S. (1924) 'The Dissolution of the Oedipal Complex', SE 19: 173–9, PFL 7.

FREUD, S. (1925a) *An Autobiographical Study*, SE 20.

FREUD, S. (1925b) 'Some Psychical Consequences of the Anatomical Distinction Between the Sexes', SE 19: 243–58, PFL 7.

FREUD, S. (1925c) ' Negation', SE 19.

FREUD, S. (1926) *The Question of Lay Analysis*, SE 20, PFL 15.

FREUD, S. (1927) 'Fetishism', SE 21: 147–57, PFL 7.

FREUD, S. (1928) 'The Future of an Illusion', SE 21: 1–56, PFL 12: 212.

FREUD, S. (1930) *Civilisation and its Discontents*, SE 21, PFL 12.

FREUD, S. (1931a) 'Female Sexuality', SE 21: 223–43, PFL 7.

FREUD, S. (1931b) 'Libidinal Types', SE 21: 215–20, PFL 7.

FREUD, S. (1933) 'Femininity', *New Introductory Lectures on Psychoanalysis*, SE 22, PFL 2.

FREUD, S. (1940) *An Outline of Psychoanalysis*, SE 23, PFL 15.

FREUD, S. (1986) *The Complete Letters of Sigmund Freud to Wilhelm Fliess (1887–1904)*, London, Hogarth Press.

FREUD, S. (1993) *The Freud Diaries 1929–1939*, London, Hogarth Press.

FROMM, E. (1990) *The Anatomy of Human Destructiveness*, London, Penguin.

FROSH, S. (1994) *Sexual Difference*, London, Macmillan.

FUSS, D. (1989) *Essentially Speaking: Feminism, Nature and Difference*, New York, Routledge.

GALLOP, J. (1982) *Feminism and Psychoanalysis: The Daughter's Seduction*, London, Macmillan.

GALLOP, J. (1985) *Reading Lacan*, Ithaca and London, Cornell University Press.

GALLOP, J. (1990) *Thinking Through the Body*, London, Routledge.

GAY, P. (1988) *Freud: A Life for Our Time*, London, Macmillan.

GAY, P. (1991) *Reading Freud*, New Haven, Yale University Press.

GAY, P. (1995) *The Freud Reader*, London, Vintage.

GEMOSKO, G. (1994) *Baudrillard and Signs*, London, Routledge.

GILLIGAN, C. (1982) *In a Different Voice*, Cambridge, MA, Harvard University.

GILMAN, H. and SANDER, L. (1993) *Freud, Race and Gender*, New Jersey, Princeton University Press.

GILMAN, H., PORTER, R., ROUSSEAU, G. and SHOWALTER, E. (1993) *Hysteria Beyond Freud*, Berkeley, University of California Press.

GIRARD, R. (1979) *Violence and the Sacred*, trans. P. Gregory, Baltimore and London, Johns Hopkins University Press.

GOLDMAN, D. (1993) *In Search of the Real: The Origins and Originality of D.W. Winnicott*, New York, Aronson.

GROLNICK, S. (1978) *Between Reality and Phantasy*, New York, Aronson.

GROLNICK, S. (1990) *The Work and Play of Winnicott*, New York, Aronson.

GROSSKURTH, P. (1985) *Melanie Klein*, London, Maresfield Library.

GROSZ, E. (1989) *Sexual Subversions: Three French Feminists*, Sydney, Allen and Unwin.

GROSZ, E. (1990) *Jacques Lacan: A Feminist Introduction*, London, Routledge.

GUNTRIP, H. (1971) *Psychoanalytic Theory, Therapy and the Self*, New York, Basic Books.

GUNTRIP, H. (1975) 'My Experience of Analysis with Fairburn and Winnicott (How Complete a Result does Psychoanalytic Therapy Achieve?)', *International Review of Psychoanalysis*, 2: 145–56.

HARROWAY, D. (1991) *Simians, Cyborgs and Women*, London, Free Association Books.

HARROWAY, D. (1992) *Primate Visions*, London, Verso Editions.

HEALD, S. (1994) *Anthropology and Psychoanalysis*, London, Routledge.

HERMAN, N. (1987) *Why Psychotherapy?*, London, Free Association Books.

HERMAN, N. (1988) *My Kleinian Home*, London, Free Association Books.

HINSHELWOOD, R.D. (1989) *A Dictionary of Kleinian Thought*, London, Free Association Books.

HIRSCH, M. (1989) *The Mother/Daughter Plot*, Bloomingron, Indiana University Press.

HOGGETT, P. (1993) *Partisans in an Uncertain World: The Psychoanalysis of Engagement*, London, Free Association Books.

HORNEY, K. (1924) 'On the Genesis of the Castration Complex in Woman', *International Journal of Psychoanalysis*, 5: 50–65.

HORNEY, K. (1926) 'Flight from Womanhood', *International Journal of Psychoanalysis*, 7: 324–39.

HORNEY, K. (1932) 'The Dread of Women', *International Journal of Psychoanalysis*, 13: 348–60.

HORNEY, K. (1933) 'The Denial of the Vagina', *International Journal of Psychoanalysis*, 14: 57–70.

HORNEY, K. (1967) *Feminine Psychology*, London, Routledge and Kegan Paul.

HORNEY, K. (1994) *The Neurotic Personality of Our Time*, London, Routledge.

HUDSON, L. (1993) *The Way Men Think*, New Haven, Yale University Press

IRIGARAY, L. (1981) 'When the Goods Get Together', trans. C. Reeder, in E. Marks and I. de Courtivron, *New French Feminisms: An Anthology*, Brighton, Harvester.

IRIGARAY, L. (1985a) *Speculum of the Other Woman*, trans. G. Gill, Ithaca, Cornell University Press.

IRIGARAY, L. (1985b) *This Sex Which is Not One*, trans. C. Porter and C. Burke, Ithaca, Cornell University Press.

IRIGARAY, L. (1992) *Elemental Passions*, trans. J. Collie and J. Still, London, Athlone Press.

IRIGARAY, L. (1993a) *An Ethics of Sexual Difference*, trans. C. Burke and G. Gill, London, Athlone Press.

IRIGARAY, L. (1993b) *Sexes and Genealogies*, trans. G. Gill, New York, Columbia University Press.

IRIGARAY, L. (1993c) *Je, Tu, Nous*, trans. A. Martin, London, Routledge.

JACOBS, M. (1992) *Sigmund Freud*, London, Sage.

JACOBY, R. (1987) *The Last Intellectuals*, New York, Basic Books.

JARDINE, A. (1981) 'Introduction to "Women's Time"', *Signs*, 7, 1: 13–15.

JARDINE, A. (1985) *Gynesis: Configurations of Women and Modernity*, Ithaca, Cornell University Press.

JARDINE, A. (1986) 'Opaque Texts and Transparent Contexts: The Political Difference of Julia Kristeva' in N.K. Miller, ed., *The Poetics of Gender*, New York, Columbia University Press.

JONES, E. (1922) 'Notes on Dr. Abrahams's Article on the Female Castration Complex', *International Journal of Psychoanalysis*, 3: 327–8.

JONES, E. (1927) 'The Early Development of Female Sexuality', *International Journal of Psychoanalysis*, 8: 457–72

JONES, E. (1933) 'The Phallic Phase', *International Journal of Psychoanalysis*, 14: 1–33.

JONES, E. (1935) 'Early Female Sexuality', *International Journal of Psychoanalysis*, 16: 263–73.

JONES, E. (1948) *Collected Papers on Psychoanalysis*, London, Baillière, Tindall and Cox (papers include 'The Early Development of Femal Sexuality' 438–51; 'The Phallic Phase' 452–84; 'Early Female Sexuality' 485–95.).

JONES, E. (1964) *The Life and Work of Sigmund Freud*, Harmondsworth, Penguin.

JUKES, A. (1993) *Why Men Hate Women*, London, Free Association Books.

KAHR, B. (1993) *Winnicott*, London, Sage.

KELLER, E.F. (1985) *Reflections on Gender and Science*, London and New Haven, Yale University Press.

KENNEDY, R. (1993) *Freedom to Relate*, London, Free Association Books.

KEOHANE, N.O., ROSALDO, M. and GELPI, B. eds. (1982) *Feminist Theory: a Critique of Ideology*, Chicago, University of Chicago Press.

KHAN, M.M.R. (1974) *The Privacy of the Self*, London, Hogarth Press and The Institute of Psychoanalysis.

KHAN, M.M.R. (1975) 'Introduction' to Winnicott, D. *Through Paediatrics to Psychoanalysis*, London, Hogarth Press and The Institute of Psychoanalysis.

KHAN, M.M.R. (1981) *The Case for a Personal Psychotherapy*, Oxford, Oxford University Press.

KHAN, M.M.R. (1983) *Hidden Selves*, London, Hogarth Press and The Institute of Psychoanalysis.

KLEIN, M. (1930) 'The Importance of Symbol Formation in the Development of the Ego', *International Journal of Psychoanalysis*, II: 24–39.

KLEIN, M. (1931) *The Psychoanalysis of Children*, London, Hogarth Press.

KLEIN, M. (1940) 'Mourning and its Relation to Manic-Depressive States', *International Journal of Psychoanalysis*, II.

KLEIN, M. (1955) 'The Psychoanalytic Play Technique' in M. Klein, P. Heimann and R.E. Money-Kyrle, *New Directions in Psycho-Analysis*, London, Tavistock.

KLEIN, M. (1957) *Envy and Gratitude*, London, Tavistock.

KLEIN, M. (1961) *Narrative of a Child Analysis*, London, Hogarth Press.

KLEIN, M. AND RIVIERE, J. (1937) 'Love, Guilt and Reparation' in *Love, Hate and Reparation*, London, Hogarth Press.

KLINE, P. (1984) *Psychology and Freudian Theory*, London, Routledge.

KOHON, G. (1986) *The British School of Psychoanalysis: The Independent Tradition*, London, Free Association Books.

KNELLER, G. (1965) *The Art and Science of Creativity*, Holt, Rheinhart and Winston.

KRISTEVA, J. (1977) *About Chinese Women*, London, Boyars.

KRISTEVA, J. (1980) *Desire in Language*, trans. L.S. Roudiez, Oxford, Blackwell.

KRISTEVA, J. (1981) 'Women's Time', trans. A. Jardine and H. Blake, *Signs*, 7, 1: 13–15.

KRISTEVA, (1984a) *Revolution in Poetic Language*, trans. M. Waller, New York, Columbia University Press.

KRISTEVA, J. (1984b) 'Julia Kristeva in Conversation with Rosalind Coward', *ICA Documents*, special issue on Desire, ed. L. Appignanesi, 22–7.

KRISTEVA, J. (1984c) 'Two Interviews with Kristeva', *Partisan Review*, 51: 1, [with E.H. Baruch].

KRISTEVA J. (1985) 'The Speaking Subject' in M. Blonsky, ed., *On Signs*, Baltimore, Johns Hopkins University Press.

KRISTEVA, J. (1986a) 'An Interview with Julia Kristeva', *Critical Texts*, 3: 3, [with I. Lipkowitz and A. Loselle].

KRISTEVA, J. (1986b) *The Kristeva Reader*, trans. T. Moi, Oxford, Basil Blackwell.

KRISTEVA, J. (1987) *Tales of Love*, trans. L.S. Roudiez, New York, Columbia University Press.

KRISTEVA, J. (1991) *Strangers to Ourselves*, trans. L.S. Roudiez, New York, Columbia University Press.

LECHTE, J. (1990) *Julia Kristeva*, London, Routledge.

LACAN, J. (1966) *Ecrits*, Paris, Seuil.

LACAN, J. (1975) *Encore: Le Seminaire XX*, 1972–3, Paris, Seuil.

LACAN, J. (1977a) *Ecrits: A Selection*, trans. A. Sheridan, London, Tavistock.

LACAN, J. (1977b) *The Four Fundamental Concepts of Psychoanalysis*, ed. J. Alain-Miller, trans. A. Sheridan, London, Hogarth Press and The Institute of Psychoanalysis.

LAPLANCHE, J. (1976) *Life and Death in Psychoanalysis*, Baltimore and London, Johns Hopkins University Press.

LAPLANCHE, J. and PONTALIS, J.B. (1985) *The Language of Psychoanalysis*, London, Hogarth Press.

LASCH, C. (1980) *The Culture of Narcissism*, London, Sphere Books.

LEMAIRE, A. (1977) *Jacques Lacan*, trans. D. Macey, London, Routledge.

LEMOINE-LUCCIONE, E. (1987) *The Dividing of Women or Woman's Lot*, London Free Association Books.

LÉVI-STRAUSS, C. (1977) *Identity*, Paris, Grasset and Fasquelle [seminar].

LEWIN, K. (1974) 'Dora Re-visited', *Psychoanalytical Review*, 60: 519–32.

LINDNER, R. (1986) *The Fifty Minute Hour: A Collection of True Psychoanalytic Tales*, London, Free Association Books.

LOMAS, P. (1973) *True and False Experience*, London, Allen Lane.

LOMAS, P. (1981) *The Case for a Personal Psychotherapy*, Oxford, Oxford University Press.

LOMAS, P. (1987) *The Limits of Interpretation: What's Wrong with Psychoanalysis?*, London, Penguin.

LOMAS, P. (1992) *The Psychotherapy of Everyday Life*, London, Penguin.

MACCANNELL, J. (1986) *Figuring Lacan: Criticism and the Cultural Unconscious*, Beckenham, Croom Helm.

MCDOUGALL, J. (1989) *Theatres of the Body*, London, Free Association Books.

MAHONEY, P. (1987) *Freud as a Writer*, New Haven, Yale University Press.

MAHONEY, P. (1989) *On Defining Freud's Discourse*, New Haven, Yale University Press.

MARKS, E. and DE COURTIVRON, I. eds. (1981) *New French Feminisms: An Anthology*, Brighton, Harvester.

MELTZER, D. (1978) *The Kleinian Development: Part 2, Richard Week-by-Week*, Perthshire: Clunie Press.

MENS-VERHULST, J. (1993) *Daughtering and Mothering*, London, Routledge.

MILLER, A. (1987) *The Drama of Being a Child*, London, Virago.

MILLER, A. (1990) *The Untouched Key*, London, Virago.

MILLER, A. (1991) *Banished Knowledge*, London, Virago.

MILLER, A. (1983) *Towards a New Psychology of Women*, Harmondsworth, Penguin.

MILLER, A. (1992) *Breaking Down the Wall of Silence*, London, Virago

MILNER, M. (Joanna Field) (1971) *On Not Being Able To Paint*, Oxford, Heinemann Educational [The first edition (1950) was published under the pseudonym Joanna Field.]

MILNER, M. (Joanna Field) (1986) *A Life of One's Own*, London, Virago.

MINSKY, R. (1990) 'The Trouble is it's Ahistorical – The Problem of the Unconscious', *Feminist Review*, 36: 4–14.

MINSKY, R. (1992) 'Lacan' in *Knowing Women*, ed. H. Crowley and S. Himmelweit, Milton Keynes, Open University and Cambridge, Polity Press.

MINSKY, R. (1995) 'Reaching Beyond Denial – Sight and In-sight – A Way Forward?' *Free Associations* 54.

MITCHELL, J. (1975) *Psychoanalysis and Feminism*, Harmondsworth, Penguin.

MITCHELL, J. (1986) *The Selected Melanie Klein*, Harmondsworth, Penguin.

MITCHELL, J. and ROSE, J. eds. (1982) *Jacques Lacan and the Ecole Freudienne: Feminine Sexuality*, London, Macmillan.

MOI, T. (1985) *Sexual Textual Politics*, London, Methuen.

MOI, T. ed. (1986) *The Kristeva Reader*, Oxford, Blackwell.

MOI, T. ed. (1987) *French Feminist Thought*, London, Blackwell.

MOI, T. (1989) *Feminist Theory and Simone de Beavoir: a reader*, Oxford, Blackwell.

MOORE, S. (1988) 'Getting a Bit of the Other – The Pimps of Post-Modernism' in R. Chapman and J. Rutherford, eds. *Male Order: Unwrapping Masculinity*, London, Lawrence and Wishart, 165–92.

OLIVER, K. (1993) *Reading Kristeva*, Bloomington and Indianapolis, Indiana University Press.

OLIVIER, C. (1991) *Jocasta's Children: The Imprint of the Mother*, London, Routledge.

ORBACH, S. (1994a) *What Do Women Want?*, London, Fontana.

ORBACH, S. (1994b) *What's Really Going On Here?*, London, Virago.

ORBACH, S. (1994c) *Between Women*, London, Arrow.

PHILLIPS, A. (1988) *Winnicott*, London, Fontana [Modern Masters].

PHILLIPS, A. (1994a) *On Kissing, Tickling and Being Bored*, London, Faber.

PHILLIPS, A. (1994b) *On Flirtation*, London, Faber.

RICH, A. (1976) *Of Woman Born: Motherhood as Experience and Institution*, New York, Bantam.

RIEFF, P. (1989) *Freud: the Mind of the Moralist*, Chicago, University of Chicago Press.

RICHARDS, B. ed. (1984) *Capitalism and Infancy: Essays on Psychoanalysis and Politics*, London, Free Association Books.

RICHARDS, B. (1989) *Images of Freud: Cultural Responses to Psychoanalysis*, London, Dent.

RICHARDS, B. (1994) *Disciplines of Delight*, London, Free Association Books.

RIVIERE, J. (1936) 'The Genesis of Psychical Conflict in Earliest Infancy', *International Journal of Psychoanalysis*, 18.

ROAZEN, P. (1971) *Freud and His Followers*, New York, Da Capo Press.

ROBINSON, P. (1993) *Freud and His Critics*, Berkeley, University of California Press.

ROITH, E. (1987) *The Riddle of Freud*, London, Tavistock.

ROSE, J. (1986) *Sexuality in the Field of Vision*, London, Verso.

ROSE, J. (1993) *Why War?*, Oxford, Blackwell.

ROSS, J.M. (1994) *What Men Want*, Cambridge, MA, Harvard University Press.

ROUDINESCO, E. (1990) *Psychoanalysis in France 1925–1985*, London, Free Association Books.

RUSTIN, M. (1982) 'A Socialist Consideration of Kleinian Psychoanalysis', *New Left Review*, 131: 71–96.

RUSTIN, M. (1991) *The Good Society and the Inner World*, London, Verso.

RYCROFT, C. (1985) *Psychoanalysis and Beyond*, London, Chatto and Windus.

RYCROFT, C. (1995) *A Critical Dictionary of Psychoanalysis*, Harmondsworth, Penguin.

RYCROFT, C., GOVER, G., STORR, A., WREN-LEWIS, J. and LOMAS, P. (1968) *Psychoanalysis Observed*, Harmondsworth, Penguin.

SARAP, M. (1992) *Jacques Lacan*, New York, Harvester Wheatsheaf.

SAYERS, J. (1986) *Sexual Contradictions*, London, Tavistock.

SAYERS, J. (1991) *Mothering Psychoanalysis: Hélène Deutsch, Karen Horney, Anna Freud and Melanie Klein*, London, Hamish Hamilton.

SCHNEIDERMAN, S. (1983) *Jacques Lacan: The Death of an Intellectual Hero*, Cambridge, MA, Harvard University Press.

SEGAL, H. (1979) *Klein*, London, Fontana [Modern Masters].

SEGAL, H. (1986) *Delusion and Artistic Creativity and Other Psychoanalytic Essays*, London, Free Association Books.

SEGAL, J. (1985) *Phantasy in Everyday Life*, London, Pelican.

SEGAL, J. (1992) *Klein*, London, Sage.

SEGAL, L. (1990) *Slow Motion*, London, Virago.

SEGAL, L. (1990) 'Sensual Uncertainty and Why the Clitoris is not Enough' in H. Crowley and S. Himmelweit, eds., *Knowing Women*, Milton Keynes, Open University Press and Cambridge, Polity Press.

SEGAL, L. (1992a) *Is the Future Female?*, London, Virago.

SEGAL, L. (1992b) *Sex Exposed*, London, Virago.

SEGAL, L. (1992c) *Straight Sex*, London, Virago.

SEIDLER, V.J. ed. (1992) *Men, Sex and Relationships*, London, Routledge

SELLERS, S. ed. (1988) *Writing Differences: Reading from the Seminar of Hélène Cixous*, Milton Keynes, Open University.

SHIACH, M. (1991) *Hélène Cixous: A Politics of Writing*, London, Routledge.

SILVERMAN, K. (1988) *The Acoustic Mirror: The Female Voice in Psychoanalysis and Cinema*, Bloomington, Indiana University Press.

SOKOL, B. ed. (1993) *The Undiscovered Country: New Essays in Psychoanalysis and Shakespeare*, London, Free Association Books.

SPRENGNETHER M. (1990) *The Spectral Mother: Freud, Feminism and Psychoanalysis*, Ithaca, Cornell University Press.

STOLLER, R.J. (1986) *Perversion*, London, Karnac.

STOLLER, R.J. (1991a) *Porn*, New Haven, Yale University Press.

STOLLER, R.J. (1991b) *Pain and Passion*, New Haven, Yale University Press.

STOLLER, R.J. (1992) *Presentations of Gender*, New Haven, Yale University Press.

STOLLER, R.J. (1994) *Sex and Gender*, London, Karnac.

STORR, A. (1979) *The Art of Psychotherapy*, London, Butterworth-Heinemann.

STORR, A. (1990) *Freud*, Oxford, Oxford University Press.

STORR, A. (1991) *The Dynamics of Creation*, Harmondsworth, Penguin.

STORR, A. (1992a) *Human Destructiveness*, London, Routledge.

STORR, A. (1992b) *Human Aggression*, Harmondsworth, Penguin.

STORR, A. (1993) *Music and the Mind*, London, Flamingo.

SUTTIE, I. (1988) *The Origins of Love and Hate*, London, Free Association Books.

TODD, J. ed. (1983) *Women Writers Talking*, New York, Holmes & Meier.

TONG, R. (1989) *Feminist Thought*, London, Routledge [chapter five, Psychoanalytic Feminism' and chapter eight 'Post-Modern Feminism'].

TURKLE, S. (1978) *Psychoanalytic Politics*, New York, Basic Books.

WEATHERILL, R. (1994) *Violence and Privacy: Psychoanalysis and Cultural Collapse*, London, Free Association Books.

WELLDON, E.V. (1992) *Mother, Madonna, Whore*, New York, Guilford Publications.

WHITFORD, M. (1989) 'Re-reading Irigaray' in T. Brennan ed., *Between Feminism and Psychoanalysis*, London, Routledge.

WHITFORD, M. (1991a) *Luce Irigaray: Philosophy in the Feminine*, London, Routledge.

WHITFORD, M. ed. (1991b) *The Irigaray Reader*, Oxford, Blackwell.

WHITFORD, M. ed. (1994) *Knowing the Difference*, London, Routledge.

WILCOX, H. ed. (1990) *The Body and the Text: Hélène Cixous, Reading and Teaching*, London, Harvester Wheatsheaf.

WINNICOTT, D. (1957) *The Child and the Family: First Relationships*, London, Tavistock.

WINNICOTT, D. (1958) *Collected Papers: Through Paediatrics to Psychoanalysis*, London and Tavistock: New York, Basic Books.

WINNICOTT, D. (1964a) *The Child, the Family and the Outside World*, Harmondsworth, Penguin.

WINNICOTT, D. (1964b) *The Family and Individual Development*, London, Tavistock.

WINNICOTT, D. (1964c) *The Effect of Psychotic Parents*, London, Tavistock.

WINNICOTT, D. (1965) *The Maturational Processes and the Facilitating Environment: Studies in the Theories of Emotional Development*, London, Hogarth Press and The Institute of Psychoanalysis.

WINNICOTT, D. (1971) *Playing and Reality*, London, Routledge.

WINNICOTT, D. (1977) *The Piggle: An Account of Psychoanalytic Treatment of a Little Girl*, Harmondsworth, Penguin.

WINNICOTT, D. (1984) *Deprivation and Delinquency*, London, Tavistock.

WINNICOTT, D. (1987) *Home is Where We Start From: Essays by a Psychoanalyst*, London, Pelican.

WINNICOTT, D. (1988) *Human Nature*, London, Free Association Books.

WISDOM, J. (1992) *Freud, Women and Society*, New Brunswick, Transaction Publishers.

WOLFENSTEIN, E. (1993) *Psychoanalytic Marxism*, London, Free Association Books.

WOLLHEIM, R. (1971) *Freud*, London, Fontana [Modern Masters].

WRIGHT, E. (1984) *Psychoanalytic Criticism: Theory in Practice*, London, Methuen.

WRIGHT, E. ed. (1992) *Feminism and Psychoanalysis: A Critical Dictionary*, London, Blackwell.

YOUNG-BRUEHL, E. (1988) *Anna Freud*, London, Macmillan.

YOUNG-BRUEHL, E. (1990) *Freud on Women*, London, Hogarth Press.

INDEX

abandonment, sense of 60

abject 182–3

Abraham, Karl 107, 164

absent father 44, 53

abuse: of children 41, 191–2; of women 82

academic practice 14–15

active aim: in women 65, 169–71; in infantile sexuality 33; in heterosexuality 58; in relation to mother 48, 50; sublimation of 60

actual father 149

actual mother 113

adaptation 13–14, 97, 117, 126–7

aggression 44; in baby 116; fear of own 84; in Klein's child analysis 91; in masochism 47, 81–2, 84; towards father 41–5; see also victim/executioner

aliveness, sense of 111

ambivalence: of baby 79, 166; of patriarchal men and women 93, 105; see also splitting, good and bad breast

anaclitic love 38

anal drives 81

anal phase 33, 81

anality (pleasure from control) 37

Andreas Salome, Lou 62

anger, girl's, of the mother 59, 50, 61

anxiety, (in baby) 78, 82–4, 87, 98–9; see also castration anxiety, castration complex, false self, psychical annihilation (threat of), social anxiety

appropriation of 'femininity' 196–7

art 123

artistic creativity 125, 127, 129–30, 187, 189

artistic imagination 123

attentiveness (of mother) 114

authenticity, personal sense of 111, 123

auto-eroticism 31–8

autonomy, sense of 123

avant-garde artists 182

baby: deprived 98, 104; phantasy of having one with mother, with father 50; see also Klein, Winnicot

bad breast 83–4; see also good breast

Bauer, Ida (Dora) 62, 73

'being' 122, 159

being and doing 121–2

bereavement 39, 95

Bernays, Martha (Freud's wife) 25, 62

Beyond the Pleasure Principle 25, 80

binary thinking 102, 211

biological instincts 99, 103

biological factors 66, 80, 90, 92, 164

biology 10, 193

birth 9

bisexuality 46–50, 56, 64, 73, 95, 170

blaming 88, 99

blind spot 112

bodily aliveness, sense of 111

bodily processes 182–3

body 10, 112; and phantasy 194, 198, 210; history and 10; in infantile sexuality 31–38; and knowledge 211; and psyche/

soma relationship 112, 118; and women 185, 188, 193
breast: envy of 95–6; good and bad 83, 92; as source of life 96
Breuer, Josef 25, 27
British Psychoanalytical Society 105

cars, symbolism of 35
castrating woman 53, 96
castration, women as symbol of 193
castration anxiety 41
castration complex 41–5, 50–1, 59; see also Oedipal crisis, penis-envy, victim/executioner
catholicism 101
change 69, 97, 171, 203; consequences of 203; in Symbolic 195–8
character traits 35–8
Charcot, Jean Martin 25
children: emotional abuse of 191–2; as extensions of self 39; sexual abuse of 41
Chodorow, Nancy 15, 104, 131, 178,
Christianity 86, 94, 184
Cinderella 80
civilisation 28, 64; see also culture, Western philosophy, language
Civilisation and Its Discontents 28
Cixous, Hélène 4, 21, 102, 153, 171, 180, 182, 197, 202
cleanliness 35
clitoris 33, 34, 47, 49, 52
combined parent figure (combined object) 84, 90, 94, 104
common sense 99
complexity 98
compliance 117, 118, 123
complementarity (in heterosexuality) 166
component instincts 31–8
compulsive 'doing' 37, 119, 122
concern for others 98

condensation 28–9
consciousness 4, 168 see also ego, culture, knowledge, language
continuous self, sense of 115
control: and anal phase 33, 37; and domination 68, 70, 193; and mother 132, 133; compulsive need for 35, 60, 122; in omnipotence 89, 99, 115; in projective identification 86
counter-transference 12
creativity: and artistic experience and expression 128–30, 184–5; in baby 117; of mother 96, 97, 100, 111, 114, 116, 173, 184–5, 209; see also Winnicott, women's writing
cruelty 98; and rivalry among women 199; see also denigration, sadism, victim/executioner, violence
culture: assumptions of 192, 201; symbolic substitutes in 36–7; experience of 117, 127; and Oedipal crisis 44, 149; and place of the father 149–52; and representations of women 68, 93, 102, 103, 160, 193; and sexual world 168–9; as substitute father 44, 149; see also language
cyclical time 183–4

dark continent: women as 48, 193
day-dreaming 112, 125, 126, 127
death; see bereavement, castration anxiety, castration complex, life and death drives, the Real, women as symbol
defences 13, 28; in paranoid-schizoid position 84–7; in depressive position 88; language as 68
Demand, realm of 146, 153, 164
democratic tendency 125
demonisation 98–9
denial 88, 95, 118: of women 193–200
denigration 84, 93, 97, 161; see also

cruelty, sadism, victim/executioner
dependence 70, 82, 132, 170; on women
    193
depressed mother 119
depression 7, 40, 59, 81; in mother 85,
    88, 117, 119, 131
depressive position 88–90, 91, 94–5
deprivation: social 99, 208; psychical
    104, 113, 115
Derrida 179, 196
dereliction, women's state of 194–5
Descartes 26,156
desire 4, 40–62
Desire: in language 138, 140, 142, 147–8,
    154–5, 157–8, 163; of mother 140–2,
    155, 165; realm of 146–8, 149, 157
destructiveness, 88–9, 98; see also
    denigration, paranoid-schizoid
    position, sadism, victim/executioner
Deutsch, Helene 95
developmental theory: and Klein; 21,
    87; and Winnicott 21, 111
différance 196, 197
difference 4, 10, 18–19, 69, 71, 142, 150–2,
    168, 170, 178, 196; see also Oedipal crisis
Dinnerstein, Dorothy 104
dissociation 20, 112, 119
disavowal 57
disembodiment 171, 173, 196
disillusionment 115, 126–7
disintegration, sense of 113
displacement 13, 29
diversity 180
'doing' 122, 172
Dora case 62, 73
dreams, symbolism in 28–9, 54
drives 31–2
drug addiction 37
dual instinct theory (life and death
    drives) 80–2

eating 36

eclectic approach 22, 206, 209
eco-feminism 13
Ecole Freudienne 137, 175, 178–9, 192
Ecrits 137
écriture feminine 197
education 129
ego 30–1; in the Imaginary 143, 144–5,
    156; see also consciousness
the Ego and the Id 25, 30, 81
ego-psychology 13
Eichenbaum, Luise 131
embodiment 202; disembodiment 171,
    173, 196–7
emotional withdrawal 68
empathy 97, 185, 208, 211
empty speech 143, 203
engulfment, fear of 68, 86, 132–3
enrichment (of baby's identity) 126
environment, mother as 130
envy: of father 94, 207; of mother 91–7,
    207; of others 97
'Envy and Gratitude' 91–7
essentialism 202, anti- 180, 182, 211
estrangement, (from self) 119
ethnocentrism 71; see other
exclusion: of others 99; from 'world-
    making' 105
external world 84, 91
excessive mental functioning 40, 119,
    210–11

faeces, symbolic meaning of 33, 54
fairy tales 80, 103, 210
falling in love 6–7
false self , 117–20, 120, 127
family, origin of unconscious in 8, 9
fantasy (as opposed to phantasy) 7
fascism 99, 123
father: actual 149; complex 101; in
    culture 69; flight from 130–3,
    idealised 149; as part of breast 90,
    101, 104; as place of the father 148–9;

substitute 49; as superego 41–6; symbolic 149

female Imaginary 193–200, 203

female masochism 47

'femininity': appropriation of 101, 197; as cultural norm 18–19, 64, 65; debates on 164, 178; denial of in boys 67; Freud's view of 45; Klein's view of 80; men's fear of 170, 210; and morality 49; rejection/repudiation of 56, 66; and wish for a baby 50, 57; *see also* women, 'masculinity'

'Femininity' (Freud's essay on) 46, 47–62; and Irigaray's critique of 200–1

femininity complex 100

feminine feminine 196

feminisation (of others) 71, 210

Ferenczi, Sandor 107

fetishism 33–4, 126

fixation 35

Fliess, Wilhelm 73

fluidity (of identity) 182, 199, 201–2

fore-play: as polymorphous perversity 35

fort/da game 67

fragmentation 87

free association 11, 27

Freud, Anna 62, 105

Freud, Sigmund: and castration complex 40–7; and 'femininity' 47–58; feminist criticism of 64, 74; feminist interest in 17; and heterosexuality 58–62, 69–70; and hysteria 27–8, 59–60; and Klein and Winnicott 17; life and career of 25, 72–5; as modernist 27; and mother's role in theory 66; and narcissism 38–40; and Oedipal crisis 40–7; and penis/baby equivalence 54–8; and penis-envy 50–4; as postmodernist 27, 66; and

precariousness 64–5, 68; and repression 26, 42, 46; and sexuality 31–8; and symbolic structure of the unconscious 28–30; theoretical overview of ideas 26–7; and unconscious 26–31; and types of women 57–8; and women, attitudes to and relationships with 17, 62, 74; and subordination of women 66

friendship 38

frigidity 96, 167

full speech 143, 174

gender categories 10, 63, 64, 66, 202

gender identity 46; fluidity and multiplicity of 182, 199, 201–2

generosity 92–3

genital phase 35

genital sexuality 34

genocide 191

God 45, 86, 94, 101–2

'going on being', sense of 111, 115

good and evil; *see* good breast and bad breast

good breast 83, 114

'good enough' mother 112–15

gratitude 92–3, 101

greed 92, 123

guilt 41–3, 81, 87, 88, 187

hallucination (of breast) 83, 115

hate, in baby 82

'having' 150, 159

helplessness: in baby 82–3, 88, 123, 132; induced by society 99

heterosexuality 34, 57–9, 63, 65, 69–70, 159, 162, 166, 167, 200

history: culture and 8–10

holding environment, mother as 112

homo-eroticism 101

homophobia 5, 71

homosexuality 35, 45, 65, 70, 74

Horney, Karen 95
hostility 61
humanism 174–5, 191–2;
humanist therapy 41
hysteria: in men 170, in women 27, 59, 62, 72–3

id 30, 133; *see also* desire, Desire, Oedipal crisis, sexuality, unconscious
id, ego, superego, joint structural concepts of 30
idealisation 61, 84, 86, 93–4, 189; and repetitive failure in relationships 93; *see also* narcissism
identification 31: boys with father 42; boys with mother 44, 54, 101; girls with father 54; girls with mother 45, 49; in the Imaginary 141; with knowledge and intellect 40, 119, 210–11; in paranoid-schizoid position 99
identity: confusion with concept of identification 196; destruction of 212; fixity of 189; in Imaginary 142, 147; myth of 143; in Oedipal crisis 40–6; primitive 83; repression of aspects of 57, 68, 70; in Symbolic 142, 152; unity of 20, 206; *see also* depressive position, transitional object, transitional space
ideology 168
illusion 124–5, 127, 128
illusionment 115, 132; *see also* disillusionment
Imaginary: concept of 141, 143–6, 158, 161, 181, 198–9; dual 198; female 193, 194–5; male 192–3, 195
Imaginary ego 144–5, 156, 167
imperfection: sense of 53; of Freud 62
impingement 105, 119, 121
impotence 167

incest: law against 40; child's incestuous phantasies 54; *see also* Oedipal crisis
incorporation 36
infantile sexuality 31–8
inferiority, sense of 53, 55, 56, 57, 66, 71; compensation for 58; and superiority 71
inner world 84
insight (emotional) 101, 108
instinctual experience 112
integration 88, 94, 97–8, 112, 189
intellectuals 203
intermediate experience 124–5, 127, 129
internalisation: *see* introjection
Interpretation of Dreams 25, 139
intersubjectivity 140
introjection 83, 86, 92
intuition 127, 188
Irigaray, Luce: and appropriation of 'femininity' 196–7; and women as castration and death 193–4; criticisms of 202; and cultural assumptions 192, 194–5; and denial of mother 194–5, 203; and dual symbolic 198–9; and female Imaginary 195–8; and intellectuals 203; and love 200; and male imaginary 191, 192; and mimicry 199; and philosophy 196; and psychoanalysis 195–6, 200–1

Jakobson, Roman 139
jealousy 92, 94–5
Jones, Ernest 164
jouissance 162, 167, 188, 194; as 'truth' 174, 187

kissing 35
Klein, Eric 79
Klein, Melanie: and castrating woman 96; and concept of phantasy 79, 80;

criticisms of 103–4; and denial 88; and depressive position 88; and Dinnerstein 104; and good and bad breast 83–4, 114, and envy 92; and father 90, 94; feminist use of 104–5; and Freud's dual instinct theory 80; and frigidity 96; and gratitude 92; and greed 92; and jealousy 92; and Lacan 164; life and work of 78, 106–7; overview of theoretical ideas 78–80; and paranoid-schizoid position 86; and persecutory anxiety 93; and phantasies of love and hate 82–4; and projection 85; and projective identification 86; and splitting 85; and symbolisation 91; and Winnicott 103; and womb-envy 95–6, 100–1

knowledge: excessive interest in as substitute identity 40, 119, 210–11, 120–1; *see also* consciousness, culture, language, Symbolic

Kristeva, Julia: and the abject other; 182–3; and avant-garde artists 182; and the body 21; and concepts of 183–4; criticisms of 188, 191; and de-centring of identity 153; and double discourse 181; and fluidity and multiplicity 181–2, 188, 201–2; and marginality 173, 180, 182; and motherhood 184–7; and political action 189; and representation of women 86; and semiotic 183; and 'stranger within' 187, 191; and womb-envy 190; and women as 'truth' 180–1, 184, 186, 187; and women's writing 188

Lacan: and bogus power 169–70; and destabilising of identity 171; and connection between psychical and social 168–9; and place of the father 148–50; and identity in the Imaginary (mirror stage) 144–6; and identity in the Symbolic 150–4; life and career 137, 175–6; and masquerade 161–2; and jouissance 161–2; and the meaning of the phallus 164–8; and men's projection onto women 170–3, 193; overview of theoretical ideas 138–44; and patriarchal consciousness 168; and the phallic signifier 158; and the phallus 150; and psychoanalysis as the analysis of language 138; problems with theory of 170–4; and provisionality 173; and realms of demand and desire 146–8; and suffering 174; and unconscious Desire 155–6; and value 174–5; and woman as the lack 153–4, 158–61; writing of 155, 163–4

lack, women as; 153, 154, 158; men's projection of 170, 193

language: and bodily phantasy 194; as consciousness 4, 155–6, 168, 211; as defence 68, 119, 210–11; identification with 152–3, 157; poetic 179; as site of change 181–2, 188, 201–2; as site of Oedipal crisis and castration 148; as substitute for loss 150; as the Symbolic 150–4; as unconscious Desire 4, 10, 138, 140–2, 146, 148, 155, 211; *see also* Irigaray, Kristeva, Lacan

latency 34

lesbian women 57, 65, 184

libido; *see* id

life and death drives (dual instinct theory) 80–2, 113

life-instinct 92, 113

listening to music 125

linear time 183

literary texts and desire 155, 173

Little Hans 42

logic and reason 129

loss: in boys 191, 208; of mother 4, 9, 58, 59, 67, 89, 95, 112, 207; of identity (self) 119, 149–50, 169; as symbolised in language 154
lost object 91, 103
love 200, 211
love and hate instincts 79
love, state of being in 6–7
lying 126

male imaginary 192–3, 195, 203
macho men 35
mania 89
marginality 180, 182–3
masculine feminine 196
'masculinity' 18–19; and Freud 41–5, 64, 65, 67–8; social construction of 168; see also 'femininity', Oedipal crisis
masculine aim: in relation to clitoris 47–8, 50, 57; lingering quality of in women 56; see also Oedipal crisis, penis-envy
masochism 47, 81–2, 113
masquerade 161–2, 166
mastery 5, 28, 81, 154, 173
masturbation 33, 42, 61
maternal environment 111
matriarchy 53
meaning: construction of 145, 198–200; challenge to 173, 182–3, 188, 207; destruction of 212
meaning of the phallus 152–3
'Meaning of the Phallus' 164–7, 168–9
melancholia 39, 81
memories 29
men: and castration complex 40–6; and danger of psychical collapse 203; and father 42–3, 45, 50, 56; and fetishism 33–4; and male Imaginary 192–3; and passive aim 65; patriarchal 93, 105; and phallic

signifier 142, 151–2; and phallus 101, 103, 154, 164, 167; and place of the father 69, 149, 180; and projection of vulnerability 160, 194, 210; and relationships with women 61; and separation from the mother 67–9; and superego 42–4; and womb envy 59, 95–6, 100–2, 172, 188, 190; see also language, 'masculinity', Oedipal crisis, power, precariousness
metaphor 139, 151, 200
metonymy 139, 199
Middle Group (of British Psychoanalytical Society) 124
Miller, Alice 41, 191
Milner, Marion 128–30
mimicry 199
mirror image, mother as 114, 145
mirror stage (Imaginary) 141, 144–6
misogyny 53, 56, 61–2, 96
misrecognition 152
modernist Freud 27
modernist theory 206
money 35
monumental time 183
moral values 43–4, 49, 187; anxiety about 44
moral panics 99
mother: actual 134; blaming of 13, 130; denial of 193–4; depressed 117, 131, 134; depriving 113; as good and bad breast 83, 114; 'good enough' 112–15; return to in heterosexuality 58–61; and Oedipal crisis 40–50; as symbolic breast 83–4, 97; symbolic representation in Christianity 184, 186; unity with 113; use of 116; see also Klein, women
mother-daughter relationship 59, 61, 194, 199
mother-son relationship 53, 55, 61, 96
motherhood 184, 185, 190; see also

phantasy, creativity, 'good enough' mother, women (envy of)

multiplicity (of pleasures, identity) 182, 195, 197, 201–2

myth 210

name of the father, law of 149, 151

narcissism: and bereavement 39; in boys 52; and children as extensions of self 39; and culture 68–9; and desire 40; and falling in love 38, 41, 167–8; and choice of partner 61; and penis-envy 52–3; as projective identification 86, 93, 99; and knowledge 119, 211; primary 145; secondary 162; theory of 38–40; and younger partner 39

narcissistic love 38

National Health Service 99

nationalism (destructive forms of) 5, 71, 99, 123

nature, culture and 101

needs 146, 148, 165–6

neurosis 35, 193; male identity as 193, 206

neurotic illness 118

Nirvana principle 81

Object-relations theory 19, 79, 83, 145, 165, 206

objects: of baby 79; good and bad 84

obsessions 35

observation (as method of knowing) 101

obsessional neurosis 60

Oedipal crisis: and aggression 44–4; and boy's identification with father 42–3, 45; and castration complex 40–6; and culture 44; and entry into culture 41; failure to enter 66; and formation of unconscious 42; and girl's identification with the mother 45; and guilt 43; and language 148; and love affair with mother 40; as

origin of unconscious 8–9; and penis-envy 45; and repression 40–6; rivalry and conflict in 40–4; and superego 42–4; and symbolic castration 42; and wish for a baby 45; see also Symbolic, womb-envy

omnipotence 88, 95, 99

orality (pleasure in incorporation) 36

oral phase 32

Orbach, Susie 131

Other 141, 147–8, 157, 165

other 71, 130

other of the same 193, 198

other of the other 198

overcompensation 100

painting, as intermediate experience 129

Pappenheim, Bertha 27

paranoia 84, 87

paranoid-schizoid position 87, 91, 93, 95, 98–9, 102

part objects 83, 84

passive aim: and father 50, 56; in 'femininity' 47; in heterosexuality 58; in infantile sexuality 32; in men 65; see also Oedipal crisis, sexuality

paternal metaphor 149

patriarchal culture 18, 60, 67–8

patriarchal men and women 102

penis/phallus 102, 103; as connector 33; and fetishism 33–4

penis-envy 17, 45, 49–54, 56–9, 63, 95

penis-baby equivalence 46, 54–6

perfection, (desire for) 72

persecutory anxiety 87, 93

perversions 35

phallic mother 181

phallic phase 33–4

phallic pleasure as source of primitive identity 37

phallic signifier 142, 151–2, 156–8, 165, 168; bogus power of 159–60, 169
phallocentrism 63, 169
phallus 154, 164, 167
phantasised mother 113
phantasy 7, 70, as concept in Klein 79–80, 84, 97–9, 194; as concept in Irigaray 194; as concept in Winnicott 115; in fairytales 103; in representations of women 68, 93, 102, 160, 161, 172; *see also* Oedipal Crisis, unconscious mechanisms
philosophy; *see* Western philosophers
place of the father 69, 149, 180; *see also* Symbolic
place of pre-Oedipal mother 180
play 85; ruthless 116, 120, 123–4, 126, 127, 128–9; *see also* artistic creativity, intermediate experience, transitional object, transitional space
play-technique 84–5, 91
pleasure: in heterosexuality 162; in infantile sexuality 31–8; as jouissance 162, 174; in Oedipal phase 49; as source of primitive identity 31–2, 92
pleasure principle 81
plurality (of identity) 180; *see also* fluidity, multiplicity
political action 14, 188–9, 197
polymorphous perversity 35; *see also* infantile sexuality and pleasure
pornography 68, 97, 132
post-modernism 16, 206; and Freud 27
post-structuralist theory 21, 138
power 17, 67, 89, 98, 102–3, 113, 132, 150, 159, 169; *see also* control, men, mother, phallus, women
powerlessness 98, 113, 160, 169
pre-conscious 30
pre-oedipal mother 49, 60, 61, 180–1, 183, 185
pre-oedipal world 180

precariousness 63, 66, 174, 206; women as male projection of 209
pregnancy 184
primary identification with the mother 70
primary process 30
primary unintegration 112
primitive greed 92
primitive ruthless love 116, 128
projection 5–7, 85–8, 125, 143, 199, 203
projective identification 6–7, 86; *see also* narcissism
prostitution 68
protestantism 101
provisionality (of knowledge) 173, 175
psyche-soma relationship 86, 112
psychical annihilation: baby and 118; threat of in men 60, 169, 209
psychical pain 42, 66; *see also* loss, castration anxiety, penis-envy, separation from the mother, womb-envy
psychical processes 168
psychical reality; *see* unconscious
psychical representations 26; *see also* dreams, symptoms
psychoanalysis: as academic practice 14–15; and anxiety produced in academic use 15–16; assumptions within 192, 195; confusion with non-psychoanalytic psychotherapy, psychiatry and ego-psychology 24; criticisms of 13–14, 97, 192–6, 200–1; and feminism 17–18; as therapeutic practice 10–13, 155, 165; and 'Truth' 15–17; strangeness of 14–15; *see also* psychoanalytical psychotherapy
psychoanalysis of children 24–5, 91
psychoanalytic psychotherapy 10–13, 97, 121, 123, 127, 143–4, 155, 189, 203
psychoanalytic theory 3, 10
psychology 3

psychosis 89, 157, 171
psychosomatic illness 86, 112

racism 5, 71, 86
rationality 149, 168; as surrogate
    mother 203
Real, the 143, 147–8, 157, 193
'reality' 211
reality principle 81
rejection: sense of in hysteria 59, 60;
    of 'femininity' 55, 56, 66
relatedness, mother and baby 114
relationships 199; involving
    compliance 118–19; involving
    projective identification 86–7;
    involving idealisation 93
religion: and reparation 89; and
    representation of motherhood 184;
    as source of idealised parent 86; as
    substitute father 44
religious feeling 126
reparation 88, 89, 95, 98, 101
repetition compulsion 81
repression 26, 42, 46, 57, 58, 64
responsibility 89, 211
responsiveness 114; see also empathy
retaliation, fear of 87
rigid convictions 123; see also
    compliance
rivalry and conflict in Oedipal crisis
    40–4, 87, 99
romantic love 38, 63; see also falling in
    love
ruthlessness (of baby) 116, 131–2

sadism 81, 100, 113
sado-masochism 133
Saint Theresa, Bernini's statue 162
sameness 146, 193, 195, 201
sanity 161
Saussure, Ferdinand de 138–9
scape-goating 99, 182, 189

science 129
secondary identification 61
secondary process 30
seduction theory 41
self, concept of 11; see identity,
    identification
self-preservation instincts 36
self-realisation 117
semiotic, the 183
separation 48, 63, 67, 88, 190
separation anxiety 67, 118
separation from the mother 53–4, 60,
    67–8, 102, 116, 120, 207–8
sexism 5, 71
sexual difference 150–1, 187, 198, 201; see
    also Irigaray, Kristeva, Lacan,
    Oedipal complex
sexual infidelity 68, 86
sexual inhibition 57
sexual relationships 103
sexuality: and character traits 35; as
    drive 31; infantile 32–5; as pleasure
    and earliest source of identity 31;
    and psychical representations 35;
    and realms of Demand and Desire
    167; and social world 168–9; and
    violence 68; see also bisexuality,
    heterosexuality, homosexuality,
    language, unconscious
shopping 37
sibling rivalry 59
sight and in-sight 101, 172
sign, 138, 152
signified 151, 155
signifier 138, 155, 158
single mothers 99, 100, 184
smoking 36
social: anxiety 98–9; change 69, 97;
    conflict 208, 100; helplessness
    99, 208; Imaginary 195; integration
    98; processes 168; provision 98, 131, 208
socialisation theory 3, 69

socialism 98
sociology 3
speculum 195
specularisation 195
speech 11–12, 137, 163, 203; empty 143; full 143, 174
splitting 84, 85, 87, 99, 167
spoiling 96–7, 209
'Stabat Mater' 184
Stalinism 99
stealing 126
structural linguistics 138–9
subject 140, 150–4; and object 129
subjectivity 71, 138, 141, 151–2, 154, 161, 169, 171, 174, 191–5, 198, 211
sublimation: and artistic and intellectual interests 37–8, 60; and civilisation 38
submission and domination 13; see also victim/executioner
suffering 174, 189
superego 30, 42–5, 49, 81, 143; see also father, Oedipal crisis, victim/ executioner
Symbolic 141–3, 150–56, 181; transformation of 195, 197–8, 203
Symbolic castration 42, 151, 153, 158–60, 169, 170, 176, 187, 189, 191
symbolic father 149
symbolisation 28–9, 91, 124–8
symptoms 28

talking (excessively) 36
talking cure 27, see also free association, psychoanalytic psychotherapy
technology 195
television watching 36
tenderness 38
theory 156, 195, 210
theoretical incompatibility 206
theorists 201, 203

thing-presentations 29
thinking 168; as substitute for feeling 40, 119, 210–11; see also knowledge, language
third term 151
tidiness 35
time 183, 186
Three Essays on Sexuality 32
toilet training 9, 61
toys as symbols 91
trans-sexuals 34
transference 12
transition from phantasy to reality 42, 44, 88, 117, 120, 129, 207
transitional object 120, 124, 125, 127
transitional phenomena 120, 125
transitional space 120, 123, 207
traumatic experiences 35
'Truly, Madly, Deeply' (film) in relation to narcissism and bereavement 39
'truth' 128, 149, 163–4, 174, 181, 184, 186, 187, 188

uncertainty 173
unconditional love 13, 127
Unconscious, the 29
unconscious: as concept 3–21, 27–31; and body 10, 211; as Desire (Lacan) 169; defences of 6–8; as disassociation (Winnicott) 112, 119; and dreams 28–9; evidence for 5–6; as language (Lacan) 150–155, 163; origins of 8–10; psychical representations of 26; as repression (Freud) 26, 42, 46, 57, 58, 64; symptoms of 3; as unconscious mechanisms (Klein) 84–8; as universal 8–10, 28; see also Oedipal crisis, sexuality
unconscious positions 87
unconscious representations 51

unintegration 113, 123
universality 8–10

vagina 34, 49, 164
values 168, 174–5, 187
vanity 58
victim/executioner 71, 186, 189, 191, 210; *see also* castration complex, symbolic castration
victimisation 99
violence 18, 98–9, 210; against women 68, 82, 97
Virgin Mary 101
vulnerability 67, 68, 70, 99; projection of onto others 160, 194, 210

weaning 9, 61
Western philosophy 192, 195; and male philosophers 196
Winnicott, Donald: and artistic creativity 123, 128–30; attitude to theory 111, 124, 127; and 'being' and 'doing' 121–2; and compliance 117, 118, 123; and criticism of Klein 104; and day-dreaming 112, 125–7; and depressed mother 117, 131; and dissociation 20, 112, 119; and disillusionment 115; and enjoyment of artistic experience 125, 127; and false self 117; and father 130–3; and fear of annihilation 132; and 'good enough' mother 113–15; and illusionment 115; and intermediate experience 124–5, 127, 129; and language 110–11, 134; life and career 110, 133–4; overview of theoretical ideas 110–13; and play 123–4; and power of mother 132–3; and transitional object and transitional space 120, 124–8, 207
wisdom 200
wish for a baby 45, 50, 57
woman, as category 182
woman, as other of the same 193, 198
woman, as other of the other 198
womb-envy 59, 95–6, 100–2, 172, 188, 190
women: as castrating 53, 96; creativity of 184–5, 96–7, 100, 103, 111, 114, 116, 197–8, 209; cultural representations of 68, 80, 93, 102, 160–1, 172; as symbol of death and castration 67, 193–4, 172, 209; denial of 193–200; envy of 56, 59, 95–6, 100–2, 172, 188, 190; as the lack 158–162; as male unconscious 160, 161, 170, 172; and motherhood 172, 209; need for control of 70, 193, 209; as the phallus 159, 166; and phantasy of as all-powerful 103; rejection of by women 56, and relationships with men 61; and relationships with women 199; subordination of 17–18, 56, 66, 113, 132, 209; as 'too much' 209; as 'truth' 186; writing of 179, 185–6, 188; *see also* bisexuality, body, breast, 'femininity', mother, penis-baby equivalence, penis-envy, unconscious, womb-envy
'Women's Time' 183–7
women's writing 179, 185–6, 188
word-presentations 29
work 35, 172
workaholism 60, 68